BROTHERS FROM BATAAN:

POWs, 1942-1945

Best Wishes,

Adrian R. Martin

Addie Martin

BROTHERS FROM BATAAN:

POWs, 1942-1945

Adrian R. Martin

Sunflower University Press®

1531 Yuma (Box 1009), Manhattan, Kansas 66502-4228, USA

ISBN 0-89745-142-2

Layout by Lori L. Daniel

Acknowledgments

Many thanks for editing and proofreading help should go to Dr. Michael P. Onorato, Professor of History at California State University — Fullerton, and to Dan Daggett and Larry Graves, teachers at New London Public Schools, Wisconsin, as well as to Colleen O'Brien Batley, a high school classmate, from Menasha, Wisconsin.

Contents

Glossary

Aeso:	Jail
Bango:	Roll call
Behai:	Living hut
Benjo:	Toilet
Bento:	Boxed lunch
Byoki:	Sick, ill
Dog Robber:	POW who worked for officers or Japanese
Honcho:	Foreman or boss
Honey Bucket:	Wooden tub used to carry POW excrement
Kumshaw:	Bribes
Kupae:	Warming shack
Lugao:	A watery rice soup
Mestizo:	A person of mixed blood
Quan:	To cook a mixture of any and all types of food in a pot or pan
Tenko:	Number during roll call
Tutami:	Sleeping mat
Vitamin Stick:	Japanese sword
Yasame:	Rest

Introduction

My name is Adrian R. Martin. I was named by my father after Adrian Raphael Martin, an uncle I never knew. He died in a Japanese prisoner-of-war camp in 1945. He had been a prisoner for 3¼ years, had survived the infamous Bataan Death March, and had spent 2½ years in three Philippine prisoner-of-war camps. He endured a gruesome ten-day trip to Japan in the hold of a Hell Ship and then spent ten months in a cold, isolated camp in northern Japan before he died. I was one year old when he died, far too young to understand the significance of what he went through.

My parents were divorced in 1951, and in the following years I had little contact with my father's side of the family. As I grew into my teenage years and became interested in athletics, the name Adrian for a boy gathered more than a passing interest. In an age when teammates and opponents had names like Dave, Joe, Rock, Rich, and Zeke, I showed up with an "Adrian" — but that never bothered me. In the back of my mind I knew a little about my uncle's story, and the name became one of pride rather than embarassment.

There were times, however, when I felt my pride being taxed. During my senior year of high school, I repeatedly received recruiting mail from the WAVES and WACS. Even today, at the age of 47, when I write a school textbook company and don't indicate my gender, the reply usually returns addressed to a Ms. Adrian R. Martin.

There have been benefits, too. As a high school student I represented our school at a large gathering of youth for a religious convention in Chicago. The hotel, one of the city's largest, knew the interests of teenagers, and their solution was to put the boys on the 20th through 24th floors and the girls on the 8th through 12th floors. When processing my reservation, they looked at my name and placed me on the 10th floor. I spent two wonderful days surrounded by girls before someone discovered the error.

My interest in being named after someone particular even extends to my family. My two sons are John Fitzgerald Kennedy Martin and Robert Francis

Kennedy Martin. I've always felt that being a namesake gave meaning and importance to one's life.

Although I share my uncle's first and last names, my middle name is not Raphael. My father had every intention of naming me Adrian Raphael, but my mother wanted neither. When I was born on a cold March Saturday in 1944, she compromised for Adrian Robert.

My efforts to write this biography actually began in earnest in October 1984. In 1973, when my mother passed away, I found an old shoe box in a closet that contained Adrian's war letters and POW cards, as well as letters written to my grandparents by surviving POWs. In spite of my parents' divorce, these obviously had been put away for me. I'm not sure, but in the back of my mind, as I went through my high school and college years, I believe that I knew of their existence. But at that age, the signficance of World War II, Bataan, and prisoner-of-war life was lost on athletics, girls, and cars.

Sometime toward the end of the seventies, however, the concept of heritage took on a new meaning with the television series *Roots*. About the same time, the country was startled with the words "hostage" and "prisoner" as we witnessed the Iranian crisis and other hostage situations. The events were not lost on me. I recall around 1982 taking all the material out of that shoe box and reading and rereading it as I waited for the Sunday evening television special, *Bataan, The Forgotten Hell*. I even searched history and geography books for references. As I watched, I recall the chill that went down my spine as the events on the screen corresponded to my shoe box letters. For a brief moment, I felt I was there on Bataan 40 years ago with my Uncle Adrian.

Not long after this, our school system in New London, Wisconsin, where I am employed as an English teacher, received a $20,000 grant to develop a program for students to study local history on an individual basis. I volunteered to be one of the teachers supervising a student. At the same time, I was working on a master's degree at the University of Wisconsin-Stevens Point and was in need of one credit, so I signed up for an Independent Writing course.

Even after the authorization of the one credit, I had no idea what to write about. Then the thought hit me. Why don't I do some historical research and writing which would help my participation in our local history project?

I finally decided to interview a 78-year-old coach from New London about what it was like to be an athlete and coach during the 1920s and 1930s. I thought that after a few hours of taped interviews and a 12-page paper, I would be done with the course. I would have my one credit. Instead, one year and three credits later, I had a 176-page biography of the man — not just sports and the twenties and thirties.

After the book was successfully marketed, many asked, "What's next?" I thoroughly enjoyed the vehicle of oral interview, and I knew I wanted to stay in the historical area. My next writing task finally dawned on me. The challenge of "discovering" who Adrian Raphael Martin was — what he stood for, and what happened to him in the Orient — and to do this by oral interview was a challenge too powerful for me to refuse.

I went to the public library and looked to see if there were any national organizations that included the men on Bataan. There was one: the American Defenders of Bataan and Corregidor. I took the eight names from the letters that I had and wrote the organizations to see if they had any of the men in their membership. They returned four addresses to me. But then I stalled. I thought of how difficult this venture would be. Would I find enough men to talk to? How much would they know about Adrian? Would they even want to speak to me?

I put aside the project for two months during the summer of 1984. Finally, one fall night while sitting in a graduate class, the professor wanted us to write down a description of a task that we had been meaning to do for some time and at which we had balked. Our homework was to do something about it. My mind was made up. The next day I sat down at the typewriter and wrote to the men whose addresses I had obtained.

By the first of October I had my first reply. By the time I completed the project, those initial interviews mushroomed to nearly 200. I have read 40 books on the topic and have attended numerous national and state ex-POW conventions. I have scanned 1,600 feet of microfilm from the National Archives in Washington, D.C., on documents, orders, medical charts, rosters, and diaries — all about the men I have been studying and interviewing. The microfilm has been a gold mine to this project.

As a youngster, when I would visit my father, he occasionally would tell me a story or two about Uncle Adrian R. Martin. When I got older, I mentioned to him a number of times that we should sit down sometime and tape his recollections. He always said, "We'll do it the next time." Unfortunately, my father died of a massive heart attack before anything was ever done.

Also, as a youngster, I spent my grade school years reading all the biographies on the classroom and library shelves. While most of my friends were into the Bobbsie Twins or some adventure story, I was captivated by the stories of George Washington, Abe Lincoln, and Teddy Roosevelt and what it was that made them achieve greatness. But as time went on, I found out that you don't have to be famous to achieve greatness. I became intrigued with looking at history not in terms of the great men or the great events, but what the common person was doing during the times of the great events or great men. Often their stories are more revealing than those of the famous. This, too, influenced my decision to begin this project.

In this book, you won't find out what was happening to General Douglas MacArthur or to General Jonathan Wainwright or to other important military leaders in the Philippines. What you will read are the actual words of the men who were on Bataan and Corregidor. They are my eyes and ears in telling the Adrian Raphael Martin story. It is important to remember that a good portion of what they experienced also happened to "Addie."

The reason for my writing this book can be found in the words of the dedication of E. Bartlett Kerr's book *Surrender and Survival*. Kerr's father, who fought in the Philippines, died on the Hell Ship, *Oryoko, Maru*. Kerr dedicated his book "to my father and the others who did not return to tell their stories." Practically everyone came back from World War II with a story. Because my uncle couldn't tell his, I'm doing it for him. This is especially important, as not one of the relatives still alive today knows exactly what had happened. One told me he died in battle, another said he died on the Death March, and a third said he perished working in a coal mine in Japan. Others mention his death in a Japanese salt mine, another his dying at Okita, and still another affirming that he died of pneumonia. None of this is the truth. Adrian Raphael Martin died of tuberculosis on 8 June 1945 at Hanawa, Japan. Even the tombstone on his grave in DePere, Wisconsin, is wrong. It says he died on 9 June 1945. For the most part, as far as his relatives and friends in the States were concerned, his wartime and prisoner-of-war life were known only to God — until now.

This project started out to set the record straight, but it became much more than that. It became a composite picture of the places and events that surrounded Adrian. And although many of the men interviewed did not know him personally, but just happened to be in the same place at the same time, many said, "I had to let you know what happened, because what happened to me affected your uncle also." Much of the material in the chapters on Las Piñas, the *Noto, Maru*, and Hanawa came from men who did not know Addie, but because they lived only a few feet from him, most likely what had happened to them also happened to Addie.

One of the real challenges of portraying these terrible years of POW life was that much of the history of those events in the Philippines and Japan exists today only in the cracks, crevices, and recesses in the minds of these 60-, 70-, and 80-year-old men. For most of what transpired in the Philippines and Japan you cannot consult a history book. Comparatively little has been written. Every event or incident that occurred truly has 360 degrees. A man's impression or interpretation is cast by the "angle" or "degree" from which he viewed it. Often, because of battle stress, physical and mental abuse, and months of slow but sure starvation, two men viewing the same incident might have two entirely different versions of what transpired and, yet, they might have been only feet apart. You will definitely find that in this book.

In May 1985, as I stood in a large ballroom of the Albuquerque Hilton, site of the American Defenders of Bataan and Corregidor Convention, an ex-POW from the 200th Coast Artillery Corps (CAC) said to me as he looked out at the 800 Bataan and Corregidor fighters enjoying the evening with their wives, "You know, every guy here has the story of what happened to him somewhat mixed up. But they all deserve to have their stories somewhat mixed up after what they went through."

That has been one of the difficulties of writing this biography. Not everyone is sure he got the story right. Another ex-POW once remarked to me that "Not everyone wants the REAL story to come out. Not everyone was a hero. Some did things they weren't proud of."

It is also difficult writing about what happened to these men during their 3½ years as POWs because for those in America it appeared that in April 1942 the earth opened up and swallowed the Battling Bastards of Bataan. Not much of what was happening to them got back to the United States. And yet some remember events so clearly and precisely that you know certain incidents are indelibly etched in the prisoners' minds.

Another problem I had in first trying to pry these stories from the men was whether or not I could be an appreciative listener. How could I, 25 years their junior and the product of the "soft" sixties and seventies, understand what they went through? How could anyone comprehend, except a fellow prisoner? Many times as I listened they asked, "Do you understand?" I would shake my head "Yes." We both knew, however, that I didn't.

Otis Yates, a cattle rancher from Clovis, New Mexico, and a 200th CAC man, told me over a beer at the American Ex-Prisoner of War Convention in July 1985, as we discussed the writing of POW books, "Nobody [POWs] tells it like it really was; nobody [writers] writes it like you really told it. How can you tell somebody about what really happened if they weren't there? How can they understand?"

My job is to tell the story the best I can, using the actual words of the men who were there.

Trying to write the biography of a man dead over 40 years and whose final 3¼ years were spent in Japanese confinement, with most of his relatives now dead, has been most challenging. One thing that helped is the fact that many of these Bataan and Corregidor men unfortunately will not be alive in a decade or two. It's amazing that so many have lived this long. I had the feeling that many of the ex-POWs realized that when I asked to interview them that it was time to unlock their minds and pour out to me that which they have never told before. For many it was a difficult experience. On more than one occasion a man has broken down and cried. Others would leave a sentence or topic right in the middle and gaze into space and then softly utter, "I don't want to go on."

This book was not solely for an audience of Adrian's relatives and ex-POWs. The intent was to demonstrate what happened to the young men of our country as they emerged from the poverty and lack of opportunity of the Depression era and were thrust into a war they did not choose. For many, in hindsight, every choice, every decision of the 1930s brought them closer to that inevitable conflict in the Pacific. For Addie, those decisions led to his death.

For myself, I have found out much. I have discovered how much Adrian Raphael and Adrian Robert are alike: in mannerisms, build, interests, and sense of humor, honesty, and positive thinking, and more. But beyond that — the *Roots* syndrome — I have found a group of ex-prisoners so tightly bound together — even after 40 years — that their feeling for one another defies description. When two strangers from Bataan embrace today, you can feel the genuine honesty when they say, "Hey buddy! You and I are one." To see that has been the most rewarding aspect of my research. As one ex-POW told me, "We're closer than brothers."

When I began, I wasn't sure what I would end up with. I felt like the man looking at the Rocky Mountains through a dense fog. He knows the mountains are there but can't see a thing. After a few hours, the fog starts to burn off and he can see more clearly until finally, later in the day, all the fog is gone and he can take in the total beauty of the mountains. When I began this work, I had no idea where I would end up. Each month some of the "fog" was lifted from the end product as I began to interview more men, read more books, and pore over microfilm. Finally the "fog" is gone, and the book is reality.

And so I am finished. I have found some answers. I have discovered things I never dreamed of finding. I feel like the man at the end of Edgar Lee Master's *Spoon River Anthology* who says at the completion of his life, "And now I pass this to you like an orange to a child. Do with it what you will."

I, too, have completed my quest. Here, World, is my book. Do with it what you will.

Chapter 1

The Early Years

Addie's Family

DePere, Wisconsin, 44.22° North, 88.4° West. Hanawa, Japan, 40.11° North, 140.48° East. DePere — a quiet Midwestern city of 6,000 — lies just south of Green Bay in the fertile farm country of northeastern Wisconsin. Hanawa, in the rugged mountains of northern Honshu, the main Japanese island, has a population of 20,000, many of whom work in the area mines. The difference in time between the two is nine hours. On the surface these two distant spots on the globe don't seem to have very much in common. But for Adrian Raphael Martin, the two were the most important cities of his short life. The former represents his place of birth, the latter his place of death.

A brief sentence in the Thursday, 5 March 1914, edition of the Green Bay *Press Gazette* announced: "A son arrived at the home of Mr. and Mrs. Wm. H. Martin yesterday." Adrian, or Addie (Ā/dē) as his friends called him, was the last of six boys born to William and Anna Martin. Older brothers Lee, Clarence, and Donald were still living at home at the time. Robert and Gerald had died previously at birth. The Martins lived in a large house on the south side of DePere, edged between the Chicago and Northwestern railroad tracks and the meandering Fox River, directly across the river from St. Norbert College. These were the same railroad tracks that would take Addie off to war in 1941, and the tracks that would return his ashes from Hanawa in 1945.

As Addie grew up in this rural setting, little did he realize that he was going to be a tragic example of what happened to the youth of his generation — a generation of youngsters emerging from World War I with the belief that this was the war to end all wars, that the world had been made safe for democracy. In his early teens, his generation was convinced that the prosperity of the twenties would continue into their adulthood. Opportunity would be plentiful. Addie, however, like thousands of others his age, would later find his hopes and dreams shattered by another world war — not only in Europe but also in the Far East.

From left to right: Addie's father, mother, Addie, brother Clarence, and an unidentified neighbor. (Courtesy of Josephine Smits)

His father also came from a long line of boys. Nine in fact. The Martin clan had moved to Rockland township in southern Brown County in 1850 from the rugged farm area of Galway, Ireland. They settled down to do what the Irish seem to know best — farm the toughest, rock-infested area of a county. Will Martin and some of his brothers, however, did not choose to carry on the farming tradition when they became young men. Two, Pat and Joe, became distinguished lawyers and had a marked influence on their nephew.

Uncle Pat, the oldest of the two, was a powerful area Democrat and a Brown County district attorney. He was generally regarded as the finest criminal lawyer in northeastern Wisconsin during the early 1900s.

Uncle Joe took his legal talents to the Supreme Court of the State of Wisconsin. He served on the court from 1934-1948 and was one of Addie's favorites. During the Depression, when Addie was attending the University of Wisconsin Law School in Madison, he made numerous trips to Joe's chambers at the Capitol to borrow money.

Will Martin, Addie's father, did not enter the legal profession, but he was by no means less intelligent than his brothers. For much of his life he made a decent living for his family by sharing in the Democratic "dole." His brother Pat, after all, was the leading Democrat in Brown County and for years the Democrats were in power. He held various jobs from beverage tax and revenue collector to supervisor of area highway construction.

Addie's parents: William Martin and Anna Lee Martin. (Courtesy of Josephine Smits)

Addie's mother, Anna, was from the Lee family and, like Will, could trace her roots to Ireland. In fact, in this part of Wisconsin, it was common for people of a particular nationality to settle in the same area, attend the same church, and usually marry someone of the same nationality.

Anna Martin appeared frail and usually kept a shawl wrapped around her shoulders, even on warm days. Despite her many illnesses, she kept the family together during the tough times with her patience and devotion to her children. Although money was scarce for new clothes, DePere parents commented that the Martin boys were always clean and well groomed.

Addie was especially devoted to his mother. As she continued to be sick, it was not unusual to see him helping her with shopping or up the steps of St.

Francis Church for First Friday Mass. His letters written home as a soldier are graphic examples of his love and concern for her.

With the emphasis upon education in his family, it was not surprising that Addie excelled when he began attending St. Francis School. He did so well, in fact, that he graduated a year early, having skipped a grade. But academics was not his only interest. One day, his and his friends' shenanigans caused the "terror" of St. Francis, Sister Lucy, to lock the culprits in a classroom to cool off. Addie and his friends made short work of her plans when they opened a window, jumped out, and made good their escape. Unfortunately, Japanese prisoner-of-war camp wasn't to be that easy.

High School Days

In 1926, DePere was a predominantly Catholic community composed of the Irish, Dutch, and German. A quarter-mile from the Martin home and near the banks of the Fox River sat East DePere High School. For Addie, a 13-year-old, wavy-haired freshman, this was his first large-scale experience with those who weren't Irish Catholics. You would expect someone a year younger than his classmates to disdain leadership, but on the contrary, Addie became a participant rather than an observer. Sitting on the sidelines wasn't in the Martin blood.

When he graduated at the age of 17 in the spring of 1931 with an 87 percent average, he had filled his four years by participating as a class officer, an orator, an actor, a yearbook editor, and a member of the football and basketball

Addie and cousins. (Courtesy of Josephine Smits)

teams. But more than this, he was remembered by his classmates for his cheerful, talkative personality.

His closest friends in high school were Jim Martin, Harold Schumerth, Jerry Kersten, and John Toonen. Jim, a cousin, lived on the family farm in the town of Rockland. Harold's family, which included 11 boys, ran the downtown furniture store next to the bridge spanning the Fox River. Their store was the social headquarters for the East DePere students. Jerry Kersten's father was one of the town doctors; Toonen's father worked at the local foundry.

Catholicism played an important part in Addie's life. As he entered high school, he continued to serve Mass at St. Francis and participate in other parish activities. He believed very strongly in his faith.

> HAROLD SCHUMERTH — Addie was a very religious kind of guy. He had tremendous respect for the clergy. Everyone in those days [1920s and 1930s] had respect for the clergy, but Addie had *tremendous* respect. If a priest said, "Jump!," Addie would say the expected, "How high?" Back in those days you never thought of going to Holy Communion unless you went to Confession first, and he used to take the longest time in his examination of conscience. He kept close to his faith. He spent a lot of time with the Lord.

But Addie spent time with others besides his high school friends and the Lord. Most high school students have difficulty communicating with the older generation, but Addie was one of those who could carry on long conversations with adults three times his age. Occasionally on his way home from school, he would stop to see his Aunt Bess, Mrs. Mark Lee, and entertain her with high school developments. When John Toonen arrived home late from work, he often found Addie and his mother already in a lively discussion. This ability to gab became a distinguishing trait that served him well in high school and college forensics. As Toonen remembers, "Addie had the ability to get along with everyone." Although he dated many young ladies, there were times, however, when he didn't always get along with the girls.

Jerry Kersten — all 300 pounds of him — and Addie were a real Mutt and Jeff combination. He frequently suggested to Addie that they call some girls and double-date in his father's new car. That was a real treat in those days when you could date with a car. But usually the evening turned out more trick than a treat with Addie on the receiving end of the trick.

> SCHUMERTH — The guy who really pulled some tricks on Addie was Jerry Kersten. He was the only one who had a car. Jerry would tell him that he's got a date and then he'd pick Addie up downtown around 7 o'clock.

High school football team at East DePere — Addie is in front row — middle. (Courtesy of Josephine Smits)

Well, Addie would be there around 6:30 [with his date] waiting for Jerry. Finally it would be 7:30, then 8:00, and no Jerry. He had no intention of showing up. He was off some place in Green Bay.

Addie stood up so many girls on account of Jerry Kersten that he was having a hard time getting dates. Everyone would kind of meet every night down by our furniture store, and some of the girls would say to one another, "I hope you don't have a date with Martin. He'll never show up!"

Yet, Addie and Jerry remained friends for years. The incident highlights two of Addie's traits. Although somewhat gullible, he was forgiving and always optimistic that better days and better times were just around the corner.

In high school, classroom work was easy for him. His inherited good memory, coupled with his speaking ability, insured accomplishment in curricular and co-curricular activities. The quotation under his graduation picture states, "I can't think unless I speak." He had roles in two operettas, "The Gypsy Rover" and "Miss Cherry Blossom." In forensics, under the tutelage of Mr. Koepke, Addie won or placed in most of the local and district contests, usually in extemporaneous speaking. He read voraciously and this gave him a large vocabulary.

JIM MARTIN — Addie won a lot of awards for speaking. He could really enunciate his words. Even today he'd stand out as a speaker. He used a lot of big words; he was that intelligent. He'd use a word and we'd say. "Now explain that word, Addie."

He'd give us a crazy look and say, "I'm not going to explain it to you dummies."

But he would explain it to the teachers.

MARTIN — He was never one to accept an answer. He'd question the teachers a lot. He read a lot so he knew a lot about what the teachers were saying. He could pick out things in what someone was saying that were wrong. Sometimes he'd say, "That's a lot of bull!" And then he'd really tell you about what the right answer was. He could practically paint a picture for you.

While he shined in school with his intelligence, vocabulary, and eloquence, none of these helped him when it came to performing manual labor. He disliked it. Working on the Irish farms south of town was not for him. In fact, when visiting Jim in the country, he stayed as far away from the animals and farm work as he could. When his friends were getting odd jobs, Addie usually

High school basketball team at East De Pere — Addie is in back row — far right. (Courtesy of Josephine Smits)

showed up just as they were finishing and getting paid. Then he'd suggest they "celebrate" the completion of the job with their new found wealth. Usually he was successful.

SCHUMERTH — Addie was opposed to hard, physical labor. He was very ambitious in moving around in society, in school work, and in trying to get to the top. But he was not a laborer in any sense of the word. He was very poor with his hands. He couldn't even paint well. We used to get little jobs like weeding beets for the farmers, but I can't remember Addie wanting any part of that. His ability was in speaking and handling people.

What's ironic about this dislike for physical work is that he played four years of high school football for Coach "Dad" Braisher. At 5′4″ and 130 pounds he was one of the smallest on the team but also one of the toughest.

JOHN TOONEN — On the football field he had guts. Oh, he had guts! No matter how big they were, he'd go after them.

But even with all his guts, there were times he couldn't escape "Dad" Braisher's dog house. The coach was called "Dad" because through the years he was more like a father to his players than a coach.

SCHUMERTH — Addie was quick — a lot faster than I was — but "Dad" never had a lot of confidence in his signal calling. The week before we played New London, we played a team, and it got to be fourth down and 25 yards to go, and Addie called a running play instead of punting the ball. Back in those days [1929], the coach didn't have communication with his signal caller like you have today. The quarterback called his own signals. Well, Braisher was just furious because Addie called a running play instead of punt formation.

So the next week we're over at New London, and we get the ball. Braisher told Addie, "I want you to run three downs and kick." Well, you know what happens. "Pop" Larson goes off right tackle on the first play for 20 or 30 yards. On the the next play, we get another 20, and on the third we make some more yardage. By now we're down on the New London 19-yard line, and Addie calls for a punt, and the kicker punted the ball right out of the field. That was the end of Addie Martin as a quarterback.

MARTIN — Addie was always in forensics, plays, the yearbook staff — a class officer — and the operetta, and "Dad" never liked that. He wanted us just to play football and basketball, and Addie used to miss practice once in a while. He used to make Braisher madder than hell.

But being into all the school activities was what small-town high school was all about during the 1920s and 1930s. Unlike today, where students tend to specialize, getting involved in a wide range of extra-curricular activities was the rule rather than the exception. For Addie, those high school experiences were positive.

After graduating in 1931, he looked forward to attending college. Going away to school at the time was out of the question. The Depression put his father out of work, so the choice of where to go was easy. St. Norbert College was a fine all-boys school just across the Fox River in West DePere, only a 1½-mile walk from his home. Tuition wasn't expensive.

Even though he disliked work, he managed to save money from various jobs. One summer he received a dollar a day carrying water during the construction of the Northland Hotel in downtown Green Bay. Actually, the job belonged to his older brother, Don, who disliked hard work as much as Addie. Don convinced his younger brother to take over. When Don wanted the job back, the workers asked Addie to stay on because he was doing a better job than Don.

Another chore he had was unloading the large Great Lakes' cargo ships that stopped in Green Bay and DePere. After a couple of days of backbreaking work, Addie looked for easier work. He thought he had found it delivering Coke, but his small hands made grasping the bottles difficult. Sometimes he broke more than he delivered. But the easiest job of all was the time Addie and his friends traveled 40 miles to Door County, an area nationally known for its cherry crop.

TOONEN — Oh, we had a good time that summer up in Sturgeon Bay picking cherries. About the only thing that Addie didn't care for was picking the cherries. Most of the time he'd work half a day, and even at that, he'd be sitting there on top of that ladder just staring at those cherries. During July and August, we lived in a tent, cooked our own meals, and ate by candlelight. Addie, Harold Schumerth, my brother, and I got along on very little money and saved most of what we earned for school.

Addie definitely wasn't used to working long hours on a physical job. In fact, he was usually more successful in *getting out* of work than in finding it.

Chapter 2

College Days

St. Norbert College

In September 1931, Addie withdrew his meager savings and strolled across the bridge to West DePere, enrolled, and paid his tuition. The St. Norbert of the thirties was a small, private Catholic college of approximately 200 male students. The Norbertine Order of teaching priests, who ran the school, attracted students primarily from Wisconsin, the Chicago area, the East Coast, and of course, DePere. Those like Addie, who lived at home and walked to school, were called the "day dogs" because the only time they were on campus was during the day.

During his freshman year, except for John Toonen, most of Addie's friends like Harry Schumerth and Jim Martin were still seniors in high school. Initially, Addie hung out with the "day dogs," but his outgoing, conversational personality soon changed all that. It wasn't long before Addie belonged to some of the other groups on campus.

There were over 70 freshmen that year in Addie's class. He was a member of the debate team and was Secretary-Treasurer of Alpha Tau Rho, the Honorary Debate Society. On Fridays he worked for the campus radio station WHBY and announced the acts for the musical program *Lamplit Hour*. And he was an enthusiastic participant in the intramural basketball and boxing programs.

He also did well in the classroom. At the end of his freshman year he had 36 credits, a large number for a freshman, and a 2.0 grade point average on a 3.0 scale.

> TOONEN — Addie was just an all-around guy at St. Norbert, and that's why everyone liked him. He was an above average student, but he could get along with anyone. I just managed to stay in school at that time. I often wondered how Addie could be in all those activities and still come up with those good grades. It was probably because of his good memory. He'd read it once and remember it.

The following September, he was joined at St. Norbert by his high school friends Jim Martin and Harold Schumerth. The "old gang" was back together again, and they were joined by another older East DePere grad, Virgil Kohlbeck, who was three years older than Addie. Kohlbeck's family ran the local dairy, and he and Addie were friends already during Addie's freshman year. The "day dogs" didn't have enough money for each to buy his books, so they often took the same course, bought only one book, and shared. During his sophomore year, Addie earned nine A's and three B's. At the end of the year, he was ranked number one in his class.

One of the activities these "day dogs" really enjoyed was entering a team in the college intramural basketball league. Virgil, Harold, John, Jim Martin, and Addie were joined on the team by another DePere native, John Fox. The college annual, *Des Peres*, described Addie's game: "Martin was the best dribbler in the league and had the habit of bringing the ball down court and then sinking a two-point."

Another sport that Addie became involved in was boxing. During his freshman year, the program, under the direction of Coach Malevich, became a major sport. Malevich had been a successful fighter/instructor from Chicago prior to coming to St. Norbert. Every day he put the pugilists through rigorous training. Nine boxing cards were offered during Addie's freshman year, and over 6,000 fans showed up at Van Dyke gym to cheer on their favorites. Addie won more than his share of fights that first year but lost the 135-pound college championship to Charles DeVett by a close decision.

At St. Norbert, Addie was interested in assuming leadership roles and moving up in the world. By his junior year he had risen to the vice presidency of the debating fraternity, Alpha Tau Rho. That year he and his partner, James Hughes, represented the college throughout the Midwest in debate tournaments. Later, he appeared in two Collegiate Players productions. In the comedy, *It Won't Be Long Now*, he had a minor role as a photographer, and in *First Night*, he ironically plays a prisoner in Sing Sing. Addie was also the Activities Section Editor of the 1934 *Des Peres*.

His interest in his religion increased during his years at St. Norbert. He remained close to the priests. In 1934, Addie was the vice-president of the school's Holy Name Society, the largest group on campus, and joined the Third Order, a religious study group. One would almost believe that Addie was possibly looking at the priesthood, but that was not the case. When it came to his campus social life, he still hung out with the "day dogs."

MARTIN — Addie had a lot of brass. He wasn't afraid to do anything. He'd see some gal, and he'd really want a date with her. He'd buy her a box of candy or maybe some flowers on the *first* date. He had that habit. He probably paid a buck-and-a-half for that candy, and then he'd never date her again.

He'd come back to me and say, "That's the girl I'm going to marry!" Then he'd never call her again.

She'd come around and ask us, "Is Addie mad at me?"

I don't think he ever got serious with a girl. I think a lot of times it was the money factor. He didn't have money, the girls in those days didn't have jobs like they do today, so marriage was out of the question.

Possibly Addie had every intention of graduating from St. Norbert. By the end of his junior year he had acquired 109 credits and had a grade point average of 2.25. He was a popular campus personality, a top-notch debater, a determined boxer, and a religious leader. But this was also the Depression, and in 1934 money for the Martins in DePere was hard to come by. His brother Don found a good job in the Records Department of the Wisconsin Telephone Company in Madison. He always had an influence upon Addie, and convinced him that his St. Nobert's success would provide a solid base for entering the University of Wisconsin's Law School in Madison and carrying on the Martin legal tradition. So despite being close to graduating with honors at St. Norbert, September 1934 found him on the University of Wisconsin campus in Madison.

The University of Wisconsin Law School

That Addie should pursue a law degree at Wisconsin was not a surprise to anyone. His grades and eloquence at St. Norbert were necessary prerequisites to succeed in Madison. His uncles, Pat and Joe, had been accomplished lawyers. What was surprising was that he would leave St. Norbert so close to graduation during the difficult financial times of 1935. In DePere, room and board were free and the cost of tuition and books was nominal. How could he afford law school?

Fortunately for Addie, Don obtained a job with the telephone company in Madison. After skipping two grades himself, Don graduated from East DePere High School in 1926 at the age of 16, and spent his next two years at Madison, Wisconsin. Because he lacked money to continue, he returned to DePere to work and supported his parents during the early years of the Depression and occasionally gave Addie some money for St. Norbert. Actually Don's goal was to be the lawyer in the family, but seeing Addie's talent and success at St. Norbert's, he decided that Addie should continue the Martin legal tradition. Although only 4 years older than Addie, according to Virgil Kohlbeck, "Don was more like a father to Addie than a brother."

When Don was a student at the University, he resided at the Norbertine

House on North Murray Street, just off State Street in the heart of the campus. Father Leo Rummel was in charge of the house. Evidently Father Rummel did such a commendable job of looking after Don when he was a freshman, he thought this would be an excellent place for Addie to live. Besides, Addie could earn part of his room and board by doing odd jobs around the building.

Academically, the caliber of student in Addie's law classes was much higher. He was not ready for the intense competition. To remain in Law School, a 74 percent average was required. After one semester he found himself with three very low grades: in Contracts a 55 percent, Property a 55 percent, and Torts a 62 percent. To remain in school, he would have to repeat these courses. But for the meantime, he decided to drop out of school for the second semester. Jobs were tough to come by. In addition to his room-and-board job at the Norbertine House, Addie passed out gum samples on Bascom Hill and donated blood, a common practice among students needing extra cash.

He returned in fall 1935, intending to really hit the books and get good grades. His weighted average was 75.5 percent, and he made up the three failed courses from the previous year. During the second semester, with the help of a summer school make-up of Contracts, his weighted average was 71 percent. The first semester of 1936, however, saw his grades take a nose dive. His average was 67 percent, and Addie decided to drop out during the second semester.

To continue to live in Madison required money, especially since he had moved out of the Norbertine House and in with other law school students. And this problem brings out another trait in his personality: he was *always* out of money, *always* wanted to borrow some, but he *always* made a point of paying it back.

> SCHUMERTH — Addie started having some financial problems. I know he never had money. He would borrow a couple of bucks from me, Don would give him some, and his Uncle Joe would help out. But he *always* paid it back.

> TOONEN — Addie would borrow money, but eventually he would pay every penny back. Even if it was only 50 cents, he would write it down on a piece of paper. He remembered everybody he owed money to.

Fellow law student Jerry Van Hoof recalls keeping three jobs just to stay in school and often asked Addie why he didn't get a job. Addie said something to the effect that he wasn't much interested in physical labor. Addie, he remembers, was good at manipulating events but not much for work. Jerry had a job near the Norbertine House, and Addie liked to stop and chat while Jerry worked. He'd ask Jerry if he could drive him down State Street in his Roadster to the State Capitol at the end of work. He and Jerry marched up to the Supreme Court chambers to see Addie's Uncle Joe, the Supreme Court Justice. Once in his office, he put the touch on his uncle for $20. Joe, who liked Addie, usually gave him the money. And on his little sheet of paper, the nephew marked down what he owed.

In April 1938, six weeks before the end of his last semester, he borrowed $30 from the Burr Jones Loan Fund for needy law students at the University of Wisconsin. To receive the cash, the student had to be recommended by the Law School Dean. The note was for 5 months at 3 percent interest and could be renewed at maturity at 6 percent annually. Addie's loan was granted on 28 April 1938. Five months later, 28 September 1938, the loan was renewed for another year. The University dug into some old, dusty files recently and found that his account showed $30 still due. The balance had not been pursued and was inactive because it showed that Addie was "missing in action."

What's intriguing is what he intended to do with the money. Though not a large sum by today's standards, during the Depression $30 went a long way. He intended to finance his education the following fall at the University of Notre Dame in South Bend, Indiana.

Notre Dame Graduate School

Addie began his studies at Notre Dame in fall 1938. Those who knew him after 1938 would have thought he had gone to Notre Dame all of his life. Addie was proud to attend Notre Dame. His "fighting Irish" spirit no doubt had something to do with it. Many of those who met Addie during the war years even thought him to be a Notre Dame graduate.

The reason why Addie chose Notre Dame can be traced to what happened to Harold Schumerth after leaving St. Norbert. Addie's long-time DePere friend attended Notre Dame graduate school in 1937-1938 with the help of a Knights of Columbus scholarship. Harold took classes leading up to a Master of Arts in Sociology, specializing in social work. After one year of school, he became seriously ill and dropped out after the 1938 spring term. Four months later, Addie appeared on campus taking almost the exact same courses as Harold. By the end of the year, Addie had 26 credits, an 84 percent average, and was close to a Master's Degree. An average of 80 percent was needed to graduate, so Addie's work at Notre Dame would be considered successful. His grades seem to indicate that he was doing a great deal of studying, but he also found time to have some fun.

On 17 November 1938, Coach "Dad" Braisher, Ray Maternoski, Jim Martin, and Harold, who was feeling better, motored to South Bend to see the

On vacation — John Collins, Addie, and Harold Schumerth. (Courtesy of Harold Schumerth)

On vacation — Collins, Addie, and John Toonen. (Courtesy of Harold Schumerth)

Addie as he looked shortly before going off to war.

Fightin' Irish play the Minnesota Gophers. Addie was to get the tickets and meet his DePere friends outside the stadium prior to game time.

> MARTIN — Addie had the tickets to the football game, and we were standing outside the stadium looking for him. Schumerth had been to Notre Dame, so he knew where to meet Addie. Well, we were waiting for him, and we could hear Addie hollering, "Get your textbook [program] of the game." We could hear his voice, but we couldn't see him.
>
> Finally he came over and said, "I sold your tickets. I didn't think you were coming." He was great for that kind of a joke.
>
> Then he said he had the tickets, "but the price went up $5.00 apiece." Braisher was ready to strangle him right then and there.

At the end of the spring term, Addie had good grades, with 26 credits, and was in need of only a few more for a Master's Degree in Social Work; but unfortunately, he was also broke.

When Addie returned home broke in June 1939, financial prospects to continue graduate school at Notre Dame were dim. Addie wasn't interested in getting work as a manual laborer, and to get into a professional occupation, he needed a college degree. By this time, he had over 200 college credits, most of them in history and sociology, but no diploma. How could he become a college graduate and not go to school that summer? If there was a way, Addie would find it. The answer was St. Norbert College. His transcript does not indicate that he took any classes that summer, but on 27 July he applied for a Bachelor of Science Degree in History. Then, on Thursday, 3 August, he received his diploma during summer graduation ceremonies. Evidently, Addie convinced the school to accept his credits from Wisconsin and Notre Dame and apply them towards graduation. He already had 109 credits from his previous stint at St. Norbert, and a student usually needed 128 to graduate.

Shortly after the ceremony, to celebrate what Addie thought would be the guarantee of a good job, he and John Toonen, Harold Schumerth, and John Collins jumped in a car and took off for a week long trip to Copper Harbor in Michigan's Upper Peninsula and points in Canada. When they returned on 9 August, Addie was ready to look for a full time "professional" job.

With his Notre Dame background in sociology, Addie took a job as a social worker in Southern California. A search of Los Angeles County Government and Catholic high school employment records does not indicate that he was employed by either. Friends and his 1945 obituary refer to his doing counseling at a "boys' home" or "boys' school," but neither indicate exactly where. With his religious background he probably worked for some Catholic organization.

When he arrived in the Los Angeles area in September 1939, he was hoping the job would lead to bigger and better opportunities. When he left in June 1940, he was broke again, homesick, and disappointed. To get back to Wisconsin he had to hitchhike. The week-and-a-half journey took him through many states that he had never seen before. His last ride took him to Kaukauna, 15 miles south of DePere. Since it was late at night, he slept in a cornfield next to the highway.

When he returned home the next day, he was tired, penniless, and disillusioned about his future. He contemplated a counseling job at the nearby Green Bay Reformatory, but with war clouds on the horizon, he also began considering a year or two in the Army. At his cousin's wedding in July, he told relatives he was considering that option.

Chapter 3

Joining the Army

The Draft

By the time Addie wearily returned to DePere in June 1940, Adolph Hitler and his German Army were already in control of much of Europe, having invaded Poland, Finland, Norway, Denmark, the Netherlands, Belgium, Luxembourg, and France. By July, Hitler had begun the battle for England. Addie, like many his age, knew that the United States would inevitably be drawn into the European conflict. Each day in 1940, his attention was drawn to the warfare across the Atlantic. Those in their twenties realized that the next Great War would no doubt be fought by them. But few young men imagined at this time that the fighting might also be to the west, where Japan had already begun its aggressive Greater East Asia Co-Prosperity Plan.

In Washington, President Franklin Roosevelt and his advisors also realized that our country's entry into global conflict was inevitable. Conscription was reinstated in September 1940 with the Selective Training and Service Act, the first peacetime United States draft. All males ages 21 to 35 were required to register with their local board in October. A lottery held in Washington at the end of that month determined the order in which men were called to service.

On 16 October 1940, Addie registered with his local draft board and received his draft serial number — 1046. The men were then given a classification according to availability, prior service, occupation, dependency, and religious conviction. Having no essential job and no dependents, Addie was Class 1-A — "available for military service." His draft card indicates that he was 5'5" and weighed 155 pounds, had blue eyes, black hair, and a ruddy complexion.

Two weeks later on 29 October, President Roosevelt and Secretary of War Henry L. Stimson began drawing the order of draft. Stimson drew the blue capsuled numbers out of the fish bowl and Roosevelt read them. As a result of the lottery, Addie was to be the 2,685th young man to be called in Brown County. His cousin Jim Martin was not as lucky. He was to be the 160th man

selected. Initially those drafted were to be in service for only a year. The draft
director, Clarence A. Dykstra, a former University of Wisconsin professor,
estimated that those with a number over 2,000, like Addie, would not be
drafted for well over a year — probably sometime in 1942. During the first few
months, only a few Brown County men were chosen. But in early 1941, as the
situation in Europe worsened, more young men were selected in the March
call, including Addie's cousin Jim. And to the surprise of many, Addie joined
Jim, volunteering a full year before he would have been drafted.

> MARTIN — Addie had one of the highest numbers in Brown County.
> His number wouldn't have come up for a long, long time. In October,
> he thought about joining the National Guard. I told him, "Christ, you
> don't want to join the National Guard! You don't have to evade the
> draft. You should be in pretty good shape — being a college
> graduate."
>
> But he was discouraged and frustrated about the job situation, and
> he was broke. If he could have gotten some kind of a job, he might not
> have volunteered. There just wasn't any work around here in sociolo-
> gy. He was ahead of his time as far as counseling jobs were concerned.

Besides trying for a job at the reformatory, Addie had also looked into some
teaching openings in area high schools but nothing panned out. By Christmas
1940, his spirits were at an all-time low. Here he was, 26 years old, a college
graduate, but without any job prospects or money. He wanted desperately to
be a lawyer, but his poor grades in law school prevented his return. There
didn't appear to be a future for him in DePere. When it looked certain that Jim
and many of his friends were going to be drafted in March, Addie believed that
after a year in the service the bleak job market in Wisconsin might improve.

As March approached, Addie, Jim, Harold, and Virgil Kohlbeck spent
many evenings at their favorite watering hole — the Union Hotel.

> MARTIN — I didn't want Addie to go into the Army. "You got all this
> education and you got a high number in the draft."
>
> One night we were all together, and Addie had a buzz on, and he
> jumped up and said, "I only have one life to give for my country."
>
> We all laughed about it then, but what a gulldarn thing that it would
> actually happen.

On Tuesday, 18 March, at 2:00 p.m., Addie and 100 Brown County men
reported to the draft board offices in Green Bay. Goodbyes between loved ones
were exchanged. Addie told his parents he'd see them in a year, he'd be sure to
go to church every Sunday, and he'd write often. At 3:10 the next afternoon 101

of the area's finest boarded the Chicago and Northwestern for the 140-mile train trip to Milwaukee. Bands played and speeches were given. The Green Bay *Press Gazette* gave front page coverage to the event. The article observed that "Adrian Martin, lightweight champion boxer in 1931 and 1932 and James Martin, varsity lineman for the St. Norbert Green Knight's football team . . ." were among those boarding.

Camp Grant

The Chicago and Northwestern passenger train slowly pulled away from the downtown Green Bay station and headed south for Milwaukee. For some on the train, there was a carnival atmosphere. In 1941, going off to become a soldier still evoked romantic ideals. Many old acquaintances were renewed.

After arriving in Milwaukee shortly after 6:00 p.m., the draftees were taken a few blocks to the Pfister Hotel, where they were fed and bedded down for the night. The next morning, the 101, along with many more young men from other draft boards, reported at 7:30 a.m. to the induction center for tests and their physicals.

Shortly thereafter, those passing were sent 40 miles to Camp Grant, located outside Chicago, where Addie and Jim were both given the Army mental exam. Both did quite well.

JIM MARTIN — I remember Addie and I took this IQ test. There were only 150 questions on it. After we got done and walked out, Addie said to me, "I got 143. There were three I had wrong and four I didn't know."

I did 115, which I thought was pretty good. I did some pretty good guessing. Addie had told me how this test would be. He said it would be multiple choice, and if you didn't know the answer, take a guess because it would be held against you if you didn't.

When the Army saw his score and his educational background, they called him in and wanted him to go to OCS [Officer Candidate School]. They tried to talk Addie into going, but he just wouldn't go, and I don't know why.

The reason was that Addie only wanted a year in the Army, and OCS would have required a much longer commitment. After more processing at Camp Grant, Addie, satisfied to be a regular soldier, Jim, and many others were put on another train on 25 March and shipped out for basic training to a relatively new camp near Houston. They arrived at Camp Wallace on the 27th.

Camp Wallace

The group sent to Camp Wallace near Galveston included not only the

Above and below: Two views of Camp Wallace near Galveston, Texas.

View of several barracks from water tower. Cars are parked on crushed seashell. (Courtesy of William A. Nolan)

Brown County soldiers, but others from the Midwest. Being the outgoing conversationalist that he was, Addie soon made friends. One of the first was Bill Nolan from Detroit, Michigan. Bill remembers well what Camp Wallace, located almost on the Gulf of Mexico, looked like.

BILL NOLAN — We were told this camp was built on a swamp area. To begin construction, logs had to be laid in three or four tiers. This area had to be drained. Then barracks were built. The parade grounds were filled and covered with broken seashells that came from a button factory. After two or three hours out on those shells, a person would return to the barracks, and place a cold towel over his eyes because you were almost blind. When we arrived on March 27th, barracks were still being built.

The new soldiers were put through the "normal" basic training exercises. To let the civilians back in DePere know what the boys were going through, Jim Martin was asked to write a letter to the *DePere Journal-Democrat* describing army life at Camp Wallace.

MARTIN — Just a few lines to my many friends in northeastern Wisconsin telling them something about Army life.

We are up at 5:30 in the morning. We stand reveille at 5:40, after which we hurry back to the barracks to make our beds, wash up, and get ready for breakfast at 6:00 a.m. After breakfast we scrub the barracks, police the grounds. All of this is done before 7:00 a.m. when we line up for infantry drill. From 8:00 to 10:00, we have artillery drill and lectures on general principles pertaining to army warfare. From 10:00-11:00, we have rifle practice, such as target practice and getting insights and windage on the range.

The dinner hour is 11:30-1:00 p.m., although we are apt to be inspected during this period. From 1:00 to 2:30, we have lectures on 3-inch guns, communication in general, or drill for a weekend parade. From 2:30 to 4:30, we have lectures on knot tying, map reading, or warfare camouflage. From 4:30-6:30 is the supper hour. We are free from 6:00 p.m. to 9:00 p.m., unless we have an hour's infantry drill. We are in bed by 9:00, unless we have a pass which is only good to 11:00 p.m. On Saturday, we have general inspection of barracks, clothes, field equipment, and arms. At 11:30 on Saturday, we are free until 11:00 p.m. Sunday night.

The weather is extremely fine since our arrival. The temperature has averaged around 83 degrees. We have had very little rain although we have had a lot of windy weather.

At the end of his letter he mentions that Addie ". . . is being groomed for the position of First Sergeant, a position he no doubt could handle." With his college background and his high IQ, Addie was again encouraged to attend OCS at Fort Benning, Georgia. But he declined, thinking one year and out was

Addie in uniform at Camp Wallace.

what he wanted. Yet his background marked him as one to be promoted rapidly. He was one of the first in this new batch of draftees at Camp Wallace to be made a First Sergeant.

Camp Wallace, however, was not all work and no play. In April, Addie, Jim, and Bill Sutton traveled 30 miles north to Houston to celebrate Easter weekend. They saw the sights, and because they had little cash, all slept in the same room on Saturday night.

> MARTIN — We got paid $21.00 per month. The first payday we got was the Saturday before Easter. We had maybe nine dollars between us, pooled it — and that took us into Houston for the Easter weekend. We got one room in a hotel. We went to church Easter morning and then went around to the other churches looking at these young babes all dressed up in their finest, like they were in an Easter parade.

That morning Addie awoke early and sent a letter to his dad on Houston YMCA stationery. He mentions that Jim, Bill Sutton, a friend from Chicago who had worked in Green Bay before being drafted, and he were just finishing breakfast and would be leaving for church shortly. At the end of the letter, he mentioned that the rumor around camp was that when they finished basic training, the men would return to Camp Grant for more training.

Bill became a good friend at Camp Wallace, and Addie helped him out with an important matter to a soldier — mail from home.

> MARTIN — Bill was never getting any mail. For months no mail came for him, and he had a girl in Green Bay. Addie said, "There's something wrong. I'll go over to the mail-call person and talk to him."
>
> Well this mail-call guy had a Texas drawl, and what he was calling was "Sutto — Sutto," and nobody ever answered. Addie came back and told Sutton to go and get his mail. The dumb corporal couldn't even pronounce his name right.

Camp Wallace was comprised of soldiers from many parts of the country. One of these groups was the uneducated Southern hillbilly.

> MARTIN — Addie was a helluva good writer. He had excellent penmanship. Back in college he would write letters for guys looking for jobs. He used to put us all to shame with his penmanship.
>
> Well, the best gun men at Camp Wallace were these hillbillies. In basic training, these guys broke all the firing records. They didn't have any brains, but boy, could they hit the target. Addie always used to say, "I want to be on their side."
>
> These guys would get letters from their girls back home, and Addie would read the letters for them and add all kinds of romantic stuff. He'd also help these guys write letters home to their girls. He'd add

Interior of barrack at Camp Wallace, Galveston, Texas. 27th Training Battery. (On back of picture was this note: "Mother this is the inside of the upper floor in our barracks. The lockers on the floor are for our clothes.")

some things like how much they missed them and how much they loved them.

He'd say, "A lot of those girls back home are lonesome, too."

Another of his good friends was Bill Wells from Berlin, Wisconsin. Bill had gone to Ripon College and was working for the power company when he was drafted. Bill was a big, powerful guy, and Addie enjoyed playing tricks on him.

MARTIN — Bill was a a good-looking guy. Later he was one of the first to die in prison camp. He was a good friend of Addie's. He'd get in more damn fights. We'd go into a honky-tonk, and it would be about five deep at the bar. Addie would sneak around and kick him in the shins, and Bill would turn around swinging, and Addie, being quick, would be gone. I'll bet Addie did this three different times to him.

One Sunday morning we were sitting in the barracks and Bill said, "I'd like to find the bastard who kicked me!"

Addie said, "I think I know who it was. It was so and so." And that guy happened to be sitting there at the time. Bill chased after the guy, and everybody started laughing.

Bill finally said to Addie, "Are you the little shit who kicked me in the shins?"

Addie would say with a smile, "No, I wouldn't do that to you, Bill."

Laughs were easy to come by at Camp Wallace, but money wasn't. A soldier in those days couldn't do much on $21.00 a month. And as usual Addie was good at borrowing money from others.

MARTIN — Addie used to come over to my barracks and ask, "Did you get your check yet?"

"Yeah."

"Well then, let's go!"

Nolan, Wells, and I never had a lot of money. Occasionally we'd get some from home. Addie never had any money, and when he'd try to borrow a couple of bucks, we'd give him hell.

"You'll never pay it back, Martin. Where's the money coming from?"

He'd say, "I just talked to my brother Don, and the check is on its way. Let's go to town."

But we usually never went to town until the end of the month when

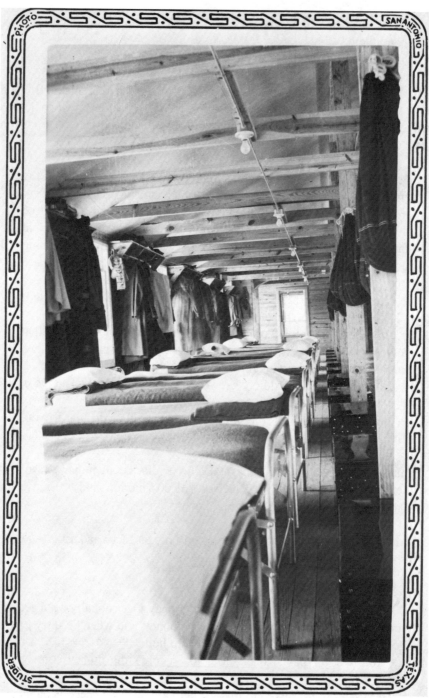

Barracks at Camp Wallace — close view of beds. (On back of picture was this note: "The pillow which has an ink spot on it is my bed. Our pants and shirt and coats hang on the racks on the wall. That is how we have to make our bed every day.")

we had payday. Galveston was a rough town, so we usually went to Hitchrock, which was only about five miles from camp.

Addie was attracted to those with money and connections. On 2 May, he and a soldier from a wealthy family finagled a weekend pass and traveled by train to Louisville, Kentucky for the running for the roses — the Kentucky Derby. They left Houston on a Friday night and got back to camp by 5:00 a.m. Monday morning. The Derby that year was memorable in that Whirlaway, with Eddie Arcaro riding, set a new record of 2.02.2. Addie shared memories of that exciting weekend with friends in the barracks. And his rich friend paid for most of the weekend.

A week later, Addie wrote a short letter home to his mother. Sunday, 11 May, was Mother's Day, and he wanted to make sure she knew she was uppermost in his thoughts.

ADDIE MARTIN LETTER — 10 May 1941 — I went to confession this afternoon and will offer Communion for you tomorrow morning. Wanted to send you a table cloth with C[amp] W[allace] insignia for Mother's Day but they ran out of them before pay day. Also hoped to send a telegram this afternoon but found out that the place for sending them was way out at the other end of Camp — just where, I don't know.

So here's a letter a little late but it's to tell you that you're the grandest mother in the world. . . .

After Mother's day there were six more weeks of basic training before reassignment. The DePere men were hoping to return to Camp Grant. That way they'd be only 200 miles from home and at least have a chance to see their families again. But that was not the case.

After 14 weeks of basic training, the Brown County soldiers were not shipped north. To their dismay they stayed in the Southwest. On Friday, 27 June, they boarded a Southern Pacific train and headed west. Two days later, after an 800-mile trip, they arrived in late afternoon in El Paso, Texas. Trucks were waiting to take them to their new home — Fort Bliss. Jim Martin observed, "Texas has to be the only state where you can take a two-day train ride and never leave the state!"

Fort Bliss

Fort Bliss was a sprawling military reservation, 75 miles long and 54 miles wide located north of El Paso. The sandy, mountainous area contrasted starkly with the low swamp land of Camp Wallace. Instead of the comforts of new barracks, at Fort Bliss the men slept in six-man tents.

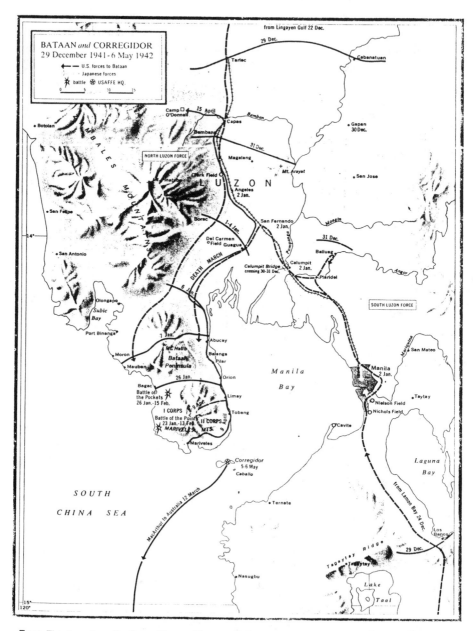

From *The American Heritage Picture History of World War II*, by C. L. Sulzberger (New York: American Heritage Publishing Co., Inc., a Division of Forbes, Inc., 1966), p. 166. Used with permission.

The men shipped from Camp Wallace were needed to fill spots in the four National Guard units training at Fort Bliss and to bring them to war-time strength. The Guard units federalized in late 1940 were the 202nd Coast Artillery from Chicago, the 206th from Arkansas, the 260th from Washington, D.C., and the 200th from New Mexico. They all had six months of training prior to Addie's arrival. The units all anticipated being sent to the impending World War, but none knew exactly where.

The National Guard units were comprised of citizen-soldiers from a particular city or region in a state. Until being called up, their training consisted mostly of weekend drills. On 4 July, after five days in camp, Addie voiced his displeasure at being at Fort Bliss with the Guard units, in a letter to Harold Schumerth.

> ADDIE MARTIN LETTER — 4 July 1941 — We're now 4,000 feet above sea level, whereas at Wallace we were only a few feet above sea level. . . . No, we didn't get back to the Chicago area as was hoped for. . . . We're with National Guard outfits now. They're a bunch of Boy Scouts alongside the regular Army men. In three months, we had more work with the rifle, machine guns, and larger guns etc. than these fellows have had since January. And what's more, these jokers have eaten up most of the ratings [promotions] already. But that's the Army.

Shortly after arrival Addie was plugged into the 200th Coast Artillery, the New Mexico National Guard, as a Chaplain's Assistant, and many of his Camp Wallace friends — Bill Nolan, Bill Wells, Urban McVey, Walter Schuette, Motts Tonelli, and Solly Manasse — were also assigned to the outfit. Many from the unit were Spanish-Americans or Indians. For some from the Midwest, adjustments in attitude had to be made. Addie was up to the challenge, but he had to adjust to having his bed in the tent with his new "friends" from New Mexico.

> JOHN L. JOHNSON — Addie and I were in the same six-man tent at Fort Bliss. The first night he was there, he went to visit some Camp Wallace boys in another battery. Some of the others, me included, short-sheeted his bed. We were in bed when he came back. He didn't turn the light on, he got into bed, then got out of bed, remade his bed hurriedly, and went to sleep. The next morning he never said anything about it.

Part of the problem initially was that many of the Camp Wallace arrivals, especially the men from the Midwest, were older and, in many cases, more

Bill Nolan, left, waiting with Addie Martin, right, for the bus at Fort Bliss.

educated than their New Mexico counterparts. They believed that many of those ranked above them were too young and not as intelligent. Addie sarcastically addressed this problem in a letter to his mother.

ADDIE MARTIN LETTER — 27 August 1941 — To be sure, mother, there are a lot of things in this Army that look inefficient as the devil and a lot of things that look unfair. For example, all the time we were at Wallace, we were with Texas fellows who ran home every other weekend. But they [officers] told us we were going back north at the end of thirteen weeks so no one complained. Then at the end of our training they send us over here to join National Guard units. Well

Addie, left, at Fort Bliss, El Paso, TX.

these National Guard outfits were ALREADY organized and all the ratings were taken up by the boys from the particular cities where the batteries come from. It's a God damn shame to see some of the punks they've got in good positions. Some of them can't pronounce anything over a two-syllable word. But as we say there are two ways of doing a thing — the right way and the Army way. So, if anyone ever asks you about progress in the Army, tell them there isn't a hell of a lot of chance for it in National Guard units.

Prior to 1939 the New Mexico National Guard was a distinguished Cavalry unit. Many of the Camp Wallace men noticed the horses on arrival in El Paso and wondered what kind of Army they were getting into. But by the time Addie arrived, the New Mexico outfit already had been converted to Coast Artillery/Anti-Aircraft units. But Addie's interest in the 200th wasn't with the guns. He saw an opportunity to put his mind to use.

ADDIE MARTIN LETTER TO HAROLD SCHUMERTH — 15 July 1941 — I'm working with Tonelli on a regimental athletic program, teaching a class in English and extemporaneous speech. . . . Motts was drafted out of Chicago. He rather hates this Army setup but neither of us is killing ourselves on the job.

ADDIE MARTIN LETTER TO HIS MOTHER — 27 August 1941 — I'm doing office work — personnel work for the most part and doing a good job of it. Haven't had to do a lot of drilling or anything of that sort for a long time.

Tonelli was Mario "Motts" Tonelli, who had been a rugged Notre Dame fullback in the 1930s. Prior to being drafted, he had been a rookie running back with the Chicago Cardinals of the National Football League. Like others, Motts expected to serve one year, and then resume his promising professional football career. The Notre Dame connection helped cement his friendship with Addie. Motts, however, had been hoping to join his hometown Chicago National Guard, the 202nd, but when he had the opportunity to head a Regimental Recreation Program for the 200th, Motts jumped at the chance. Addie assisted him, and they both worked out of Chaplain Howden's office.

Besides helping with the Recreation Program and doing some teaching, Addie spent most of his time doing clerical work. There were men in the 200th who could neither read nor write, and Addie occasionally helped them. He was also busy writing dependency discharges. Soldiers from families with money problems could request a discharge to return home and help their families. With the United States still at peace, the Army considered these petitions. As war approached in late 1941, these discharges became harder to get. With his mother ill and in the hospital during summer and fall 1941, and with his father out of work, Addie considered applying for a discharge to return home and help his family.

ADDIE MARTIN LETTER — 27 August 1941 — I'm not sorry I joined up — this time will go fast enough. Don't worry, at the end of a year if we're still at peace, I'll get out on a dependency discharge or some other similar method. I certainly draw up enough applications for the other fellows with less deserving cases.

But there was also time for fun. On several occasions Addie, Jim Martin, Bill Nolan, and others went into El Paso and Juarez just across the border in Mexico. For the Midwestern soldiers this was their first experience with the "South of the Border" culture. Both cities offered extensive shopping opportunities.

Addie got to see the sites in Juarez once for a few hours. Most of his outings, however, were to El Paso, but even then, there were parts of El Paso the soldiers were warned to stay away from. When a fellow soldier who went to the wrong side of town was knifed, practically all of the Fort Bliss men blamed it on "the Mexicans." Addie was one of the few who said the incident never would have occured had the soldier stayed where he was supposed to. Addie was tolerant and understanding in that regard. The issue, rather than *who was involved*, usually swayed his judgement. That's why he got along well in the 200th, a unit with a very strong Spanish-American and Indian flavor.

His speaking ability often defused tense situations. That ability received a

Jimmie Martin of DePere, Wisconsin, left; Bill Nolan, center; and Jimmie Barrett, right, of Detroit, Michigan. Tents of Battery "H" 200th CAC, El Paso, Texas, Fort Bliss. (Courtesy of William A. Nolan)

Addie Martin, left, 28 August 1941, and Jim Martin, right, El Paso, Texas.

severe test when Jim and Addie stopped at one of their favorite taverns in Logan Heights.

MARTIN — We used to go to this tavern and we all would order Schlitz beer.

The bartender used to say, "Aw, go back to Milwaukee you dumb Germans!"

We used to have a helluva time with him. I guess he had tended bar in Milwaukee once.

"Anyone who orders Schlitz beer out here, well. . . ."

He expected us to order Texas beer. He was our buddy. A lot of the Wisconsin guys liked to hang out at this place. He told us about these two guys in the back room that were going to go AWOL. There was a guy from Appleton and a guy from Green Bay. Addie went back there and told them what would happen if they did and talked them both out of it.

Being able to talk someone out of something became a Martin trademark. Often it worked with some outside help.

MARTIN — I had this Jewish guy in my outfit from Washington, D.C. He told us that if we went into a Jewish-owned store in El Paso early in the morning and a shirt was marked $2.00, if we offered them a quarter they'd take it. The Jewish people thought it was bad luck to lose their first sale of the day.

Addie and I went down early one morning and bought two short sleeve dress shirts. We offered them 50 cents and they took it.

Another new Army friend was Solly Manasse of Las Cruces, New Mexico. Ironically Solly was not in the New Mexico National Guard. Like Addie he was a draftee and sent to Camp Wallace about the same time. Although Solly was from New Mexico, he and Addie had much in common. Solly had spent the summers of his youth at a camp near Madison, Wisconsin. The area so impressed him, that when the time came to go to college, Solly decided to attend the University of Wisconsin. Although they didn't know each other at the time, Addie and Solly were on the campus together in the thirties. Being college graduates, their intellects were similar. Because both were older than most of the New Mexico guard unit, age also helped cement their friendship. They remained together during the War and prison camp experience.

A difference in age had an effect upon Addie's circle of friends. Your close friends socially were those your age. That was certainly true with Bill Evans, a young Guard member from Deming, New Mexico, who was part of Addie's Headquarters Company, Second Batallion. By the time the two first met, Addie was 27.

BILL EVANS — At Fort Bliss, Addie and I were not close, buddy-buddy friends like some others in the outfit. I knew him to be a fine, honorable man. He was considerably older than most of us. We were just kids. We had a Motor Sergeant that was 35 years old. We called him "Pops." If you were over 20 you were bordering on middle age in the 200th.

Chaplain Howden

Chaplain Fredrick B. "Ted" Howden, Addie's Fort Bliss boss, was one of the most respected officers in the New Mexico National Guard. Born the son of the Episcopal Bishop of New Mexico, Chaplain Howden was educated at Yale but returned to New Mexico to enter the Episcopalian ministry. He was a very tall, slender man with deepset eyes and a high forehead accented by a receding hairline.

Prior to Fort Bliss, he had been a Chaplain at the New Mexico Military Institute at Roswell, where he was also a swimming coach. A devoted family man, his decision to join the Guard and then follow the unit to Fort Bliss was difficult. He and his wife, Betta, had three young sons, Ted, Alfred, and John. When the 200th received their orders to go to the Philippines, the decision to follow was extremely difficult. His age and family situation permitted him the option of remaining behind. But his sense of duty to the men in the unit was strong. His wife was rather bitter when he departed Fort Bliss in late August and left her to care for the three small sons.

Bill Evans of Headquarters Company was one of those who drove a truck and helped move the Howdens at Fort Bliss. Howden's religious task in the 200th was made difficult by the fact that most of the unit, including Addie and Motts, were Catholic, and he was Episcopalian.

> FRED BREWER — Chaplain Howden was the religious leader for the regiment although a great number of the men were nominally Catholic. He was the son of the Bishop of the Episcopal Conference for all of New Mexico.
>
> I was drafted as a Protestant assistant to him doing office work, helping with Sunday services, playing piano for the hymns, and doing correspondence for the men, many of whom were Navajos, Hispanics, and even Anglos without schooling. I also kept track of games, library holdings, and social activities.

Jumping ahead, it's fascinating to find out what happened to this Episcopalian chaplain during the war. When the 200th arrived in the Philippines in September 1941, waiting to meet them was the legendary New Mexico Catholic priest, Father Albert Braun. Legendary because Father Braun's ministry spanned two world wars and many decades of working with the Mescalero Apache in New Mexico. In her biography of the good father, *Among*

The Mescalero Apaches, Dorothy Emerson details how Chaplain Howden, an Episcopalian with a unit predominantly Catholic, prevailed upon Father Braun to come to Bataan from Corrigedor to celebrate Mass for the Catholics in the 200th. Being from New Mexico in the first place, Father Braun already knew many of the soldiers. Father Braun and Chaplain Howden formed a close working relationship that continued during the early days of the prisoner-of-war camp.

In October 1942, Father Braun and Chaplain Howden were transferred with over 1,000 other prisoners to Davao Penal Colony 700 miles south of Manila. Along the way Chaplain Howden became very ill and was near death. He asked Father Al and Father Herman Baumann to baptize him a Catholic. Shortly after arrival at Davao, Chaplain Howden died a Catholic. Not many knew of the conversion. Father John Duffy, who later became a close friend of Addie's at Fort Stotsenberg in the Philippines in the few months before the war, revealed some of the particulars of the conversion in a letter to Addie's parents after the war.

FATHER JOHN DUFFY LETTER — 27 November 1947 — Both Adrian and Motts [Tonelli] helped their own Chaplain [at Fort Stotsenberg] who was an Episcopalian. Howden, I believe his name was. But with over 60 percent of that regiment Catholic it was a great help to me to have such swell Catholics in the Chaplain's office. Howden was a good fellow. In fact, exceptionally good. He died in Davao prison camp in early '43 or the last of '42. Asked Father Braun to receive him into the Church. Received all the sacraments and died a Catholic. Some of the Protestants did not like it and none of us have told his wife as we thought that there was no need to disturb her. We feel that he can do far more for her up above pulling a few strings with St. Peter.

The Episcopalian minister, who died a Catholic, was seized from this earth in his prime. Like Addie he had dreams and a family to come back to. What interaction and impact the two had on each other is unknown, but Addie's cousin Jim, who wasn't aware of the circumstances of the Chaplain's death, remembers, "We knew Addie's boss at Fort Bliss was a non-Catholic Chaplain. We always said, Addie would convince him to become a Catholic priest."

Chapter 4

Call to the Philippines

Departing Fort Bliss

Since January 1941, the 200th CAC had undergone extensive training at Fort Bliss with their "new" anti-aircraft equipment. Most of the New Mexico guardsmen had entered the service when it was still a cavalry unit. Working with these large guns was challenging, but even more challenging was the fact that much of the equipment and ammunition was World War I vintage. The purpose of anti-aircraft is not just to shoot the enemy out of the sky but also to disrupt their bombing pattern. Jim Martin recalled watching the 200th train and seeing their equipment. "The 200th had no equipment to speak of. They couldn't have shot if a bird came at them. They had just lousy equipment."

Even with poor equipment, the guard stood a chance to improve if they could fire at real targets. In 1941, a tow-target squadron finally arrived at Fort Bliss. Their job was to tow gliders and drones to where the 200th CAC could fire at them. But sometimes this practice had mixed results.

> JOE STEMLER — We got to fire at targets at Fort Bliss, but we damn near hit the tow plane instead of the target. The pilots, they didn't want to fly anymore.

But despite an occasional errant shot, the gunners of the 200th must have distinguished themselves to the Army observers from Washington. In early August, the Guard toured New Mexico to "show off" their equipment in front of friends and family. For a week beginning 8 August, a National Guard convoy of 1,700 officers and men and over 250 vehicles went around the state. Stops were made in Deming, Hatch, Hot Springs (Truth or Consequences), Socorro, Belen, Albuquerque, Roswell, and Carlsbad. In a July letter to Harold Schumerth, Addie referred to the impending August maneuvers but "from there we don't know just where we'll be going." The suspense didn't last long. On 17 August, two days after returning to Fort Bliss, the 200th

received their secret overseas assignment of great importance — Fort Stotsenberg in the Philippines.

Although the destination was not explicitly given to the men, most guessed
that the Pacific assignment was the Philippines.

> ADDIE MARTIN LETTER TO HIS MOTHER — 27 August 1941 —
> [his last letter from Fort Bliss] — We expect to leave [Fort Bliss]
> Sunday or next Tuesday — either one. We'll be going to San
> Francisco, then I believe on to the Philippines by way of Hawaii.
> That's the story and that's about all there's to it. Rather glad to be
> moving out of this sand and stone country.

The First Battalion had already left Fort Bliss on 20 August. After saying
good-bye to Jim Martin, who remained with another guard unit, Addie and the
Second Battalion boarded a train on Sunday, 31 August, for the trip to San
Francisco. By this time the First Battalion had already left for the Philippines
on the SS *Pierce*.

After an uneventful two-day trip through New Mexico, Arizona, and
California, the Second Battalion arrived at Fort McDowell on Angel Island in
San Francisco Bay. Troops going overseas usually stopped here for shots and
sun tan uniforms. Although uneventful for most, for Addie it was a miserable
trip because he had dysentery, a cruel foreshadowing of problems to plague
him and other prisoners during their POW years. On Sunday, 7 August, Addie
wrote a letter to his mother explaining his illness and also expressing his
excitement about seeing the world, but at the same time longing to be back in
Wisconsin.

> ADDIE MARTIN LETTER — 7 September 1941 — It's a cool and
> beautiful fall afternoon on Angel Island here in San Francisco Bay.
> We've just finished noon dinner so before doing anything else this
> afternoon, I'm going to write this letter to you. It will likely be the last
> letter to reach you for a while as we're supposed to sail tomorrow
> afternoon.
>
> I might tell you that I'm still in the hospital here but expect to be
> released tomorrow morning in time to get ready to board ship. Have
> been in here for four days now but right now feeling okay again. I had
> a case of the dysentery which began a week ago yesterday and
> continued for about a week — that stuff is really bad. I can appreciate
> how Dad must have suffered. However, it is all over with now and the
> appetite is right back where it belongs. I was all set to leave here today
> but they never release anyone on Sunday — so I'll have to wait until
> morning. I understand we're sailing on the COOLIDGE.

I'd certainly like to be back in Green Bay watching the Packers this fall and to be with you. But since that is next to impossible, it's better not to talk about the whole thing. Everything will turn out okay and I'll get back there in due time. Meantime mother I always think about you, Dad, Leo, Don, and Moon [Clarence] and pray for you all each night and hope that you're doing likewise for me.

I know that I'll enjoy this trip — for I've always wanted to see as much of this old world as I could. And now I'm getting a chance to do just that. Yet, when this is all over, I'll be perfectly willing to settle down to a normal life.

Two days later, 9 September, the 200th CAC departed Angel Island at 9:00 p.m. Addie and many of the other men stood on deck and looked back at the Golden Gate and the San Francisco lights as the SS *Coolidge* headed west into the Pacific sunset. For most this was to be their final glimpse of the United States for over four years. For some, like Addie, this was their last.

President Coolidge

The ten-year-old *President Coolidge* was one of two Dollar Line luxury ships in trans-Pacific service taken over by the Army in 1941. On her smoke stacks were the characteristic Dollar signs. Steaming west she transported troops, and returning she would evacuate civilians.

On the second day of the 7,000-mile voyage, Addie discovered some of the *Coolidge's* stationery and began a day-by-day letter to his mother describing the trip. On a boat with over 2,000 soldiers crammed into every available space, sometimes there wasn't much to do except write home. The journey was rather monotonous as every morning the men awoke, looked out the portals, and saw nothing but miles and miles of ocean. Still there was some excitement.

ADDIE MARTIN SHIP DIARY — Wednesday — 10 September 1941 — We've been out to sea now for two days and won't land in Honolulu until Saturday morning [Sept. 13]. That will be the first chance we'll have of sending off any mail. Anyway I'll start this letter now and probably add to it tomorrow and the next day.

Did not experience any sea sickness at all and likely won't now anymore. We're on the COOLIDGE a ship built in 1931 — a fine ship. San Francisco with all its lights aglow presented a beautiful sight as we cleared harbor Monday night and pulled out under the Golden Gate Bridge. San Francisco you see is built on hills as are Oakland, Berkley, and other cities located on San Francisco Bay.

Starboard side view of the *SS Coolidge*, 15 September 1941. The 200th CAC and 194th Tank Battalion were on this ship. (Courtesy of William Nolan)

Am bunking with Tonelli in the lower berth of a double-decker-bed — a little crowded but okay. There are 2200 soldiers aboard. We had a life boat drill this afternoon and will probably have one each day now. Outside of that there hasn't been much of anything else. A few improvised offices have been set up. I have to report for one hour a day.

We may stay in Honolulu for a day or two and then again we may only stay a couple of hours before leaving for Manila.

Anyway mom, this is an experience a person will never forget.

I've covered a lot of miles since I left DePere but I've never ceased thinking of you and all the family. I'll be glad of course when this is all over and I'll be able to get back to normal life.

Am afraid I have to shove off for evening dinner in a few minutes so will have to add more to this later.

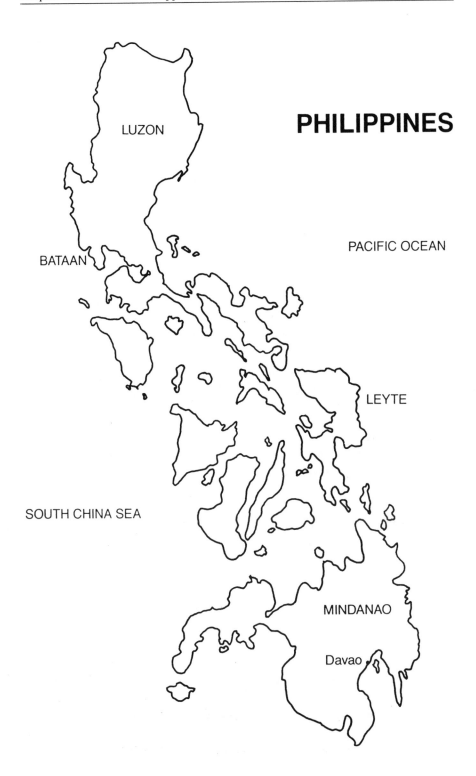

And it was the race to dinner that provided the first bit of excitement on board. One of Addie's friends in the Headquarters Battalion provided the entertainment, and because it involved boxing, Addie attended the excitement.

JACK ALDRICH — The Second Battalion, 200th CAC, sailed for the Orient on the *Coolidge*. Also aboard were elements of the 194th Tank Battalion.

Now I suppose every Army has its chow-hounds, and we certainly had our proportionate share on board ship. These fellows would line up for dinner far in advance of the meal announcements that came over the PA system. Boredom during the long days and nights at sea was probably the underlying reason.

As time wore on, a few scuffles and fist fights developed as the chow hounds jockeyed for position at the head of the chow line. Finally, the situation got so bad the mess officers decided to arrange a contest between the tankers and the artillery men to determine "first-in-line rights." Further it would provide entertainment for the troops on board.

A boxing match was the decision, and the two units were asked to choose their best fighters for the contest. The artillery men chose Bob Rutledge, a member of the Headquarters Battery, Second Battalion from Clovis, New Mexico. Bob was a Golden Gloves fighter whose prowess had sent him to the national finals for two years running. The name of the tanker escapes me, but the artillery men won the bout and the first-in-chow-line rights.

Once it was decided who was going to eat first, the soldiers also found entertainment inside the dining room. Because the *Coolidge* would transport civilians from the Philippines on its return trip, some of the amenities of a cruise ship were still available.

EVANS — The one thing I remember about the *Coolidge* was that when we would go through chow line with our trays, we had regular GI-type chow, but there was a string orchestra in tuxedos that played chamber music. Inquiries about this found that the *Coolidge* was still designated a luxury liner. It was used as a troop ship to go to the Philippines and was picking up American civilians and others to return them to the United States. The musicians' union said, "We are being paid to play music, so we'll play for the soldiers, too."

ADDIE MARTIN DIARY — Thursday — 11 September 1941 — 6:00

Addie in front, Motts Tonelli behind. Two on side are unidentified.

p.m. — One more day out at sea has passed. We had another life boat drill. Sat out on deck for a couple of hours. Slept for a little while and will see a show tonight. We're only a day and a half out of Honolulu now. You can begin to notice a rise in temperature — will most likely notice it much more between Honolulu and Manila. Heard part of Roosevelt's speech over the loud speaker system this afternoon. You see we're losing time right along. When we pass the International Date Line we will have lost a full day.

Friday — 12 September 1941 — 10:00 a.m. — Saw a show last night on the sun deck — "Abraham Lincoln in Illinois" — hadn't seen it before so enjoyed it. Just found out that mail costs 20 cents per 1/2 oz. air mail from the Islands. That's going to be a little expensive. Of course regular mail is only 3 cents as in the States but the Lord only knows how long it would be in transit to you. After this I won't be able to send anything until we reach Manila and that's a good distance from Honolulu. We'll be on the ship for some time yet.

It's gradually getting warmer as we go farther westward. After we leave Honolulu we'll still have 4,881 miles to go before reaching Manila. It's 2,051 from San Francisco to Honolulu — so you can see this is a pretty long trip.

Saturday — 13 September 1941 — 6:45 a.m. — Have already passed several small islands this morning. We'll pull into Pearl Harbor in an hour or so. Seems good to see land again.

Can't add much — want to get cleaned up a bit before going ashore for a couple of hours.

Hours later Addie left the boat, mailed his letter to his mother, and briefly enjoyed the sights. By 5:00 p.m., all were back on the *Coolidge* and the liner set sail for the 13-day trip to the Philippines. This part of the voyage was more cautious as the vessel neared that part of the world controlled by the Japanese. The *Coolidge* traveled by blackout in a zigzag course and was escorted by the destroyers *Astoria* and the *St. Louis*. Several times during the trip smoke was spotted on the horizon. The *Astoria* was dispatched to investigate, but nothing of concern was found. Other than that, the trip in Addie's opinion was boring and uneventful. He began another day-by-day letter to his mother that he mailed once the boat docked in Manila.

ADDIE MARTIN DIARY — Saturday — 20 September 1941 — Here's the start of another letter. This one will have to wait to be mailed until we get to Manila. We left Honolulu last Saturday and we'll be another six or eight days in reaching Manila. We've been convoyed since leaving Honolulu with a blackout of all lights aboard ship in the evening. All this probably hasn't been necessary, but

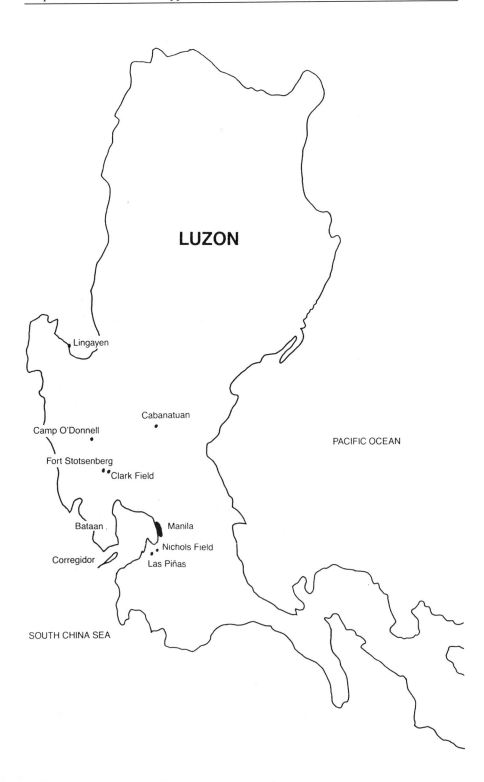

they've been doing it nevertheless. We'll be glad when we finally reach Manila. This has been an awfully long boat ride — nearly 8,000 miles. And it's been getting warmer each day. Then too, 2,500 men is somewhat of an overload for this ship.

We passed the International Date Line and lost a day this week. Actually it is only September 19 today back in Wisconsin. Certainly hoping you're listening to the Packer games this fall.

Honolulu was a fine city with a marvelous climate. Much cooler than where we're going. It's pretty much a vacation spot, however.

Understand we'll be stopping at the island of Guam for water tomorrow and will be able to send out mail from there.

Sunday — 21 September 1941 — 11:45 a.m. — Well we're not stopping at Guam today as we figured we might — the fact is that we just won't get that far today.

Suppose the Packers are playing the Bears or Cardinals today. Not much new otherwise. Got about eleven hours sleep last night. We had rosary today in absence of a Catholic priest aboard ship. Expect to eat the noon meal today and forget about tonight's meal — spend the rest of the day out on the deck just taking it easy.

Monday — 22 September 1941 — 9:00 a.m. — Expect we'll get into Manila Friday. Will be glad to land as it is getting a little tiresome aboard ship right now.

Tuesday — 23 September 1941 — Just a few days and we'll be in Manila. Expect to arrive Friday morning.

Meanwhile things remained unchanged — scenery is still water.

Wednesday, 24 September 1941 — 10:00 a.m. — Raining today so everyone is staying inside the ship. Not much to do except sit around, eat, and sleep. We'll leave the ship Friday morning. I think everyone will be glad to hit land again. Mom, send the Monday issues of the PRESS-GAZETTE. You can send them ordinary mail for 3 cents. It will take a while before they reach me but the football articles will still be news.

Thursday — 25 September 1941 — Am closing this letter now, Mother. Am feeling fine and we'll be coming into Manila tomorrow morning. Hope you're all well and I'll write again somewhat later. This air-mail is costly. Love to all and hello to all.

Chapter 5

Waiting for the Japs

Fort Stotsenberg

On Friday, 26 September, the *Coolidge* steamed into Manila Bay and docked at the famous Pier 7, touted to be the world's longest pier. Bill Rust, one of the boarding party, had a cup of coffee with Addie. As part of Headquarters Company, Addie had a minor role in organizing the unloading of the 200th CAC. Once off the boat, the 200th and the 194th Tank Battalion proceeded 75 miles north to their new home, Fort Stotsenberg, adjacent to Clark Field.

American civilians then boarded the *Coolidge* and headed back to the safety of the United States. On 1 November, the *Coolidge* left San Francisco with another load of troops bound for the Philippines. A year later the luxury liner met an inglorious end. On 26 October 1942, while carrying over 5,000 soldiers, it hit two U.S. mines as it entered the harbor of Espiritu Santo in the New Hebrides Islands (now Vanuatu). An hour and a half later, the ship was at the bottom of the harbor, but, fortunately, most of the troops made it safely ashore.

After the 200th CAC had arrived at Fort Stotsenberg later that night of 26 September, the men unpacked and enjoyed their first sleep back on solid ground. The next morning Addie wrote his mother describing his new surroundings.

ADDIE MARTIN LETTER — 27 September 1941 — Arrived here last night after reaching Manila yesterday afternoon. Manila is a study in contrasts — a million new things. We were taken by buses to this fort which is about sixty miles out of Manila and up towards the mountains. The Coast Artillery will form a protective group for the air base [Clark Field] located up here. Couldn't begin to tell you everything in a single letter.

Later in the letter, Addie continues his complaint about the high cost of the

mail. While at Camp Wallace and Fort Bliss, Addie's letters include his usual
intention of sending money home but can't until the *next* payday. He continues
that practice at Fort Stotsenberg.

> ADDIE MARTIN LETTER — 27 September 1941 — Don't want you
> to ever worry about me if you don't hear from me for sometime. Boat
> mail is notoriously slow. Air-mail is expensive and you don't have to
> write me air-mail because you can't afford it. We haven't been paid
> this month, and because of the shift again it likely will be late.
> Otherwise I'd send you a couple of dollars because I should end up a
> few dollars ahead this month, and never worry about me — we'll have
> a good camp here soon.

Fort Stotsenberg was a big change from what the men had been used to.
Besides the new climate and open-air barracks, the Philippines provided an
entirely different culture.

> BILL NOLAN — The barracks were built of wooden floors, bamboo
> sides, and roofs made of leaves. As we jumped from the trucks at our
> barracks, I wondered when the natives would come running and
> hollering with spears and swords held high over their heads. It looked
> like the end of the world. As I learned in the next two or three weeks,
> the mountains to the north and east of us was unexplored territory. Just
> roads for lumber crews to remove large mahogany and travel, by
> horse, to the coast, where fishermen lived. Showers were just a large
> building with sides about 3 feet high, and a roof and about 10 or 12
> shower heads. Toilet facilities consisted of 12 or 14 holes in an
> outhouse.

With temperatures usually in the nineties, most of the barracks and hangars
were either completely or partially open on the side. The climate of the
Philippines is divided between wet and dry seasons. The wet or monsoon
season occurs in the spring and summer and the dry in the fall and winter.
When Addie arrived at Fort Stotsenberg, the wet season was ending, and the
dry season was just beginning.

Once settled in, Addie again worked out of Chaplain Howden's office. He
performed clerical work but because most of the 200th was Catholic, Addie
also helped one of the Catholic priests already stationed at Stotsenberg. Father
John Duffy from Toledo, Ohio, was a Notre Dame alumnus, and Addie, Motts
Tonelli, and he spent many relaxing moments together that fall.

FATHER JOHN DUFFY LETTER — 27 November 1947 — From the

time Adrian and Motts Tonelli came to Stotsenberg, I used to take them to my quarters on Sunday morning after the last Mass and we would have breakfast together and discuss the happenings at Old Notre Dame. I had my own home on the Post and it gave them the opportunity to get out of the barracks and to relax in comfortable chairs and be themselves. My Filipino house boy and cook used to be able to turn out some very good groceries and I always felt that Adrian and Motts enjoyed those Sunday morning breakfasts. We had a lot of fun in those days before the war, swapping yarns and planning on what we'd do when we were hoping that there would be no war. The Philippines was a swell place in those days before the war, and Adrian got around a little to see the beauty of the place.

Addie continued to be a conscientious Catholic, while in the Philippines. His old tentmate from Fort Bliss, John Johnson, remembers some of that religious concern.

JOHNSON — One time we were walking back from the PX to the barracks, and Addie wanted to stop in the church. I went in with him, and he went and knelt down and started to pray. I asked what I should do because I had never been in a Catholic Church. He told me just to sit in the pew and be quiet.

We also had this one guy in the barracks who used to go down to "Sloppy Bottom" [a barrio near the Fort] looking for women to screw. Addie used to get on him and remind him that he better leave a trust fund for the education of all the children he was fathering because we'd be back in the States in a year.

Addie said this tongue-in-cheek, but the incident exemplifies the cultural shock that faced many newly arrived soldiers in the Philippines. Prior to the troop build-up in the summer and fall of 1941, the Philippines was an idyllic military assignment. The duty was easy; seldom did the men work past noon because of the heat, and there were numerous "fringe" benefits when it came to sex. Increasing world tensions in 1941 were to put an end to this life. Bob Stewart and Forrest Knox, 192nd Tankers from Janesville, Wisconsin, made the following observations.

BOB STEWART — The people [military] who had been over there [Philippines prior to 1941] had been there for some period of time. They were career Army and Navy men, and they were going to take the easiest and sweetest road out. It didn't make any difference to us because we thought we were only going to be there for one year, but it turned out to be more than that. The regular Army men weren't over there to soldier. They were over there to have a helluva good time. The Philippines was the softest duty station in the world, and that's the reason they stayed there. If you found a good bunk boy all you had to do was hold the rifle at inspection. He did everything else for you.

FORREST KNOX — The morality in the Philippines was different from America. It took a long time to get this setup explained to me. The military's got a tremendous problem with venereal disease. In order to control this, the medical department wanted our guys to shack up with a Filipino woman, but have her checked first.

Now if you could get a woman shacked up, say you were there for a three-year hitch, she'd try and get pregnant as fast as she could. If she could have two kids before you left, you could acknowledge this fact to the Finance Department that she was your common-law wife, and the two kids were yours. Then she would get so much per month for each of those kids. Now if she lucked out and this guy was a short-termer and a new guy comes in, the first thing he does is ask the new guy if he's got anything against native women.

He would transfer his family to the new guy. He would take him out and introduce him and try to get the new guy to move in and take over his shack and squaw and raise the kids for him. Now these kids still belonged to the first guy, but if the woman could get passed on for two or three hitches and have five or six kids, the per diem for these kids got to the point where she could live in the high society part of town. She was getting an income that was up to the businessman. If you're talking about morals, they didn't look down on what she was doing. Hell, every Filipino woman had a c ____. She was just lucky to have one she could sell. This was her outlook — that it was worth something. The rest had to give it away for free. Once she had three or four kids she lived in a better part of town. These women were in competition to snag a soldier if they could.

Around here in the United States, a soldier has to hassle around for quite a while to find one [woman] that will even put out. Over there you had to beat them off you. Some guys just couldn't understand it. They'd say, "The Philippine morals was bad." It was the Philippine finances that was bad.

Although Bob and Forrest's estimation of prewar Philippines might be an oversimplification, few would argue that this tropical duty in the 1930s wasn't "soft." In light of what was to come, the "country club" atmosphere became an Achilles Heel. Certainly during the thirties this military lifestyle was in stark contrast to what was going on in the Japanese military.

Many of the troops in the Philippines in September 1941 had a cavalier attitude toward a war in the Pacific. Few believed that conflict with the Japanese was imminent, and if it was, once the firing began, the war would be over shortly. Some seemed more interested in seeing the sights than in preparing for an invasion.

By October, the 200th CAC had become accustomed to Fort Stotsenberg. Those who hadn't strayed off the post to enjoy the "pleasures" of the surrounding area or had received a pass to go to Manila, found plenty of entertainment at the Fort. Besides the typical barracks hijinks, there was more organized recreation on the Post. Many tried the golf course, tennis courts, softball diamonds, and athletic equipment.

If a soldier at Stotsenberg were fortunate enough to get a pass, he usually traveled to Manila. In Addie's 23 October letter he mentioned that as yet he hadn't been to Manila but planned to go in early November. Father Duffy recalled that Addie and members of the Holy Name had a Sunday outing in Manila. Later Addie, Gunnar Sacson, and two others from Headquarters Company spent a weekend there.

> GUNNAR SACSON — Addie and I and Bob Bell and Henry Wiedler went into Manila around the second week of November. We spent the night at the Army-Navy YMCA. We made a few of the clubs, did a little sight seeing up and down Dewey Boulevard, and did a little shopping for Christmas in the Walled City. Then on Sunday morning we took a boat ride out and went aboard a submarine in Manila Bay, looked it over, and then came back. In the afternoon the truck for the 200th was waiting, and it drove us back to Clark Field. Addie was a real nice guy. He liked to talk and shoot the breeze.

If Addie took an Army truck to Manila rather than a Philippine bus or train, he missed an experience of a lifetime. On the bus and train the soldiers had the opportunity to mix with the Filipinos and witness some of the native "culture" firsthand.

> NOLAN — During the first three months [at Fort Stotsenberg], I received four passes for weekends in Manila. Now if you did not get a ride in a military truck, you had to ride an old train — open sides, wooden seats, and just a roof. The engine looked like a train of the old wild west movies in the year 1800. People climbed and hung all over the roof, sides, and carried children, chicken, pigs, pots, and pans with them. When the train stopped at a small village, the natives

would buy fruit and sugar cane. The soldiers did not buy anything because we had been warned about disease from these items. It was just like a trip to Mexico today — do not drink the water or eat the fruit or vegetables.

When we arrived in Manila, the downtown section was beautiful. We stayed at the Far Eastern Hotel. We slept three to a room, and each room had a ceiling fan. Of course, every bed had a large netting covering the bed. This was needed because of the flies, bugs, and mosquitoes.

STEWART — It was an education going to a foreign country. When we landed in the Philippines we went to Fort Stotsenberg, and the next day we came back to Manila to pick up our trucks. Women were carrying everything on their head in these straw baskets. Nobody ever told us anything. We were green from the States. We didn't know what's going on.

We went through this barrio, and we saw this woman alongside the road with this big load of things on her head. We see her squat down, and we don't know what's going on. We scratched our head and wonder what's that supposed to be. But here she was urinating and we didn't realize that. When you put things together, it made a lot of sense. Why should she take this big heavy thing off her head and go set it down when she could accomplish the same thing. She relieved herself, and she didn't miss a beat. The load was on her head, and that's an education to see that. People from different countries have different customs.

KNOX — If you got on one of the Philippine buses that went from town to town, they would pull over alongside the road for a relief call. Everybody got out and relieved themselves right alongside the road.

When you ride a Greyhound bus [in the States], you stop at a terminal and get off to go to the bathroom. In the Philippines there was so much confusion as they were loading and unloading, and the seats had curtains on both sides, so every seat had two exits, and you could get on or off on the sides. The whole top was covered with a luggage rack, and there were chickens and pigs up there, but in the confusion there wasn't time for going to the bathroom, so you had to have a piss call. The bus would stop and everyone would get off. The men would stand in one place and the women in another.

A Story of Oranges and Rainbows

Mao Tse-tung wrote about war, "Know your enemy and know yourself, and you can fight a hundred battles without disaster." In retrospect, one of the problems encountered in the war in the Philippines was that the Americans by and large underestimated the fighting ability and perseverance of the Japanese. After all, the United States knew little about military defeat. They had become so accustomed to winning that victory in an anticipated Pacific war, unfortunately, was expected and not to be earned. History books are filled with examples of overconfidence, but sometimes military leaders are blind to the obvious.

During the 1930s, when Japan embarked on the Greater East Asia Co-Prosperity Sphere, their aim was to rid the Orient of American influence. While many viewed the policy as a political and economic move, some experts in the Philippines and Washington also saw military implications. They contended that in order to rule the vast area of the Orient, Japan needed military control of countries outside of Japan.

During the 1930s, the Japanese war machine assumed increased control of and influence over their government. During this time there was a tremendous build-up of the Japanese Army and Navy. Ironically, the United States helped. During the War many soldiers remember finding Japanese weapons made with parts from the United States.

And as troops in Japan were increased in number, so, too, was the ancient fighting warrior code of Bushido strengthened. This Japanese military philosophy was built on a soldier's absolute obedience to superiors and his being prepared to make the ultimate sacrifice for his country. Surrender was never permitted.

Over a decade before World War II, while Addie was still in high school, personnel in the War College had anticipated a conflict with Japan. Hypothetical situations led to hypothetical solutions. The Philippines, especially Manila Bay, would be expedient to Japan's grand design. The Japanese Navy, they envisioned, would attack Lingayen Gulf, 50 miles north of Fort Stotsenberg, the obvious site of an invasion. Our Navy would steam from Pearl Harbor, defeat the Japanese in the South China Sea, and the war would be over. If for some reason the Naval fleet did not arrive in time and the Japanese made a successful landing, the American and Philippine Forces would retreat to the jungles of Bataan and the island of Corregidor protecting Manila Bay. By delaying tactics, they could stall the advance of the Japanese for six months until the Navy negotiated the 5,000 miles to Manila and achieved a victory.

This grand design for the defense of the Philippines was called WPO3 or War Plan Orange. In 1935, when the Philippines became a Commonwealth, our nation was responsible for their defense until 1946 when the Philippines were to become independent. Our military advisor to the Philippines, General Douglas MacArthur, initiated a plan to train Filipino soliders and officers to the point where no country would even consider invading that Island.

During the time Addie was studying at the University of Wisconsin and Notre Dame, Japan was waging war with China. It was obvious to some that their next step would be the Philippines, which was protected by the United States. By 1940, relations between Japan and the United States were rapidly deteriorating. But so, too, was the Allied relationship with Germany across the Atlantic in Europe. One of the dangers was that we could be drawn into war across two different oceans, militarily an impossible task.

In 1941, MacArthur insisted that the Philippines were rapidly advancing to the stage where they could protect themselves without the necessity of our Navy as seen in the Orange Plan. He now believed that the Philippine Army could meet any invasion on the beaches of Lingayen Gulf and repel the invaders. No retreat to Bataan was necessary, especially if the Philippines had adequate air power. To protect the air fields like Clark Field next to Fort Stotsenberg, MacArthur wanted anti-aircraft weapons and tanks. When he finally convinced the War Department during the summer of 1941 that the Orange Plan wasn't necessary, Washington decided to send him the 200th Coast Artillery Corps and two tank battalions, the 192nd and 194th.

MacArthur contended that if Japan would attack the Philippines, they would wait until the hot season — April 1942. By that time the General envisioned his Army ready to meet the Japanese on the beaches. Supplies, therefore, were removed from storage on Bataan, as called for by the Orange Plan, and stashed in central Luzon closer to the beaches, where the action would be.

What MacArthur didn't realize was that in July the United States and England held secret meetings in Washington to discuss strategy for the impending world conflict. The result of this conference was War Plan 5 — The Rainbow Plan. Our country's intention was to pursue a "Europe first" strategy. In the Philippines, MacArthur would have to fight a defensive war for six months until help arrived. A few military experts in Washington, though, knew the truth. The Islands were too far away to defend adequately. Ultimately, surrender might be inevitable.

While MacArthur was removing supplies from Bataan in August and September, he was oblivious to the Rainbow Plan. He envisioned that the Orange Plan, the retreat to Bataan, would deliver the vast majority of the Filipino citizenry to the hands of the Japanese. After hearing of the Japanese atrocities in China, in conscience, he could not do this to them. He had to meet the enemy on the beaches. Finally in October, two months after the Rainbow Plan had been adopted, he was informed of its existence. Naturally, he disagreed with the plan.

For most of the fall of 1941, negotiations concerning the United States's role in the Far East occurred on almost a daily basis between American and Japanese diplomats. Fortunately, our cryptographers had broken the Japanese diplomatic code, so our negotiators knew the Japanese demands almost before they were brought to the table. Still, no compromises were reached. In early September, as Addie pulled out of San Francisco on the *Coolidge*, the Japanese government had already determined that if diplomacy couldn't resolve the issues between the two countries, war would result. On 26 November, the Japanese Naval Task Force that attacked Pearl Harbor moved out. They were in position by 3 December. Japan resolved that if no breakthroughs in negotiations occurred by 29 November, their war machine would be put in motion. The American cryptographers deciphered these messages and our government *knew* that Japan was ready to attack somewhere in the Pacific. Most suspected the Philippines; few guessed Pearl Harbor. And no one knew when.

Addie's last two letters from Fort Stotsenberg portray his concern over the growing world tensions, but also his overconfidence.

ADDIE MARTIN LETTER — 23 October 1941 — We over here are of course watching developments in the diplomatic crisis between the U.S. and Japan. We don't however feel anything will come of it — only if Germany should be overwhelmingly successful in Russia and that doesn't seem to be the case.

And then one week before the War. . . .

ADDIE MARTIN LETTER — 1 December 1941 — We're standing by here waiting developments in the Japanese situation. Frankly, most of us wish that if there is to be any trouble that it get started soon so that we can get it over with and get back to the States.

That was his last letter that his family would receive. Ironically, in his October letter, he mentioned that he had written Mrs. Bishop, who was in charge of the Brown County Draft Board, to see if he could receive presumably a dependency discharge and return to DePere. His December letter mentions nothing about whether he had heard from Mrs. Bishop. That last letter ends in typical Addie fashion — "Don't want you worrying about me. Go ahead and have a good Xmas. Had hoped to send a few dollars but can't see how in the hell I can this time."

Exactly a week after that last letter, 8 December 1941, his life became anything but typical.

Chapter 6

The War Begins

Bandits Over Clark

The bombing of Clark Field, adjacent to Fort Stotsenberg, on 8 December 1941 (Philippine time), is completely overshadowed in history books by the Japanese bombing of Pearl Harbor on 7 December. Yet each event had about the same impact on MacArthur's plan of Philippine defense. One took away his Navy, the other his Air Force. The similarities of these two setbacks, ten hours apart, almost defies belief. Nobody knows for sure why Clark was destroyed in the manner it was. No one was willing to accept blame. But the confusion of that day and the days before the bombing had a catastrophic impact upon our defense of the Philippines.

By the end of November, Fort Stotsenberg and Clark Field were on alert. Soldiers weren't getting passes for outings in Manila. Many were in gun positions around the airfield. Others were busy digging bunkers. A few soldiers jokingly considered these precautions a waste of time. But by 2:00 p.m. on 8 December 1941 no one at Clark disputed Japan's ability to wage war.

In the days before Pearl Harbor, rudimentary radar sets along the western coast and air reconnaissance spotted what was believed to be Japanese planes over the South China Sea. Some even suspected the planes to be over the Philippine mainland. But orders were to assume a defensive posture and not to fire unless attacked.

About the same time, in Manila and the villages near Clark, many of Japanese descent disappeared mysteriously. Businessmen/spies vanished. A Japanese air strike seemed imminent. Clark, everyone surmised, would be a primary target. And the tension mounted.

Why was Clark so vital to the defense of the Philippines? Many of the B-17 Flying Fortresses were headquartered here. These large bombers that would be so successful in the war in Europe were a necessary ingredient in MacArthur's aggressive plan to destroy the Japanese *before* they landed on the beaches of Lingayen.

Because of the International Date Line, the events of Sunday, 7 December, at Pearl Harbor, actually occurred on Monday, 8 December, in the Philippines. While the men at Stotsenberg and Clark slept, the Japanese, without a declaration of war, launched a surprise attack on Pearl Harbor. Approximately 150 to 200 fighters, bombers, and torpedo planes attacked ships and planes in Hawaii, resulting in a damaging loss of fighting equipment and personnel. These were the very ships that were to "bail out" the retreating soldiers in Bataan under the Orange Plan.

By the time Addie awoke that Monday morning, high-ranking officers at Stotsenberg and Clark knew about Pearl Harbor. Over the next few hours, the enlisted men, usually in small groups, were informed of the tragedy. Some heard news reports on the radio. Most realized that the next Japanese attack would occur soon in the Philippines — most likely at Clark.

Because of the resulting confusion of that day and subsequent years of prison camp, an accurate accounting of what happened at Clark is extremely difficult. Suffice it to say, that like Pearl Harbor, where the vessels were not in the Pacific Ocean but moored in convenient rows, at Clark, when the Japanese flew over, the Flying Fortresses were *not* in the air but also on the ground — many awaiting refueling and in convenient rows.

By breakfast, most of the B-17 bombers and P-40 fighters from Clark were circling central Luzon. Shortly after Addie finished breakfast and reported to Headquarters, Baguio in extreme northern Luzon had been bombed by the Japanese. By mid-morning, Addie called on Father Duffy. At approximately the same time, the 54 Japanese bombers that would attack Clark had taken off from Formosa and were rendezvousing over the South China Sea.

> FATHER JOHN DUFFY LETTER — I was with Addie about an hour before the first attack at Stotsenberg on 8 December 1941. We knew of the attack on Pearl Harbor which had taken place at 2:30 a.m. We were looking for the Nips and we expected Clark Field to be hit. I remember telling him to get out of the buildings when the Nips came and hit the ground.

Many of those in headquarters of the 200th vividly recall the events of 8 December. Although a tense atmosphere hung over Stotsenberg and Clark, activity was almost "leisurely." That Japan would try to attack Clark just didn't seem possible, especially in light of the fact that, to many, Pearl Harbor appeared more rumor than fact. Addie was just finishing lunch when the Japanese arrived.

> ALDRICH — On December 8th, I remember waking up to a clatter of noise in the barracks and people talking excitedly. The Nips had

bombed Pearl Harbor in Hawaii, evidently without a declaration of war. The regiment had been on an alert for more than a week due to the fact that our radar had picked up unidentified aircraft flying over the tip of northern Luzon.

When we went to chow and later to duty, we made sure we had our helmets, weapons, ammunition, and gas masks because if an officer or first three-grader discovered anyone without any — or all — of these, a royal butt chewin' followed. Clark Field, adjacent to Fort Stotsenberg, was buzzing with great numbers of aircraft taking off and landing. The strategy here was lost to us as we reported to our duty area. Our anti-aircraft weapons were dispersed around the airfield, but headquarters was functioning in its regular quarters on the Fort proper. Headquarters was my duty station. Reports began to filter in verifying the Pearl Harbor attack as well as some of the losses, and the consensus was that we were now in a real shooting war.

Returning to headquarters after lunch I heard some shout, "Look at the planes — they must be Navy!"

Someone else yelled, "Look at the insignia — that's not the Navy. Look at the meatballs on the wings — Hell!! Those are Japs."

At about 20,000 feet, two waves of bombers in perfect formation — nine, nine, and eight — then nine, nine, eight — floated lazily overhead. I remember an eerie whistling sound, and over on the airfield, a geyser of dust sprang high in the air. The noise of explosions filled the air, and the ground trembled underfoot. The bombardment of Clark Field had begun.

Dust and smoke filled the air. I saw some guys in a ditch across the road, and I ran over and joined them. I quickly slammed a clip of ammo into my rifle — adjusted the chin strap on my helmet as concussions from the explosions kept the thing bouncing up and down on my head.

The bombers flew straight on and suddenly the big explosions ceased. Black smoke filled the sky and dust was settling on everything. An occasional explosion could be heard, probably inside the many burning buildings.

EVANS — When the bombing occurred on December 8th, I had just finished eating. I had gone back to my barracks, and we were listening to the news broadcast from Don Bell. Don Bell was called "the Walter Winchell of the Philippines." He was giving us a run-down and said, "It has been reported that Clark Field had been bombed but reports say that if they had been bombed, they haven't been hit." We all got a big laugh out of that. And just about that time, Nelson Apple, who was a member of Headquarters Battery and our communications Master Sergeant, said, "Look at those Navy planes!"

I walked outside, looked up, and saw all these planes coming over high and I *knew* they weren't Navy planes, but I didn't want to say that. So I walked back into the barracks, got my helmet, put it on, picked up my rifle, rifle belt, and gas mask, and started back out when the bombs hit. And sure enough, they weren't Navy planes. They were Japanese, and that's how the war started for us.

Whereas Addie and the men of Headquarters spent the two-week alert within Fort Stotsenberg, the men in the gun batteries were dispersed in the fields around Clark. And that's where most of them were when the 54 Japanese bombers flew over Clark. Most felt frustration as they realized that their guns could not reach the bombers.

URBAN McVEY — My commanding officer had called our unit together and told us about the bombing at Pearl Harbor and that war was going to probably break out in the Philippines. We went and got ready for the Japs, and I remember there was a lot of confusion. We had a bunch of B-17s on the ground at Clark Field next to Stotsenberg, and I was by our anti-aircraft guns getting ready. We saw this big, beautiful V of planes coming across the sky, about 60 of them, and we thought they were ours until all of a sudden I saw the bomb doors open underneath them. Then I knew they weren't ours.

They were too high up. The guns were left over from World War I. I think the shells were too, because most of them either didn't explode in the air or exploded on the way up. The Japs knew our guns couldn't reach them.

A collective sigh of relief went out as the men watched the bombers leave in a southeasterly direction. But that feeling left shortly as the Japanese Zeros engaged in low-level strafing of the airfield. Anything that moved they shot at. Many remained in the trenches until the planes left. Japanese machine guns dismantled the B-17s and P-40s that weren't destroyed by the bombs. Because the strafers were often only a few hundred feet above the ground, the guns of the 200th knocked a few Zeros from the sky.

ALDRICH — The sound of our gun batteries firing away reached us about the same time the Jap pursuit planes came swinging in on low-level strafing runs. Overhead smoke drifting by hid most of the air activity from view, and as the noise of small arms fire began to increase, we tried to get lower in the ditch. Rounds from the strafing aircraft caused little puffs of dust to pop up in straight rows here and there. Again the strange metallic taste filled my mouth. I was to associate this sensation with just plain old unadulterated fear.

Whenever a low-flying Jap plane appeared in an occasional clearing in the smoke, everyone fired their rifles as rapidly as possible at the target. The raid lasted about 53 minutes, but we stayed in that ditch for some time. Covered with dirt, and uniforms wringing wet with sweat, we laid there and talked about our shooting war with Japan.

Someone — probably a medic — was runing around inquiring if anyone was injured. It was a relief to learn that no one in our vicinity had been hit. In the distance, the sound of the Regimental Band could be heard playing peppy march music. Our spirits were high, but we couldn't help but wonder what tomorrow might bring.

For Addie tomorrow brought a new outfit, a transfer unit to Manila, and a full-scale war.

515th to Manila

Hindsight allows the opportunity to see that moments after the Japanese bombers and strafers left Clark, Addie's destiny in this war was practically sealed. With an impaired Navy in Pearl Harbor and a thoroughly destroyed Air Force in the Philippines, it was only a matter of time before the Japanese conquered the Philippines. But in the hours after the attack at Clark, few enlisted men even recognized this fact. Most were thinking that the Japanese might have been "lucky" and victory in the next encounter certainly would fall to the American and Filipino Forces.

After the bombing, Addie sought Father Duffy, and they compared experiences. By mid-afternoon, the 200th was notified to select 500 men and form a new Anti-Aircraft Regiment to be sent to defend Manila. By later afternoon, Addie was told that he was to be a First Sergeant in Headquarters of this new outfit, and by 8:00 p.m., he was in the blacked-out city of Manila. For equipment the batteries uncrated anti-aircraft guns that had just arrived in Manila from the States. This new outfit was later designated the 515th Coast Artillery Corps/Anti-Aircraft.

NOLAN — I was sent to Manila and reported to an Army warehouse on Manila Bay. We were issued 37-mm anti-aircraft guns and old Springfield rifles. This equipment was 1918 issue and still packed in oil and grease.

The 515th was needed in Manila because without an Air Force, the city was virtually defenseless. Although there were very few planes left at Clark, the majority of the 200th was still needed to defend the field in case plane reinforcements were forthcoming. Many of the batteries spent the night readying the guns in position around strategic sites in the city. Protected were Nichols Field, Fort McKinley, the Port Area, the oil tanks, and United States Air Forces Far East (USAFFE) Headquarters in the famed Walled City. Addie was stationed at the Walled City with General MacArthur and his staff. Accompanying the 515th to Manila were elements of the 194th Tank Battalion that had been at Clark.

MORGAN JONES — It appeared that the Commanding Officer picked the men to go with the 515th. There seemed to be an equal mix of "goof-offs," nonfavorites being sent, and apparently the CO of the 515th also picking some of their desired choices. We left after dark, arriving in Manila before midnight, and spending the remainder of the night on the polo field. Eventually Headquarters was quartered in the Walled City, sleeping in barracks on top of the Wall, and using the same bomb shelter in the wall with General MacArthur and his staff.

The Intramuros or Walled City was the older, historic section of Manila. Men remember its beauty in the prewar days. It was almost like entering another world. There was a beautiful park nearby, and inside, flowering balconies hung over the street, and occasionally monkeys could be seen scurrying about.

The threat of Japanese bombers wasn't the only problem facing the 515th. Japanese sympathizers spied on troop movements and often helped guide the incoming Japanese bombers to their targets.

JOHNSON — A couple of days after we arrived in Manila, I remember Addie talking to some guys at the Walled City who were telling him some stories of seeing some Japs. He thought they were exaggerating and was questioning them pretty close.

And the Filipino citizens didn't help matters either. Excitable by nature, the site of Japanese bombers flying overhead at 20,000 feet sometimes caused them to fire randomly with pistols, trying to shoot the enemy down. More often than not, the ones worried about getting hit were their own troops.

On 10 December, and for days after, the Japanese bombed Manila. Flying above 20,000 feet, they were greeted with puffs of artillery fire that usually exploded a few thousand feet below them. Without an Air Force, the 515th had the inevitable responsibility of keeping the Japanese bombers from destroying the Philippine capital. During these days of bombing, Addie, who was stationed with Morgan Jones in Headquarters, saw MacArthur in person.

> JONES — In the Walled City, we mostly just waited for something to happen — awaiting orders to draw equipment, guns [anti-aircraft], and searchlights. We were in a holding pattern. We were in an air-raid shelter in the Wall several times with USAFFE officers, most of whom seemed frightened during the air raid. As it was extremely hot therein, and as General MacArthur stood outside during the raids, several of us followed his lead. If and when he would start to run for the shelter, I would have been just ahead of him.

Though the 515th performed admirably, their stay in Manila lasted only slightly more than two weeks.

After the bombing at Clark, the Japanese landed troops at various points on Luzon. The main landing, however, occured on 22 December on the very western shores that MacArthur had long anticipated — Lingayen. These are the shores on which MacArthur, with air support, expected to provide an aggressive resistance to the enemy. Meeting little opposition, however, the Japanese moved south toward Clark Field and Manila.

Two days later, another large landing force landed at Mauban in Lamon Bay on the eastern side of Luzon, 50 miles to the southeast of Manila. The 515th and 200th were now caught between two pincers — the two landing forces that were making steady progress each day toward Manila. Sensing the impending danger, MacArthur discarded the Rainbow Plan, and ordered the American and Filipino troops into the Bataan Peninsula as part of War Plan Orange.

Why retreat to Bataan? The Bataan Peninsula is 30 miles long and 20 miles at its widest. Its southern tip is only miles from the island fortress of Corregidor at the mouth of Manila Bay. To first conquer and then govern the southern half of their Far East Empire, especially Australia, Japan needed Manila Bay. To control Manila Bay they needed the island of Corregidor, which stood at its entrance. To subdue Corregidor they needed the high ground at the southern tip of Bataan.

The success of War Plan Orange depended on Allied troops fighting a delaying action for six months until the Navy won its way to Manila Bay and victory. Despite fighting on a peninsula only 30 miles long, the terrain of Bataan allowed the undermanned and underfed Americans and Filipinos to keep the Japanese at bay for six months. Bataan was a dense jungle, full of deep ravines, small streams, rugged mountains, and on the eastern side, damp swamp land. Bataan had only two roads for motor travel but thousands of trails. The Japanese would be fighting a force of 70,000, which they could not see but knew were there.

But the first challenge facing the 515th and 200th was to get to Bataan before being cut off by the advancing Japanese Forces. To reach the jungles of Bataan both units, the 200th from the north and the 515th from the south, had to retreat to the Calumpit Bridge, the "gateway" to the peninsula. To get there in all haste meant that rice, medicine, and other supplies stored in central Luzon, supplies so necessary to existing on Bataan, had to be left behind for the Japanese. MacArthur, in accordance with the Rainbow Plan, had moved supplies from Bataan to central Luzon. Now retreating troops had no time to remove them.

By Christmas Day, the 515th had left Manila, crossed the Calumpit Bridge over the Pampanga River, and was getting into position to defend Pilar Air Field at the northern end of Bataan. But that trip itself was not without danger.

NOLAN — On December 25th, Battery H was ordered to pull out of Manila and head for Bataan. On December 26th, the 515th set up at Pilar. I was then ordered to take a large 4x4 truck and return to Manila to pick up other batteries of the 515th. I made three trips, all at night, because of the Jap fighter planes. The roads to Bataan were two-lane, black-top roads with ditches on both sides. On two of these trips my truck went in the ditch. The truck had to be pulled out by other trucks. I hurt my back, my right knee, and had a bruise on my forehead.

By New Year's Day, 1942, the last of the American-Filipino Forces had crossed into Bataan. The bridge was blown up and the battle of Bataan was about to begin. The 515th continued to provide air defense to keep Japanese planes off our frontline infantry and artillery. But on 13 January, Addie's outfit transferred to Cabcaben in southern Bataan. Addie remained here for the rest of the war awaiting the advancing Japanese.

Fighting on Bataan

What happened on Bataan during the 100 days from the time of the destruction of Calumpit Bridge to the 9 April surrender is difficult for the layman to describe. Every important battle of World War II had its *hell*. But Bataan had *many hells*.

The Japanese believed they could march quickly through Bataan and conquer Corregidor by the end of January. But they underestimated the spirit of these men who became known as the "Battling Bastards of Bataan." The story of Bataan is a story of soldiers without adequate food or medicine, fighting an enemy superior in number, air power, and ammunition, but not in determination.

Addie was not at the front but near enough to the action to be concerned. And when the Japanese bombers flew over Cabcaben airfield, the action was

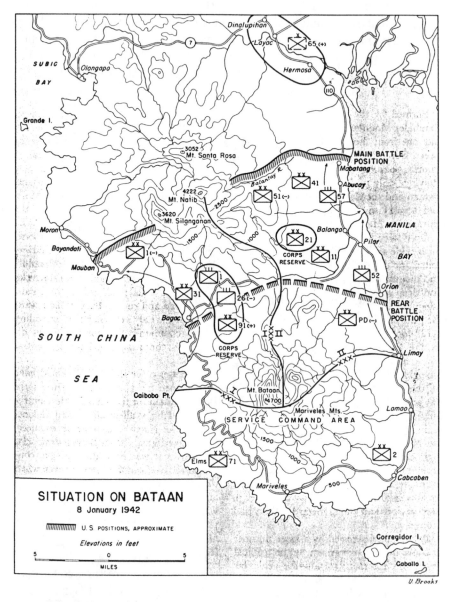

SITUATION ON BATAAN
8 January 1942

U.S. POSITIONS, APPROXIMATE

Elevations in feet

5   0   5
MILES

U. Brooks

In January, the 515th arrived in Bataan and set up near Cabcaben. Addie stayed there until the surrender. Each month the Main Battle Position line was pushed closer to the southern tip of Bataan. (U.S. Army) right on top of him. Critical to the Bataan soldier were food, medicine, and staying alive. Addie and his friends in the 200th and 515th faced these challenges daily.

Almost immediately upon arriving in Bataan, the troops were put on half rations. Napoleon noted, "An army marches on its stomach." But on Bataan there wasn't much choice. Much of the food had previously been stored in Luzon and, with a hasty retreat, could not be gathered up and brought back to Bataan. Part of Addie's job in Headquarters was acquiring nourishment for the 515th. Supplies were occasionally ferried across from Corregidor but as time went on, most soldiers weren't even getting half rations. Headquarters often purchased food from civilians, but many had to resort to eating the Bataan wildlife and vegetation to survive. Horses, mules, and even the Filipino water buffalo, the carabao, found their way into the empty stomachs of the Battling Bastards. Addie's friend, Motts Tonelli, shot a crow and reluctantly tried to eat it.

> NOLAN — Our rations every day in January was a little rice and some fish. We also hunted food in the jungle — mostly monkey, wild chickens, lizards, and anything we could eat. Later no food could be found.

> McVEY — We were down to half rations a day. Actually toward the front lines you ate a meal when you could. We ate the cavalry horses — that wasn't half bad. We ate monkey, iguana tail, and carabao. They were tough. And we didn't always get to cook the food. Sometimes you ate it raw — just to get something into your stomach.

Addie weighed 150 pounds at the start of the war. By the time of surrender in April, he was down to about the 130s. All of the troops lost weight, and this only aggravated the medical problems.

Under normal circumstances few people would want to visit the steamy jungles of Bataan. The extremely warm, swampy area was a natural breeding ground for malaria. Most of the troops at one time or another came down with the disease. Even 40 years later men vividly recall the alternating periods of fever and chills. Quinine was the only effective cure, but it soon became scarce.

Others, including Addie, suffered from dysentery. Cleanliness during a war is always a problem, but on Bataan, under the constant bombardment and pressure from the Japanese, it was a nightmare.

Two field hospitals were established along the road from Cabcaben to Mariveles on the extreme southern tip of Bataan. Most of the time they were filled beyond capacity with malaria patients and the wounded. And to make

日本帝国軍は降伏する所の隊員を殺さない。無益なる戦いを即刻止め降伏せよ。あらゆる降伏をカモフラージュせよ。見えなければマッカーサー元帥はあなたたちを見捨てた。

The Imperial Japanese troops never kill those who surrender to them. Stop this futile fighting and surrender. General MacArthur has deserted you.

Left: Surrender leaflets dropped by the Japs on Bataan, 20 March 1942. Some captured Americans found with these leaflets were executed for apparently disobeying a direct order by not surrendering in March.

TICKET TO ARMISTICE

USE THIS TICKET, SAVE YOUR LIFE, YOU WILL BE KINDLY TREATED

Follow These Instructions:

1. Come towards our lines waving a white flag.

2. Strap your gun over your left shoulder muzzle down and pointed behind you.

3. Show this ticket to the sentry.

4. Any number of you may surrender with this one ticket.

JAPANESE ARMY HEADQUARTERS

matters worse, Japanese bombs were sometimes dropped on the hospitals. Addie stopped on two occasions to visit Father Duffy, who was recovering from wounds.

Despite the food and medical problems, the men on Bataan put up a gallant, heroic fight. It's impossible to determine the amount of ammunition that Japan expended in subduing Bataan, but it was immense. Each month the American and Filipino troops were pushed back toward the southern tip of Bataan, as Japanese infantry, artillery, and planes laid down death on a daily basis. Besides protecting the small airfields on the peninsula, the 200th and 515th kept the Japanese bombers and fighters off Allied infantry and artillery. But with outdated equipment, the task was challenging.

> STEMLER — If we could have had the right ammunition, there would have been a helluva lot more planes shot down. The ammunition we had was all corroded. After you took the corrosion off, a lot of them had holes in casings and you couldn't use them. When you set the fuses, you couldn't set them accurate because the ammunition was so damn old.

> JONES — The gun batteries set up around Cabcaben to fire at planes bombing. The first time the searchlights were hooked up to our early type radar, the first night we had a bombing raid, the lights centered on the planes, the three-inch guns fired and blew the radar as the cables were too short and too near the guns.

By 7 January, the American and Filipino troops had established their east-west line of defense across northern Bataan at Abucay. By 26 January, they had retreated 12 miles to form the Orion-Bagac line. This line remained steady against the Japanese onslaughts until April. By this time the lack of food, medicine, and sleep had taken its toll on the men. Soldiers slept in their foxholes at the front, and this wasn't always an advantage. John Johnson remembers that one of the men from Battery B snored so loud they were afraid he would alert the Japs to their position.

And it didn't take the men long to realize that the "promised" help wasn't coming. This point was especially driven home on 11 March when MacArthur, under cover of night, slipped past the Japanese and left Corregidor for Australia. Most of the Battling Bastards didn't debate the strategy of his departure. All they knew was that "Dugout Doug," who seemed to run the war from the security of Corregidor, was now gone. As the line of defense slowly slipped to the bottom of Bataan, so too did the men's thoughts of victory. While Addie's job before the 9 December bombing was working out of the Chaplain's Office, after the war started, he did less of that and more

Japanese Propaganda Leaflets.

assignments for Headquarters. One of the chores was to prepare for the upcoming rainy season. Headquarters built several huts of bamboo, just like the American settlers did with logs. Makeshift nails were fashioned from bamboo.

Addie did, however, continue to see the Chaplains on a daily basis. On Bataan the work of the Chaplains like Chaplain Howden, Father Duffy, and others was evident. The padres went from unit to unit, trench to trench, and foxhole to foxhole boosting the spirits of the men. After 120 interviews I have heard a Bataan veteran occasionally condemn an officer or doctor, but *never* have I heard one criticize a Chaplain. Their heroics have occasionally been portrayed in various books about this era, but few have done justice to the clergy's work. The tremendous pressure they worked under from 1941 to 1945 demanded heroism, and they accepted the challenge — and most went well beyond the call of duty. Whether it was saying Mass from an altar of ammunition boxes, hearing a foxhole confession, or encouraging the wounded in the hospitals, the work of these "soldiers of God" played a major role in buoying the spirits of the men.

For the most part though, the front line soldier didn't see the Chaplains on a daily basis. As Father William Cummings observed on Bataan. "There are no atheists in foxholes." With bullets flying overhead every day, most made their own "arrangements" with God.

> McVEY — I got to know Father Mathias Zerfes from Wisconsin and Father John Curran from Illinois pretty well, but during the fighting I didn't get to see many priests. I think all the time from December to April I went to Mass once. You had to carry your conscience in your heart.

The spirits of the American and Filipino Forces needed continual uplifting. Besides the lack of food and medicine, and being outnumbered, the soldiers were bombarded with Japanese propaganda encouraging them to quit. After being denied the victory in Bataan in January which they had expected, the Japanese dramatically increased their written and verbal messages, as they realized that each day of fighting delayed their plan for controlling the southern half of the Greater East Asia Co-Prosperity Sphere. Looking back, most of the men recall the humor of the Japanese diatribe.

> STEMLER — They used to drop one leaflet that said, "The beautiful isle of the Philippines" and "What are you fighting for?" and it had some Japanese writing on it.

> JOHNSON — We always figured the message asking us to come forward to surrender — on the other side in Japanese it said, "Shoot the sonofabitch in the back!"

The Japanese had a propaganda mill second to none. Not only did they have to demoralize the enemy, but they had to control the thinking of their own troops and the citizens back home. Fortunately, the Americans could see the humor in some of the Japanese "stories." While most of the propaganda was directed towards the Americans, one leaflet was aimed at the Filipino troops. MacArthur and other military advisors had once envisioned the Philippines capable of its own defense. But that would take time and training. The bombing at Clark ended that possibility.

The best Filipino fighters were the American-trained Scouts. These dedicated, disciplined, and fearless soldiers were to be the backbone of the Philippine Army. Steeped in tradition, these men were well respected by their American counterparts. Often the Scout tradition was passed on within a family from generation to generation. But the soldiers in the regular Army were altogether different. MacArthur believed these soldiers would be combat ready by April 1942. Unfortunately the war started four months too soon, resulting in four months of disciplined training being sorely missed. Of the 70,000 troops defending southern Bataan, 50,000 were Filipinos, most in the regular Army.

> McVEY — The Scouts, their best, select fighters, who were trained by our officers, were tough. They were fierce fighters. The regular Army, however, wasn't very tough. They just couldn't take the guff that you had to take when fighting a war. I remember we'd issue them shoes and pretty soon they had sold them and were marching along barefoot. Most of them were used to bare feet anyway. Most of that regular Army was undependable.

Often when placed at the front, men in the Philippine regular Army would get up and move to the rear. When stopped by Americans, they would say they were the "sole survivor" of their company. Occasionally during a 12-hour period, several "sole survivors" from the same company would move to the rear.

Surrender on Bataan

Toward the end of March, the Japanese brought in reinforcements for the final assault on Bataan. By this time the American and Filipino troops had been stretched to the limits of human endurance. They had exhausted most of their food and medicine. Since MacArthur's departure, many had long forgotten about the promised reinforcements and final victory. Some of the antiquated equipment began to malfunction under daily use, and the troops began running low on ammunition. Besides, the Japanese kept up a daily barrage of bombing and artillery fire.

After MacArthur's departure, Wainwright was evacuated to Corregidor to run the war from the *Rock*. On Bataan the troops were under the control of Major General Edward King. Enormous burdens were placed upon King, the most significant being President Roosevelt's statement that the American flag in the Philippines "will be defended by our men unto death." To many the implications were quite clear. Defend Bataan until death. *Do not* surrender. In fact, the word "surrender" was not a term often found in the military history of the United States. But to General King to have 70,000 American and Filipino Forces needlessly slaughtered was out of the question.

That last week on Bataan seemed a month in *hell*. The Battling Bastards had fought the "good fight" against insurmountable odds. Surrender, to King, rather than slaughter, seemed a more viable solution.

By the beginning of April, the American and Filipino Forces had retreated to the bottom one third of the Bataan peninsula. There was no place to go, and Corregidor couldn't and wouldn't take 70,000 men.

Addie spent most of his three months on Bataan many miles behind the lines at Cabcaben on the southern third of Bataan, and saw the Japanese rapidly approach. By the first week of April the enemy was only eight miles away from his postion and closing fast.

Beginning on Good Friday afternoon, 3 April, the Japanese made their long awaited assault. After two days of extraordinarily heavy fighting, the American and Filipino Forces disintegrated. On 7 April, General King merged the 200th and 515th and some infantry to form the Provisional Coast Artillery. This outfit lasted a mere 30 hours. In fact, during the final hours, most of the anti-aircraft guns were destroyed, and the Provisional Coast Artillery was more infantry than anti-aircraft. By 8 April, this newly formed group established a defensive line just south of Cabcaben Airfield. Streaming toward them were many American and Filipino units heading for the rear. The front line was rapidly disintegrating, and the Provisional Coast Artillery became the *last* line of defense. Wainwright wired MacArthur and the War Department in Washington:

IT IS WITH DEEP REGRET THAT I AM FORCED TO REPORT
THAT THE TROOPS ON BATAAN ARE FAST FOLDING UP

On 8 April, as the end neared, orders were given to start destroying equipment, so the Japanese couldn't use it. The most important were the ammunition caves near Mariveles. Shortly before they were blown up, nature at 9:30 p.m. provided a harbinger that the end was near — an earthquake, whose epicenter was at Cabcaben not far from Addie.

DWIGHT CABLE — I remember the earthquake the night before the surrender very well. I was in the back of the truck, and the vibrations were so strong that a small tree, about six inches in diameter — about three feet from the truck — almost touched the truck as they both swayed.

Early in the morning of 9 April, the Provisional Coast Artillery was ordered *not* to return Japanese fire. General King was preparing to go forward to surrender. In the early dawn hours near Cabcaben Field, Addie saw General King begin his anguishing journey to surrender to the Japanese Imperial Army.

NOLAN — On April 9th, General King surrendered Bataan. At this time I weighed about 135 pounds — down from 170 pounds — very bad shape with malaria and dysentery. The Jap soldiers made us gather on a small hill off the main highway. At the same time, Jap artillery moved in a valley behind this hill. There were over 500 to 600 American soldiers on this hill. The Jap artillery started to fire on Corregidor. The first three rounds of return fire from Corregidor were short of the Japanese artillery and landed in the center of the group of American POWs. This shell landed about 25 yards from where I was sitting.

After the explosion, I found myself laying on the ground, blood coming from my nose — very large cut and swelling on the left side of my head. Also both ears hurt, and I could not hear. We were made to stay on this hill as the Jap artillery continued firing shells at Corregidor.

The next shells from the Americans came closer to the Jap position and then hit their guns and ammunition dump. We were made to sit on this hill until the next morning, April 10th. During this 12 to 14 hours, we had no water or food. The temperature was 95 degrees — hot sun. Many men fainted during the day but recovered at night.

CABLE — I was in the first group to turn ourselves in to the Japanese at Cabcaben. They had us squat down at the east end of the airfield. As we squatted there, waiting, several low-powered explosive shells dropped in amongst us, digging small craters — two or three feet in diameter — and throwing up a lot of dirt.

Chapter 7

POW Life Begins

The Death March

Surviving POWs recognize that history books erroneously used the sensational words "Death March" to refer to their three years and four months as prisoners. The Death March actually was less than a week of that total. For Addie it was less than 24 hours.

When Wainwright heard that King had surrendered, he immediately informed MacArthur in Australia:

> AT 6 O'CLOCK THIS MORNING GENERAL KING . . . WITHOUT MY KNOWLEDGE OR APPROVAL SENT A FLAG OF TRUCE TO THE JAPANESE COMMANDER. THE MINUTE I HEARD OF IT I DISAPPROVED OF HIS ACTION AND DIRECTED THAT THERE BE NO SURRENDER. I WAS INFORMED IT WAS TOO LATE TO MAKE ANY CHANGE, THAT THE ACTION HAD ALREADY BEEN TAKEN. . . .
> PHYSICAL EXHAUSTION AND SICKNESS DUE TO A LONG PERIOD OF INSUFFICIENT FOOD IS THE REAL CAUSE OF THIS TERRIBLE DISASTER. WHEN I GET WORD WHAT TERMS HAVE BEEN ARRANGED I WILL ADVISE YOU.

MacArthur then informed the world:

> THE BATAAN FORCE WENT OUT AS IT WOULD HAVE WISHED, FIGHTING TO THE END [OF] ITS FLICKERING FORLORN HOPE. NO ARMY HAS EVER DONE SO MUCH WITH SO LITTLE AND NOTHING BECAME IT MORE THAN ITS LAST HOUR OF TRIAL AND AGONY. TO THE WEEPING MOTHERS OF ITS DEAD, I CAN ONLY SAY THAT THE SACRIFICE AND HALO OF JESUS OF NAZARETH HAS DESCENDED

UPON THEIR SONS, AND THAT GOD WILL TAKE THEM
UNTO HIMSELF.

As news of the surrender spread across southern Bataan, soldiers poured
out of the hills and climbed out of the foxholes and gathered in groups along
the winding highway between Cabcaben and Mariveles at the extreme
southern tip of Bataan. The Japanese were surprised to see 70,000 American
and Filipino troops. They expected much less. And the 12,000 Americans who
surrendered were unprepared for the treatment the Japanese accorded them.

Few Americans understood that the Japanese Bushido fighting code made
surrender impossible. For the Japanese, death was the alternative to surrender.
Because of this, the Battling Bastards, in the eyes of the Japanese, were
humanity in its lowest form. Humiliation rather than respect for a courageous
battle was their reception. Prisoners were searched. Watches, pens, and
seemingly valueless items ended up in Japanese pockets. Those who didn't
cooperate were beaten and sometimes killed.

The Japanese hadn't anticipated so many troops being on Bataan nor that
the Americans would surrender. Because of this, plans for disposition of the
prisoners were woefully inadequate. They hoped to have enough vehicles to
transport the prisoners the 65 miles out of Bataan to Camp O'Donnell. But the
enormous number of men, the lack of vehicles, and the hunger to capture
Corregidor resulted in the tragedy known as the "Death March."

As the prisoners congregated along the highway, the Japanese began putting
them into groups. Rank and previous unit meant little. Soldiers hoping to
remain with friends often found themselves with others they didn't know.
Many prisoners today don't recall the entire march or who was beside them.
Memories come in bits and pieces — not in chronology. To avoid the agony,
most marchers used the same technique that one uses in a dental chair.
Concentrate on something else more pleasant to alleviate the pain of the
present. Therefore much has been forgotten. Four months of intense fighting
on little food or medicine left most concerned with just putting one foot in
front of the other — not with observing where they were, who was next to
them, and where they were headed. Those who surrendered near Cabcaben
were the first to begin the march. That's where Addie was, but his story of the
Death March was different than most.

The 200th/515th, which had formed a defensive line at Cabcaben Ridge,
were some of the first to be received by the Japanese. This included Addie and
the members of Headquarters Company. To 98.5 percent of the captured
Americans, the Death March was many miles of forced marching under
intense heat with no food or water. Fifteen miles were in oven-like boxcars.
This journey on the average took four to five days. But luckily for Addie, most
of his trip was by truck. Two hundred members from the 200th/515th, most

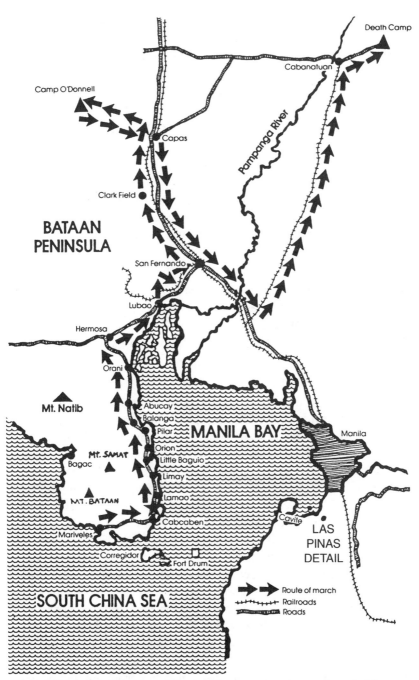

Route of Death March to Camp O'Donnell. Addie fortunately rode a truck most of the way and arrived on 10 April. On or around 2 June he was transferred to Cabanatuan. (Adapted from *Cabanatuan: Japanese Death Camp,* by Vince Taylor (Waco, TX: Texian Press, 1985), p. 40.

from Headquarters and many Sergeants like Addie, arrived at Camp O'Donnell within 24 hours of the surrender. Their memories of when and where they jumped on the trucks differs slightly. No list of who rode ever existed, but with his past record of getting out of physical labor and getting what he wanted, it is easy to imagine Addie was one of the 200. Some in the 200th/515th, who staggered into Camp O'Donnell a week later, remembered that Addie was already there and appeared in great shape. Given his disdain for physical labor, Addie would never have survived the full 65-mile Death March.

CABLE — As I understand, the Japanese were telling Colonel Sage [of the 200th/515th Headquarters] that we would have to walk to Camp O'Donnell. He told them in the strongest possible terms that we had been on short rations and were very weak and could not possibly walk that far, and that the Japanese must get trucks and take us to O'Donnell by truck.

Two others from Headquarters, Sergeant Lee Pelayo, who would end up at Hanawa, Japan, and Master Sergeant Jesse Finley were also on the truck to O'Donnell. What did Addie and the others miss by being trucked to O'Donnell? Addie's friend Bill Nolan recalls the horrors of the Death March.

NOLAN — On April 10th, 1942, the Jap guards started us walking from our position at Cabcaben, going north as fast as the guards could walk. Myself with a very sore head, ears hurt, could not hear . . . very thirsty . . . no food or water. The temperature reached 95 degrees and prisoners would faint or pass out on the march. These prisoners that could not get up were shot or bayoneted to death and left along the road. Some were run over by Jap trucks bringing Jap soldiers for the invasion of Corregidor. As these trucks passed American soldiers, they would hit and club Americans on their head and shoulders. Many fell and died under the wheels of Jap trucks. We walked from 6:00 a.m. until 6:00 or 7:00 p.m. Again no water or food. Calvin Graef, my First Sergeant, and myself both dipped water from the ditch on the side of the road.
   This ditch contained water covered with green slime, dead horses, and American soldiers killed by Japs. Everyone suffered from malaria and dysentery. We had no quinine since February, '42. That night we slept on the ground on the side of the road. During these stops, Jap soldiers would strip us for our rings, watches, and pen-and-pencil sets. On dead American soldiers Japs would cut off fingers to get the rings. They took our canteens, gun belts — and left us with shirts and

pants. Our helmets were knocked off and left on the road. So no hats for the rest of the march.

These conditions continued for four days until we reached San Fernando. Here we received our first cup of rice and some tea. While waiting in line for food, I passed out. When I came to, I was lying on the ground and had another large bump on the back of my head and was very dizzy.

We stayed here overnight, and the next morning at daybreak, all prisoners were marched to the railway station. At the siding were small, metal box cars. We were pushed by bayonets into these cars. About 100 prisoners in each car . . . could only stand up . . . and no room to sit down. The door was locked by the guards. Again the temperature reached 95 degrees. The metal sides of these box cars became so hot, we could not touch them. The ride lasted until dark when we unloaded. During the ride many prisoners became uncontrollable from the heat with no water or toilet facilities. Everyone had dysentery, and everyone went on the floor and over prisoners lying on the floor. These prisoners had passed out or were dead. I believe 10 or 15 men died in each box car during the eight hour trip.

The courage of the men on Bataan and Corregidor postponed Japanese plans for invading Australia and thus controlling the South Pacific. The delay permitted MacArthur a base of operations in Australia to stage his triumphant return to the Philippines and the subsequent conquest of Japan.

To the prisoners, however, the day of surrender marked the beginning of a three-year four-month odyssey, while it appeared to family and friends back in the States that the earth had opened up and swallowed the men of Bataan.

Camp O'Donnell

In the first days following his arrival, as his friends in the 200th/515th staggered into O'Donnell, Addie learned how lucky he was to have ridden part of the Death March. But if Addie could envision what was to happen to him during the next 27 months, he might have chosen to perish on the Death March. That might have been more humane.

Camp O'Donnell was located a few miles west of Capas in Luzon and 12 miles north-northwest of Clark Field. The name of the area came from a family of early Spanish settlers. In 1941, O'Donnell was used as a training facility for the Philippine Army. The camp was totally inadequate for 70,000 tired and ill troops. Housing was deficient. Men often slept under the barracks rather than in them. And water was almost nowhere to be found. Doctors lacked both facilities and medicine to treat the myriad of illnesses that beset the Battling Bastards of Bataan.

If the march from Mariveles and Cabcaben to O'Donnell was a *death march*, then Camp O'Donnell surely was a *death camp*. In its seven-week existence, 1,500 Americans and 20,000 Filipinos perished. Upon staggering into O'Donnell, the soldiers were required to stand in the broiling sun to listen to the humiliating rantings of the Japanese Commandant.

Addie's group probably didn't get the sun treatment, but they got to listen to the ranting and raving of the Japanese Commandant. The fact that 200 men including Addie were there so quickly after the surrender caught both the American Headquarters and the Japanese by surprise.

Gary Anloff was an Adjutant to General King and recalled his move to O'Donnell. On 10 April, 133 men from the General's Headquarters convoyed to the camp in 34 cars and 2 Ford trucks. To his surprise Addie and others from the 200th/515th were already there.

GARY ANLOFF — That night we found that there were a very few officers and men from the 200th/515th who arrived before we did. They also were transported by truck. How this happened, I don't know. I heard that when they surrendered, a truck was available and someone talked the Jap officer into getting them started.

JOHN E. OLSON — About 200 officers and men from the Provisional Tank Group and the 200th/515th CAC gathered near Cabcaben during the morning of April 9th. They seem to have had some organic vehicles still functioning and convinced the Japanese in the vicinity. Apparently, an English-speaking officer was the prime factor in the situation. The senior U.S. officer, Brigadier General James Weaver, led the group. Through fortuitous circumstances they rode the whole way, arriving the afternoon of the 10th. Though they were shaken down once enroute, a number failed to shed Japanese souvenirs and paid with their lives.

According to James Hamilton in *Rainbow Over The Philippines*, the Japanese executed four officers and three enlisted men in Addie's group for having Japanese trinkets or coins. After listening to the harangue of the Commandant, Addie ate and bedded down for the night. The meal was his first in over 24 hours.

Upon awaking the next morning, and with only 383 men in camp, the prisoners got a chance to view O'Donnell. What they saw was not a pretty sight. The open-air barracks were similar to those at Fort Stotsenberg. But there were too few to house 70,000 American and Filipino prisoners.

Each morning Addie watched by the front gates for Death March survivors to stumble in. His vigil the first few days was in vain. Not until 13 April did any marchers arrive. That day 1,500 men stumbled in. By 24 April over 8,000 men were in camp and practically all from Bataan.

One of those was a Brown County friend, Urban McVey. Addie poked him in the ribs to keep him up and moving. Lying down to die at O'Donnell became easier than living. Little food, less water, and a scarcity of medicine were characteristics of O'Donnell. The few water spigots dripped rather than flowed. For nourishment Addie ate small quantities of rice, lugao — a rice soup, and an occasional green. About the only things in abundance at O'Donnell were confusion, flies, and exhaustion.

With the lack of food, water, and medicine, disease ran rampant. Few were spared dysentery or malaria. To receive *any* medicine was almost a godsend. Those who did and survived never forgot.

DAN STOUDT — I still have a soft spot for our doctor, Alvin Powliet. When I got to O'Donnell and got my first attack of malaria, he gave me a couple quinine pills. To get a couple quinine pills from someone was really something. It was unreal.

NOLAN — On April 13th I arrived at Camp O'Donnell. As we entered the camp we were searched by Jap soldiers. Anyone found to have Jap money or papers, was pulled from line and shot. Of course, anyone at the rear of the line threw away any Jap material. Camp O'Donnell had some barracks but most of the American soldiers lay on the ground. We had no tents, blankets, and no hats in this 90-degree temperature. We only had the clothes on our back. Just a shirt, pants, and shoes. The next day 5,000 American soldiers were lined up and made to stand in the hot sun for about four hours. At this time, a Jap officer mounted a large platform. He spoke Japanese and had someone repeat it in English. His two-hour speech told us we were nothing as we surrendered instead of fighting to the end. We would not be given any food, medicine, or housing as everything on the islands was to be given to the Jap soldiers. Therefore all American material taken from us would be for the Jap Army.

I found a place to lie under the floor of a small building. I was able to hide some medicine and sulfa tablets. We found four or five water taps for the whole camp. This meant you stood in line all day to get a canteen of water. The Japs gave us a cup of watery soup made from rice weeds. As everyone had malaria and dysentery, everyone just lay on the ground. We also found out that a toilet problem existed. This meant large holes had to be dug and used for toilet facilities. The next couple of days men were found lying dead in the holes. They were too weak from dysentery and fell into these holes. Therefore American

HEADQUARTERS GROUP II

JUNE 22, 1943

OCCUPATIONAL BREAKDOWN OF PERSONNEL

NON-TECHNICAL

Farmers, Poultry	0	Cooks	103
Farmers, Agricultural	111	Bakers	14
Farmers, Stock	10	Teachers	10
Farmers, Dairy	3	Students	54
Farmers, Truck	1	Meteorologists	0
Businessmen	112	Musicians	2
Typists	7	Professional Soldiers/Sailors	218
Clerks	144	Laborers	174
Chauffeurs	32	Seamen	6
Truck Drivers	165		
Bus Drivers	4	TOTAL	1176

GROUP II TECHNICAL

Radio Operators	10	Engineers-Electrical	2
Radio Technicians	5	Engineers-Mining	15
Telephone Operators	0	Engineers-Highway	0
Telephone Repairmen	5	Painters	10
Telephone Lineman	11	Welders	11
Electricians	13	Petroleum	0
Machinists	10	Foundry	11
Mechanics	70	Textiles	1
Carpenters	18	Miners	12
Plumbers	12	Railroad	6
Riggers	2	Glass	1
Cement Workers	0	Printers	6
Surveyors	1		
Engineers-Mechanical	9	Total	361
Engineers-Chemical	3	non-technical	1169
Engineers-Civil	17	total-group II	1430

(Courtesy of National Archives)

soldiers had to stand guard and try to help the weaker ones from falling into this waste water. Because of the unsanitary conditions, about 40 to 60 Americans died each day and had to be buried outside of camp.

Across the road was the Filipino camp. These soldiers had been in the service of the Philippine Army on Bataan. We could see them burying 200 to 300 men a day.

Over 25 Americans on an average were dying every day during May. To combat boredom Addie's friends, Urban McVey and Solly Manasse, volunteered to haul the bodies from the hospital to the mass graves being dug north of the camp.

By the first week of June the conditions were getting worse instead of better. The Japanese command decided to ship the Americans to a trio of camps near Cabanatuan.

O'Donnell to Cabanatuan

On 6 May 1942, the island fortress of Corregidor fell. The Japanese now had more prisoners to worry about. They decided to move the prisoners from Corregidor and Bilibid and merge them with the bedraggled O'Donnell prisoners at new camps near Cabanatuan City, approximately 100 miles north of Manila in central Luzon.

The three Cabanatuan camps were numbered #1, #2, and #3. Originally they had been a Philippine Army training complex. Camp #1 was approximately four miles to the east of Cabanatuan City. Camp #2 was four miles further on and Camp #3 was six miles past #2. A small dirt road connected the camps.

Many of the Americans in Bataan field hospitals were brought to #3 in late May. Shortly thereafter, the men who surrendered at Corregidor arrived at #3. When #3 was filled, the remainder from Corregidor were placed in #2. When no water supply was found there, they were transferred to #1 in the first days of June.

Each Cabanatuan prisoner, and possibly all Philippine Island prisoners, had a number assigned to them, presumably by the Japanese. Addie's number was 4209. (I have not interviewed a single prionser who knows anything about a number. I have asked Colonel John E. Olson author of *O'Donnell — Andersonville of the Pacific* of their origin. He has no idea but is certain the men didn't get them at O'Donnell. The fact that these numbers appear on Cabanatuan documents and include men from Corregidor who were *not* at O'Donnell seems to support the idea that these numbers were assigned at Cabanatuan. But what do they refer to? The order of arrival at Cabanatuan? Rank? For every guess there appear exceptions. Many of the 200th CAC and the 515th

CAC have numbers between 4,000 and 7,000, but there are numerous exceptions. And just as those near Addie's number of 4209 are First Sergeants or Staff Sergeants, there, too, are many exceptions. My guess, with the help of Bill Nolan's recollection, is that the number was assigned according to rank.)

BILL NOLAN — These conditions of no food, water, medicine, and toilet facilities lasted until June 1942, when we were told to get ready to move. As death seemed to cover the camp, everyone was ready to leave. Anything could be better than Camp O'Donnell. We also heard that Corregidor had surrendered on May 10th or 11th. We were placed on trucks or on trains. After a four- or five-hour ride we arrived at Cabanatuan, a much larger camp. At this point the Japs tried to separate everyone by rank. Officers in one area, Sergeants in another, and the rest in another area.

When Addie and the approximately 6,000 men who came to Cabanatuan from O'Donnell arrived, they anticipated a clean camp with adequate food, water, and medical supplies. What they found was almost another O'Donnell. Groups started the 50-mile trip on or around 2 June, and this movement continued for several days. Some were trucked the entire distance. Others were packed in box cars and rode to Cabanatuan City and then marched from the rail station to the camp.

When the O'Donnell prisoners arrived, the Corregidor prisoners already at #1 were shocked to see the condition of the men. Many had lost 40 or 50 pounds. Their bodies were racked with malaria, dysentery, and other diseases. Clothing was torn. Many Corregidor prisoners had difficulty recognizing old friends. The diseases and conditions that brought death to O'Donnell continued at Cabanatuan.

Hundreds of men died during those first months. Some from disease, others through malnutrition, and many just gave up.

In the fall of 1942, the Japanese began moving some of the "healthier" Camp #1 prisoners to work details. On 8 October 1942, 1,900 men were shipped to Mukden in Manchuria.

In late October, 1,000 men, including Addie's Notre Dame friend Motts Tonelli and his 200th CAC boss Chaplain Howden, were shipped to Davao Penal Colony in Mindanao to perform slave labor. After the men left for Davao, Cabanatuan #3 was permanently closed and the remaining men transferred to #1.

In early November, 1,500 more men were transferred to Japan. By the end of 1942, Camps #2 and #3 were closed permanently, and the remaining prisoners who were not shipped out or who had not died now lived in #1. Most would find Camp #1 to be their home for at least the next 24 months.

By early 1943, illness and death had been stabilized, food was more plentiful, and the men were put on local work details. Camp #1 was then divided into three groups. Each group had its own officers, chaplains, and physicians. To further aid the Japanese in utilizing the men correctly, the officers were asked to classify their men according to technical and non-technical abilities.

These groups were called simply Group One, Group Two, and Group Three. By 1944, because of the dwindling population at Cabanatuan caused by outgoing work details, the camp was divided into just Group One and Group Two. Addie initially was assigned to Group Two. On 22 June 1943, Major G. B. Cross presented an occupational breakdown of Group Two to the Group Commander. There were two divisions — technical and non-technical. Evidently the Japanese wanted to know the talents and abilities of the men so they could best utilize them.

Group Two had 1,430 men categorized 261 technical and 1,169 non-technical. Because many personnel documents were not destroyed before the surrender, the Japanese had the ability to cross check the list to make sure that the men weren't lying. The technical occupations were broken down into categories such as Radio Operators, Telephone Repairmen, Machinists, Plumbers, Engineers, Welders, etc. The non-technical occupations were farmers, businessmen, clerks, teachers, truck drivers, laborers, etc.

Addie listed himself as a laborer. In spite of his over 200 college credits, and in spite of his extreme distaste for physical labor, it's ironic that he would classify himself as a "common laborer." Was he pulling a fast one on the Japanese by not trying to do for them what he was best suited?

The 174 men who were listed as "Laborers" were placed in order of rank. As a First Sergeant, Addie was #3. To add further credence that maybe all wasn't on the up and up, one can look at the case of Addie's friend Walter Schuette. Walter was a native of Green Bay and was inducted the same day as Addie in March 1941 and went through basic training with him and later was a member of the 200th CAC. The reason he gladly signed up for the draft was the absence of a good job in the Brown County area. With only a high school education, the best job he could find was part-time bartending. What did Schuette give the Japanese as his prewar occupation? Chemical engineer. Only three men were listed under that job. Maybe Walter was thinking that a mixer of drinks in a tavern *is* a chemical engineer.

This was the information the Japanese used to assign details. They were especially interested in the men with technical skills that they could put to use repairing trucks and communication systems. The rest were usually assigned to more "routine" details at Cabanatuan.

Chapter 8

Cabanatuan

Maps and Diaries

Of all the Japanese prisoner-of-war camps in the Philippines, more has been written about Cabanatuan than almost all the others combined. The information in the Cabanatuan section will add to the excellent information in books by Calvin Chunn, Donald Knox, Dr. Eugene Jacobs, Bill Evans, Vince Taylor, and G. Bartlett Kerr and others. The topics covered will be those which others have not yet touched or information relative to Addie's activities during his 16-month stay at Cabanatuan #1.

Included is a map of Cabanatuan #1 sketched by Dr. Jacobs. When I have shown the map to other prisoners, some disagreed with portions of the layout. One of the reasons was that the camp was constantly changing. As more work details were sent from the camp, there was consolidation. Also the buildings could be picked up and moved to different locations. Finally, some prisoners' recollections reflect 1942 Cabanatuan and others 1944.

Also a great help was locating the diary of Private Ernest Norquist, who was a prisoner from June of 1942 to August of 1944. Norquist was a 1941 graduate of the University of Minnesota and an army medic. His detailed diary, — now a book *Our Paradise, A GI's War Diary* — including sketches and diagrams, most importantly provides a day-by-day account of the events of Cabanatuan — some trivial, some mundane, some ironic, and others tragic. His efforts to keep the diary were not without danger. If caught by the Japanese, he most certainly would have been punished — possibly executed.

During his incarceration Private Norquist spent as much time with the clergy as he possibly could. He performed clerical work for them, sang in the choir, and so respected their work at Cabanatuan that after being released in 1945, he entered the Presbyterian Ministry and was ordained in 1949. He is retired and today lives in Beaver Dam, Wisconsin.

Many of his fellow POWs knew he was keeping a diary that might be useful later, so they helped him secure paper. Truck drivers who left camp would

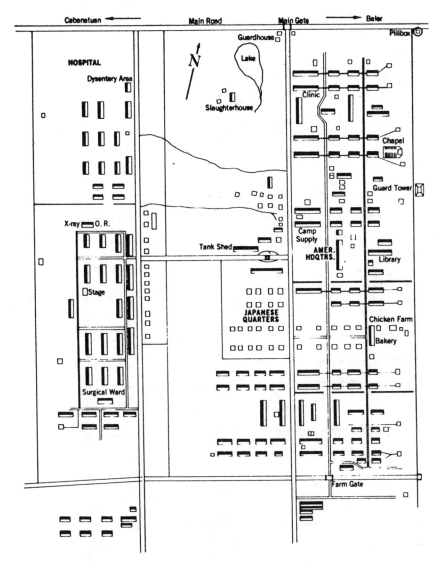

Japanese prisoner of war camp Number 1 at Cabanatuan. (From *Blood Brothers: A Medic's Sketch Book,* by Colonel Eugene C. Jacobs (New York: Carlton Press, Inc., 1985), p. 45.)

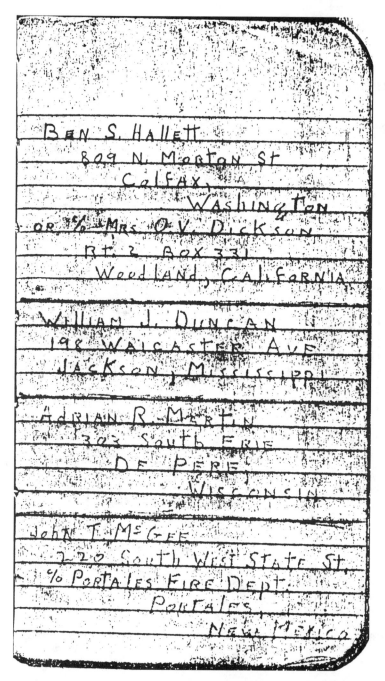

These men were entered in this address book probably in the first half of 1943, at Cabanatuan. (Courtesy of Bill Evans, 8-19-85)

bring back paper, sometimes notebooks. Others saved cigarette wrappers for him. And Norquist himself was able to steal paper from the Japanese because he occasionally had to do typing. During his 27-month stay at Cabanatuan, he hid the manuscript periodically in the church altar, sometimes in the ditches and culverts surrounding the camp, and occasionally had friends keep it for him.

When he left Cabanatuan in August 1944, he buried his diary in an unlabeled food can that was sealed tightly. It was later unearthed by a Filipino family in 1945, turned over to the Army, and returned to his parents in St. Paul. Today the original is found in the State Historical Society Museum in Madison, Wisconsin.

Medical Problems

The starvation, illness, and death that hung over O'Donnell followed the prisoners to Cabanatuan. In the first seven months approximately 2,000 men died. It took months for the doctors to stabilize the medical situation in camp. Not until the middle of January in 1943 did a day finally pass without a death.

Makeshift hospitals were set up to keep the sick from the "healthy." Medicine and food had to be found. Doctors and medics were assigned wards. Many prisoners thought they were treading quicksand as dysentery and malaria consumed their bodies.

With little medicine all doctors could prescribe was *hope*. Some men survived on this; others became too angry to die, but many just quit. Death for them was easier than living.

When the medical staff established their various wards, they numbered the buildings, starting with one. When they realized that they had no number for the building that housed the hopeless who were to die shortly, they named it the "zero ward." Soon the words "zero ward" became synonymous with *death*.

Besides the lack of medicine, the doctors' job was made more difficult because of the unsanitary conditions. It was customary for cuts and abrasions to become infected. Band-Aids and gauze wrappings were cleaned and used over again. Many of those not sick enough to be in the hospital tried to be designated "quarters" so they wouldn't have to go on a work detail. Seldom did those inspected by Dr. Emil Reed achieve this.

McVEY — I remember we had this one doctor, "Death Rattle" Reed. If you were sick and couldn't go out to work, the doctors would write that you couldn't work that day. Well, Dr. Reed wouldn't write that you couldn't work until he heard "death rattling" around inside of you. Later his name changed to "Rigor Mortis" Reed because we thought you had to be dead before he'd keep you out of work.

We used to have these straddle trenches that we used to go to the bathroom in. It seemed like everyone had the dysentery at Cabanatuan. I can remember the doctors telling us not to eat the candy that the natives made and kids sometimes threw into camp. It was made from sugar cane and wasn't too clean. Addie always had diarrhea and he would constantly eat this candy. Sometimes it was covered with flies, and it only made your dysentery worse. Sometimes we'd be sitting around, and we'd see this guy get a sudden attack. We'd bet our next meal of rice whether or not the guy made it in time to the straddle trench.

BROWNELL COLE — The guys with the mild cases of dysentery could make it to the straddle trenches on their own, but the guys who had it bad would go right where they were laying. And then you could hear them retching all the time. All you could see was mucus and blood everywhere.

I remember one of the treatments was charcoal. We used to get it from the burned rice. They would boil the rice in these huge caldrons, and then they'd pour the rice out, and there would be black crusts along the bottom. We'd scrape that out and use it for medication.

McVEY — After a while we had almost no medicine to speak of. The Japs wouldn't give us any that might be coming in to us from the Red Cross. They kept that for themselves.

So many of the doctors had to rely on medical practices that went back centuries. I remember that if you had pellagra, you'd get these awful sores on your leg. In order to get the dead skin off the sore so that it could heal, the doctors put maggots on the wound, and they would eat the dead flesh away.

If someone had a foot infection, the doctors used to treat it with tannic acid. When we ran out of that, they didn't know what to use, so one doctor remembered that urine contained tannic acid, so guys were standing around in urine in order to cure the foot problems. And most of the time these things worked.

And sometimes when the American doctors asked the Japanese for help, humor — not medical relief — was the result.

BOB LUCERO — I heard this story from someone who heard it from someone etcetera.

Anyway, some of our camp doctors were real concerned about scurvy and pellagra [two vitamin deficiency deseases], which were causing prisoners to lose some of their teeth, because any sores in and around their mouths or any parts of their bodies or any cuts or scratches wouldn't heal properly and just remained open and festered.

And since they hadn't or couldn't get any medicine for malaria, dysentery, beriberi, dengue fever, diphtheria, etcetera, they went to see the Jap bigwigs about some vitamins and anything else they could get. About that time they didn't know about daily minimum requirements and hadn't discovered very many types of vitamins.

Sure enough, a couple of days later a bright, smart aleck, smart ass of a Jap delivered 20 to 30 bottles of Lydia Pinkhain's Compound [Elixir] for Women for those trying days of the month. He pointed out the vitamin contents and mineral contents and left.

Thank God the Japs hadn't read the fine print on the bottle because Lydia Pinkhain's Compound for Women was also good for Liver Spots, Gout, Acne, Arthritis, Fever, Headache, Falling Hair, Pimples, Fallen Arches, Hemorrhoids, and a whole host of other ailments!

The best part of all was that Lydia's Compound worked — as far as I know none of us ever got pregnant or had pain and cramps on "those certain days of the month!"

Occasionally prisoners sought medical help from sources other than the doctors. Through trading with fellow prisoners or the Japanese, or through purchasing medicine on the black market that was operating at Cabanatuan, some prisoners were able to come up with their own supply of the precious quinine or sulfathiazole.

But even with medicine, not everyone pulled through. After months of starvation and illness, some just didn't have the strength to fight off death. Addie's good friend from Berlin, Wisconsin, Bill Wells, was one such example. A big, strong youth who enjoyed the hijinks with Addie at Camp Wallace and Fort Bliss, Bill was one of those who died in the early months of Cabanatuan. He was diagnosed as having dysentery on 15 November 1942, was admitted to the hospital on 20 November, and died at 2:30 p.m. on 28 November at the age of 27.

In the early days of Cabanatuan, the burial detail was a daily occurrence. In the first few months, as many as 30 or 40 men would die every day. Dysentery, malaria, and starvation were the main causes. The burial detail men would report to the hospital area, load the dead often on the *behai* (living huts) shades, and carry the bodies to the makeshift cemetery just out of camp in a southeasterly direction.

LUCERO — Sometimes we took the bodies to the cemetery on shutters from the barracks, and if they were dead for a while, the body might stick to the shutter. You had a problem trying to get them off.

Because Cabanatuan was located in swampy lowlands, burial was not an

IMPERIAL JAPANESE ARMY

1. I am interned at the Philippine Military Prison Camp #1

2. My health is — excellent; good; fair; poor.

3. I am—uninjured; sick in hospital; under treatment; not under treatment.

4. I am — improving; not improving; better; well.

5. Please see that _____ MOTHER _____ is taken care of.

(Re: Family); _____ SCHUETTE AND ME _____

_____ ease give my best regards to _____

IMPERIAL JAPANESE ARMY

1. I am interned at the Philippine Military Prison Camp No. 1.

2. My health is — excellent; good; fair; poor.

3. I am — injured; sick in hospital; under treatment; not under treatment.

4. I am — improving; not improving; better; well.

5. Please see that MOTHER

6. (Re: Family) is taken

regards to DON & TOONER

Opposite page and this page: Cabanatuan POW cards sent in late 1942 and early 1943.

easy task. The prisoners could only dig down a few feet before striking water. Graves were shallow but wide, and sometimes 15-20 bodies were placed in the same grave. Usually a Chaplain accompanied the men and said a few prayers. Often during the rainy season, the dirt on top of the graves would wash away and expose parts of the decaying bodies. Once one of the living was thrown into the grave. He was Larry Holt, a popular Navaho Indian from 200th CAC of New Mexico.

Holt and other Navaho Indians in the 200th CAC played an integral part in the defense of Bataan. Japanese Intelligence knew most of the codes and the languages of the world. When the Americans used their field phones during battle, the Japanese could listen in and tell what was going on. Because the Navaho language was known only to a small group and basically never spoken off the reservation, the Japanese knew nothing about it. That's where Larry Holt came in.

McVEY — We had two Navaho Indians, Lawrence Holt and another guy. To prevent our information being stolen by the Japs, we would send Holt out to the enemy lines to scout around and then call back. One of the other Navaho Indians would answer and Holt would report the information in Navaho. The Japanese could never figure out what the hell was going on. They couldn't decipher what was being said. That sure worked well.

But at Cabanatuan the Americans weren't the only soldiers to get sick. The Japanese also suffered from malaria, dysentery, and other Philippine diseases, but they usually had adequate medical supplies, so their illnesses were short lived. Japanese doctors wouldn't think of providing the necessary medicine to ease the suffering from a non-battle injury. So the guards looked elsewhere for medical help, and the enterprising American prisoners were ready to take advantage of the situation.

COLE — I remember the prisoners were making these tablets out of corn starch and trading it to the Japanese for cigarettes. The Japs thought it would cure their VD. They found this corn starch in this big warehouse up around Tarlac just on the other side of Clark Field. The Japs figured it must be worth something if there's so much of it. They figured the Americans would know what to do with it so the Japs brought in bags of the stuff to Cabanatuan.

Prison Camp Mail

For all Addie's family knew about his welfare, the day the Americans surrendered, 9 April 1942, the earth opened up and swallowed him. No communication was received by his family until several months later while he was at Cabanatuan. When families back in the States initially heard nothing, many assumed their loved ones were dead.

The prisoners at Cabanatuan were allowed to send a brief message on a prepared post card. The first statement dealt with where they were located. The Cabanatuan prisoner was in "the Philippine Military Prison Camp #1." The second statement concerned his health. He could underline "excellent; good; fair; poor." Additional lines indicated physical status and condition and ended with the prisoner's concern for those back in the States.

The cards had no date and the recipient could not tell where the cards came from outside of the statement "Philippine Camp #1." It wasn't until after the war when the prisoners returned that the relatives knew what camps they were in. The cards were censored by the Japanese, and you can bet that any cards marked "poor health" or "not improving," or containing some comment the Japanese didn't want, would not make it back to the States.

The cards were typed by a fellow prisoner after he was given the messages to send, and then each prisoner signed the card. When the parents saw their son's signature, they knew he was alive.

Addie was able to send two cards from Cabanatuan. His first, sent probably in 1942, indicated that his health was "good," he was "uninjured," and that he was "well." He indicated that "McVey and Schuette" were okay. That was the first that these two Brown County families knew that their sons had survived the Death March. He ended by sending his best to "all."

His second card was sent in early 1943. On later cards prisoners requested items from home.

Work Details

The Japanese intended and the American prisoners expected that some kind of work would become part of the daily routine at Cabanatuan. Whereas the Americans expected the Japanese to follow the terms of the 1929 Geneva Convention Relative to the Treatment of Prisoners of War, the Japanese had other ideas. Their Bushido code did not permit a Japanese soldier to become a prisoner of war, and although they signed but did not ratify the Geneva Articles, they paid *little* attention to the following articles.

LABOR
Article 30

The length of the day's work of prisoners of war, including therein the trip going and returning, shall not be excessive and must not, in any case, exceed that allowed for the civil workers in the region employed at the same work. Every prisoner shall be allowed a rest of 24 consecutive hours every week, preferably Sunday.

Article 31

Labor furnished by prisoners of war shall have no direct relation with war operations. It is especially prohibited to use prisoners for manufacturing and transporting arms or munitions of any kind, or for transporting material intended for combatant units.

In case of violation of the provisions of the preceding paragraph, prisoners, after executing or beginning to execute the order, shall be free to have their protests presented through the mediation of the agents whose functions are set forth in Articles 43 and 44, or, in the absence of an agent, through the mediation of representatives of the protecting Power.

Article 32

It is forbidden to use prisoners of war at unhealthful or dangerous work.

Any aggravation of the conditions of labor by disciplinary measures is forbidden.

Instead, the Japanese adhered to their own 1904 regulations for handling prisoners, but they often deviated even from that. During the early days of Cabanatuan, jobs usually concerned running the camp properly. Weeds were cut, pathways were created, latrines and drainage ditches were dug, and barracks were picked up and moved. Later the carabao, wood, and farm details became part of the daily routine at Cabanatuan.

The carabao detail was a small group that drove the carabao carts to Cabantuan to pick up 100 pound sacks of rice and other supplies. It was a detail desired by many but given to few.

EVANS — I was very fortunate to get on the carabao detail. There was about nine or ten of us that drove carabao carts into the city of Cabanatuan daily to pick up rice and other rations and haul them back to camp. Now this was an all-day trip so it afforded us a lot of opportunities to get extra food and smuggle in contraband.

Another detail that allowed some contact with the outside was the wood detail. Wood was needed to fire the mess hall stoves. Details of approximately 50 men were trucked to nearby woods and given an ax for every two men. Trees were chopped down, cut up, and then trucked back to camp. The work wasn't as demanding as other details and afforded the men a change of scenery. Some even found the duty humorous.

LUCERO — We picked out all of the balsa trees. They were real light wood. You make cigar boxes and model airplanes out of it. We cut them with an ax and hauled the wood back. We thought we were lumberjacks like Paul Bunyan.

The main work detail at Cabanatuan, however, was far more strenuous. In late 1942, the Japanese decided to start a farm just to the south of the compound. If successful, more acres were to be turned into farm land. The Japanese expected to use the vegetables to supplement the POWs' diet. As it turned out, much of what was produced made its way to Cabanatuan, where the Japanese traded it for other items.

The work was difficult. The Japanese forced the men to work in an uncomfortable erect position. They were not allowed to bend the knees or kneel. Often the men worked barefoot, and talking was usually not permitted. Indiscretions by the POWs resulted in beatings. Many times the men tried to make "quarters," but the Japanese and doctors, like "Death Rattle" Reed, thought the physical activity, although difficult, was better for the men than languishing all day in camp.

Beans, corn, squash, sweet potatoes, and rice were the usual products. The men dug, hoed, and planted by hand. Before the war, little manual labor was done in the Philippines during the midday because of the intense heat. The Americans arrived on the farm around 6:00 a.m. and worked until 11:00 a.m. They marched back to camp for lunch and then worked from 3:00 p.m. until 5:30 or 6:00 p.m. By 1944 approximately 4,000 men were working daily at the farm, and still more were employed in the "honey-bucket" brigade carrying refuse from the Japanese latrines to the farm to be used as fertilizer.

The Americans were even successful later in convincing the Japanese to use some of the compound for farming, and men planted little gardens of okra, eggplant, and sweet potatoes.

McVEY — At Cabanatuan we were off working in the farm fields. We had to do all the work by hand. For every three kernels of corn that they gave us to plant, we usually ate two. It was really hot out there and sometimes they made us work ten hours in the sun. We weren't allowed to talk much to one another, or they'd come around and hit us.

I remember one time some guy was eating the tops of the onions out in the field. The Japs came in the barracks and lined us all up and checked everyone's mouth. They found this guy with green stains in his mouth and suspected him to being the guy who ate the onions. They hauled him out and beat him as an example to the rest.

WALT MASON — We kept telling ourselves that the Americans will win the war and we will be saved. At Cabanatuan when we planted rice, it took six months before we could harvest it. When the Japs no longer had us plant rice because they might not be there to harvest it, we knew the Americans were coming, and the war was winding down.

Cabanatuan Guards

Although the Cabanatuan work details are still etched on the minds of the POWs, probably remembered more by some was the treatment by the guards. The Japanese guards were not the most intelligent soldiers on the island. Some were older, some had been wounded, and some were just not smart enough to do anything else but guard prisoners.

The Americans enjoyed tricking the guards even at the risk of a beating. Being the lower echelon of the Japanese Army, the guards had been beaten often by their superiors, and they delighted in being in a position to turn the tables. The POWs came up with nicknames for the guards, which were often quite humorous. Ask any Cabanatuan prisoners today to mention some of the guards, and most likely they'll mention "Donald Duck," "Air Raid," "Big Speedo," and "Little Speedo."

These guards and others were often the purveyors of the beatings. As expected, the prisoners were beaten for lack of cooperation and for stealing, but many times just because they couldn't understand the directions often given in Japanese. And sometimes they were beaten just because they happened to be there.

JOHNSON — We had one guard called "Donald Duck." He was called that because of the way he walked. He was in charge of a detail planting rice. We had to stand all day in water and mud.

McVEY — Someone told him that the reason we called him "Donald Duck" was that "Donald Duck" was a big movie star in America. He thought he was really great, that he looked like a famous movie star. Actually he was called that because he was always yakking like "Donald Duck" does.

Well, one day the Japs got a hold of some movies and they called us together to show them to us for some entertainment. One of the movies happened to be a "Donald Duck" one. When he found out who "Donald Duck" really was, boy, did he get mad! The next day out on the farm he hit just about everybody. You stayed away from him for quite a while.

I remember one time we had to get the hoes out to work on the fields. They were all stored in this shed. They were made out of wood, and that's what we worked the ground with. They were hanging horizontally, not up and down, and one of them was stuck as the guy pulled it off the rack. Well, "Donald Duck" thought he wasn't moving fast enough, so he starts hitting the guy with his cane. Well, the guy told him to hold on, come close, and see that it's stuck. Well, "Donald Duck" got his head close, and when he did, this guy yanked the hoe loose, and the front end of it hit "Donald Duck" in the head and knocked him out. Of course that's what the guy had in mind all the time. Well, did we scatter. Nobody wanted to be caught in there when they found him, because they would have killed us.

MANASSE — The farm detail was a horrible experience for all of us but it was an area where if you were in Cabanatuan, that's where you worked. Before I got on the farm, I spent a couple of months on the wood detail. It was great because we left the camp early in the morning and we came back at night. But as far as the farm was concerned, we had some pretty horrible Japanese guards who used clubs to get what they wanted. I remember one of them by the name of "Air Raid." That was the name we gave him. Every time we saw him coming, we would yell "air raid" so we would start to work so he wouldn't catch us loafing on the job.

McVEY — Two of the main guards were "Big Speedo" and "Little Speedo." They were called that because if you were slow in your work they would holler *Speedo*. "Big Speedo" didn't beat up the prisoners. "Little Speedo" did, and he was much bossier than "Big Speedo."

Whether Addie received beatings at the hands of "Donald Duck," "Air Raid," or "Little Speedo" is unknown. His beatings were to come later at Las Piñas.

But the Japanese weren't the only "guards" at Cabanatuan. Traditionally, one of the "duties" of a prisoner is to attempt to escape. To solve the problem the Japanese divided the camp into ten-man squads. If one man in your group of ten escaped, the other nine were executed. The Japanese didn't do this every time but did do it enough to keep the Americans uneasy about escaping. To further prevent prisoners from sneaking away, the Americans themselves posted *inside guards*. Before he was sent to Davao in 1942, Addie's friend Mario Tonelli, the ex-Notre Dame and Chicago Cardinal fullback was one of these guards.

According to a recovered 1944 memo, the Camp Patrol was a night patrol consisting of two posts with the watches divided as follows: 9:00 p.m. to 2:00 a.m. and 2:00 a.m. to 6:00 a.m. Post #1 ran from the fence between the Hospital Area and Group One, along Broadway, through Group Two Gate, and through the Group Two Area to the latrine line of Group Two. Post #2 ran from the fence between the Hospital Area and Group One along Fifth Avenue to the fence between Group One and Group Two.

Members of the patrol did not have to follow the routes exactly and could move as they deemed necessary so as not to establish a pattern. Their duties included apprehending any individuals out of their barracks without authority after Call to Quarters, preventing stealing from the gardens, and carrying out other duties coming within the purview of General Orders for Sentinels. Offenders were escorted to their barracks and reported to their barracks' leader. The guards were allowed to carry nightsticks and arm bands.

With the use of the outside Japanese guards and the inside American guards, escape attempts were kept at a minimum.

Addie's Work at Cabanatuan

If there was any way possible for Addie to get out of the work details, he probably made the most of it. His life-long "fear" of animals kept him from getting on the carabao detail; his distaste for physical labor forced him to keep his distance from the wood detail; and his inability to withstand intense sun made the farm detail undesirable. Because a majority of the Cabanatuan prisoners at one time or another were on the farm detail, Addie made a brief appearance planting seeds and pulling weeds. After all, he did give the Japanese "Manual Laborer" as his prewar occupation. But Addie spent some of his time on the details within the compound. It was common for a prisoner to perform at Cabanatuan a service similar to that which he did before and during the War. Addie's chicanery and his love and respect for his religion certainly put him in a position where he could be of service to the priests.

But initially religion was suppressed by the Japanese. Not until the end of 1942 were religious services conducted on an "official" and regular basis. If there ever existed work at Cabanatuan that Addie would volunteer for, it would have had to be some chore to help the Chaplains.

After the Japanese divided the camp into Groups One, Two, and Three, they assigned Chaplains to each group. Assigned to Addie's Group Two were Catholic priests Fathers John Wilson, James O'Brien, and John McDonnell. Also assigned to Group Two was Edward J. Nagel, who had been a missionary in the Islands when the War broke out.

Each group had its own small chapel as did the hospital area. Later a larger chapel for the entire camp was made out of the east end of the library, but the group chapels still remained. Some of the wood that was brought back to camp by the wood detail was dried and made into benches for the larger chapel.

Addie spent a great deal of his 15½ months at Cabanatuan working with the Chaplains. He helped prepare the altar for Mass, did errands and chores for the priests, and was an active participant in the bull sessions held after the evening Rosary. His religious efforts did not go unnoticed.

FATHER STANLEY REILLY LETTER — 23 July — It is easy to recall Adrian who often was my companion in the prison camps. At Cabanatuan Adrian and I often passed the time of day in each other's company. I noticed always his devotion and loyalty to his faith and his priests.

JOE ROMERO — Addie would help the Fathers prepare for the evening Mass held on a makeshift altar of bamboo and boxes on week days and on Sundays. He would also accompany the Chaplains to the barracks to see if the men wanted to go to Confession. Many would go, and many men regardless of their religion wanted moral comfort by talking to men like Chaplain Howden. Addie didn't look like he was in bad shape or very sick. He was always smiling and would talk to many of us after the Masses were over. Of course he had many friends he knew very well and hung around with. Everybody in camp liked [Addie] because he treated everybody there the same. He had a special feeling and love for every POW that was in that prison camp with him.

At Cabanatuan the POWs formed friendships in various ways. Sometimes their friends were those from their original unit, sometimes those from their city or state, and sometimes those of the same nationality as themselves. Before the war broke out, Addie's good friend at Fort Stotsenberg was Father John Duffy, who was both an Irishman and a Notre Dame graduate. At Cabanatuan, Addie continued to be helpful to Chaplain Howden, who was from the 200th CAC, Addie's original outfit, but he also became friends with Father Mathias Zerfes, who was from Addie's home state, Wisconsin, and with Father James O'Brien, who like Addie was an Irishman.

Part of his responsibilities for Mass included getting the wine and hosts ready for Communion. Procuring these in a prison camp was extremely difficult if not impossible. According to Father John Wilson, only one candle was used during the Mass and an eye dropper used for a few drops of Altar wine when quantities were low. Fortunately, the Japanese allowed the Chaplains to order the wine and hosts from Father Buddenbroch, a Belgian priest in Manila, and from Archbishop Michael O'Doherty, also in Manila. For example, on 1 February 1944, the Catholic Chaplains ordered one dozen bottles of Mass Wine, 1,000 small hosts, 1,000 larger hosts, 1 chalice, 2 dozen candles, 500 holy medals, 12 dozen rosaries, and a small grip to carry Mass equipment. Most of the Protestant requests that day were for musical necessities — 400 hymnals, sheet music, 2 organs, and a Victrola.

An interesting sidelight to the work of the Chaplains was the difference between the Protestant and Catholic services. The Catholic services were nearly always in Latin, very traditional, and seldom varied from week to week. The Protestants, on the other hand, changed their worship services every week — new prayers, different songs, and a different topic for the sermon. Usually the Japanese had to give approval for each service. The Catholics seldom were hassled by the Japanese authorities because they seemed to be doing the same thing week in and week out. The Protestants, however, ran into problems occasionally with getting approval for what they wanted to do. And whereas the Catholic services were either Mass or the Rosary service, the Protestants had prayer services and Bible study, besides the Sunday devotions.

On 16 June 1943, a religious survey of the camp was conducted. Of the 5,885 prisoners that were surveyed, there were:

Protestants	4,015
Catholics	1,520
Jewish	114
No Religion	236

This report was submitted to the commanding Officer at Cabanatuan by Curtis T. Beecher, Lieutenant Colonel, U.S. Marine Corps. The knowledge of how many men of each religion there were in camp and who those men were helped the Chaplains better serve the spiritual needs of the prisoners.

Each month the Chaplains had to turn in a report as to their activities for the month. According to these reports, the Protestants had fewer services than the Catholics, but they in turn spent more time visiting the men in the barracks. For example, in July 1944, the Protestants had:

Church Services:

Sunday:	20
Weekly:	12
Bible Classes:	13

The Catholics meanwhile had:

Church Services:

Sunday:	25
Weekly:	125
Rosary:	93

But in the area of contacting the men in the barracks, the Protestant Chaplains made 315 visits and saw 2,214 men while the Catholic chaplains saw 250 men on their 37 visits. Confessions, even in a prison camp, must have taken some time.

Because of the large number of services that the Catholics performed, it was necessary that the Chaplains had prisoners that would help them in organizing and setting up these services. This is where Addie played an important role. When someone was needed to prepare the altar for Mass or to lead the evening Rosary devotions, it was Addie.

Group Two held their Rosary devotions every evening at 7:00 p.m. at the chapel. The daily Rosary after supper was a time for the men to relax, pray, and meet friends. After the service, Addie and several of the men would sit and talk with the Chaplains about religion, their lives at Cabanatuan, and what the future held in store for them. Father John Wilson was one of those who led the men in the Rosary.

FATHER JOHN WILSON — Every evening at 7:00 p.m., we gathered outside the chapel, formed a circle, and said the Rosary, the Litany of the Blessed Virgin Mary, and a Prayer for a Happy Death. I knew the Litany and the Prayer for a Happy Death by heart. We had no prayer books of any kind.

The following is the Prayer for a Happy Death that Addie and the men said each evening after the Rosary.

> Life is short — and death is sure.
> The hour of death — remains obscure.
> A soul you have — an only one,
> If that be lost — all hope is gone.
> Waste not your time — while time shall last,
> For after death — 'tis ever past.
> The all-seeing God — your Judge will be,
> Or heaven or hell — your destiny.
> All earthly things — will fleet away.
> Eternity — will ever stay.

Besides the Rosary services, the Catholic Chaplains were able to later convince the Japanese that a religious retreat would be beneficial for both the Chaplains and the men. Each priest took a different day to lead the retreat, and for that week the priests didn't have to report to the farm for work.

An important part of any religious service was the singing. Both the Catholics and Prostestants had choirs. Bernard Fitzpatrick from Minnesota, a member of the 194th Tank Group, was one of the organizers of the Catholic choir that sang during the High Masses. The Catholic hymns were often more traditional Latin numbers and to the Protestants might appear dry and lifeless. Their choir usually chose different songs from one week to the next. Often the choir was under the direction of elderly Neville Baugh, who was a distin- guished Manila musician prior to the War breaking out. Baugh was one of those who later died during the daring liberation of Cabanatuan in 1945 by Mucci's Rangers.

Memorial Day of 1943, honoring soldiers who have died in battle, was a moving experience for the Cabanatuan prisoners.

> NORQUIST DIARY — 30 May 1943 — Memorial Day — sans dinner at the Forum, sans holiday atmosphere, sans flags, and sans picnic journey in the country. But there was a great Memorial Service here. At a little after 8:00 a.m. we assembled to march to the cemetery. At the lead were ranking officers and the chaplains, as well as one cantor, a civilian with a patriarchal beard — followed by our glee club and that of the other side of the camp. There was a bit of rain, which passed, leaving a clear, warm sky. A gentle wind blew. We counted off, then walked over the cobblestone pathway to the cemetery. Those of us who have wooden shoes had a hard time walking. We reached our destination and began a long wait for the service to begin. The place had changed in appearance. A concrete memorial stone had been erected and the graves had been banked and ditched. At length the Japanese Camp Commander arrived.

> HENRY FLUGGER DIARY — Services at the prison camp ceme- tery. 1,500 prisoners allowed to attend. The Japanese Major presented a wreath. Prayers in Hebrew, Latin, and English.

According to a C. S. Maupin memo, for those patients in the hospital area and those prisoners on duty, a separate service was held at the stage in the hospital area at 10:45 a.m. Those in the dysentery ward, however, were not allowed to attend. The Program included:

Invocation	Chaplain Talbot
"Lincoln's Gettysburg Address"	Major Kagy
Patriotic song	Hospital Glee Club
Taps	Pvt. (Ernest) Norquist
Benediction	Chaplain Zimmerman

Because the 1943 Memorial Day observance was so successful, the prison- ers requested another program the following year. According to a 9 May 1944 memo, Lieutenant Colonel Curtis T. Beecher, Commander at Cabanatuan, requested of the Japanese that the prisoners be allowed to hold a 45-minute observance at the cemetery honoring the war dead. He requested that this occur at 7:00 a.m. on Tuesday, 30 May 1944, and that the Chaplains and prisoners desiring to attend be permitted to do so.

Recreation

Soon after arriving at Cabanatuan, the American officers realized that unless the prisoners were occupied by some activity other than religious services, many might die just by giving up. If all the men had to do each day was eat their meager rice ration and work long hours on the farm, or lie in a hospital ward, POWs might choose death over living. Fortunately the officers, often with the help of the Chaplains, organized activities to keep the men busy during their free time. And some of the prisoners themselves invented their own diversions.

The Japanese confiscated most of the playing cards, but prisoners made their own by drawing numbers and figures and played poker and other card games in their *behais*. Some played chess. Others organized clubs by cities, states, religion, etc. There were bingo games held occasionally with money often the prize. To keep the mind active, some questioned one another about state capitals or baseball players and their teams. But there were also events scheduled that were on a larger scale.

Addie chose, however, to participate in activities that weren't physically demanding. Since his youth, he enjoyed mental challenges. In camp he made use of the "Cabanatuan College" and the library.

The college courses were held in the medical area. After having earned over 200 college credits, education seemed natural for Addie. The Chaplains, doctors, and many of the officers were college graduates. Keeping the mind active was important for the prisoner's survival. Unfortunately, the college only lasted for a short period of time during the early Cabanatuan months.

MANASSE — I know that Addie helped around the educational area in these camps. He was always interested in that, and that's why I believe I enjoyed talking with him as much as I did. Both of us were well educated, I would say, and at least we had something in common. Most of the men did not have this type of education, so there was a little bit of a difference on who you could talk to and how you could vary your conversation. Addie helped in the chapel on a regular basis and in the educational attempts that were made to keep the men busy. I did not participate in any of this, as I felt the best way to survive was to keep as busy as I could and accept any work that we were asked to do.

Chaplain Albert Talbot was Dean of the College and students who com-

Class schedule

February 1943 -

	1.00-2.15	2.15-3.00	3.00-3.50	3.50-4.15
Monday	Fundamental ology General Compar- ative linguistics Ch. Talbot	English Grammar Composition Spelling Ch. Zimmerman	History Ancient and Medieval Sgt. Jackson	Japanese Language Capt. Weinstein
Tuesday:	General Compar- ative Linguistics Fundamental Sociology	Anatomy for Medical Corps Capt. Boland	Music Theory History Appreciation Neville R.Baugh	History Ancient and ? Sgt.Jackson
Wednesday:	Ch. Talbot Sociology General Comparative Linguistics C ept.Roland	Anatomy for Medical Corps Capt.Roland	Astronomy Elementary and Advanced Sgt.Gillfoyle	Japanese Language Capt.Weinstein

Thursday

Sociology	English	Basic	History
General	Grammar	Theory	Ancient
Comparative	Composition	History	and
Linguistics	Spelling	Appreciation	Medieval
C. Talbot	Ch. Zimmerman	Orville K. Bauch	Sgt. Jackson

Sociology	Anatomy	Astronomy	Japanese
General	for	Elementary	Language
Comparative	Medical	and	
Linguistics	Corps	Advanced	
Ch. Talbot	Ch. Roland	Sgt. Guillotte	Capt. Weinstei

Saturday

History	Anatomy	Lettering	Lettering
Ancient	for	in	in
and	Medical	Mechanical	Mechanical
Medieval	Corps	Drawing	Drawing
Sgt. Jackson	Capt. Roland	I. Norquist	E. Norquist

3). All the students who fulfill the requirements of diligence in work, regular attendance in class and do the work assigned and pass the final examination will be given a certificate of proficiency in the subject or subjects taken.

Albert D. Talbot, Dean

Albert D. Talbot, Dean
Captain U.S. Army
Chaplain

pleted the necessary work were to receive a certificate of proficiency.

FATHER WILSON — Father Albert Talbot was the Chaplain for the hospital area. He was the one who began the classes. Those classes could not function in the area everybody had to work, which was all of us on our side [duty side] of the fence. We had to work every day. The men in the hospital area could not work so they were the only ones able to attend class. But there were a few classes even in our [duty side] area. A couple of Japs came in and conducted classes in Japanese. Very few signed up. Several Spanish speaking doctors from New Mexico and Arizona conducted classes in Spanish. They were held only on days when there was no work.

There was also one class in Gaelic, which attracted Addie's interest. Whether any men ever received their certificates of proficiency is unclear, but the college was a diversion that attracted Addie.

He would also have found interesting the four or five libraries within the prison compound. The main library was located in the same building as the chapel just to the east of the American Headquarters. Since he spent most of his time at the chapel, Addie had easy access to the books. There were also smaller libraries at various locations in the medical area. Books and magazines came from the men themselves. Many had been carried by the prisoners from Bataan and Corregidor. Occasionally books or magazines might come from an outside source such as Manila, and the Japanese even donated some of their propaganda material. Surprisingly, most of the reading materials were real literature and not trash. There were dictionaries, classics, and contemporary literature. In all there were over 3,000 books and magazines, and they were used extensively. The heavy use and moist conditions caused damage to the books, but librarians did an excellent job binding them and keeping them readable. Occasionally, a page might be ripped out so that a prisoner could roll an infrequent cigarette, but for the most part the men used and respected the books. The library had check-out procedures and "fines" for overdue material.

Food

When you ask any Cabanatuan veteran what his meals consisted of, he is mostly likely to reply, "RICE! RICE! AND MORE RICE!!" One prisoner recalled, "The nice thing about rice — it goes with anything." The prisoners expected that rice would comprise most of their diet, but they often wondered what else would go with it. And how much food would they get?

At Cabanatuan each Group had its own mess. Each Group was subdivided into Companies, and each Company drew the food for its men. Rice was steamed in large caldrons, and each prisoner usually got two or three mess kits of rice per day. Sometimes they were given a watery Japanese rice soup called "*lugao.*"

Various types of "greens" growing around the camp eventually found their way into an American-style soup. And on rare occasions, two or three small pieces of carabao were placed in the soup kettle, but few men even noticed the protein as that kettle of soup sometimes fed 100 men. One of the purposes of the farm, as mentioned before, was to supply food for the prisoners, but little found its way into the mess. That prompted several of the men to grow their own within the Cabanatuan compound. Suffice it to say, the prisoners at Cabanatuan were not fed an adequate diet by any standards.

The following Cabanatuan hospital menu from 1 August 1944 found on microfilm from the National Archives points out some of the nutritional problems and ironies of prison camp life.

HOSPITAL — REGULAR STRENGTH 533

BREAKFAST	LUNCH	DINNER
Rice	Rice	Rice
Tea	Gravy with Gabi	Braised Carabao
Limes	Corn on the Cob	Boiled Greens
		Pudding

	Grams	Calories
Proteins	53	212
Fats	38	342
Carbohydrates	458	1832
	Total Calories	2386

Ask any healthy Cabanatuan prisoner if he ever received this much food in a day, and he'll probably say, "Never!!" Those on the duty side averaged between 1,000 and 2,000 calories per day. The American medical community believed that in order to get a sick man back on his feet, he had to be fed well. This sound medical philosophy met its opposite in the Japanese doctors. When they were in a position to determine the dietary requirements of the sick and healthy American prisoner, the sick were given less to eat.

Besides the gardens within the compound, the prisoners were able to augment their diet in three different ways. Addie, who was fairly healthy when he left Cabanatuan for Las Piñas in September 1943, used the first two.

First, Red Cross boxes were distributed occasionally to the men. Prisoners had their choice of consuming the contents on the spot or allowing themselves so much food per day to make it last.

McVEY — I remember getting a Red Cross package. I don't remember what all we had in it, but I remember a Kraft cheese wrapper that I had kept from the package. I know I tried to make the food in the packages last as long as I could. I would mix a little each day with the rice that we were fed. I know Addie ate his right away. And then he had the habit of visiting you when his food ran out. He was good at getting food out of *your* Red Cross box.

When the Red Cross packages came in, the feverish trading reminded prisoners of the New York Stock Exchange.

Secondly, there was a commissary, and if the prisoners had money or something to bargain with, they usually could pick up additional food that was sometimes smuggled into camp by outside details.

McVEY — I remember little kids would take a peso and tie a string around it and tie the other end to a rock and then throw it through the fence at us. The Japs thought the kids were throwing rocks at us to annoy us, but there was money attached to it. We could then use the money at the commissary that was run inside the camp.

The commissary listed the prices of the products for sale. Often the cost was inflated by the law of supply and demand.

NORQUIST DIARY — 30 APRIL 1944 —

COMMISSARY PRICES

peanuts . . . . 2.50 pesos/cup	peppers . . . . .30 cup
chicken eggs . . . . .61 each	beans . . . . 3.00 cup
notebooks . . . . 2.00 each	ground pepper . . . . . . 2.00 oz.
coconut candy . . . . 1.60 bar	garlic . . . . .25 bulb
limes . . . . .03 each	coconuts 60
camotes (sweet potatoes) .65 kilo	

Addie dealt with the commissary. At Cabanatuan there were those with outside connections who ran a black market and would often lend money at a high rate of interest. Whether Addie did business with them, borrowed money from the clergy, or charged goods at the commissary will never be known, but he did sign promissory notes.

MANASSE LETTER — 22 November 1945 — Adrian spoke to me of a brother, Don. In the Philippines, Adrian and I signed certain promissory notes, which we used to buy food. If any of these are ever presented, Adrian informed me to let Don know of their authenticity.

Finally, when the men became desperate enough, there was vegetation and animal life that eventually found its way into the prisoners' stomachs, especially during 1944 when food became scarce.

JOHNSON — After work one night we were lined up on the road to be counted and we were waiting for the food to be brought in by "motorsickle." One time they brought it in on a three-wheeled "motorsickle" with a box on it. One night they were bringing in a horse for us to eat. Well, it went by with the head hanging over one side and the legs, cut off, were hanging over the other. We were all standing there getting counted and one of the guys near me said, "Well, there are people in the states that never had horseshoe soup."

STEWART — These Mexicans from the 200th CAC were very adept at living, it seemed to me, in Cabanatuan. How they got hold of them, I don't know, but they would get hold of those red hot peppers and put them in a bottle and set them in the sun and that would make a juice for their rice.

The proteins the Americans received were few and far between. As time wore on and food became scarce, what the prisoners considered pets in 1942 was food in 1944.

Rumors

One of the traits of the Cabanatuan prisoners was their eternal optimism. They fervently believed that MacArthur's return with Yanks and tanks was just a few days away. But, as the war dragged on, that belief had to be fanned frequently by rumors to keep it from going out. Cut off from news, the Americans had to resort to a variety of methods of getting information about the War. The Japanese did not permit radios and newspapers at Cabanatuan, although on occasion some were smuggled in. The Philippine people in the area tried to get information to the men as often as possible.

JOHNSON — We had a detail of men that would go down to the Cabanatuan dump to get fertilizer for the farm. The Filipino women would come by and sing us the news so that we could know what was going on. The Japs just thought they were just singing a song.

Many of the rumors that might have started with an element of fact, soon turned into exaggeration with each retelling. Private Norquist kept a record in his diary of the rumors floating through Cabanatuan. Fellow prisoners encouraged him to publish a book of the rumors. He considered calling the book *The Third Hole,* referring to the alleged source of many of the rumors, at the latrine. During the 2¼ years Private Norquist was at Cabanatuan, he consulted with camp "experts" as to cost of publication. The following are just a small portion of the Cabanatuan rumors that are in his diary. Some are serious, some humorous, and others totally ridiculous, but all portray the dogged hope the prisoners possessed that Cabanatuan was not to be the place they would spend the rest of their lives.

1942

Roosevelt said in a speech we would be home by September 15.

Henry Ford will give every Bataan man a car when we return home.

Ships have left Ecuador to get us.

There was a big successful naval battle west of Guam in which the Nipponese lost over 60 ocean ships.

1943

We have been bombing Formosa and Japan heavily from aircraft carriers.

We have launched seven aircraft carriers since the start of the war.

President Roosevelt gives Japan to March 15 to make an unconditional surrender or else he will turn everything possible loose on Japan.

So many Japanese ships have sunk in the South Islands that the water is full of bodies.

The Americans blasted the Panama Canal, thereby bottling up the Japanese fleet in the Pacific.

In February, in the U.S. one shipyard launched 14 ships, outfitted 13, and laid the keels for 14 more.

We will all move soon. The sick to Bilibid and the well to Japan.

Five Japanese boats left Manila Bay. Several explosions were heard by men on Corregidor who are now here. Only one Japanese ship returned, and it was beached on Bataan. It was loaded with Japanese civilians going back to their homeland.

Medics will be given Lincoln Zephyrs when they get to the States.

There were 6, 60, or 600 ships sunk 6, 60, or 600 miles south of Sicily by 6, 60, or 600 airplanes from Rome, home, or Nome.

Someone told Chaplain Taylor (Baptist) that the Pope of Rome has been converted to the Baptist faith and peace reigns in Italy.

Each man from Bataan is to be given a kangaroo apiece in token of their magnificent bravery which saved Australia.

Every man who wants it will be given a land homestead when he returns to the U.S.

Eskimos have landed on the coast of Africa and are advancing by dog team.

1944

The Nips have found Amelia Earhart on one of the Pacific Islands. Some say that Richard Halliburton and three kids were there too.

They tell me about one man here who had left a new Buick with his wife. Now, in the Philippines, he gets a letter and a picture — of herself and a handsome but strange man sitting in the Buick with "The guy in the car is my NEW husband" written in explanation. Another fellow is rumored to have received a letter from his wife in which she says, "Why did you give up, you coward?"

By June we shall all be out of here. Everyone will go out on detail.

The Yanks are moving too fast for the Nips to get us out of here.

F. D. R. made a speech in which he said the war will be over in 44 (by election time). Yeah — it will be over; all over; all over the world!!

Someone just came by saying that all the States (except Arizona, New Mexico, and Oklahoma) are paying $2.50 per day bonus — up to $1,500. The three named states will give land.

A detail of 500 men will leave here soon. Some medics are on it. No
chance for me though. [This rumor proved partially true. A week
after he heard this rumor, Private Norquist and 516 others, including
Addie, were shipped to Bilibid awaiting transfer to Japan.]

Chapter 9

Las Piñas

The Move to a New Camp

During September 1943, rumors spread throughout Cabanatuan that another outgoing work detail would be formed soon. So far Addie felt fortunate to have escape the details that were sent to Davao, Clark Field, and Nichols Field. It made no sense to the Japanese to send sick men on these details, as they did little work and usually spread the illness. They looked for those who appeared to be the most healthy. Although Addie had been ill part of the time at Cabanatuan, he had not been assigned a great deal of back-breaking chores, so he was in fairly good shape in September 1943. Most men had no choice anyway as to when they would leave on a work detail or where they were going. On 18 September, 800 men, including Addie, knew they were leaving Cabanatuan the next morning, but none were aware of the destination.

MANFRED KIRK — The detail was selected by those supposed to be in the best physical condition. By that time about everyone was in the same condition — not good. Of course there was always a few who knew how to miss those details by talking to certain people, better known as brown nosing.

ROMERO — Our American camp doctors gave the Japanese the list of able-bodied men for the work detail for Las Piñas. My health was fair at the time, but not good according to American health.

JOHN CICHA — I think we were the last detail to leave Cabanatuan and the last of the able-bodied men. My health was fair under those conditions. From camp to Cabanatuan City we walked, the trip to Manila was by train, and from Manila to Las Piñas by truck.

ALDRICH — One day late in September, I was informed by the

Barracks' Leader, after returning from a hard day's work on the wood detail, that I would be leaving before sunup the following morning for an airfield detail near Manila.

I didn't sleep well that night, and it was still dark outside when Jim Alsobrook shook my leg vigorously to wake me up. I hurried over to the mess hall and got a cup of hot tea and a scoop of *lugao* — rushed back to the barracks to finish my meal and grab my gear.

Forty or fifty of us were herded onto the old wood detail truck after being counted by the Japs. We pumped the Jap guards for information as to where we were headed. The only news we could get from them was that our new guards would meet us in Manila. It was just beginning to turn light in the east when we turned up the main road to Cabanatuan City.

Upon arrival in Cabanatuan City, we were taken straight away to the railroad station. From my position on the truck, I had not seen many Filipinos on the streets, but I spotted an occasional "V-for-Victory" sign from the buildings' interiors and windows as we rolled by.

The wait at the rail station was a short one. We loaded into a box car and were soon on our way to Manila. What a difference between this trip and the earlier one from San Fernando to Capas on the way to Camp O'Donnell at the end of the Death March. The doors were left open so the air could circulate, and we enjoyed more room.

Suddenly, one of the old timers announced that we were probably on our way to Nichols Field. He based this observation on the fact that our new guards were Jap Navy, and we were on the road leading out to Paranaque.

Nichols Field was run by the Jap Navy and had the worst reputation of all the camps on Luzon, and it was located near the barrio known as Paranaque. Nichols was run by an extremely cruel commandant known as the "White Angel," who took particular joy in severely beating Americans.

The old feeling of fear returned, and the old metallic taste returned to my mouth . . . stark fear. The truckload of Americans became very silent. We rode along in silence as each of us coped with individual feelings. I was convinced that if the Jap commandant was cruel, the guards under him would be of the same bent. The future looked bleak. I prayed hard for help and guidance.

Suddenly someone announced, "There's Nichols." Sure enough, a short distance from our road, the many buildings of the airfield were quite visible. Ironically, the front gate structure was painted white. But the trucks didn't turn into the road leading to that white gate.

My first thoughts were that my prayer had been answered. Slowly the talking on the truck began to accelerate, and soon we were all laughing and slapping each other on the shoulders and back.

The guard noticed the immediate change, and I think was flattered when we told him we were happy to be going to his camp rather than Nichols.

EVANS — My friend Y. C. Lindsay and I had some contraband that we had acquired at Cabanatuan. We had some sulfanilamide tablets that we had procured from the Japs out of one of their warehouses. We wanted to take these pills with us, as they had a high value if we could find an outlet in wherever we were going. I taped my contraband to the inside of my thigh, and Lindsay ripped open the seam of a small pillow. He placed the pills in the center of the stuffing and then sewed the pillow up. We didn't have any problem there. The Japs never found anything, and at about 6:00 a.m. we were counted and recounted until everything checked out to the Japs' satisfaction. Then we started the nine-kilometer march to the city of Cabanatuan, where we were to board a train. This march was somewhat different than the one these men had made over a year ago. At least we had rice in our belly and plenty of water. The march was uneventful, except for an occasional Filipino man making a victory sign with his fingers or smiling or waving when the Japs couldn't see them.

Most of the prisoners housed at Bilibid or Cabanatuan lived in fear of being sent to Nichols Field also known as the Pasay Work Detail. During 1943, rumors were rampant concerning the brutality of the evil Japanese commandant, the "White Angel." Practically all of the men on the trucks on 19 September thought their destination was Nichols Field, which in actuality was only a few miles away from the Las Piñas Work Detail. Today, over 40 years later, few survivors talk about what went on at Nichols Field. Most of what is known is basically rumor.

KNOX — Just a few stories got out about Nichols Field but it had a terribly bad reputation. The bad part of Nichols Field was the Camp Commandant. I've heard him called the "White Angel." He was a pure sadist and in their military hierarchy there was no check on him. He could do as he pleased, especially with prisoners. If he killed off a batch, he'd just call Cabanatuan and order some others.

The guys who died at Nichols Field, they put them in coffins and delivered them to Bilibid with orders to bury them without opening the coffin. They got their kicks by torturing people. They always talk about the *black bean*. In Mexican executions if you drew the *black bean* out of the cup it was your turn to die. You never knew when it would be your turn to be the *black bean*. This is what destroyed the men at Nichols Field. At Las Piñas it was bad, but once you were inside the gate, nobody bothered you. You were safe until the morning *tenko* [roll call]. At Nichols you were never safe.

They might come in at three in the morning and take someone in order to kill somebody. This is what destroyed the prisoners. They had to live under it 24 hours a day instead of just 12, and it turned them into zombies.

They said anyone who got sent to Nichols Field twice had bad luck. Anyone who got sent three times was a born loser.

STEWART — All I know about Nichols Field is hearsay. I do know that at Cabanatuan we would never volunteer for an airport detail because you might be sent to Nichols Field. There was a lot of wild stories about what happened at Nichols Field, and there's no reason in the world why I should deny them, but one story I do know, and I don't remember who told it . . . but one day the prisoners were marching four abreast out to the air field for work and there was a chicken along one side of the road. As chickens will do, they will want to get to the other side of the road, and this chicken jumped up and tried to fly across the column. An arm reached up and grabbed the chicken and the chicken absolutely disappeared. They ate him raw right there on the way to work.

MARVIN SHEARWOOD — At Nichols Field I saw men tied up by their thumbs until they died. Men were shot with a firing squad and then had their heads cut off by the "White Angel." He used to tell us, "Cut off your head or worse, shoot it."

BURTON "SWEDE" GALDE — I was sent to Nichols Field in July of 1942, and I was sent back in September of 1942 because of malaria and dysentery. I lost 80 pounds in two months. I lost the use of my arms and legs too.

Most on board the trucks thought their passing Nichols Field for Las Piñas was the greatest thing that had happened to them as prisoners. Later, many would say that Las Piñas would be the worst possible detail. But the men's spirits were high as they pulled into the new Las Piñas compound.

EVANS — When we arrived, it had started raining. Not a steady downpour but that light drizzly type of downpour of rain that chills your body and spirits. The rain had turned the dirt road into mud so that when we dismounted from the truck, we sank about six inches into it. It was almost dark when we entered our new home, marching in single file and very slowly so we could be counted again. Our camp, as we later learned, was to be called Las Piñas. It was made up of seven buildings, four of which were quarters for the men. One was to be a kitchen, one for the American officers and Jap guards' quarters, and one was for the guard house and Jap commandant.

Each of our buildings was divided into four rooms, 50 men to a room. As you entered the door from each room there was a narrow aisle to the right and left of the door the width of the room. Then there was a platform composing the rest of the room about 25x30 feet for the men to sleep on. The buildings were made of rough wood with corrugated tin roofs. The whole camp was surrounded by two barbed wire fences running parallel to each other with about ten feet between fences. Our host made it clear as we entered the camp that if anyone should get caught between these two fences, it was punishable by death. As we entered the compound, we were dropped off 50 men at a time in their rooms until everyone was in. Of course there was considerable confusion at this point, and nobody seemed to be in the right place, so it was decided to wait until morning to straighten things out — a decision that took the Japs the better part of the night to make.

After we were bedded down we were all given a small quantity of rice. This was mighty welcome [and was] all we had had to eat since leaving Cabanatuan. These rice balls were made by wetting your hand with water and forming a ball with steamed rice to about the size of a baseball. After our supper we spread out on the floor and tried to sleep.

First Days

In 1944, Bill Evans was able to draw a map of the Las Piñas compound. Inside, there were four parallel barracks running east to west. Each barracks was divided into four sections, each housing 50 men. Two of the sections, in the first prisoner barracks as they came into the camp, were for the hospital and officers. Most of the Navy and Marine personnel were in the last barracks, the one farthest from the gate. The rest of the sections were made up of Army. Between the barracks were shower areas. To the east of the barracks were two latrines and immediately east of that, the kitchen and supply area. A barracks just south of the first American barracks housed the Japs. The camp had a

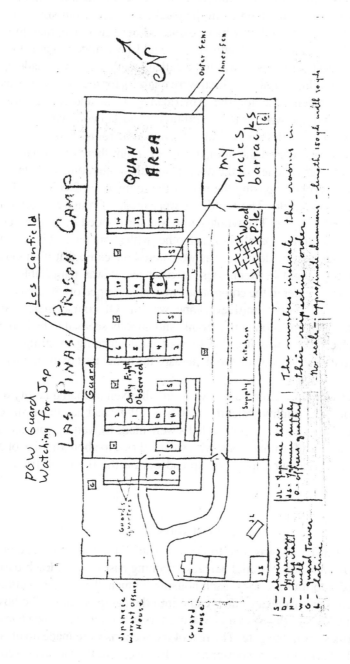

(From *Koral*, by William R. Evans (Roque River, OR: Atwood Publishing Co., 1986), p. 82.)

large wall around it, and in the American section there was an inner barbed wire fence. The Japanese wanted no one to be between the two fences.

ABIE ABRAHAM — When we arrived at Las Piñas, it was getting dark, and we stood in the rain while the Japanese counted us off, again and again. Finally, we were released and ended up sleeping on the hard wood floor in our wet clothes. After arriving at Las Piñas, we didn't work for at least five days as it rained every day.

EVANS — In the morning, we had roll call and were counted again and assigned to rooms which were to be called companies. Each company [was led by] one American officer. During the trip from Cabanatuan, Lindsay and I had gotten separated. I was assigned to Company Eight and he was assigned to Company Six. We managed to find a man in my company who wanted to be in Company Six, so we made the swap, and Lindsay came over to Company Eight. Lindsay and I had stayed together until then, and we didn't want to split up at this stage.

Our Company Commander was Captain Myers, who later got killed. He had been a P-40 pilot. I was elected Commissary Clerk, in the event we would ever make any purchases from the Filipinos. In our company was a fellow named Dick Breslin. His dad was American and his mother Filipino. Lindsay and I joined forces with Breslin. Dick's dad was killed on the Death March, and Dick himself had fought with the 31st Infantry. He joined after the war started. The three of us joined up and decided to split three ways on any- and everything.

The next day we spent getting everything straightened out in the camp. Up to this point we had no idea what kind of work we were going to do, but we soon found out.

ALDRICH — The buildings of the camp appeared to all be made of wood and seemed to be new and in good shape. Most of the structures were three feet off the ground and supported by cement pilings. There were porches on each barracks building, with steps on each end, and railings running the entire length. The barracks were all alike. At the entry, the floor was at porch level for about three or four feet back from the wall, and a bay was raised at chair height the length of the room, affording an area to sit down and remove shoes — and these were left at floor level. We climbed up on the raised bay area to get back to the assigned bunk area.

The latrines were the Navy type [long trough with running water to

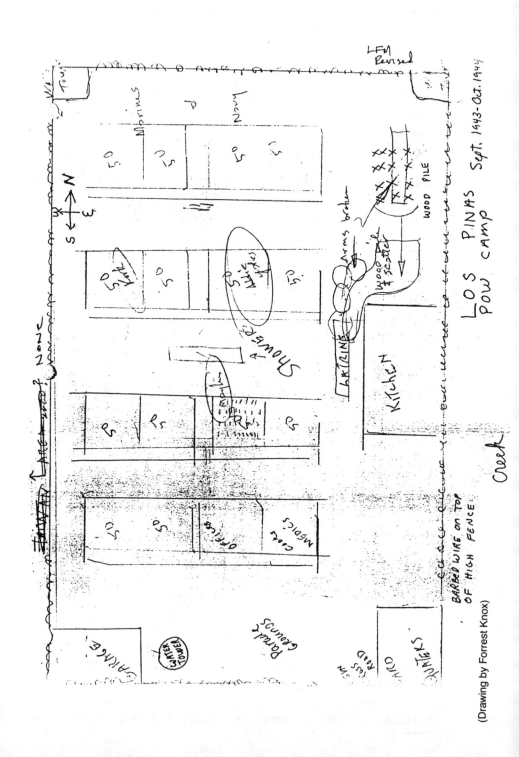

(Drawing by Forrest Knox)

carry off the waste] protected on one side and at each end — one long side was open, and there was a roof for rain protection. The kitchen and supply room was along one side equidistant to the barracks and near the compound fence.

DAVE KIMBALL — We had bed bugs and lice on the straw mats we slept on. You could turn the lights off at night, wait a few minutes, switch back on the light, and the mats were black with bed bugs.

Addie lived in the third barracks from the gate, in section eight just to the right of the corridor, according to the Evan's diagram. Most of the men in that area were from the 200th or 515th CAC. Although the work was easy at first, 15 days later, on 11 October, 200 replacements were sent from Cabanatuan to Las Piñas. Floyd Meyer was one of those sent back to Cabanatuan after only two or three weeks in camp. He recalls that the Jap doctor gave the customary glass rod ameobic dysentery test and sent back the carriers. The Japs had a profound fear of amoebic dysentery.

After the first week, the prisoners were introduced to their work — to turn a rice paddy into a runway for the Japanese to train pilots. Each day the men lined up for roll call and at the crack of dawn marched two miles in a southeasterly direction.

KNOX — In front of the guard shack was the parade gounds, where we all had to line up and count off and then go out the gate to go to work. Anybody who was sick, on quarters, was allowed to sleep in their own bunk, but they had to stand at parade in the morning, because, before anyone left the compound, they had to have a complete and total count of everyone in the compound. If the count didn't come out right, they'd do it again. When we were finally ready to leave, we went out the gate, up the road with the guard marching alongside.

Now all the time I worked with the Japs, they never had the time right. They never had regulation time; they kept jostlin' with the time. I used to harass the bastards for years because they couldn't set the right clock. And the reason for that was that you couldn't go out the gate before daylight, and so they'd wake you up before daylight, give you your breakfast, get you ready and get you counted, and they did a half-ass job of getting you counted.

We move the clock back an hour for daylight savings time, but not them slopeheads. They'd move it back ten minutes at a time when it started getting daylight sooner. That way they'd get us to work an extra ten minutes at the field.

Far Eastern University of Engineering

Hardly a prisoner that I have interviewed hasn't made some kind of comment about the Japanese way of doing things. Whether it was their obsession with taking roll call, their fear of the mentally ill, or their system of discipline, it didn't take the Americans long to realize that the Eastern way was quite different from theirs.

This difference was never more graphic than in the Japanese engineering skills. Las Piñas was located seven miles southwest of Manila and subject to a variety of weather — all of it scorching hot. During the months of May to September, the area was under monsoon conditions as the moist air came off Manila Bay, a scant two miles away. The rest of the year was extremely dry. For part of the year, there was too much water — for the rest not enough.

The Japanese intended to use the 800 men to build an airfield to train their young carrier pilots. The spot they selected was a large rice paddy completely filled with water. The area was only a few miles from the Nichols Field detail, and some of the prisoners at first believed their job was to build an extension for Nichols Field. Today, Las Piñas and Nichols Field are only a few miles from the large Manila International Airport. But in September 1943, the prisoners questioned the mentality of anyone who wanted an airfield to be constructed on a rice paddy.

KNOX — We used to laugh amongst ourselves, "Trying to make an airfield in this kind of muck. They'll never land an airplane here."

Why, the American engineers tried for years to make runways at Nichols Field and they still couldn't land on most of it. But you know, being Oriental they knew how to do it. First, we dug a monstrous drainage ditch around the field. After they got the field leveled off, it was so soupy you could hardly walk across it. They had these Filipinos making these rushed mesh mats, and they'd come in sections about 60x30 feet. They'd carry them out to the runway and lay them down and overlap them. We was watching this, and we still couldn't believe it.

And then we went to the quarry and started dynamiting rock, and we hauled it up and put it on the runway. Then we'd break it up with a sledge hammer. All that was holding up this rock was this bamboo mats. Then we put a very thin layer of concrete over it. We thought, "These slopeheads don't know a thing about concrete," but all it was was a water seal because everything they did had a crown to it. If they could get the water to run to the drainage ditch and not to the soil underneath it would work.

When the planes first hit that damn field, it looked like they were on rubber — and these planes would come down and just settle on it, and

I was fascinated by that. I thought they were going to go right through into that muck. It worked just as slick as can be. When the cement got hard, the water would roll right off, and as long as the water didn't get to the soil, it was okay. It was quite an education as far as tropical engineering was concerned.

ART ROSS — As far as engineering skills go, I called the Japs magicians. They would make you do impossible things — things you never thought humanly possible. In Tayabas they built a road through the jungle. For years the American and Philippine governments couldn't do it, and they had all the heavy equipment. The Japs did it though — and by hand.

ROMERO — The Japanese were very clever, using many engineering skills unknown to us. We were seeing them for the first time in our lives.

By the end of the first week most of the prisoners were introduced to this Japanese "engineering project." Each day after *tenko* the men marched out the gate and trooped approximately two miles in a southeasterly direction to the airfield. The road was rocky and often muddy, especially near the bridge that passed over a creek. The daily trek was especially difficult during the rainy season. Many thought the brush flourishing alongside the road might be ideal for some kind of guerrilla contact later on.

During those early September and October weeks, the men were busy building a drainage ditch and tearing down the dikes surrounding the rice paddy so that the water could drain off.

EVANS — On the morning of our third day there, we were ordered to fall out at the crack of dawn into our respective companies, in front of the guard house but inside the main compound. There was large yard there about the size of a tennis court. At this point, each company was joined by a Jap civilian who had a club about the size of a pick handle.

From there we started marching out of the compound and went on a dirt road in the opposite direction from the town of Las Piñas. Of course, there were Jap soldiers in the front, rear, and both sides, armed with rifles and bayonets. These Japs were of the JNLP, which is the Japanese Naval Landing Party, which is the equivalent to our Marines, which didn't please us too much as they were the same group that were at Nichols Field. After marching for 1½ kilometers, we came to a huge rice paddy that was fairly level and had several large swells in it. We were given tools, which consisted of hoes, shovels, picks, and baskets to carry off dirt. We were then spread out, and each company was given an area to start working on. Our job was to break down the dikes between the paddies and spread the dirt around. The first day passed rather slowly, and there were very few men beaten. We began to think that maybe this wouldn't be too bad after all — at least so far as the treatment of the men went. How wrong this bit of optimism proved to be. It didn't take us long to figure out that our Jap hosts were going to have us build an airfield for them. It was amazing to me that there was no machinery to do it with, only the Americans and some Taiwanese forced labor from Formosa.

ALDRICH — The first labor at the camp was performed at a point about a mile south of the creek. Each man was assigned a work quota of digging a drainage ditch one meter long, one meter deep, and three meters wide — a quota that clearly was beyond our capabilities. And we were kept there until dusk to achieve this. This went on for several days, and finally the Jap honcho — our direct Jap supervision was by older Japs in Navy uniform who were campaigners that had been wounded in battle or in accidents — called his superior over, and he confronted Major Miller. I must say that Miller stood up nobly in the defense of his slave-labor crew, maintaining all the while that the quota for each man was too large. This argument was quite heated, and suddenly the Jap hit Miller with his vitamin stick [sword]. The blow broke Miller's watch, and it went to pieces. The Jap then left, but not before announcing he expected the crew to dig their quota the following day.

The next day we all felt sorry for Major Miller. We tried like hell to meet that quota, but it was impossible for us to achieve it. Sure enough, later that afternoon the Jap came back and confronted Miller. Another shouting match followed, and as the Jap again raised his club, Miller said, "You broke my watch yesterday, and another blow like that might break my arm." Sure enough the Jap hit him again, and this time broke his arm. I helped tie a makeshift splint on his arm.

Major Miller wore a splint on his arm for some time, but the "honcho" let the work crew get away with just the amount they could dig each day.

KIMBALL — My first job was chopping down the grass and weeds on the terraces of the rice paddies. Our tools consisted of hoes made out of 55-gallon drums. They were homemade and very flimsy.

I had one of my most frightening experiences happen to me at this airfield. Of all the bombs, shells, beatings, etcetera, this ordeal scared me the worst I was ever scared in my life. I'm from West Virginia, and we have a lot of copperheads and rattlesnakes, and I don't like snakes. Here I am barefoot with only a G-string on and chopping away at the tops of the paddies, when all at once I see this snake. Before I could say "Jack Robinson," here comes this cobra right at me. It seems to me about eight-foot of him up in the air with hood flared and really moving fast. At this time, I really put that hoe to work. This all happened within seconds, and when the guys close to me heard me scream "cobra," they and the Jap guards came running over. That snake was in about six pieces, and I was white as a sheet. The Japs told me to go to the shed and "no more work" that day.

And where there is one cobra, there is two. They soon found the second one, and it was really a side show. A POW killed it, and I am told the Japs took their remains to camp and ate them. A guy by the name of Pete Peterson from Des Moines, Iowa, said, "Dave, the best way to tell you what you looked like swinging that hoe was a propeller on an airplane."

After the rice paddy was drained, the men had to make the area level. Filipino surveyors had already come in and placed grade stakes. Because of the undulating terrain, dirt had to be hauled from the high ground by small rail cars on tracks and dumped in the low-lying areas. When one area was level, the tracks were moved to another area. Practically all of the work was accomplished by manual labor under very difficult conditions.

PAT HITCHCOCK — Once we had broken through the dikes and had drained the rice paddies and had allowed the ground to dry, the Japanese brought in narrow-gauge track, from the mines at Baguio, and ore cars. We would dig out a cut and lay the tracks moving the earth from the high places on the field to the low places, where we leveled it off, much the way you would today with a bulldozer, but this was all pick-and-shovel work.

LESLIE CANFIELD — We worked in teams of four — two pushing and unloading the ore carts and the other two digging away at a bank about four feet high. The bank was mostly clay with large rocks. My little area was pick-and-shovel reducing the level of the land. Every so often, all hands would be required to help move the tracks to get the cars closer to the bank.

GLEN REAM — The narrow-gauged tracks extended about a hundred yards; when we finished leveling that, we would move another ten yards. We worked on rail cars — four men on a team taking turns. Two dug between 500-1000 pounds of dirt; two would load the large flat-bed car, then push it down, tip it over, and dump. There were about 50 men to a track.

FRANK MAYHUE — To level the airfield the Japanese brought in mining cars with their rails and ties. We set the rail line so that we could fill the cars from the high places and dump it into the low places, moving the tracks as we went. Sometimes the tracks would be moved by prying iron bars. At other times, we would stand between the rails and ties, and lift the rails over to the new position. In this manner, we would shift the rails from one work area to another, sometimes up to a couple of hundred yards. Then of course we had to move the mining cars. As many men as possible would get around the car and push, pull, and shove, with the Jap guards beating and screaming.

But trying to break up the dirt and shovel it into the cars presented problems, depending on whether the prisoners were working during the monsoon season or the dry season.

KNOX — When we got there, it was the monsoon season. When this volcanic ground turned to muck, instead of sinking to your knees, why, you could sink right out of sight. Some guys had the soles of their shoes sucked right off. But when it was dry, we would cut out a piece as big as a refrigerator, and we had a hell of a time breaking it into smaller pieces. But when it was wet, it was just like goo, and when it was dry, it was extremely hard.

The long hours and the changing weather conditions made the work at Las Piñas difficult. But to make matters worse, the equipment used in the construction of the airfield would seem rather primitive.

REAM — The American-made picks and shovels were used whenever possible since the Japanese-made tools were easily bent.

ALDRICH — As time wore on, so did some of the tools we used. Ironically, some of the guys would run from formation to pick out tools that were in good shape. This behavior drew the wrath of most of the work crews because the Japs displayed pleasure as they misinterpreted the eagerness of a few Americans. For the most part, these eager beavers were not well liked. "Tweedy" Davis was the most notorious of the characters who would run to get the best pick of tools.

He was only a kid that had lied about his age and had to have his parents' consent to get into the service. He was a hillbilly from the South. Too small to hit, but was cussed out loudly by everyone in the camp.

Weather

Most of the Las Piñas prisoners had previously been at Cabanatuan, where, because of its central location in Luzon, the weather was more stable than at Las Piñas, located near large bodies of water. The best way to describe the weather is simply to let the men tell the story.

ALDRICH — Few days passed without rain of some kind. Las Piñas, located just south of the city of Manila, was actually on a narrow strip of land with Manila Bay on one side and Laguna De Bay — Philippines' largest land-locked lake — on the other. These two large bodies of water certainly must have contributed to the excessive amount of moisture in the air. Misting rain or light showers were not sufficient cause for the Japs to stop us from working. They would take us to the rest house to wait out the showers, if they were wet, cold, and uncomfortable.

December through May was the dry season, and the work was hot and dusty on the airfield. Though I had no way of measuring, it always felt as if the humidity was at least five or ten degrees higher than the temperature. I would guess the temperature was between 90 and 100 degrees Fahrenheit.

It rained almost every day — not counting the fine mist that was evident every morning. During the rainy season, it really rained, and the airfield became a quagmire. There were times when the pelting rain was so strong, the raindrops came down like buck-shot, and we would be herded by the Japs to the rest shack. They made us run because, in their infinite philosophy, this allowed less drops to hit the body, and therefore one would not get so wet.

I was usually chilled when I woke up each moring. When I got wet in the rain, I would shake as if I had the ague or malaria. Having to work in the rain in wet clothing just made a miserable situation much worse.

In November, a typhoon hit Las Piñas and kept the men in the barracks and off work for four days. It seemed to the men that it made no difference if they were in the rainy season or the dry season.

KNOX — Rain or shine, you were always miserable. If the sun was shining, it was hot and you were never in the shade. So you were dripping with sweat and hot as hell. If it rained, well you were wet again. Only now you were cold and miserable. So it's a state of mind. It got so I never paid any attention — just live through the day.

Lack of Clothing

The question of what one wears while working in a rice paddy during 100-degree temperatures was often on the men's mind. Most of the clothes the men brought to Las Piñas were almost rags to begin with. They soon became stained with salt from constant sweating. Any kind of shoe deteriorated rapidly in the muck. Humidity tore the stitching out of the shoe, and occasionally when a prisoner stepped into the mud and sank up to his knee, upon removal of his leg, his shoe had remained behind. Occasionally, men received additional clothes, either from packages from home or from extras the Japanese rounded up.

JONES — I recall that we received 50 pieces of clothing during the rainy season. In our barracks we had 50 men. Each piece of clothing was written on a piece of paper and put in the hat. We each drew out a piece of paper which contained the name of the article we had won. Included was a rather heavy-knitted cap with ear flaps and was the prize each of us wanted. Funny, but the last man to draw was the First Sergeant, and he won the hat. We later figured out he had placed that paper in the sweatband of the hat so he would win it.

If a prisoner wore too many clothes to work, he chanced sweating too much. If he took his shirt off, his skin stood a chance of damage from too much sun. Most chose to wear just a G-string, no shirt, and no shoes. Few had caps. Some had straw hats. In fact, most prisoners shaved their heads because of bed bugs and lice. This in turn allowed their entire head to be exposed to the burning sun.

Many of the prisoners from the Southern part of the United States and those who were either of Spanish or Indian descent adjusted quite well. Those, like Addie, who were fair skinned and blue-eyed received sun burns that eventually blistered and caused discomfort and infection.

Without proper diet and vitamin intake, prisoners exposed to too much sun were susceptible to many tropical diseases. One of these was pellagra, a surface eruption of the skin caused by too much sun and a lack of niacin. Many, many prisoners, including Addie, contracted pellagra during their stay at Las Piñas. More notable yet is the fact that the prolonged exposure to the sun affected the men long after they had left the Pacific. Of the 50 Las Piñas men

I've interviewed, five are currently being treated for skin cancers. Most feel they are the result of the prolonged exposure to the Las Piñas sun.

KNOX — Some of the guys burnt something terrible. I just wore a G-string and it took me until 1947 to get rid of the tan line from Las Piñas. There was this one guy who wore a uniform all the time. He wore a blue jacket and blue pants — a big floppy hat — and he was the only prisoner that was issued gloves. The back of his hands would break out with these great big blisters from the sun.

Now, working at the airfield you would sweat, and the place where your arm rubbed against your shoulder as in the shoveling motion — everyone would get blisters right along that area from the friction. Guam blisters is what we called them. I had them so thick on my back you couldn't touch them. I was worried they were going to get infected, and I didn't know what to do about it. There was a hose by the kitchen, and I got a brush, and some GI soap and had the guys scrub them blisters off my back. It felt just like they had set me on fire. I got rid of them without getting infection, which was what I wanted because there was no way the doctors could get any medicine for it. I had big white scars for years because of them.

ROBERT JOHNSTON — I was fair skinned, had severe sunburn, and still bear the scars. I wore a white Navy jumper, but it developed many holes, and I got badly burned through the frayed jumper. I eventually got pellagra.

The Walk to Work

The daily two-mile walk to the airfield caused more anxiety than the return trip. Most weren't sure what the day at work held for them. Most knew it would be difficult and often result in beatings. The return, however, was usually more relaxed. Work was done, and the men were coming back to the relative safety of the compound. Often the guerrillas left food alongside the road. Sometimes the men were permitted to jump in the creek for a quick bath. And occasionally there was some humor.

KNOX — We were walking to work one day, and there was a bunch of women lined up along the road. One of the side effects of starvation is that you lose all of your sex interest. We went by all the Filipino "girls," and some of them were beautiful. After we had walked by, I mentioned to one of the guys, "Hey, those are some beautiful Filipino girls there."

He said, "Why you dumb son-of-a-bitch."

"What do you mean by that?"

"Those are all benny boys."

"You're shittin' me?"

"No, most of them were, but there were a few women there."

Benny boy was just a common name for homosexuals. You'd hear about a soldier shacking up with one of them and not knowing that they had a benny boy. They had half a coconut for tits and hair that hung down to their waist. When you go into a foreign country, there are always these little comic sayings that you have, and the one we had in the Philippines was, "You can screw all the women and most of the men."

LEROY COOKINGHAM — We were allowed to wash mud off in the tidal creek on the way back to camp until the doctor decided we were getting skin problems from the dirty water.

JONES — It made the Japs very mad for us to sing on the march back to camp after a hard day's work. They would then try to work us harder the next day.

ROSS — On the way back to camp these Filipinos would leave bananas and sugar cakes, which they fed to their horses. I would pick them up and bring them back to camp and trade or sell them.

ALDRICH — Our American Commander's name was John Davis, and he was lovingly called "Carabao." This was due to the fact that his stride was not unlike the lowly Filipino beast of burden — the water buffalo.

One morning at *bango* [roll call] just before going to work, the Japs told "Carabao" that from this day forth the Americans would emulate the Japs when passing the guard station at the camp gate. That meant that the ragtag POWs would be formed up in a column of fours and march at attention — not American style but Jap style. When the Japs marched at attention the legs went stiffly out without bending the knee and were brought down smartly as the step was completed. Very much like the German goose step.

"Carabao" fussed and fumed and worried all day as to just how to get approximately 500 doing the goose step when passing the Jap guard post when they came in from work.

We started our trek back to camp at the end of the work day. "Carabao" had no problem getting us into a column of fours and marching at attention because he used American Army commands to get us that far. We're stepping along at 120 per, and looking pretty sharp — notwithstanding the fact that we were in rags.

As the detail neared the guard post at the main gate, "Carabao," who had been marching out in front of the column, stepped up to the Jap sentries, snapped to attention, and tossed the finest highball we'd seen in many a day. He quickly did an about face, and we all knew the crucial moment was at hand.

As the first elements of the column drew abreast of the guard post he bellowed his preparatory command, "Goose Step," followed by the command of execution, "Goose!"

The Americans stopped, and the air was filled with laughter while tension eased away. We noticed the Japs were laughing too! Watanabe informed "Carabao" that he could just forget that marching at attention bit, and the incident was soon forgotten.

Guerrilla Contact

Once the American soldier in the Philippines became a prisoner in 1942, he wasn't completely shut off from information about the war, or from aid. Many soldiers who had escaped to the hills of Bataan in April 1942 joined loyal Filipino guerrilla units trying to disrupt Japanese operations. Their hit-and-run technique that was advised by MacArthur proved successful. One of their other functions, however, was to provide food, medicine, and money to the prisoners.

Many of the prisoners at Cabanatuan were part of a secret system of smuggling contraband into camp. When Las Piñas opened, the guerrillas immediately established contact, and those men who previously had contact at Cabanatuan naturally looked to reestablish contact in Las Piñas. In some ways this effort proved easier than at Cabanatuan. Las Piñas was closer to Manila, there were daily truck trips leaving the compound, and the terrain between the camp and work area offered opportunity for contact. Although it is impossible to get an exact count, aid from the guerrillas saved many prisoners' lives.

Y. C. LINDSAY — Dick Breslin was a Filipino *mestizo*. His father was American, his mother Filipino. Because of his father, he joined the 31st Infantry. At Las Piñas, we made contact with the guerrillas through Dick. He had relatives in Manila, so he could not help bring the stuff into camp. The Japs would have retaliated against his family had he been caught. We used the sulfanilamide tablets we had snuck in and traded with the guerrillas for things we needed. We almost got caught once bringing some stuff in. They would have shot us had they caught us. This is just a small part of what we did. I could tell stories all night.

ALDRICH — In the areas strung out along the airfield where the Americans were working, an amazing discovery was made. As the crews reached the work place, they were finding notes, money, and food that had been hidden there the night before by the Filipinos. The notes carried words of encouragement and some war news. The money — Jap war script — was taken into camp and given to the truck drivers to buy food if the opportunity presented itself. The food was shared with the immediate work crew and consumed on the spot but out of sight of the Japs. This contact with the Filipinos didn't happen every night. I recall this happening to my group only a couple of times. Rice wrapped in banana leaves was our prize.

MAYHUE — It was a real treat to be on a detail during which we could surreptitiously talk to a Filipino. We could always count on news of how the Japanese were advancing on all war fronts — to the rear. Sometimes the Filipino would have a little tidbit of rice cake, candy, or such to give us. I will always love and respect Filipinos as my brothers and sisters. They were just as patriotic as we Americans were. And they did risk life and limb to help us in some way or another.

Food

When the 800 men arrived at Las Piñas, most had been captives for 17 months. Gradual starvation had already subtracted substantial weight from each prisoner. Like Cabanatuan, the men found food constantly on their mind. Las Piñas, however, offered chances for the men to improve their diet. The backbreaking work at the airfield, on the other hand, quickly decimated any weight gain. In short, although many found the food and opportunities to enrich their diet more plentiful at Las Piñas, the overall effect was that the men became weaker each month.

Besides the daily menu of rice and more rice, the prisoners supplemented their diet with area flora and fauna. Some used creative methods to obtain and prepare their food. Within the compound, men were allowed additional food. Some used the food supplied by the Japanese, and others used the money the guerrillas snuck in to buy food. The men were usually given three meals a day: one was eaten before marching to the airfield at the break of dawn; a second meal of steamed rice was brought to the airfield at noon; and a third was given shortly after returning from work in the evening.

ALDRICH — The breakfast ration usually consisted of *lugao* and tea, and on rare occasions a small amount of sugar — about ½ teaspoon — to go with it. Lunch, or perhaps I should call it midday meal, usually

was steamed rice — ½ canteen cup — and water soup — ½ canteen
cup. The evening ration after work usually had a little more substance
— larger amount of steamed rice, thicker soup — about ¾ canteen
cup full. A piece of fish or carabao on occasion. In no way were the
meals constant or reliable.

Weeds harvested out on the airfield, they grew wild in watery bogs,
made excellent soup. Tasted very much like turnip greens.

Now and then we could supplement our food. The Japs let us have
"quan" fires between the kitchen and the wood pile. "Quan" is a
designation to anything that has no name. It is a handy word.

As usual the buddy system was in effect at all times, and you could
work out a system where one would start the "quan" while the other
bathed — then exchange places until the "quan" was finished.
Guarding the pot was mandatory since some thievery went on.

CLEHAN DEWEY — The kitchen received fish heads quite often
and some starchy vegetables, which they mixed with the rice. We
received a gumbo type of soup with a burnt rice-coffee mixture in the
mornings. We received a mess kit of steamed rice at noon carried to
the field from camp. The supper meal most always had a little meat or
fish mixed with the rice. One day, a large shark was carried into the
kitchen, full of maggots, but the kitchen personnel cut it up and
cooked it with the rice. I knew they were in the rice but it didn't bother
me.

ALDRICH — Pete Pyetski was on an errand outside the camp work
detail one day when the truck driver ran over a small pig. The driver
stopped the truck, and a Filipino came running out of his hut —
yelling and screaming at the American driver. The Jap guard that
accompanied the work detail was sitting on the passenger side and
wasn't noticed by the Filipino until it was too late. The Jap guard got
out and approached the poor Filipino and yelled at him to stand at
attention. Yelling at the top of his lungs, the Jap beat hell out of the
poor Filipino.

Pyetski jumped off the truck and threw the pig up onto the bed, and
he and the other American burrowed it into the sand — I think that is
what they were hauling — and hid the pig under the load. The guard
left the Filipino alone when the poor guy slumped to the ground semi-
conscious.

When they got back to camp, the sand was dumped near the
kitchen, and in order to keep the guard from seeing the loot, Pyetski
hustled the pig into the kitchen. The cooks were goggle-eyed, but

sensing some good chow they helped hide the animal. Arrangements were made for cooking, and the three of us had two fried pork chops apiece that night. So many people had to be paid off — the American driver and Pyetski's helper as well as the cooks who hid the animal — that we didn't get much out of that venture. After the cooks took a choice cut or two, the balance was cooked in the evening soup. So we had our pork chops and the soup that night was unusually rich. I had the runs the next day, but the memory was sublime.

BERNARD SAUNDERS — One POW we nicknamed Doby devised a trap to catch rats around our latrines which he supplemented his rice with.

DEWEY — To show you we still were not getting enough to eat, one man in our barracks took a stick and killed a large rat and cooked it for himself. The camp officers put a stop to that because they were afraid of a cholera epidemic.

KIMBALL — Some guy was stealing food out of the kitchen and was caught. He became very unpopular. So to show him that crime didn't pay, they got him between the barracks and made him fight. Anybody who desired could punch him for a short time. I am sure he got the message.

REAM — Someone was caught stealing from the supply room. For punishment he was given the silent treatment — no one would talk to him, and he had to fight three POWs barehanded, one at a time.

Fights

It's almost incomprehensible today, to consider that fights between POWs erupted almost daily at Las Piñas. When you consider that the men were underweight, underfed, and overworked, it's inconceivable that they could summon enough energy at the end of the day to engage in fisticuffs. But they did. Although there was an occasional disagreement at the airfield, most of the fights were staged between the last two barracks. The back barracks housed the Marines and Navy, and many of the fights involved these men. In fact, one of the Marines, who often refereed the fights, was a former heavyweight boxer.

On occasion the men at Las Piñas were fed well by POW standards. When the men were getting their chow, they had more energy and fights were more frequent. When food was scarce, so were the fights.

MAYHUE — Arguments and fighting were a fact of life in Las Piñas. Due to circumstances and attitudes, there were many fights between or among the POWs both inside and outside the barracks, and I had my share of them. These fights could erupt from any conceivable thing — words, unequal quantities of rice being dished out, etcetera, but mostly because of short tempers. As long as the parties involved used only their fists, no one was hurt because we were all too weak to work up a good swing. Sometimes we had to fight someone to keep them from working themselves to death — at other times we would fight for the simple reason we hated each other.

There was one fellow, who while drinking would get raucous and loud, so much so that sometimes the guards would come in to investigate. We would get around their investigation by telling them that the guy was touched in the head. They did not get near someone that was strictly looney-bin material. Somebody would have to go out and kick this guy in the butt at times to quiet him down.

GALDE — The fight I was in wasn't very much. We had worked over 50 days without a day off, so when we did get a day off this guy was beating on his mess kit trying to make it bigger. The racket got to me, so I asked him to knock it off. He said, "Make me."

I got up on one foot and one knee and hit him in the ribs and that ended it. I didn't know that I had broken his ribs, until the war was over. I went to see him because he lived 40 miles from here [Arlington, Washington], and he said to his mother. "This is the guy who broke two of my ribs." I felt like running away because his mother didn't exactly like me.

CICHA — I'm sure glad Swede Galde was my friend. I'd sure hate to have him get mad at me. He was a big man around 200 pounds. Before the war he was a lumberjack in Washington. He had a lot of good stories about timber cutting. His mouth was full of gold teeth from bar fights with other lumberjacks.

HITCHCOCK — There were more fights when we were getting fed better. I never had any fights. In fact, I would go a long ways to avoid one. I was always concerned that I might injure myself as a prisoner and not have any way of correcting it. The last thing in the world I needed was some broken teeth, an injured eye, or some other injury for which there was no help.

All of the fellows in the barracks I was assigned to were Marines, some from Shanghai and some from Cavite. There was one of the

Cavite marines I had known that discovered that he was a pretty handy fighter while at Las Piñas. He found out he could move his hands fast and hurt people before they could hurt him, and he gloried in this newfound ability that he had. He was fighting all the time.

The two places I saw a lot of fights were at Las Piñas and in the hold of the *Haro, Maru* going to Japan. The fellows fighting in the hold of the ship were so weak that there was almost no way they could hurt each other. Now and then someone would get hit with a canteen, but even that didn't do any harm. In contrast to that, the men at Las Piñas were strong and able to do a great deal of damage to each other. Some got cut up pretty badly.

I knew Jack Taylor, the heavyweight fighter. They called him "Jock" Taylor. I know they said he had fought Primo Carnera, who was the former heavyweight champion. At the time they were building Carnera up for the championship. The story seems to be that they fed Primo a lot of set-up fights so that he could get a shot at the championship and eventually become the champion. There seemed to be a feeling that "Jock" Taylor went into the tank for him.

The Marine, Jack Taylor, was indeed a heavyweight fighter before the War. Primo Carnera on his march to the heavyweight championship fought 25 fights in 1932. One of them was against Jack Taylor in Louisville. Carnera defeated Taylor on a second round knockout on 17 October 1932, just four days after Carnera had defeated another "opponent." He won the title on 29 June 1933 by defeating Jack Sharkey. Carnera was 6' 6", 270 pounds, and a carnival side show "freak" in Italy. Most of his fights in early 1932 were in Europe. Taylor was one of his first American fights. Carnera didn't last long as champion, as others cut him up badly in later fights.

But not everyone in camp was interested in fighting or even watching the fights. Survival was more important than entertainment.

Life in the Barracks

When the prisoners returned to camp at dusk, except for the fighters, most had food and rest on their mind. Recreation and visiting required too much energy that could be used for survival the next day at the airfield.

Fortunately, POWs Bill Evans, Pat Hitchcock, and Walter Gilles were able to keep diaries. These offer a glimpse into the everyday life at Las Piñas. Diaries were scarce for a number of reasons — lack of paper and pens and if the Japs discovered the writing, death was often the punishment.

KIRK — By not knowing whether there would be another tomorrow, everybody talked about food mostly. Every so often one would mention a car. Of course you had those characters who would steal false teeth or anything they could get their hands on. The majority of the men at Las Piñas were better than other camps. Everybody talked about milk shakes and sundaes.

CANFIELD — Life in the barracks was usually made up of groups of individuals that had gravitated to their respective groups by likes and dislikes and their ability to associate amiably with each other. I used to play chess and discuss daydreams with fellows that shared our little group. Mostly it was live and let live as best we could.

ALDRICH — Barracks life was humdrum at best. The rare day off was spent washing sweat-salt stained clothes, and airing the pallets we slept on. Sometimes rain storms would prohibit airing the bedding. Got a little gamy.

Pyetski, Thennell, and I looked after each other — guarded each other's meager possessions, and nursed whoever might be ill, even to the point of giving the sick a bath. We were bound and determined the Japs wouldn't get the best of us. With the rigorous work schedule on the field, we got as much sack time as we could.

One of the few pleasures the men had in the barracks was smoking. That desire never left. For some it became stronger as the POW experience wore on. The Old Gold Company sent millions of cigarettes to the Philippines, but not all the cigarettes wound up in the prisoners' hands. Cigarettes were an important medium of exchange, whether to buy goods, to trade, to sell, or even to bribe a Japanese guard.

WILLIE ARTERBURN — We got Old Golds from the Red Cross packages and on the back of the package it had something like, "Freedom is our heritage," etcetera. The Japs didn't like it, so they started pickin' up the Old Golds, so I went out behind the barracks and buried mine before they took my Old Golds. Whenever I needed a pack I'd go out and dig one up.

What was on the back of the package that raised the Japanese ire? The Old Gold Company had printed:

> Our heritage has always been freedom —
> We cannot afford to relinquish it —
> Our armed forces will safeguard that heritage
> If we too, do our share to preserve it.

Red Cross Packages

Those cigarettes were part of the Red Cross boxes. Prisoners also received cards, letters, and packages from home. All were censored or had items removed, but at least the prisoners knew that someone cared. For many, the items supplemented their diet; for others it was the difference between life and death. Most packages contained Spam and corned beef, Klim — a powdered milk — cigarettes, various forms of chocolate, and vitamins.

JONES — The Red Cross packages were well received and sometimes parceled out to us a little at a time. We received an English Red Cross package on 12/25/43, and an American one on 1/1/44, a Canadian one 1/23/44 and parts of one on 12/23/43, 1/16/44, 2/14/44, and the last of it on 4/8/44. The package from my parents I received on 3/14/44. The packages from home, we were most happy to receive as we then knew that we were not forgotten, and included many things the Red Cross package did not have, such as combs, toilet paper, and other toilet articles.

ALDRICH — I was issued a Red Cross box sometime around Christmas, 1943, and I'd be hard pressed to determine the most valuable item. Items I remember getting were: one large can powdered milk — brand name Klim; one package cheese; one tin sardines; one tin Oleomargarine; one tin corned beef; two bars sweet chocolate; one package sugar; one package prunes; one tin instant coffee; one tin plum pudding; one small can sweetened evaporated milk; and two packages cigarettes. I spread the items out [used sparingly] and finished the last of the box five months later.

About a month after receiving the Red Cross box, I got a personal box from my parents. They had sent mostly personal items: handkerchiefs, shaving items, socks, a large tin of Sir Walter Raleigh pipe tobacco. There was a map of New Mexico inside the box, and had been wrapped around something. The reason for this became apparent when letters from home were passed out. My parents had moved from Clovis, New Mexico, to a small community near Ruiduso named Captain. The map helped me locate it.

The four letters I received had been censored by the Nips, and some items had been cut out — probably had reference to the war.

HITCHCOCK — The first Red Cross boxes and mail from home that any of us received came in while we were at Las Piñas, and that was a couple of years after we were captured. Some fellows got so high on the caffeine in the George Washington dehydrated coffee that they were unable to sleep all night. In fact some of them were staggering around as though they were drunk.

MANASSE — The package I received from home had been strafed, and all the cigarettes had been taken out of it, which didn't bother me a great deal. I treasured the vitamin capsules that were enclosed, and I believe I warded off a very bad case of pellagra and beriberi by judiciously taking these pills over a week or two.

CICHA — We got portions of the Red Cross packages. There was a little of everything — t-shirts, corned beef, butter, dried fruit, English pudding, cigarettes, instant coffee, dried whole milk, etcetera. I remember one guy broke into *our* storage, where Red Cross items were kept, and stole some. The Japs did not know about this, but our officers turned him loose to whoever wanted to give him a beating. He was beat up pretty bad by several of our men.

HITCHCOCK — Most of the prisoners took the position that anything we stole from the Japanese was great; anything stolen from another prisoner should be dealt with severely.

Glen Ream of Albuquerque received a package from home. It was sent by his father on Glen's birthday, 20 August 1943 and was received by him at Las Piñas on 16 March 1944, seven months later. The identification tag which he has kept through the years indicates what the package contained:

> 2 lbs. dried prunes
> 2 lbs. dried raisins
> 3 lbs. hard candy
> 1 lb. malted milk powder
> 3 pckgs dried soup mix
> 4 pckgs boullion cubes
> 2 pckgs razor blades
> 1 styptic pencil
> 1 tooth brush
> 1 handkerchief
> 10 safety pins

As Pat Hitchcock noted, the first packages and mail from home were received at Las Piñas. According to the prisoner diaries, the packages from home were distributed in March 1944. Supposedly they were brought to the

IMPERIAL JAPANESE ARMY

1. I am interned at—Philippine Military Prison Camp No. __4__.

2. My health is—~~excellent~~ good; ~~fair poor~~.

3. Message (50 words limit)

Hope all at home are well. Merry Xmas to all.

Regards Uncle Joe, Torner, Harold, Fox, Kersten,

Virgil and everyone. Everyone take care of mother

and Dad. Trust you are receiving fifty dollars

allotment regularly. All love to Don and brothers.

Keep chins up; will do likewise.

_____

Signature

IMPERIAL JAPANESE ARMY

1. I am interned at—Philippine Military Prison Camp No.—4

2. My health is—~~excellent~~ good;~~fair~~ ~~poor~~ x

3. Message (limited to 25 words)

Am well. All my love to you and family.

Signature

Opposite page and this page: Las Piñas POW cards sent in late 1943 and early 1944.

Philippines by the Red Cross ship the *Gripsholm*. Many of the letters took a long time getting to the Philippines.

> GALDE — I received one letter, and it left Seattle to New York to Stockholm then to Berlin to Rome and on to Japan and finally the Philippines. It took eight to ten months. When the letter was written, my dad was alive and healthy. By the time I received it, he was dead.

Addie also received packages from home. One of his three POW cards sent from Las Piñas acknowledges this. The return address on the post card-type letter from Las Piñas was PHILIPPINE MILITARY PRISON CAMP NO. 4. Some typed information on the back indicated the camp the men were in and their health (excellent-good-fair-poor). Most men regardless of their condition indicated their health as good. They didn't want to unnecessarily worry their families, and besides, the Japanese wouldn't permit a letter to go home indicating that the prisoner's health was fair or poor.

The bottom half of the card contained five lines in which the prisoners could either write or have a typed message. These messages could be either 50, 25, or 10 words in length. At Las Piñas, Addie had two 50-word cards and one 25-word card all typewritten. The cards were censored, of course, and any damaging comments were deleted, or the Japanese conveniently lost the card. Addie's three cards indicated his health as "good."

The typed message on Addie's first card, sent around Christmas 1943, was "Hope all at home are well. Merry X-Mas to all. Regards to Uncle Joe [Martin], [John] Toonen, Harold [Schumerth], [John] Fox, [Jerry] Kersten, Virgil [Kohlbeck], and everyone. Everyone take care of Mother and Dad. Trust you are receiving fifty dollars allotment regularly. All love to Don and brothers. Keep chins up; will do likewise."

Underneath the message was Addie's signature.

The second letter sent in early 1944 contained a short message: "Am well. All my love to you and family."

The final letter obviously was sent after the distribution of packages from home in March 1944. Addie indicates he received one and put in an order for subsequent packages. "Overjoyed at receipt of your packages and letters. All my love to you. Next time send shoes, 6-1/2 D, pants, shirt, and food. Am well, and God willing, hope to see you in due time. Congratulations to Don from whom I've heard [a reference to his passing the bar exam in 1943, his marriage in 1943, or the expected arrival in March, 1944, of the nephew that would be named Adrian]. Have monthly allotment raised ten dollars if you desire."

The cards also took a while to return to the states. Glen Ream's family received his three cards in August 1944, January 1945, and May 1945, eight to ten months after they were written. The cards, if nothing else, at least gave hope to relatives and friends in America that their loved ones in the Philippines were still alive.

The Medical Situation

When details were sent from Cabanatuan to various points in the Philippines, accompanying the prisoners were one or two American doctors. Occasionally, a Japanese doctor was also present. At Las Piñas, a Dr. Nogi, who was the chief medical official for the Japanese at Bilibid in Manila, would drive out to the camp.

Interestingly, few men can recall the names of the Las Piñas doctors. Such is not the case when asking the prisoners to name doctors at Cabanatuan, Davao, Clark Field, or some of the camps in Japan. Maybe it was because of the fact that the men spent most of the daylight hours at the airfield. As time wore on and the work became more demanding, many prisoners sought out the doctors to get out of work. Because there was a quota of how many prisoners the Japanese would allow on quarters, often the doctors had to send a man back to work, when under "normal" conditions he would be put to bed. Possibly some of the men resented this. Nevertheless, I found a significant number of Las Piñas prisoners who didn't recall the doctors' names and didn't want to talk about them. Some POWs gave me names of doctors they thought were at Las Piñas but actually were at other camps.

Most of the prisoners, however, recall their own illnesses, and they were many. Some recall medical problems of those around them. Las Piñas was a brutal work detail under terrible weather and sanitary conditions. The men suffered from malaria, beriberi, pellagra, and Guam blisters. And some of the "illnesses" later on were self-inflicted.

HITCHCOCK — As far as medical treatment, the doctors had almost no medicine and very little to work with. I think the doctors were doing a very difficult job under trying circumstances. It must have made them sad to realize they had patients that they could cure, if they only had the medicine.

On the other side, they were reviled by some of the prisoners who thought they should be kept in. But if the doctors kept too many people in, then the really sick people would be forced out to work. They were damned if they did and damned if they didn't.

If you were going to be kept in from work, it had to be something that the Japanese could either see, touch, or smell. So you had to have a fever, broken bone, or dysentery. If you had a problem that did not fall within these parameters, such as cardiac arrest, you had to keep working until you stopped breathing.

JONES — I was injured one day by being run over by some of the rail cars and was dragged a short distance. Unfortunately, the medical cure was nearly as bad as the accident. The main medicine for cuts, scrapes, and bruises was gentian violet and to discourage the men from running to the medic with minor cuts, a strong astringent was mixed in. In treating my mass of scraped skin, they had to use that medicine. The medic was quite apologetic for the pain he caused.

MANASSE — Some of the fellows would use all kinds of ruses to get off of work. It was very trying and difficult. Many were injured by guards around the airfield for not doing what they were supposed to do. I worked almost every day, and finally I got good and tired and needed a rest. One day, when I got back to camp, I found someone in the medical line to give me a hot cup of water, which I drank and ran right into the infirmary and had my temperature taken. It was 115 degrees, but it did get me a couple of days off.

CANFIELD — Sometimes some of us could miss a day of work by drinking hot water before sick call and complain of aching. Worked pretty well until one nut held the hot water in his mouth too long and had an indicated temperature of 108 degrees. He was set down for observation and rechecked. Then his temperature was normal.

AUGUST DE BAUCHE — To get out of work some of the guys would get some green bamboo, wring the water out of it, and then drink it. It would sour their stomach and make them vomit. Hopefully, that would be enough to keep them out of work that day.

ALDRICH — Pete Pyetski was pulled out of *bango* one morning to be placed on a special work detail to haul sand and cement into camp for some sort of expansion in the kitchen. The detail lasted for several days, and he was asked on a couple of occasions to deliver some chow over to sick bay. He learned that one of the sick guys had a circumcision and as a result was flat on his back, with some guy delivering his food to him.

The rest and attention did not escape Pete's attention, and he went on sick call after the sand and cement detail was over and requested a circumcision. He got his rest, and his chow delivered to the sick bay; but he also got an infection shortly after coming back to duty. The more I think about it, the more I'm sure he rubbed dirt into the operation to promote the infection. This gave him a couple more days rest, however.

Rest was exactly what many of the men needed. That and food. The prisoners would eat almost anything they could get their hands on. As work at the airfield intensified, many were willing to seriously injure themselves to escape work.

EVANS — There were a lot of self-mutilation jobs at Las Piñas. There were people who were desperate. You don't do these things unless you're desperate. I was standing next to a guy working. He was standing on my left, and I can't remember his name, but he was from Albuquerque. We were working away. He had a pick, and we were barefoot. Most of us were barefoot because we didn't have shoes. He had a long needle-nose pick that he was using in digging out those rice paddies. All of a sudden I heard him say, "I'm never going to work for these son-of-a-bitches again" and *thunk*; he had driven that pick down through the top of the instep to his left foot and into the ground and pinned himself there.

I ran over, and he had sat down by then, but his foot was still pinned to the ground. He was white as a sheet, but he had kind of a sickly smile on his face.

He didn't say anything. I tried to pull the pick out by putting my foot on his toes. When I did, the blood flew, and then we called the Japs over. I don't remember if he ever worked again.

SAUNDERS — I remember a POW from Black, Missouri. He was an older soldier with the 31st Infantry, 10-15 years older than most of us. I became very friendly with him. He was very tough. One day before he went to work, he said, "Saunders, I'm not going to work for these SOBs any longer."

I didn't know what he planned to do, but when we loaded our first train of cars as they came down the track, he fell and threw his arm under the first car, and it was cut to the bone.

EVANS — In the early summer of 1944, things were very bad at Las Piñas. They were literally working us to death, and anybody that could get out of work would do it, and they would go to any extreme. My friend Lindsay said that a fellow could get a broken arm, and he could be off work for a month or six weeks, or maybe he'd be shipped back to Cabanatuan. He set up a deal where he'd break a guy's arm for a half a ration of rice for one meal for all the time the guy didn't have to work.

Between each barracks there was a well. These were water wells like you'd find on an old farm in the states. It had a pump, and they were never used, but they were there. It had a cast iron pump handle. It was held in with a large cotter pin. This is what Lindsay used to break arms with.

When he had a "patient," he'd take that cotter pin and pull it out and take that handle off and take it to one of the barracks. He had a place to put the guy's arm between two blocks and *whacko*.

Now business got so good for Lindsay that he asked me to help him, so I was the assistant. My job was to console these guys and tell them that everything would be all right, and I'd put a towel over the left forearm so there wouldn't be any break of skin, and Lindsay would pop them. My job was to keep the guy's attention off what's going to happen. Lindsay was an expert at this. He knew how hard to hit them.

Now you can't run up to the medics and holler that you got a broken arm because that's no good. All of these were performed early in the morning. The reason for this was we'd break their arms just before we went out on work detail, so they'd have a minimum amount of suffering before they'd turn themselves in.

Now this is also a coaching job that I had to do. You had to coach them how to fake a fall off one of these carts. How to do something in front of the Japs, so it appeared like a legitimate break, because this is the only way the thing would work. He'd break the guy's arm early in the morning, and then the guy would go to work and go through his fall, or however he did it, and we'd be on the payroll as far as he was concerned.

Now this went on for some time. I have no way of knowing, but I would say Lindsay broke about 30 arms. What happened was that the Japs talked to the American doctor and inquired as to why there were so many guys breaking their left arms. Of course, the doctor had no idea, but he passed the word down. When we got this information, we decided it was about time to go out of business, and we did.

Well, a guy from West Virginia came to us and said he wanted his arm broken, and we said we were out of business because the Japs were getting wise as to too many broken left arms. He said he was left handed. So we broke his right arm, and that was the last job we did. We never did another one, and we never got caught.

LINDSAY — The first arm I broke was a guy who was working with Breslin, Evans, and me. We were actually trying to talk ourselves into it, but we talked him into it instead. He wrapped his hand in a rag, so it wouldn't bruise, and held his hand on the top of the handle on the box. I took a pick off the handle, and when he was looking the other way, I hit it with the pick. The first time I didn't hit hard enough, but I did the next time.

Later I broke several arms, and I cut Bill Evans' hand real bad, and a guy named Anderson. I cut his foot real bad. I can't remember the name of the guy from West Virginia. He was the last arm I broke.

MAYHUE — Some of the arms had a decided bend in them when "healed." Rightly or wrongly the men reasoned that their arms could be rebroken and reset when they got back home. You can rightly assume that conditions were pretty bad to cause a person to break his arm to miss five or six days of work.

ALDRICH — People in the close vicinity kept an eye out for the Japs, and stuck together with their versions of the accident when the injuries were made. Two guys would get out of work by helpin' the Jap guard take the injured to the medics back at camp. After the arm was set and in a sling, the Japs made them do light duty anyway.

But Lindsay and Evans weren't the only two operating a broken-arm scheme. There was competition.

HITCHCOCK — A Marine operated the broken-arm scheme under our hut, and he had a thriving business. We used to hear him get up in the middle of the night, slip out, and he used two 4x4s, over which he laid a blanket and then laid another blanket over the individual's arm between the two 4x4s. Then he hit him with a 2x4. It got to be almost amusing to hear these two whispering under the hut, and you could hear him say "steady." We used to imagine we could hear the *swish* of the 2x4 and then the *thump* and the choked cry and curse, and the deed had been done. The person who had his arm broken would go back and lie down, because it had to be broken in the field to be official. He'd go out to work and fall down and say, "My arm is broke, my arm is broke!!"

Of course, the arm would be swelled by that time, and it wouldn't take much of a medical person to tell that the arm had been broken many hours before. When the Japanese really began to view it with suspicion was when they noticed it was always the left arms that had been broken and not the arm that was used for eating.

MAYHUE — Conditions were so bad that a number of the fellows went out of their mind so to speak. One such instance was more extreme than usual.

This fellow had only a G-string to wear like the rest of us. One day he suddenly became a raving maniac, and we could not quiet him down or control him. We tried to pin him down and hold him so that he would not hurt himself, but he broke loose and went screaming and running around the airstrip waving his G-string.

After a short time, he began picking up rocks and throwing them at the Japanese. This boy really looked wild. And strangely enough, he only threw rocks at the Japs. He did not throw anything at the POWs. The Japanese tried to keep out of his way as best they could and did their best to keep this guy from touching them. This action by the Japanese certainly seemed strange and not in keeping with the usual brutal Japanese behavior.

We found, however, that the reason for the Japanese behavior in not intefering with the guy was their superstition. The Japanese believed that if they harmed a crazy person, that either they or one of their family or relatives would also go crazy.

GALDE — The guy who went crazy was a Navy man, Howard, and he slept next to me. He supposedly made warrant officer, but he couldn't prove it. He dwelled on this because as an officer he wouldn't have had to work. He was taken away and, as far as I know, we never knew just what happened to him.

Bilibid medical records on microfilm confirm that an R. L. Howard RM1/c of the Navy was admitted from Las Piñas on 20 March 1944. He was diagnosed as having dementia praecox — schizophrenia.

Although Addie's health was good enough to get him on the Las Piñas detail, once the work began, his health deteriorated rapidly. As his strength left him, various tropical diseases wracked his weakened body. By the end of his ten-month stay, Addie spent most of his time in camp.

MANASSE — Adrian was in the infirmary when I went in with the 115-degree temperature, and he had been sick and spent most of the time in camp. And I could see why. He did not look well and was not well.

ARTERBURN — Addie had a lot of blisters all over him from the sun.

MAYHUE — I don't know when Addie came down with malaria and dysentery, but I do know that he often worked while he was sick — he was forced to do so. Addie was confined to the sick ward, but the truth was he was in again and out again. The Japanese gave no one the chance to really recuperate in the sick ward. They would walk through the ward every day and at the slightest excuse would "kick" the sick man out of the ward to the work detail. I do not use the word "kick" as a figure of speech. I am being literal.

Addie was sick when we went to Las Piñas, so you can understand that standing half the night in the drenching rain upon our arrival did not help matters. In the Philippines during the rainy season, it gets cold, especially if a man is dressed only in a G-string. This does not mean that the temperature is low, but the wind blows a chill right into your bones. It has been said that we were all a bag of bones with big eyeballs.

Addie had tropical blisters and ulcers, but he also had malaria, dysentery, and beriberi.

Alcohol Consumption

You wouldn't think that alcohol would be a problem in a prison camp, but for many at Las Piñas it was. Alcoholism in the military was a problem in the Philippines, and it continued after the surrender to Japan. An assignment to the Philippines before the War was "soft" duty, and many men thought the Islands a great place to end their military careers. With this kind of attitude, there were some who put in as much time drinking as they did soldiering.

When the war started, alcohol became scarce, but the desire for it didn't diminish. At Las Piñas those who wanted alcohol found a new source — the Japanese vehicles.

STEWART — Drinking was a problem over there before the War anyhow. How this started out was this mechanics' detail. Part of their job was to fill the Japanese trucks. They were using funnels and pouring this stuff into the tank of the truck, and the fumes of it — man that smells good. That smells like alcohol. That smells like the stuff back in the states — the bootleg stuff.

So they tasted it and that got the ball rolling. Before I left there, we were coming in from the airfield one night, and they were carrying half the mechanics in. They were *sick* and the Japs couldn't figure out why they were *byoki* [sick]. These guys were carrying alcohol back to camp in their canteens.

To make a long story short, before we left Las Piñas, when we would come in at night from our work detail, the Japs would have us unscrew our canteens and turn them upside down as we walked by them. That's how they stopped the drinking in camp.

MAYHUE — We Americans had no soap or towels, but enterprising POWs manged to steal three or four towels from the Japanese. These towels were not used for drying off after bathing. They were in much more demand to obtain alcohol from the fuel tanks. This was accomplished by taking a stick and poking as much of the towel as possible in the tank through the fill spout. By holding one corner of the towel with one hand and the stick in the other, the towel could be twisted the right amount, and then pulled from the tank quickly, held over a canteen cup, stripped down, and then squeezed. If a person had practice at this, he could get over half a canteen cup of alcohol each time he withdrew the towel. The doctors did their best to persuade everyone not to drink the alcohol. They told us that any vitamin B we were getting was nil and that the alcohol would void any possible chance of our body to metabolize vitamin B, even if we did eat something containing vitamin B.

ALDRICH — If a POW went to work thoroughly intoxicated, the Japs, surprisingly enough, weren't too harsh on them. We decided the reason for this was the Japs stood in awe of crazy people, and probably thought the drunk had too much sun and had gone off his rocker.

Working around a running motor, such as one of the trucks, was a giddy experience. The humidity around the bay area was so high that the alcohol that was used for fuel didn't evaporate in exhaust very rapidly, and if one kept breathing it, lightheadedness would result.

HITCHCOCK DIARY — 4 March 1944 [Addie's 30th birthday] — A large amount of P-40 juice [alcohol] is being carried into camp and last night a couple of men in here got stinko and raised hell from about 12:00 to 2:00 A.M.

HITCHCOCK — There were lights at the airfield run by alcohol. The alcohol was "straffed" — that was a phrase we used to mean stolen — from generators and the fellows brought it into camp, and then it was drunk. There was not a lot of alcohol drunk — just an occasional canteen that was brought in, and then was shared around with a group of people. By the same token our resistance was very low, so it didn't take very much to get us high. There was one Army fellow, who had been a mechanic, and the Japs were using him on their trucks to keep them running. He had access to alcohol and drank a great deal of it to the point where he became very puffy. Later his skin broke out into all kinds of boils and eruptions. He got into just terrible shape, probably because of an insufficient diet and too much alcohol.

CICHA — The Japs asked for two volunteers to splice steel cable, and being a Navy man and having some experience with steel cable, I volunteered. I spliced cable in the storage shop, and when that job terminated, I went into the motor pool and worked on the trucks. I used to sneak alcohol to my friends in my canteen, and the fumes were quite intoxicating. That stuff was 190 proof, therefore almost 100 percent pure. It could burn your insides out, so it had to be diluted with water.

The Japs brought in all gasoline and alcohol in 50-gallon drums, and if it happened that the drum had a little gasoline and then was used for alcohol, it produced a bad barrel of alcohol. By pouring it in water you could tell. If it turned milky in color, then it was bad stuff. When you ran into a good barrel, we would fill a disabled truck tank with it, and from there we would bring it to camp.

I used to take a bath in alcohol quite frequently at the end of the day at the motor pool.

Coconut oil was used in the trucks and was brought in in 50-gallon drums. It was not refined enough for human consumption. It would hang in your throat and have a choking effect. I remember fellows from the Southern states talking about making whiskey and using charcoal for purification. A light came on in my dome, and I said to myself, if it worked for whiskey makers, maybe it will work with this coconut oil, so I brought some into camp and tried it. I had a pound coffee can. Got some hot coals from the kitchen and some charcoal. I got a fire going and put my oil on the fire and started cooking. The oil was boiling, and we were wondering how long to cook the stuff, and after some time the charcoal started to sink to the bottom. When it all sank, I took it off the fire and let it cool, and that did the trick. It was edible then, and needless to say my friends and I had plenty oil for our dry rice.

SAUNDERS — This guy from Missouri kept getting high in camp, and we could not figure how anybody could get drunk in a POW camp. We soon found out that when the trucks came in camp to unload the rice, he would sneak around the truck and take a rag and stick it in the truck and squeeze out enough alcohol to get on a binge. This guy was something else. One day we were talking, and he said "Saunders, you know I believe we have died and are in hell and don't know it." This camp was just a little bit of hell.

ART SMITH — I knew some of the truck drivers and mechanics. I had a couple of canteens, but I used it for medicinal purposes — with hot water and a little sugar like tea, and for sores I rubbed myself with it.

PAUL KERCHUM — You sure could smell that alcohol. One of the men got loaded from it while we were working, and he got caught. It was very hot, and they made him hold a sheet of roofing metal over his head and every time he dropped it, they would beat him. When I saw that, I forgot all about alcohol.

Christmas 1943

In a camp without calendars, it's difficult to know the exact date. For the prisoners, however, their cultural background made them aware of when Easter, Memorial Day, July Fourth, and Christmas occurred. The Japanese often wouldn't permit any observance of American holidays, and if they did, the ceremonies were usually subdued. With no Chaplains assigned to Las Piñas, celebrating religious holidays fell upon the men. At Las Piñas, according to Willie Arterburn, Addie was known as "Chappie's Boy" because of his prior work with the Chaplains. There were many 200th/515th CAC men in camp, and they gave him that nickname. Many of the men recall that 1943 Christmas at Las Piñas, and Addie had a role in it. Red Cross packages were distributed, and those who were rested enough enjoyed some physical recreation.

MAYHUE — We did not have any organized religious activities at Las Piñas, but we did have a service for Christmas, 1943. The only one who knew how to go about this was Addie.

The Officers

Whether an enlisted man or an officer, being a prisoner of war was a struggle. Often I've heard an enlisted man claim that the officers had more chow and less work in the various POW camps. Under the Prisoner of War Articles of the Geneva Convention, officers were not required to perform manual labor. But some officers chose to work with the enlisted men. Those who did are still remembered today by their men. They left an indelible imprint.

As mentioned previously in the chapter concerning the doctors, many of the Las Piñas men don't remember the names of the officers. Some remember features and some recall incidents involving the officers. But few can attach names. Forrest Knox had a theory on this phenomenon.

KNOX — By the time I got back to the United States, I was pretty near homicidal. I got a brain somewhat like a computer — it's a file system. I hated those doctors at Las Piñas pretty bad, so there's a self-protecting device we have. I erased their names from my memory.

That's probably what happened to many of the men at Las Piñas. Because of the strenuous work, inadequate food, lack of proper medical care, and the constant threat of beatings, many simply erased from their minds the names of the officers that they "hated" or "envied." The following stories involving the officers sometimes include names and are, for the most part, stories about the unpopularity of their leaders.

ROSS — In order to survive in Las Piñas you had to be in a clique with a clique. I got in good with the doctors and officers and that helped me survive.

KNOX — This officer in charge of Las Piñas was living high on the hog for an officer. He was supposedly married to a Filipino gold mine heiress, and she kept him totally supplied. She bribed the Jap camp commander. They fixed it up so this officer walked around with starched fresh suntans on every day. He looked like he was on civilian duty. This is what caused friction in the camp with the other people. He was totally different than anybody else.

Now we must have had 25 officers and two doctors, and those two we had at Las Piñas was absolutely and totally useless. I went to the trouble of trying to be friends with these assholes because I figured that if I got to be friends with them, I could get a little help.

MAYHUE — The Chinese made Filipino-Japanese currency as fast or faster than the Japanese. An officer, through Filipino contacts, could borrow money from a Chinese money lender. An enlisted man, however, could not. Let me hasten to say that all officers did not have this privilege — only a few of those that had been in the Philippines long enough to establish credit or a bank account. At any rate, officers fared much better than enlisted men. They could buy medicines and food. As would be expected, the death rate among officers was much lower than that among enlisted men.

Here I am beating around the bush because I hate to make accusations, but I will go ahead and say what I believe to be true. When our packages from home arrived at Las Piñas, the American officers held them for two or three days before giving them to their rightful owners. The officers handled all matters such as this. When they did give us our packages, all of them had been opened and something was missing. Usually there was a vacant spot, where it looked as if only one thing had been removed. The packages were packed pretty tightly. Some packages had the flaps opened or holes torn in the cardboard boxes. My package had a hole torn in the corner with a small vacant space in that corner. I asked the officers who had broken into the packages, and, of course, they blamed the Japanese.

This was confusing to me, because I knew that if the Japanese had broken into the packages, they would have taken such things as American cigarettes, candy, razor blades, and such. But none of those types of things seemed to be missing.

This question was not resolved until I got home. I asked my folks to help me reconstruct what they had sent in the package. The first thing they named was vitamin pills. They told me their instructions listed vitamin pills as the most important item on the list. Bottles of vitamins, back in those days, did not have cotton packing to keep them from rattling.

Now the Japanese did not have vitamin pills and did not know of their value. In view of this, I think it not too far-fetched to imagine that the six or eight officers shook the packages and cabbaged on to our vitamins. Why was only the corner of my package torn open? It has been said that time heals all wounds, but may God forgive me, for I believe there are exceptions.

HITCHCOCK — This First Lieutenant Marshall may have been Army Air Corps and periodically was placed as the leader of our work company since he was not required to work. He was usually in pretty good spirits, and his responsibility was to sing us rollicking good songs as he marched us out to and back from work each day.

SAUNDERS — This fellow Marshall was one that always seemed to get in trouble in camp. He was tough. I don't remember what he did, but the senior officer in camp . . . beat this Marshall pretty bad. [This officer] was the cause of a lot of beatings in camp. I personally gave an affidavit to the Americans when I was debriefed. I don't know what happened to [him]. I always hoped he would be questioned about the beatings.

But there were officers who earned the men's respect. Frank Mayhue recalls one nameless officer who did his duty to help the enlisted men.

MAYHUE — I suppose the incident that gave the men the idea to break their arms stemmed from the beating the Japanese gave an

American Captain. You see, each work detail had an American honcho who the Japanese used as a go-between to explain what they wanted us to do. Of course all of us acted dumb as if we could not understand the Japanese language. By this, we could cause a lot of lost time and confusion.

I regret that I do not remember this Captain's name because he was one of *very, very, few* officers who attempted to help us dogfaces and try to make life easier for us. He did not forget his position of leadership and responsibility as an officer. During these trying times, we did not expect any help from our officers because none were inclined to offer any help. In general, American officers did not have to work, but sometimes Captains and Lieutenants were put in honcho positions in the field. Usually, they stayed in the barracks or compound and did no work. In this position, they could do the least harm also.

Anyway, this Captain made a point of arguing with the Japanese about our heavy work load and lack of food. He kept trying to make the point that we could not work unless we received an adequate diet. He continued to argue with them about how much work they expected us to do and about the brutal treatment we received.

The Japs would put up with this for some time, even though they would pound him up with their clubs from time to time. Finally, they told him he was a dishonorable officer and must be punished. Essentially, they told him he was inferior to all of us, a bad person, lacked "dissiprin" [discipline], failed to take orders from his superiors, the Jap guards, and that he was insubordinate. The Japs went on and on and told him that since he was such a big disgrace, he must be punished in front of all the American "Sojirs." This they proceeded to do by beating him senseless. "Senseless" as used here means that a person is beaten within an "inch of his life" but still remains on the verge of consciousness.

The beating took place on a small piece of high ground that had not been leveled as yet and took about two hours. Aside from being beaten to a bloody pulp, the Captain sustained a few broken ribs and a broken arm. The next couple of days the Captain was taken to the air strip and made to stand at attention until he passed out. He was then left laying there after a few more kicks until he was helped in at night.

After a couple of days the Captain was taken from camp, and I do not know what happened to him. I have related this story because the Japanese hardly ever beat an officer. Usually this amounted to slapping around for a few minutes only.

The Taiwanese

After several months at Las Piñas, the Japanese realized that their timetable to build an airfield was falling behind. To solve the labor problem they brought in over 1,000 Taiwanese. Taiwan had been ceded to Japan in 1895 by the Chinese Empire, and its males provided slave labor.

The Americans had little contact with the newcomers who lived in barracks outside and to the west of the American compound. Contact at the airfield was also minimal as the Taiwanese usually worked the night shift and the Americans the day shift.

REAM — The Taiwanese work detail toiled on the tracks at night while we worked during the day. The Taiwanese stayed in different barracks. They would use rags soaked in coconut oil for their torch lights.

HITCHCOCK — At some point it became evident that the Americans were not going to get the airfield done on time no matter how much they beat us or worked us, so they brought in a group of Formosans [Taiwanese] and put them in the camp next to us.

We didn't have much communication with the Formosans, who were working nights. As I recall, we may have passed them on the road. We never had much opportunity to visit with them. Of course, I don't know how we'd visit. We didn't speak Taiwanese, and they didn't speak English.

They had an epidemic of diarrhea or dysentery that raced through their camp and laid them up for several days. They brought a Japanese doctor in to look at them and with wonderful Oriental logic he resolved the problem.

He said the reason the men don't work is because they *benjo* [toilet] all the time. The reason they *benjo* is because they eat. Therefore if we don't feed them, they can't *benjo*, and if they don't *benjo*, they can work.

So they cut off all food to those laid up with dysentery. This cure continued until they buried quite a few of them. Then they must have asked somebody for a second opinion and went to another way of correcting the problem, because they later came back to work again.

Guards, Honchos, and Punishments

In September 1943, when the 800 prisoners left Cabanatuan for an unknown work detail, many thought their heading southwest out of Manila was a sure sign that their destination was the dreaded Nichols Field. What made it so feared was that the men there were never safe from Japanese abuse, whether at work or resting in camp. At Las Piñas, once inside the compound each night, the men were left alone. The Japanese didn't make it a practice to walk through the barracks threatening prisoners. At the airfield, however, it was a different story.

Each 50-man work group was supervised by one or more Japanese guards and/or civilian honchos and later by young Taiwanese. Usually, the same guard worked with the same work group so after a while the men got to know the guard and honcho, his name, and personality, and vice versa. On the surface, this relationship might seem to the prisoner's advantage, but some later regretfully found out otherwise.

Punishments, usually meted out with a club, were sometimes administered to everyone in a work group and at other times only to an individual. The prisoners often had difficulty trying to predict the Japanese mentality towards discipline. But one thing the POWs were sure of — the Japanese loved to hit people, and they did it effectively.

ROMERO — The Japanese Prison Commander was a Navy Captain by the name of Watanabe. The Japanese civilian bosses who were in charge of the beatings at Las Piñas all had nicknames. First the Big Honcho "Number One Boss" in charge of all the work done at the airfield was called "The Pig." He fitted the name pretty good. The Number Two man was "The Bull." This guy used the pick handle pretty often. I was hit with a shovel by him for not working fast enough. He hated Americans because he lost two brothers in the war. The third was "The Angel." He liked to punish the prisoners by making them stand in the hot sun for hours. Last, the "Little Jap." He was the interpreter, and often gave the wrong message to the Japanese, causing many POWs getting beat up.

GALDE — There were beatings at times most always related to work. The Japs were experts at this, and the reasons were many, but it was sometimes our fault. Like when the interpreter fell off the water truck and it ran over his legs. Of course we cheered because he wasn't very good at his job and often misinterpreted what we said or did, and of course we suffered.

ROSS — If the guards were beating you and you put your hand up to block a punch, you got it ten times rougher. Some of the guards were Taiwanese.

JONES — I do not believe the guards were as bad as at Nichols Field.

They did beat us at times, especially the young kids the guards had helping them. The guards in camp did not create much of a problem.

ALDRICH — After we had been at Las Piñas for three or four months, the Japs brought in a few Taiwanese to act as assistants or helpers to our Jap honcho. Now, in addition to the Jap soldiers, and the honchos, there was another factor that could cause ill-treatment.

Kozono San was the honcho that I was most often aligned with during my tour of this camp, and as time wore on, he and I did become friends of a sort. Kozono San appeared to be less volatile than the other honcho, and on rare occasion would offer a Jap cigarette to be shared by POWs in his vicinity. If we appeared to be falling behind the other crews on the other revetments, he would get a stern look on his face and cluck like an old mother hen, until we gained the pace he thought to be proper. Seldom was he provoked enough to really beat a POW.

Now Iconomas San was a different story. My close friend Les Morrison worked on the crew supervised by this cruel and sadistic Jap. Instead of the usual vitamin stick, Iconomas San carried a truck fan belt and would beat POWs with that at the slightest provocation.

Contact with the Jap guards came during *bango* or *tenko* and marching to and from the airfield. An impropriety here brought a few blows about the head and ears, not the concentrated beatings the honcho would administer.

Kozono San's Taiwanese assistant was named Go-Ju. Go-Ju's mission was to inspire the work detail by yelling and beating. The Japs thought we were not working hard and fast enough and this was a truism.

While pushing the little rail car one day, Go-Ju came up behind me and hit me with his vitamin stick. The blow was in the kidney area and it knocked me down. God, it hurt! Though I was in great pain, I jumped up and lashed into him verbally. I told him just what I thought of him and his ancestral lineage. He raised his stick to give me another whack, and Kozono San stopped him. Though Go-Ju yelled at me many times after that little incident, he never struck me again.

HITCHCOCK — The name of the honcho in the company I was in was Kuwana. We had to call him Kuwano San. He was a reasonably peaceful citizen. Occasionally, he would hit one of us with a pick handle, but it was more as a reminder rather than any intent to hurt us very badly. You could tell his heart wasn't in it.

MAYHUE — When Kanimatsu suspected me of being the instigator of the shovel incident and work slowdown, he told me that he should and could have me shot but that he would not do this, but he would discipline me each morning and each night and also in between.

He told me that I did bad things and needed to learn respect. This may sound strange, but after a person gets beaten for so long a time, he then gets numb and feels only the hardest blows.

One of Kanimatsu's favorite punishments was to line us all up and beat us with a hoe handle or a walking stick made from a tree limb. Another method of receiving punishment was to be made to kneel down on your feet and knees, bend over, and have a welding rod applied to your back. Another punishment is the sun treatment, where a POW is forced to stand at attention in the hot sun for about three days with only our usual G-string — no water or rice.

Some of the worst moments was having to stand at attention waiting for a decision as to what punishment would be meted out. Besides a severe beating, we would many times be held until the eveing meal was dished out, so we would get none. All in all, to really understand the punishment received by the POW, a person would have to suffer through it himself — heaven forbid!

Frank Mayhue became a close friend of Addie's at Las Piñas. In his attic he keeps his war mementos. One of them is a piece of paper torn from a dry cement package used at the airfield. On it he wrote the names of close Las Piñas friends that he wanted to renew acquaintances with, once the war was over. In the lower, left-hand corner of the paper is written:

Adrian R. Martin
303 S. Erie
DePere, Wisconsin

Addie and Frank were in the same work group and often involved in promoting work slowdowns and in general disrupting the Japanese effort. When Kanimatsu caught them, he had his method of dealing with them.

MAYHUE — Kanimatsu was big and stocky with a mouthful of gold teeth. Kanimatsu's face was covered with a black shadow, even though fresh shaven most of the time, but it never cracked a smile. He directed nothing but disparaging remarks to us — even when directing our work. He carried a tree limb as a walking stick and enjoyed beating us so much that he never missed the opportunity to line a bunch of us up and slap us around or use the stick on us.

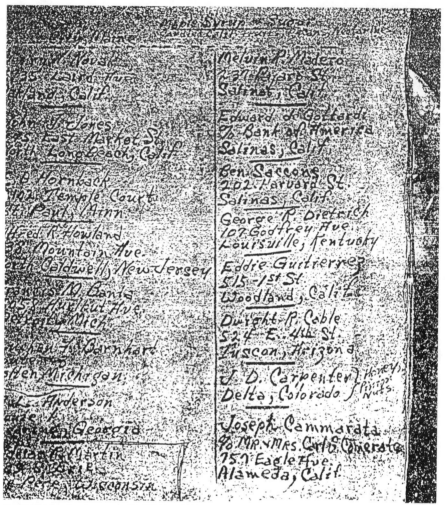

Frank Mayhue kept names of POW friends on a dry cement bag at Las Piñas. Addie's name is in the lower left-hand corner. (Courtesy of Frank Mayhue)

One such instance, I managed to be on the end of the line on Kanimatsu's right. This was usually the best place to be because hopefully the Jap would start to let up, as he would always start on his left. Addie was the third from the end with one man between us.

When Kanimatsu got to Addie, he had not let up at all, and he worked Addie over so fiercely that I could not keep from saying "son-of-a-bitch" under my breath. However, it was not under my breath because Kanimatsu stopped with his fist in midair, took one step, and then lowered the boom on me.

He cuffed my left ear with the palm of his right hand and ruptured

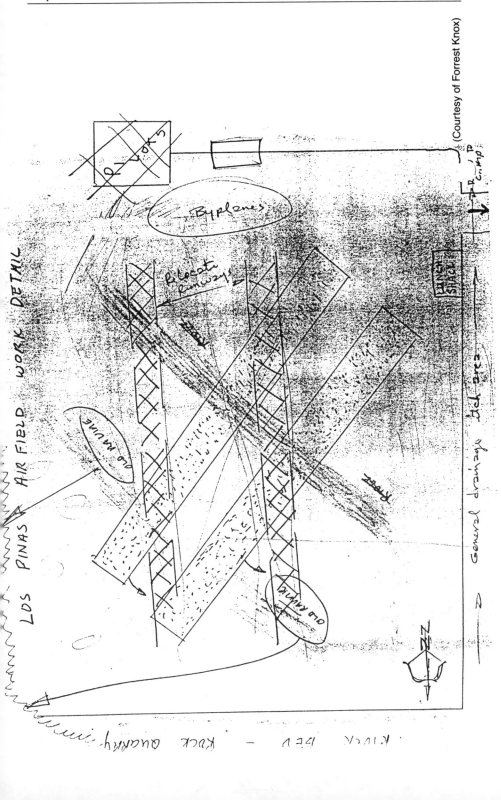

(Courtesy of Forrest Knox)

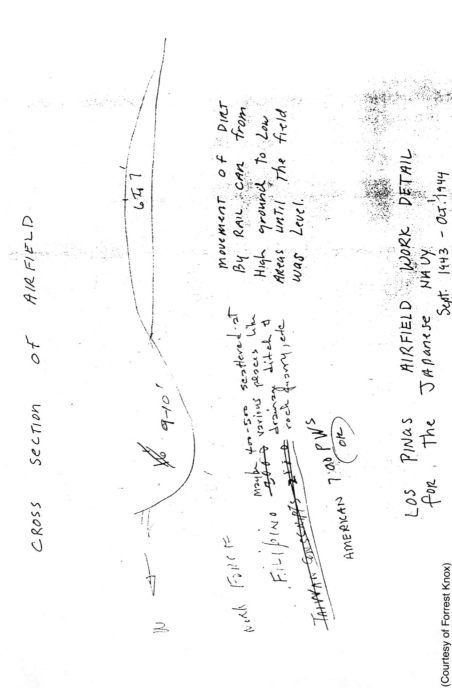

CROSS SECTION OF AIRFIELD

9-10'

movement of Dirt By RAIL can from High ground to Low Areas until The field was Level.

North Force

Filipino Maybe 400-500 scattered at various places Wh a drainag ditch & rock from pit etc

JAPANESE CONCEPTS

AMERICAN 7,000 P.W's OK

LOS PINAS AIRFIELD WORK DETAIL For The JAPANESE NAVY Sept. 1943 - Oct. 1944 my eardrum. Ever since, I have had a ringing in my ear. The upshot of this was that Kanimatsu forgot about the man between Addie and I, and he came out unscathed.

All in all, the guards at Las Piñas were not as bad as Cabanatuan to me. I mean the guards were hard on the other POWs but they knew that I was Kanimatsu's whipping boy. That is not to say that Kanimatsu did not beat anyone else, because he did — including Addie.

Airfield Construction

October and November of 1943 found the men breaking down the dikes and draining the rice paddies. This was difficult, but not backbreaking when compared to the work done during the 1944 months.

The construction of the airfield was judged an absolute necessity by the Japanese. The conquerors expected the field to be ready in early 1944, and as the deadline approached, the pressure to complete the project increased. Some men recall that the chow was increased as they worked longer, harder hours. But most remember the increased physical and emotional demands placed upon them.

Initially, the work schedule called for six days of work and *yasame* (rest) on Sunday. It didn't take long for the Japanese to insist on seven and no rest. Interestingly, the men were paid for their work. It wasn't much, and with working everyday of the week, it doesn't seem possible for the prisoners to spend money. But they did. The men established their own commissary and pooled their money. Often when the truck drivers had to go to Manila to pick up Japanese supplies, they also returned with items — food, cigarettes, medicine, etc. — purchased by the men through their commissary.

GEORGE FOX — The commissary carried fruit, mongo beans, native tobacco, cigarettes, and cigars. We were paid 10-15 centavos a day, which could buy a couple of bananas or a mango. There were also counterfeit occupation pesos coming into camp. I believe we were spending 15,000 to 20,000 pesos a month in the commissary.

As time went on, the men got an unfortunate lesson in supply and demand. Even though their pay remained the same, as items became more difficult to get, and the demand for them increased, the prisoner's buying power diminished.

One of the reasons for the decline in buying power was that the men were working for weeks at a time without *yasame*. They were trying to purchase more food, which wasn't always available. One of the reasons for their increased work was a foul-up at the airfield.

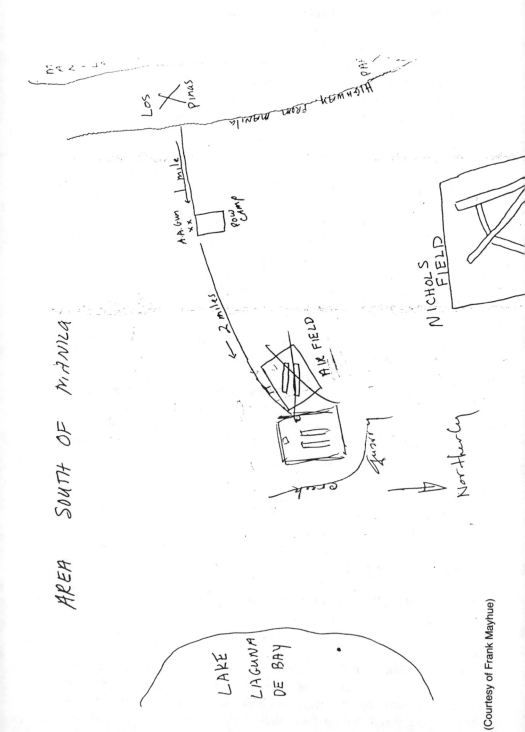

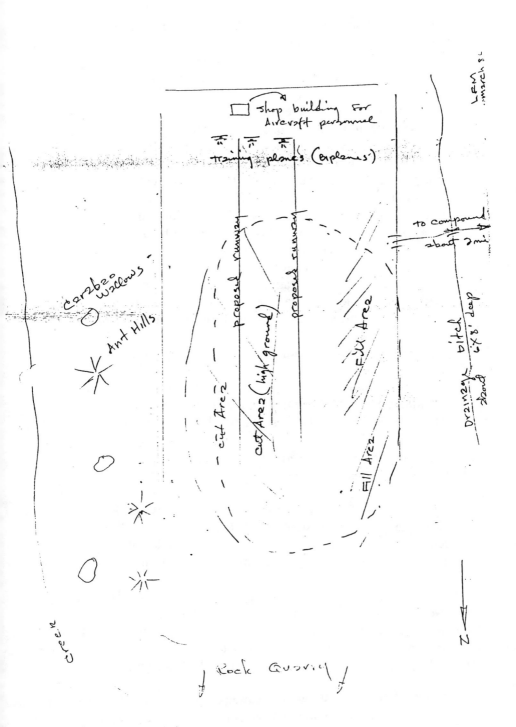

After the initial surveying of the rice paddy to insure a level runway, the men transported dirt from the high ground to the low areas. The grade stakes told them how much dirt to put in each area. As the field neared completion, the Japanese noticed that the runways weren't going to be level.

HITCHCOCK — I have a recollection that it seems to me the original surveying might have been done by a Filipino crew, who after they laid out the field, went back into Manila and disappeared. At any rate, we were working from the two sides of the field towards the middle. When we got close to the middle, it became apparent that there was going to be about a six-foot drop off in the middle of the field. As a result, they had to go back and start all over again and work that six-foot difference out. That's when the pressure began to come on, because it was obvious that we were not going to meet the deadline that had been set. We started working longer hours, more days, and there were a lot more beatings on the field to keep everybody humping. Evidently they had some sort of timetable that they were responsible for meeting, and this put them substantially behind.

CABLE — The story I heard was that the Filipino surveyors who did the survey work for the Japanese deliberately staked it so that when the two portions of the field, being leveled from opposite sides met in the middle, they were not at the same level but differed by several feet. The story was that the Japanese shot the Filipino surveyors.

Some of the prisoners believed the sway in the runway was caused more by the type of soil rather than sabotage.

ALDRICH — The airfield runway was definitely not level. The Americans prepared no stable base for the runway. If the heavy rains left depressions, loose dirt was tossed in and leveled off. Rock was used in some holes that appeared after the thing would settle.

Whether it was faulty surveying, sabotage, or poor earth, the runway was not level, and it took the prisoners weeks of long hours to correct the situation for the Japanese. This further delayed the opening of the field. To make matters worse, some prisoners orchestrated a work slowdown while others devised their own sabotage schemes. Even Addie had a hand in this.

COOKINGHAM — We were supposed to have Sunday off, but when the Japs got in a hurry to finish the field, we went 58 days without a day off. We ended up working from the first light to the last light.

DEWEY — We were required to do so much work per day. We had cars on the track like coal cars, about eight to ten to a track. All cars had to be loaded at the same time to keep the cars rolling to the dump end at the same time. If you did not get your car loaded in time, you were in for a hard hit with a stick. If you were sick or received a tin, cheap shovel, you would have a bad day.

ROSS — The Japs said, "You do ten cars and we'll go back to camp — *yasame*." I told the guys not to do it. They can't take us back to camp anyway.

This other guy kept saying, "Let's do it." Well, they did it anyhow and by 11:00 in the morning they were all done. They rested for the remainder of the day. But the next day, the quota was 10 cars a day. Not long after that, they raised it to 15. But no matter if you worked in rocky soil or soft, all cars had to be filled and moved at the same time.

EVANS — The guards tried to make us do more work than expected, but they ran into a stone wall there. We had a situation worked out where no one was allowed to work more than the other guy and throw a burden on somebody. We just didn't permit that. The Japs could never figure out why every car would be loaded at exactly the same moment. They couldn't understand, but they were. We had that worked out to a science.

We also put big clots of dirt in, so that there would be huge hollow spaces in the carts, and the Japs thought they had a full cart of dirt, and they didn't. Little *mickey mouse*, pseudo-sabotage things we would do to them.

Addie had a distaste for pick-and-shovel work since his youth. He certainly wasn't adept at this type of work, but he did aid the work slowdown.

ARTERBURN — Addie and I worked on the airfield together and then makin' revetments [three-sided dirt mounds that protected the airplanes]. That work we had to do on the airfield was actually hard on him. He didn't know a God-blessed thing about a pick and a shovel. He didn't know what work was. It was hard on that little bugger. I had to use a pick and shovel half of my life. I was pouring concrete when I was in school. I knew all about it, but Addie didn't know that kind of stuff, that poor little bugger.

MAYHUE — I was what might be called a rabble-rouser. I didn't call it this. Addie agreed with my philosophy and between us we agreed that no pressure should be used. We should only *urge* the others to help. Then we agreed that I would move up and down the track at various times to urge work slowdown, and that he would have the say in whether I was going overboard in my urging.

In reality Addie was one of the best persons I have ever known. Being a POW tends to bring out the best and the worst in a person — man or woman. Mostly it's *dog eat dog and the devil catch the hindmost*. But that's not the way it was with Addie. He maintained his equilibrium and helped others like me with theirs.

Addie could always more or less calmly evaluate things or what might or might not come to pass. Addie helped me calm my stubborness and my defiance to the Japanese. At times I lost my ability to reason, but Addie brought me back to reality. So you see, if it were not for him, I might not be here today.

Addie's personality was such that it prompted people to *buddy up* to him, to philosophize or obtain solace from. He was a solid-type person, which caused people to take seriously what he might have to offer. He was not a big mouth like I was. And while I knew him, his morale was high, even though our position was cause for dismay. He never forgot that patriotism was a key point to our lives. He certainly was a man of substance and honor.

In April, some of the men were taken off the runway detail and were used to build revetments for the anticipated Japanese airplanes. The revetments were three-sided hills of dirt, which would provide protection for the planes in case of bombings. Willie Arterburn, Morgan Jones, Swede Galde, George Fox, Paul Kerchum, and Addie were part of this detail.

Often dirt was carried to the site by the Chinese bucket-carrying method, and at other times rail cars were used. Sometimes the prisoners buried their shovels in the revetments, which antagonized the Japanese who couldn't figure out why there was a shortage of tools. This detail must have been a small one, and only for a short duration as most of the men interviewed don't recall it at all.

Arrival of Japanese Planes

The purpose of the Las Piñas airfield was to train carrier pilots. The Japanese had hoped to land planes at the field in early 1944. The work slowdowns and sabotage delayed the completion of the first runway for many weeks. Ironically, according to the Hitchcock diary, the first plane to land at Las Piñas touched down on 11 March 1944, the day I was born. Later that month more arrived.

HITCHCOCK DIARY — 23 March 1944 — Have a total of 42 planes permanently assigned to the field. Two low wing and 40 biplanes. They are painted a brilliant orange and are, to all appearances, advance trainers.

These smaller planes did not have much problem landing on this rice-paddy runway. That was not the case, however, with a larger plane that landed later.

EVANS — There was a plane that came in with some bigwigs on it. They were coming in to officially open up the runway. The concrete on the runway was too thin. The Jap band was out there and a company of infantry to present arms. When that plane, about the size of a C-47, landed, it went through that concrete and tipped over on its back and unfortunately it didn't catch fire. We're over about 100 yards away working on this other runway when all of this was happening. It was the second time during the war that I wet my pants trying to keep from laughing at this Mack Sennett comedy over there. They opened the door on the plane, and these Japanese big wheels were falling out on the runway. The Jap infantry and band was hustling over to get everything repaired. It was probably the funniest thing I had seen during the war.

MAYHUE — I was probably one of the first to learn that someone had decided to mix cement with dust for the runway. When Kanimatsu told me about it, we were working on a water pump. I asked him, "What silly son-of-a-bitch thought of that idea?" I had no sooner said it when he slapped me to the ground and then beat the hell out of me.

But we mixed enough cement and dirt to form a narrow runway for the trainer pilots to use. When the runway was completed, Kanimatsu made a special point to remind me that the trainer planes had been using the runway, and he asked, "Now what do you think of the runway?" But I told him I would rather not comment because he would probably beat me again.

Then he told me that a transport plane was due to land in ten minutes, and if the plane landed successfully, then he would beat me.

Sure enough the plane came in, landed, and broke through the cement. When I saw this, I immediately put distance between Kanimatsu and me, because I knew that he could not fail to be furious. After this incident, we had to go back to fill work for a couple of days, and I wondered what the Japs would do next.

Kanimatsu told us we would start over again and use rock for a foundation this time. He then came up to me and whacked me across the back with his stick and told me to come with him.

He began walking north and said, "We will inspect for rock quarry." On the way back to our work area he said, "I told them [supervisors] that I did not think the cement and dirt make a good runway." Then he said that because I was right, "You can rest for two days, and I will not beat you."

Because of the planes breaking through the runway, the Japanese thought a crushed-rock base might offer more stability. Just to the north of the runways was a rock quarry. Dynamite was used to blast the rock, picks were used to break the rock into smaller pieces, and rail cars were used to transport the material to the runway, where it was dumped, spread out, and compacted with a steamroller.

COOKINGHAM — We ended up digging out limestone rock from the creek to put on the runway. One of the runways was completed with sod from the lawns of Manila. Training planes were using it, but sod kept flying in all directions. So another runway was laid out, and we started putting rock on this runway using rail cars from the creek. We would shovel dirt off the rock ledge, bore holes, and blast the rock loose. Then we would load it in cars and push it to the runway. This is what we were doing the day the Americans bombed the field in September.

As the men continued to prepare the west runway, the young Japanese navy pilots continued to practice on the east runway. For the prisoners, watching the Japanese training methods was almost as interesting and amusing as their engineering skills.

STEWART — Now the wind at Las Piñas only blew in two directions. It either went towards the bay or blew in from the bay. It never went crossways, so they didn't have to build two sets of runways — just two parallel runways. Now these pilots were being trained to be carrier pilots, so they had to hit a certain spot when they came down on the runway. They'd come down, hit it, and then take off again. They'd circle and come back and try it again. If they goofed up and overshot the spot long or short, or bounced when they hit, the guy in the rear cockpit would stand up and hit the pilot with something like a rolled-up billy club.

KNOX — Now these guys all wore the regular flying suit with the zipper, and if anyone screwed up, like getting the plane stuck in the muck, then the entire contingent had to do double time around the damn airfield with their helmets and full uniform on. We was stripped to nothing but a G-string, so you can imagine how them little bastards was sweatin' in them suits. If anyone lagged behind, the officer was right behind them to beat on them until they caught up. I imagine the guy who goofed up got hit by 40 other ones when he got back to the barracks.

ALDRICH — The Jap flying school was on the other side of the runway, and the buildings and hangars were finally complete. By that time our work had carried us slightly beyond, but not so far that we couldn't see the figures moving around. The students always moved at double time.

The planes were two-wing Jennies with two cockpits. This, we were to learn, was one for the student and one for the teacher.

Soon these planes drifting over our heads prior to landing became commonplace. As the student aligned the plane to the runway, preparatory to landing, he would reduce the power for a short time and then return to full power and swoop down for a landing. It was not unusual during the periods of reduced power to hear the instructor yelling at the top of his voice to the student. If the student really made a bobble, in addition to the screaming, the instructor would flail away at the guy about the head and ears with a vitamin stick. Oddly enough, the system seemed to work because I don't recall a single crash.

KIMBALL — This pilot training was a three-ring circus. The planes were two seaters with the student in the front seat and the instructor behind him. And when they really goofed up, the instructor would make them do double time around the airfield two or three times. It was comical to us. They were just young Jap kids.

DEWEY — One time I was laying water pipe below the ground. I remember walking over to a building to get some more pipe when someone in the building called me in English to come inside.

Inside I saw about 30 Jap pilots. They were all clean-cut, young, and several spoke English. One pilot said he went to college in Chicago, Illinois. They were all friendly and were cussing the "Damn War!"

The Closing of Las Piñas

Las Piñas literally ended with a *bang* in September 1944. In July, Addie and approximately 200 other prisoners said farewell. Most of these were too ill to get much work out of anyway. The remaining men labored through August and early September preparing the second runway. But rumors persisted that the Yanks were getting close. Men who went to Manila returned to camp and observed how fortified the city had become. Even the camp had anti-aircraft near the front gate. The men gazed at the skies each day expecting to see American bombers. They didn't have to wait long. On 21 September they got what they were hoping for.

ALDRICH — We were working away on a balmy day in late September when the sound of airplane motors over the Manila Bay area caught our attention. We saw black specks maneuvering in the sky, and the staccato sound of gunfire reached our ears along with the roaring sound of straining motors. Work stopped immediately. An orange-colored arc smeared across the sky, closely followed by several more, convinced us that the fight was real.

Our excited Jap guards and honchos began screaming for us to move over into the center of the airfield. We lined up in a column of fours and were being told that we were going to return to camp.

At that moment a blue aircraft — we thought it was on fire but the wing guns firing spouted orange flame with short puffs of smoke trailing behind — came swooping low over our heads streaming directly for the hangars and aircraft on the other side.

The Japs disappeared into fox holes along the edge of the field and the Americans just stood there cheering and yelling encouragement. We were not quite sure these were American planes attacking us because the insignia was a star and bar while during our war the star had been in a circle.

Several more planes attacked the airfield and to our amazement these pilots were waggling their wings as they approached us on their swoop to give 'em hell on the other side. We were waving our hats and yelling at the top of our lungs.

All too soon it was over. The Japs came running back to us, some all wet because they had jumped in the stream, and made us run back to camp. In the rush, tools were left at the work site. Running along, a lot of smoke was spiraling up over toward Manila. We could hear explosions. God had answered our prayers.

EVANS — The Japs were using the runway for landings with these little biplanes when the Americans bombed us on the 21st. As a matter of fact, I was in the creek bed obtaining crushed rock for the base of the second runway when Admiral Halsey's aircraft hit the Manila area, and they strung bombs down the freshly built runway and that was the end of that.

MAYHUE — As a person gets older he tends to remember the best things and the worst things more vividly than the things in between. One of the happiest, and yet one of the most anxious moments that I experienced as a POW, was on September 21, 1944 while working on the airfield at Las Piñas.

The first attack that day began around noon. It's hard to remember how long the attacks lasted. After the fighters started their sweeps, our dive bombers arrived for their part in the melee. I would guess that this first attack lasted about an hour. Anyway, when the attack was over, we were called in, lined up, and marched back to our compound. For all practical purposes, our barracks were in ruins. The American pilots evidently thought the buildings housed Japanese military — strafed to pieces.

The next day, September 22, 1944, we went back out to work on the field, and I witnessed another attack on the Manila area. This attack incurred little opposition compared to the day before. The opposition that did occur came from anti-aircraft and Japanese ship small-caliber guns, which of course is bad enough.

During the second attack, we just stood out on the field and watched. After the attack was over, we were lined up and marched back to our compound again. We did not go back out to the field again, and on October 1st we were loaded on the *"Benjo, Maru."*

ALDRICH — After chow that night, too excited to sleep and pondering our fate, there was a brilliant flash of light — bright enough to light up the inside of the barracks. Seemed like five or ten minutes later our building was rocked by a gigantic explosion. It was either an ammunition dump or a ship loaded with high octane fuel.

We continued to work at the field after that first night. Several days later someone found a note from a guerrilla outfit and signed by an American officer. In essence, it said for us to divide ourselves into squads of ten and to wait their action as they planned to attack our camp guards.

But a day or so later, orders came to pack up and prepare to leave. By midday we were ready, and I was really upset because someone had stolen my canteen. I grabbed a tin can, about two-pint size, rectangular in shape with a round screw on cap, and filled it with water. We gathered on the parade ground in front of Watanabe's headquarters for a final *bango*.

After loading onto trucks, we were moved directly to Pier 7 down in Manila Bay. There was a very small ship tied up there, and it soon became evident this was for POW transportation to some other location.

Chapter 10

Japan by *Noto, Maru*

Transfer From Las Piñas

By the 21 September bombing, Addie and several Las Piñas men were already in Japan. They had fallen victim to the Japanese plans for POW transfer.

During the early summer of 1944, two things occurred to the Japanese authorities in Manila and Las Piñas. One was that MacArthur, who had begun his counteroffensive in the fall of 1942, was successful in his "island-hopping" strategy and was coming close to his March 1942 "I Shall Return" promise. Secondly, the airfield at Las Piñas was nearing completion, and the 800 laborers might be a liability. The ramifications were clear — close Las Piñas and other work details as soon as practical, and ship the prisoners to Japan. But why Japan?

The reasons, although obscure to many in 1944, are rather clear today. First, the Japanese had to save face. They could not afford freeing the prisoners to the approaching MacArthur. That would be psychological suicide. Besides, after all the suffering and torture the prisoners were subjected to in those 2¼ years since the fall of Bataan, it would be folly to leave witnesses behind who could eventually testify to the Japanese brutality. And finally, the Japanese simply needed these men to augment the work force back home which had been decimated by conscription.

In July, Addie and approximately 200 others, many of whom were ill, were shipped from Las Piñas to Bilibid to await transfer to Japan. The process of sending men to Japan was not pleasant. It was, to put it simply, inhumane. As many as 1,000 men were loaded like cattle into a hold, 40x60 feet, in Japanese freighters. That's less than 2½ square feet per man. Temperatures in the hold were well into the hundreds. Food, air, medicine, even the opportunity to relieve oneself — all were at a premium. Thus the term — "Hell Ships."

From July until December 1944, there were at least five separate shipments of men to Japan on these "Hell Ships." As the months of 1944 ticked away,

American submarines and planes began controlling the South China Sea, the
shipping link between the Philippines and Japan. The Japanese chose not to
mark the ships in some way that would designate them as carriers of prisoners
of war. Instead they loaded the POWs on unmarked ships, suitable targets for
the submarine packs and planes roaming below and above the seas looking for
Japanese supply convoys.

1944 Hell Ships

2 July 1944 — *Canadian Inventor* — Ship captured by Japanese — On 26
June approximately 1,200 prisoners had returned from the Davao Penal
Colony on Mindanao in the southern Philippines. Seven hundred were shipped
to Cabanatuan while 500 joined another 500 from Bilibid and Cabanatuan and
together they boarded the ship on 2 July. The next day they sailed but turned
back for unexplained reasons and sat in Manila Bay for 15 days until finally
sailing on 16 July. Addie's Notre Dame friend Motts Tonelli was on board.

They finally arrived in Japan on 1 September. Bad weather, submarine
evasion, and convoy problems delayed the *Canadian Inventor*. *Maru* in
Japanese means much the same as our putting SS before an American ship.
The prisoners refered to their Hell Ship as the "*Mati-mati, Maru.*" In
Japanese *mati* means "wait."

17 July 1944 — *Nissyo, Maru* — This ship contained 1,500 men, including
some from the Las Piñas detail. Addie's hometown friend Urban McVey and
Father Stanley Reilley were part of this group. The convoy containing the
Nissyo, Maru was attacked by American Naval Forces one night. Many ships
in the convoy were sunk, and it looked like the *Nissyo, Maru* might join the
others at the bottom of the China Sea. The sky was lit like daytime with the
fiery glow from burning tankers. When the Japs threw the hatch cover over the
hold, many panicked at the thought of imminent and sure death. Father Reilley
came to the rescue.

> URBAN McVEY — One night as we were packed in the hold of the
> ship he [Father Reilley] yelled, "Does anyone have a rosary?" He
> wanted to lead the men in the rosary that night. Well, I lent him mine
> that night and never got it back. After the war I tried to locate him
> back in the states, but I never got the right organization to get his
> address. He died a few years after he returned to the states.

The *Nissyo, Maru* arrived in Japan on 5 August.

1 October 1944 — *Haro, Maru* — Most remember this Hell Ship as the
"*Benjo, Maru.*" *Benjo* in Japanese means "toilet" and was coined to describe

the conditions and the smell emanating from the hold. Most of the Las Piñas men who witnessed the September bombing were on this ship. Thirty-nine of the 1,100 prisoners had died by the time the ship arrived in Formosa on 5 November. Jack Aldrich of the 200th CAC remembers the horrors of the *"Benjo, Maru"* voyage.

ALDRICH — Aldrich, Amos, and Argeanas were the first three in line as the names were called out from a roster on which we were apparently in alphabetical order. Walking up the gangplank the old foreboding feeling returned, and as we climbed down the long metal ladder to the floor of the hold, the metallic ring again formed around my tongue — abject fear — the taste of abject fear.

The bottom of the hold was covered with coal. As more and more people came down that ladder, we were pushed further back until the first three on the ship were standing in the farthest corner. Loading didn't stop until the hold was packed with everyone standing up. There was not room to sit down or lie down. The temperature shot up as the day wore on.

Soon everyone was dehydrated in the sweltering heat, and the water that had been carried on in canteens — can in my case — was exhausted. The damned ship lay at anchor for several days in the bay.

Water and food were almost nonexistent. Four five-gallon cans were lowered up and down from the hatch above, and these served as our latrines. Now and then a can of human waste would tip and shower those below with its contents. It was only natural then that the POWs called the ship *"Benjo, Maru,"* which in English translates to "Toilet Ship."

The water ration leveled off to about three tablespoons full each day. The food amounted to about ½ a canteen cup each meal. The rice was usually cooked to a watery gruel with a trace of vegetable now and then. Two meals a day if we were lucky.

Some few Americans worked above decks cooking and emptying the "honey buckets." Until the ship got under way, a couple of medical officers were allowed on deck to treat some extremely ill POWs there.

When the *"Benjo, Maru"* finally hauled anchor and began steaming out of the harbor, the rumor from the medics that had been on deck was that there were between 13 and 18 ships in our convoy.

We were to learn also the name of our vessel was *Haro, Maru*, but those who made this journey would forever call it *"Benjo."*

While the ship was under way a breath of fresh air could be captured occasionally because the hatch cover was left off. If the Japs determined the POWs in the hold were making too much noise, they would threaten to close the hatch.

Sergeants Amos, Argeanas, and I soon learned the bulkhead we were jammed up against was the separation between the hold and the boiler room. I devised a way to hook my blanket on the ship's siding and began sleeping there at night. Discovered an added bonus here — a plate had buckled on the ship's side, and I could observe the stars at night through this very narrow slit.

Later people began to drink the sea water that was sent back down into the hold in the latrine buckets. Guys who did this became absolutely insane at night and would leap around the hold, jumping on many people in the process, like animals belching a phosphorescent glow. I thanked God my blanket hammock was above and out of reach of these monsters. Someone, usually a person that had had enough, would beat these madmen into insensibility.

A few slashed their wrists and drank their own blood. These usually bled to death. There were one or two cases where a deranged guy would try to bite someone else's throat. The attempt would awaken the intended victim, and he would beat off the threat.

Strangely enough, this morbid activity did not happen during daylight hours. Those who had died in the night were passed down to the ladder, and someone there would ask permission to haul the body topside. The body was carried to the side and dumped into the sea.

After we had been at sea a few days, a pinging sound became evident at night. Sailors on board informed us the sound was good old U.S. Navy sonar, probably from submarines tracking the convoy.

Sure enough, it wasn't long until we heard explosions. The convoy was under submarine attack. People working up on deck were sent down into the hold, but they saw a large tanker and another vessel take torpedo hits. We learned later that night that the tanker had been hit because there was a huge explosion, and I saw the sky light up like day through the ruptured plate.

We heard other explosions on the voyage, but none so spectacular as that tanker. Yet the sonar pinging could be heard every night.

Inadequate food and water, coupled with inactivity, caused almost everyone to sink into a lethargic state. The violent activities of the crazies seemed to taper off at night, and the Chaplains seemed to contribute to the calm atmosphere by getting the entire detail to sing "God Bless America" every night. They told stories, prayed, and got people to help with the care of the sick.

Upon awakening one morning, discovery was made that the ship was not moving — no vibration — and the guys were talking in whispers. Scuttlebutt from above was that we were anchored in Hong Kong harbor.

After a short layover in Hong Kong and then a two month stay in Takao, Formosa, the men of the *"Benjo, Maru"* were put on another ship and arrived in Japan in January.

11 October 1944 — *Arisan, Maru* — Approximately 1,800 POWs were on the roster. In the late afternoon of 24 October, the ship was torpedoed by an American submarine with only eight men surviving.

12 December 1944 — *Oryoko, Maru* — In the most publicized of the Hell Ship experiences, 1,619 POWs descended into the hold of a relatively new and fast Japanese vessel, the *Oryoko, Maru*. Like the others before her, she was not marked in any way to indicate that she was carrying prisoners. On 14 December she was attacked by American Navy planes, with many prisoners being able to swim to shore and survive the sinking. These survivors were taken to Lingayen Gulf where they reluctantly boarded the *Brazil, Maru* which arrived in Formosa on 2 January 1945. Eventually, these survivors were placed on the *Enuri, Maru*, and they arrived in Japan on 29 January 1945, 48 days after they boarded the *Oryoko, Maru*. Only 500 of the 1,619, who started the voyage, arrived in Japan. About 100 were so weak from the trip that they died in the following weeks.

Shipment to Bilibid

But to Addie's good fortune he was not on any of the "Hell Ships." When Addie and the 200 Las Piñas prisoners were brought to Bilibid on 12 July, they found the compound teeming with men from Cabanatuan and various other details awaiting shipment on the *Nissyo, Maru*.

HARRY LISKOWSKY — Bilibid was a beehive of activity at that time, a desperate and franctic effort by the Japs to get all the able-bodied men to Japan. In fact, a ship had arrived from Singapore when I was waiting my departure. It was a horrible spectacle seeing these men brought to Bilibid from the ship. They were half dead, dehydrated, sick, and filthy. The stench of this large group could be smelled all over the camp in the tropical heat.

All prisoners were given a visual once-over to see if they looked healthy enough to survive the voyage and were capable of doing work in Japan. Bob Stewart of the 192nd tank outfit from Janesville was rejected because he appeared too thin. Addie, who had endured a number of illnesses at Las Piñas, was also rejected. Those who were not included on the *Nissyo, Maru* roster were sent to Cabanatuan.

Commander Thomas Hayes, a doctor, in the book *Bilibid Diary* described Addie and the rest of the new arrivals this way.

> HAYES DIARY — Over 400 human derelicts from Pasay [Nichols Field] and Las Piñas arrived on open trucks through a cold and miserable rain. They are an ugly mob of disorganized, degenerated, misdirected robots — reflex animals mostly. . . . All the men are sick with beriberi, pellagra, amoebic dysentery — you name it.

Addie was so ill that he was placed in the Bilibid Hospital. His illness was diagnosed as pellagra, which literally means "rough skin" and involves the gastrointestinal tract, the skin, and the nervous system. Symptoms include fatigue, listlessness, headache, loss of weight, loss of appetite, and general poor health. Those who saw Addie at the end of his stay at Las Piñas would attest that he had all of these. Its incidence is heightened during times of intense sunlight, which certainly describes the spring and summer months at Las Piñas, especially when one is walking around in nothing but a G-string. Besides that, since youth, Addie was never one to take even the Wisconsin sun very well. The Las Piñas diet did not supply the niacin necessary to combat the pellagra. Addie's hands blistered, and his arms became dry and scaly, not unlike what they looked like in his high school days when he was out in the sun. Nausea, vomiting, and diarrhea were common side effects. He was put in Ward 18B towards the back of the Bilibid compound and given daily doses of nicotinic acid for ten days. He was also treated with Paregoric to combat the vomiting and diarrhea.

During this 20-day stay he was reunited with his Stotsenberg pal Father John Duffy. The priest had recently been captured after many months as a guerrilla after escaping the Death March.

> FATHER DUFFY LETTER — 1947 — Adrian had been on a detail of POWs who were building an airfield south of Manila. I remember well when the trucks came into the prison bringing these POWs and one of the first persons I recognized was Adrian. He spotted me and gave me a cheerful salute. Came to rosary devotions that evening and afterwards we sat down by the little outside altar that was covered like a Japanese shrine and had a big talk. He was quite hopeful that at least the Americans were coming back and that we had a chance of being delivered from Oriental slavery.
>
> We talked about the fact that many of us would be killed, if not all of us, and that our position was very doubtful. We had quite a chatty talk

that night. We joked and kidded about the situation and we were really ready for any eventuality. Adrian had not been to confession for some time when he came in so he went to confession. There was no priest with the detail he had been on. He was at Mass every morning for the next ten days that we spent at Bilibid.

On 29 July the ten days were up, but Addie was diagnosed not to have recovered sufficiently from pellagra, so he was kept at Bilibid for ten more. On 8 August, he was found fit and was shipped back to Cabanatuan to join the other Las Piñas men who had been taken there on 17 July.

Preparing for the *Noto, Maru*

NORQUIST DIARY — Wednesday — 16 August 1944 — Well, 500 men will leave camp tomorrow to go to Japan — via Lingayen Gulf, it is said. The men are allowed to carry very little gear, just a blanket, mess gear and one suit of clothes plus very little else, I understand. A 15 day's supply of medicine and a medical staff go with us.

By 19 August, Addie and the others knew exactly who was going to Japan — the roster was made public. His final two days at Cabanatuan were filled with organizing what little personal property he had and in saying good-bye to his friends, especially the Chaplains.

NORQUIST DIARY — 21 August 1944 — At 2:15 a.m. we got up, dressed and drew rations for our journey to Japan on trucks. Before dawn we arrived at the village of Cabanatuan where at 6:00 a.m. we were crowded into box cars. . . . At about noon, we reached Manila and were taken to Bilibid prison. The place was crowded with thousands of men. There were 1400 in one building alone. There was a great deal of hustle and bustle with everyone getting ready for the sea journey which was said to be imminent.

With Bilibid jammed to the rafters with men, Addie and the other Cabanatuan arrivals spent their nights sleeping on the floor.

The men who made up the *Noto, Maru* roster came from four sources. One hundred fifty came from Bilibid, 517 from Cabanatuan, 345 from Clark Field, and 150 from Camp Murphy (Nielson Field) for a total of 1,162 men. Although the *Noto, Maru* held 1,035 men, extras were needed to fill in for those who became sick during the days before boarding the boat. A man whose name appeared on the list surrounded by two other POW names, usually had those same two names also surrounding his on the *Noto, Maru* list. For example, on the Cabanatuan roster of those who were leaving for Bilibid, Addie's name is surrounded by Alfred LeBeau and James Mathieson. On the roster of what men made up the *Noto, Maru* his name again appears between that of LeBeau and Mathieson.

But as "organized" as this transfer of men might seem, there were changes. In fact, from the original roster there were 38 changes. Many of these resulted from men being judged not healthy enough to withstand the rigors of the trip to Japan. Some changes, however, had nothing to do with illness.

CAPTAIN E. PEARCE FLEMING — Before coming to Bilibid I had been the Senior Officer at Clark Field for 19 or 20 months. About six or eight months before we left for Japan, an MP Captain was assigned to Clark Field, and he was certainly way senior to me. I believe he had been a Captain before the war. Now the Japanese refused to let him take over as the Senior American Officer at Clark, so I continued in that capacity. I don't think he stayed more than a month, and the Japs shipped him to Bilibid or Cabanatuan.

In any event, along comes Captain Charles Samson to Clark Field, who was also senior to me. So we went over to speak to the Japanese. They probably knew we were going to Japan in three or four months anyhow, so they said just leave things as they are.

When we got to Bilibid, here is another MP Captain [Charles Mueller], who is assigned as our Senior American Officer on our trip up North. I had known this man slightly before the war or during our captivity at Cabanatuan, and I wanted Captain Samson to be this Number One guy on the ship. He and I went to a Japanese Warrant Officer and, without the benefit of an interpreter, we succeeded in persuading him to take this other Captain off and putting "Sammy" in his place.

When we did this, we got people that we knew to fill the key positions of leadership. I was responsible for getting Sammy being changed over. All you had to do was tell the Jap Warrant Officer that the other guy was an MP. Japs didn't like MPs anymore than we did.

Some of the other changes in leadership included First Lieutenant Davis Kirk replacing Phillip Farley as Commander of Company One, First Lieutenant Peter Perkins replacing Second Lieutenant Charles Bennett as Commander of Company Two (Addie's company), and First Lieutenant Richard Pullen replacing Captain Samson as Commander of Company Five.

Most of the other changes, however, were legitimate. Some prisoners were simply too sick. Those with malaria or dysentery were judged too ill to withstand the trip. Floyd Meyer and August DeBauche from Wisconsin were two who were last minute replacements. Nearly all the replaced men were later shipped to Japan on 11 October 1944 on the *Arisan, Maru*, the freighter that had been sunk by an American submarine with the loss of all but eight men.

One of the men who was replaced, however, was not sent to Japan. That was Bill Garleb of the 31st Infantry. Bill returned from Davao on 26 June 1944 and was given the glass-rod exam for amoebic dysentery and found to be too ill to board the *Canadian Inventor*. He stayed in Bilibid until 17 July, when he was shipped to Cabanatuan. In August, he, Adrian, and 515 others were returned to Bilibid. Although on the original *Noto, Maru* roster, he wasn't sure if he wanted to go or not. He felt that General MacArthur was enough of an egomaniac to make good his "I will return" prophesy of 1942, and that his chances might be better if he stayed in the Philippines.

> BILL GARLEB — I was slated to go to Japan. Another man who was scheduled to stay wanted to go; I couldn't make up my mind because we had heard that the food was much better in Japan. But I had the feeling that MacArthur would retake the Philippines, and I would be liberated early, so the Sergeant said, "Garleb, if you don't make up your mind, I'm going to kick your ass." So I stayed. It saved my life.

Garleb was liberated at Bilibid on 4 February 1945 and was back in the states two months later.

Another who faced a similar situation was Captain Dan Golenternek, a young pediatrician from Beverly Hills. He had arrived in the Philippines shortly before the war broke out, only to find that most of the families he was to take care of had already been sent back to the states.

> DR. DAN GOLENTERNEK — Before our ship left, another medical officer, a guy by the name of Rivers or something that had to do with water, came up to me and said, "Look, I hear that you don't want to go to Japan, that you feel that the Yankees are coming soon." And I did feel that way.
>
> "Well, let's go and see if I can take your place and go to Japan, and you'll take my place and stay here."
>
> I thought about it, and finally I said, "You know I think I'll take the hand that's been dealt to me." So I stayed on the *Noto, Maru*. His ship, the *Oryoko, Maru*, was later sunk. He survived. I was not a swimmer, and I would have drowned. My feeling as I left was "*que sera sera.*"

The *Noto, Maru* was filled by five companies, approximately 200 men each. Company One was led by First Lieutenant Kirk, Company Two by First Lieutenant Peter Perkins, Company Three by First Lieutenant George Sense,

Company Four by Captain Fleming, and Company Five by First Lieutenant Richard Pullen. Within each company, the men were arranged in numerical order by rank and within a rank by alphabet. Although the bulk of the companies making up the *Noto, Maru* were Army, there were approximately 196 Navy and Marines, 11 civilians, (9 Americans, 1 Estonian, and 1 Norwegian) and 1 British sailor. In addition, there were 6 doctors, 20 medics, 2 Chaplains, and 1 interpreter — a total of 1,035 men.

Addie was in Company Two, number 210, and was the eighth highest ranking man in the 200-man group. In the few days before boarding the *Noto, Maru*, Addie and the others were busy making preparations for the journey.

> NORQUIST DIARY — 22 August 1944 — Up refreshed having slept on a concrete floor overnight — just my blanket under me and nothing else. I can sleep on anything now. Had lugao with grated coconut for breakfast. Had a shower. . . . Heard that on the sea journey we can have both hold and hand luggage. Money was pooled so that everybody could get something from the commissary. This is the best way to do it.
>
> 23 August 1944 — Got vitamins for breakfast. Men lined up for seconds on food this morning. There was considerable quantity left over after the first serving. Everyone got an extra share that wanted it. . . . had a clothing issue. Got trousers. Weather is fine and the men are in good spirits. We hear we sail tomorrow.

Addie was also busy getting ready for the trip, and along with the physical preparation, Addie also took care of the spiritual. Besides being reunited with Father Duffy at Bilibid, he also saw other Chaplains. After the War, Elmer Domroehs from Fond du Lac, Wisconsin, wrote Addie's parents and told them the night before the *Noto, Maru* trip, they spent the evening with a Chaplain from Fond du lac. Elmer was also on the *Noto, Maru*, and the priest was Father Mathias E. Zerfas, who was assigned to St. Marys in Fond du Lac. Father Zerfas and Father Duffy were part of the nine Catholic Chaplains assigned to the December 1944 *Oryoko, Maru* trip. Father Duffy was the only one of the Catholic Chaplains to survive that "Hell Ship."

But while the men busied themselves with the physical and spiritual preparation for the voyage, at least one man had been busy trying to insure that the American submarine packs would not hunt down the *Noto, Maru*.

> FLEMING — We got word to the guerrillas by Philippine Scouts — one in particular named Felippe Maningo. He was a Personnel Sergeant before the War, and the Battalion Commander promoted him to Second Lieutenant, and he survived O'Donnell. When they paroled

the Filipinos, after about 25,000 of them had died, he went back to his barrio around Stotsenberg [next to Clark Field]. A lot of my Scouts worked for the Japanese. It was the only way they could make money to eat. He was one of them. When they learned that I was one of the Senior Officers at Clark, I had many contacts with the guerrillas. The only one I trusted back and forth with information was Maningo.

We got information in rice bags. There was a woman in Manila named "High Pockets" — Clare Phillips. We would be told that in a certain bag of rice, there would be some information. I don't know if they marked the bag or what, but the Japs never figured it out. She usually knew things seven to ten days in advance. We knew we were leaving Clark and the ship was the *Noto, Maru*. I think we knew that about a week before we left Clark. We didn't know that there would be people from other camps. We assumed it would be Clark Field en masse being shipped. Unfortunately, that message never did get through to the submarine wolfpacks operating in the straits between North Luzon and Formosa. Several of the ships in our convoy were sunk on the way up there.

NORQUIST DIARY — 24 August 1944 — Lined up at noon. Went out of Bilibid at 3:00 a.m. through Manila. A few Filipinos smiled at us. Japanese were riding by in new-looking American cars. Our start turned out to be a false alarm. We returned to Bilibid.

Loading the Hell Ship

For whatever reason, the *Noto, Maru* was destined to leave the next day, 25 August. Whether there were problems getting the convoy together, fear of submarines or planes outside the entrance to Manila Bay, or the Japs needing more time to get the POW accommodations ready, no one knows for sure. But early the next morning the 1,035 prisoners lined up in their companies and again marched through the early dawn streets of Manila to the same pier that so many of them had arrived at in the Philippines just three or four years before.

NORQUIST DIARY — 25 August 1944 — Up at 3:00 a.m. After an early rice breakfast, off at dawn to the port area through Manila streets. Our ship is the *Noto, Maru*, 1,035 men crammed into a hold for cargo, 40 by 60. So crowded we couldn't all even sit down, much less lie down. Twelve men fainted with the heat in about an hour. Men could go only singly to the toilet, three holes and one urinal. Heat terrible. We are told it will be about a four day trip. Supper: pomelo, rice and radish-fish soup.

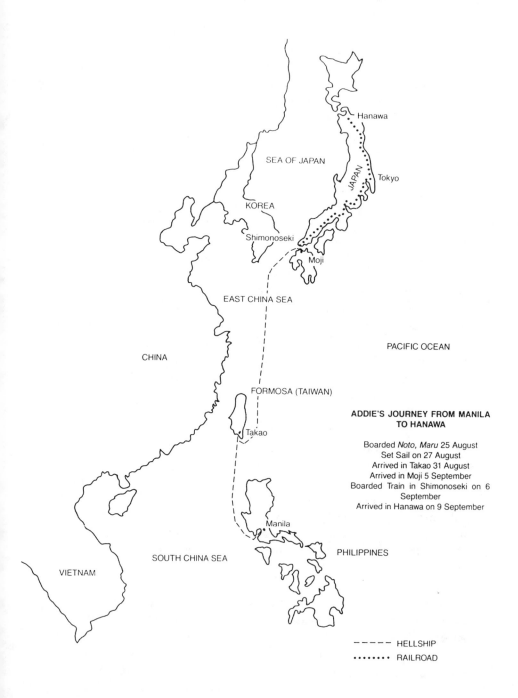

Hanawa

SEA OF JAPAN

JAPAN

Tokyo

KOREA

Shimonoseki

Moji

EAST CHINA SEA

PACIFIC OCEAN

CHINA

FORMOSA (TAIWAN)

**ADDIE'S JOURNEY FROM MANILA
TO HANAWA**

Takao

Boarded *Noto, Maru* 25 August
Set Sail on 27 August
Arrived in Takao 31 August
Arrived in Moji 5 September
Boarded Train in Shimonoseki on 6
September
Arrived in Hanawa on 9 September

Manila

PHILIPPINES

SOUTH CHINA SEA

VIETNAM

– – – – – HELLSHIP
• • • • • • • RAILROAD

COLE — I remember sitting in that terminal in Manila and looking up and seeing *Noto, Maru*, and I said I'm never going to forget that name.

STEWART — We were treated like animals. American farmers would not treat their cattle like we were treated on these Hell Ships.

DICK FRANCIES — I'll never forget it. My final impression of that trip can be expressed as a can full of slimy earthworms crowded into a small place. We were told to go down into the hold of the ship, forming straight lines. Then when all 1,035 of us were in the hold, they told us to sit down. That was to be where we would stay until we arrived in Japan. It was impossible to sit in a comfortable position. Arms, legs, and bodies were all interwoven. Toilet facilities were a large wooden tub in the center of the hole. When it was full, the Japs would use a winch and dump the contents overboard.

JOHNSTON — In my sitting spot in the hold there were some damp burlap bags. After I got situated, I started folding them for more padding. It was then I saw they were squirming with maggots. The heat was unbearable. To make matters worse, the night before we left, someone stole my canteen, my most precious possession, so I had to get along on a meager water ration — about one canteen cup per day.

After the *Noto, Maru* was loaded, it did not immediately leave Manila Bay. Possibly waiting for Japanese civilians to board, or waiting for other ships in the convoy to get ready, caused her to wait for about 24 hours before attempting to leave.

NORQUIST DIARY — 26 August 1944 — Barley in place of rice. Reminds me of Quaker Oats. Slept literally on top of each other. Cramped and hot last night. Had buckets at night for latrine. Breakfast this morning was rice and oats with a little sweetened water. Still lying in the bay. Our ship is a vessel of about 8,000 tons riding high with no cargo except us and some Japanese.
    27 August 1944 — We sweltered. Ship pulled out this morning. Water ration comes twice a day. Much noise and confusion.

Meantime Addie was wedged into the hold with the rest of Company Two. When he was told to sit down he found himself in the lap of Asbury Nix, a lanky Texan. Addie's *Noto, Maru* number was 210 while Asbury's was 219, which put them in close proximity.

ASBURY NIX — The *Noto, Maru* trip was my first encounter with a very short soldier named Martin, who sat in my lap because of the crowded conditions. We shared our canteens and our food. Because of the close proximity of each individual, there was nothing personal. Everything was shared with each other. I didn't know Martin before I got on the ship, and it was only by happenstance that we wound up in the same group of 200 men.

Depending on where you were in the tiny hold of the *Noto, Maru*, who you were with, and your physical and mental condition at the time determined your remembrances of those dark days on board.

DESIRE PELTIER — Real, restful sleep was out of the question due to the cramped conditions. The filth and squalor that existed still makes it seem like a long ago nightmare, and some may even have thought it an impossibility to ever clean ourselves completely.

GERALD STAUDENRAUS — I have some recollection of men fighting over water and hitting others with their canteen. I am sure that some almost lost their minds. I don't recall men dying but do remember passing bodies over heads, hand to hand, to the center for some air.

KIMBALL — Our sanitary facilities was a wooden tub about 2 feet high and 12 feet wide. When the tub was occupied you had to climb the ladder and use the one on the side of the ship.

The night before we boarded the ship, the Filipinos somehow gave us some coconuts and garlic. You can imagine the results. God, I can still smell that horrible stink and anybody down in that hold will never forget it.

A buddy of mine had to go, and the tub was really occupied, so he had to climb the ladder. All he had on was a G-string. He was climbing the ladder with one hand and trying to hold his other hand over his rectum, but human waste was squirting from him.

JOHNSTON — It was living hell below deck in the hold. Our latrine was a wooden tub, located in the center of the hold. A man using it had to step over other POWs to reach it. There was no toilet paper. The only way to clean our mess kits was wiping them out with a towel or article of clothing. The stench was overwhelming.

LISKOWSKY — It was sheer madness. A page out of Dante's *Inferno* couldn't describe the spectacle of humans sunk to the level of animals — painful memories of sickness, humiliation, living like animals in a cold, dark, rancid-smelling hold with filth, human excrement, sweating dirty bodies ready to scream in despair and anguish.

During the early portion of the voyage, the *Noto, Maru* was still in tropical waters. The heat in the hold was well into the hundreds, almost unbearable. Many passed out, while others tried to escape the intermingled mass of humanity and lack of air by stringing up a makeshift hammock in the hold.

JOE ZORZANELLO — Once they saw that the hold could hold all of us, they ordered us to sit down. We could only sit in each other's laps. This is when the heat exhaustion struck us. I was one of those that passed out. After I came to, I took the blanket I was carrying and strung it between the I-beams on the overhead of the hold. That helped ease the overcrowding. Others who had blankets and rope did the same.

GRAYFORD PAYNE — Each man had one GI blanket the Japs gave us for the trip and about three feet of small rope. The blanket was rolled and horsehoed around your shoulder slanted across the body. After the first day, I got a rope from a buddy and we hung a hammock [the blanket] from I-beams overhead and put a small man in it. Within a very short time there were hammocks everywhere. This was the best thing that happened the whole trip. The other men had room to sit down.

The first days of the voyage, especially those in the tropics and with the hatch cover nearly closed, were *hell*. Many passed out and some began to go out of their minds with the thought of death. Their thrashing around and screaming just added to an already impossible situation. One officer, First Lieutenant George Sense, found an effective way to keep those around him quiet.

NIX — Sense was a very large man — maybe 6′ 2″. During the voyage in the tropical weather when they closed the hatches, some people temporarily lost their minds for fear of suffocation, and in order to control them, Lieutenant Sense used one of these socks of soap, [usually tied to one's waist to avoid detection], to subdue an individual who became belligerent or lost control. Lieutenant Sense was also on Corregidor with me, and when we washed out mess gear, some of the guys would go and wash them in the sinks and any residue of rice would get in the traps in the drains. Lieutenant Sense put a sign up. "DO NOT wash your mess kits in the sink for if you do there will be a number 12 shoe in your backside." This was very effective.

FLEMING — We tried to maintain some semblance of discipline in order to avoid as much unpleasantness as we could, but we did have a few men that went out of their head. George Sense filled a sock with soap and mashed it up so it wouldn't hurt somebody. Occasionally, he would wop somebody with that sack of soap and that would calm them down some. It was something that you normally wouldn't do, but under the circumstances I think it was appropriate. When you took this soap and mashed it up, it became sort of a resilient substance. And as far as I know, we were the only ship going from Manila to Japan that year that didn't lose a man.

Danger in the South China Sea

By 28 August, the *Noto, Maru* was out in the South China Sea heading north toward Taiwan. Because most of the prisoner's time was spent in the hold, few had the opportunity to see how many ships were in the convoy. Initially, officers, medics, and occasionally a sick prisoner were allowed to come on deck.

The convoy consisted of seven or eight Japanese vessels: freighters, destroyers, a liner, and a gun boat. To avoid detection by the American submarines, the convoy followed a zigzag course after leaving Manila Bay on its way to Taiwan. But even with all the precautions, the convoy did not escape the submarines. By 31 August, the ship was anchored at Takao, Taiwan. On 1 September the *Noto, Maru* hoisted anchor and made the run to Japan. Sometime after leaving Manila Bay on the 28th and arriving in Takao, Formosa, on the 31st, American submarines came upon the convoy.

ARTERBURN — One time we heard planes during the trip and then those depth charges. We knew that if the Japs closed the hatch covers, we were going to be goners if we got hit. It was bad — damn right. It wasn't no picnic.

COLE — The Japs kept the hatch covers open, and by the way, that's important because on so many of the Hell Ships where the guys died, they kept the hatch closed. So we got some air. With the hatch open I could hear the Japs on the top deck a screamin' and hollerin'. They were pretty excited about something. Then pretty soon we could hear this thunder, and what it was. They were rollin' depth charges off the aft end of the ship because of our submarines. Believe it or not, I hoped to hell we got hit. Kill us all. Blow us sky high. Then pretty soon it calmed down.

Later they took us on deck and hosed us down. We were somewhere near Taiwan because I asked the Jap what those cliffs were off in the distance.

Several of the men, usually in groups of 10 or 20, were later taken on deck during the trip to be hosed down — a salt water bath. Many were covered with the filth and stench of diarrhea and vomit from the hold. Not everyone got on deck, however. Some didn't emerge from the hold until they landed at Moji. There appears to be no reason why some got on deck and others didn't, except for the fact that many who didn't were in Company One. These men were the first to descend into the hold and were the farthest from the hatch covers. In fact, in those early hours, when the heat was tremendous and air to breath was at a premium, many of those who passed out were from Company One. Of course many who got out were the officers and the medics and the men that were relatively close to the hatch cover. Robert Johnston faked passing out in order to get on deck for some fresh air.

JOHNSTON — At one point, I pretended to pass out, and I was hoisted on deck and washed off with the salt water hose. We were still in tropical seas, so that was a real treat — salt water and fresh air. I got to stay on deck two or three hours. I didn't want to make myself too obvious, so I just lay close to the hatch coaming, watching a Jap destroyer that was escorting the convoy. Saw only a couple of other ships, both freighters, but figured there were more.

Below deck, the medical staff of six doctors — Majors Ralph Artman and Calvin Jackson, Captains Max Bernstein, Adanto D'Amato, and Dan Golenternek, and First Lieutenant John Lamy — and 21 corpsmen were busy administering to the needs of the sick. Besides the usual problem of diarrhea, vomiting, malnutrition, and men passing out from the lack of air, the doctors also had to deal with the dreaded Guam blisters. Jack Sharp described those Guam blisters "as close to *hell* as I have ever been."

The two Catholic Chaplains on board, Father Albert Braun from New Mexico and Father Herman Baumann from Pennsylvania, moved around the men attending to the spiritual and emotional needs. Father Braun was from the 200th CAC, Addie's former outfit, and whenever possible Addie assisted him.

DR. CALVIN JACKSON — Both Chaplains were good friends. Father Braun was a Prince of Princes. He was a *real* Christian and tried to help his fellow man and often at his expense. We were friends until his death. I saw him frequently, and I'm not even Catholic.

After the *Noto, Maru's* run-in with the American subs, the Japs must have decided to let the ship go as fast as it could to Japan. The newly constructed ship, at least compared to the others in the convoy, was aptly described by prisoner Floyd Meyer: "That sucker could really fly." After leaving Taiwan on 1 September, the men on the ship spotted Japan on the 4th as she steamed up the edge of the island of Kyushu. By the 5th, the ship had arrived in the harbor at Moji, a major port at the northern end of Kyushu. As the ship lay at anchor on the 5th, Japanese doctors came on board to give the glass-rod dysentery test, looking for those with ameobic dysentery. Those with the illness were segregated. Finally on the 6th, the men were allowed to crawl out of the hold and leave the ship. Many recall how thankful they were to leave. Joe Zorzanello remembers the first thing he did was make a sincere thanks to God for surviving the *Noto, Maru*.

After reading the description of the 12-day voyage in the dark, cramped, and filthy hold of the *Noto, Maru*, it's somewhat ironic to read the following comment by M. K. Martin who had read of other Hell Ships.

M. KEITH MARTIN — My memory of our trip to Japan in the *Noto, Maru* was that it was a pleasure cruise compared to the hell times the other people experienced in the ships. At the time we didn't see how conditions could have been worse. We had it good considering.

On 6 September 1944, Addie and 1,034 other POWs had nothing to compare their trip to, but most thought their journey a hellish nightmare. Although no one died during the 12-day voyage, unlike the other 1944 Hell Ships, can a person's imagination conjure worse conditions if what was just described is today regarded as a "pleasure cruise?"

Since the end of the war a number of POWs have taken a vacation cruise. Often during quiet moments on deck looking out at the peaceful ocean, they have reflected on that 1944 voyage. On one cruise Captain Fleming, while lounging peacefully on deck, recalls thinking, "Well, no submarines are going to sink us, and the bell is going to ring soon for our fifth meal of the day."

After depositing the 1,035 prisoners at Moji in September, the *Noto, Maru* continued in the service of the Japanese military. On 1 November 1944, the *Noto, Maru* transported Japanese reinforcements and equipment from Manila to Leyte in an attempt to delay MacArthur's return to the Philippines. After the soldiers left the ship, as it lay anchored in Ormoc Bay on the evening of 2 November, workers made preparations to unload the trucks, horses, and ammunition. Suddenly the sky became filled with American B-24s from Morotai. One of the bombs disappeared down the smokestack of the *Noto, Maru*. Several explosions followed. Within the hour all the equipment and the *Noto, Maru* lay at the bottom of Caragara Harbor, a fact significant in the collapse of the Japanese defense of Leyte.

Unloading at Moji

After ten days on board the *Noto, Maru*, 1,035 men emerged from the hold into a new country filled with a kaleidoscope of unforgettable sights and sounds. The upcoming trip from Moji to the various Japanese camps offered vivid memories. Some recall the ferryboat ride to Shimonoseki, some the little box lunches served on the train, some the lush Honshu countryside, and some the efficient Japanese rail system. Everyone's story of what happened after they left the bowels of the *Noto, Maru* is a little different from the next prisoner's. As they stumbled away from the dock, no one knew for sure his final destination, but all knew they were now in Japan and that their hour of rescue had been set back by months, if not years.

NIX — We arrived in Moji, at which time we were screened and deloused. During the inspection at Moji in a big warehouse or open area, they made you lay all of your possessions on the open ground, and the Japanese would come through and they selected the items they wanted to confiscate. It may be a fountain pen. It may be anything that may have material benefit to them, or maybe no material benefit to them. We always looked to save soap because it was a very critical item. One way to avoid detection was to tie a bar of soap into two socks and then hang it in the crotch of our baggy-type trousers. The Japanese would never think to look in the crotch at least for hanging bags of soap. Another way of avoiding confiscation of items of value that you might want to keep was to wait until the inspection party had passed a line, and then subtly pass the item to that line, and then get it back after you are checked.

JOHNSTON — It was nice to get off that ship. On the dock was fresh water taps. I just drank my fill and then let it pour over my head. Guess that was the best water on earth.

MANASSE — It was an overcast day in the afternoon. We disembarked, and for the first time we found a hose with running water. We washed ourselves off, filled our canteens, and proceeded to an armory, where they said we would spend the night. We were fed. About two in the morning, however, they woke us up and marched us down to the docks. We went through what looked like a ship building area, and finally we came to the ferry. We got on, and it took only a very, very short time, and we were in Shimonoseki. We also marched quite a while to a railroad station, and all I remember about this railroad station was the numerous clocks. Precision was the Japanese rule, and the trains all arrived on time. Finally, one came into the station, stopped, and we were literally shoved into these cars, perhaps twice as many people per car as they would hold.

Of the over 60 men that I have interviewed who were on the *Noto, Maru*, most remember the trip from Moji to Shimonoseki, a distance of only a few miles by ferry boat. There is, however, a handful of *Noto, Maru* men and some from other Hell Ships who recall that they went under the strait through a tunnel much like the Holland Tunnel connecting New Jersey with New York. After getting to Shimonoseki, the prisoners were led to a rail station, where they boarded a train that took them north; they were dropped off at various camps along the way. Most thought there was no rhyme or reason as to where they would be getting off, but according to microfilm records of material recovered at Bilibid in 1945, there was a list of which men were going to which camp. By the time they completed the 550-mile trip to Tokyo, all but 500 were left off at various camps. The final 500, including Addie, boarded another train for the 300-mile journey to Hanawa in the mountains of northern Honshu.

Tokyo by Rail

Although some disagree as to what method they journeyed from Moji, they are unanimous in affirming that the train ride north and the food served were the best part of their travel to their Japanese camp.

COLE — We were put on a passenger train and started north on the island of Honshu. Many men got sick on the train ride because they drank the polluted water in the containers that were built into each car. When the fellows started getting sick from the water, we didn't drink any. The train stopped at various places on the way north to let various numbers of POWs off at different work details.

NIX — The train did not have enough room for everybody. Sometimes to get rest you had to get down underneath the seats on the floor of the train while others sat on the seats, or you kind of just laid in the aisles. This was usual for the Japanese because they pack the most into a train that they can get. The shades were pulled down over the windows, we were told, to protect us from the people who felt

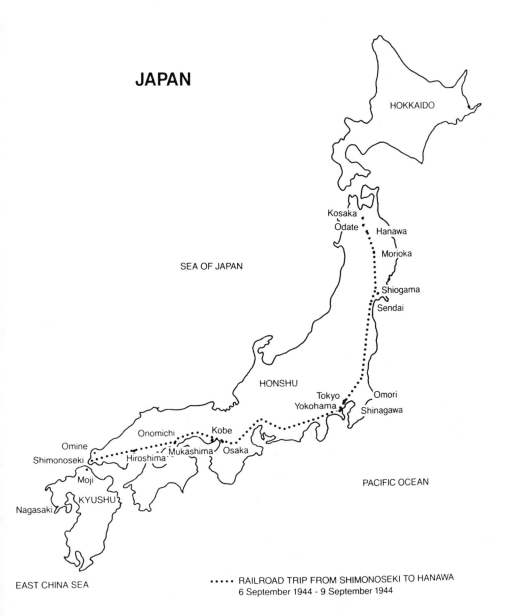

JAPAN

HOKKAIDO

Kosaka
Odate • Hanawa

Morioka

SEA OF JAPAN

Shiogama

Sendai

HONSHU

Tokyo Omori
Yokohama Shinagawa

Onomichi Kobe
Omine
Mukashima Osaka
Shimonoseki Hiroshima

PACIFIC OCEAN

Moji
KYUSHU

Nagasaki

EAST CHINA SEA

•••• RAILROAD TRIP FROM SHIMONOSEKI TO HANAWA
6 September 1944 - 9 September 1944

strongly about the Americans. We found the Japanese people more curious than antagonistic. Rations were given to us at preselected points, where a small box of rice, a sour cherry or pickled crab apple, or some piece of vegetable was given.

FLEMING — The Japanese countryside was absolutely beautiful. The thing that impressed me most, though, in riding through the countryside, was all the industry — hustle and bustle. Everybody was busy, and the thought ran through my mind that we had a long way to go to whip these folks.

RAY THRONEBERRY — All shades were drawn, and we we were not permitted to raise them. I remember getting a box lunch aboard the train, a box about four inches by four inches which contained a little rice, maybe some squid, and some seaweed. It was the best meal I had in Japan.

As the train carrying the prisoners continued northward, small details were left off. A group of 50 was deposited at Omine Machi, 25 miles from Shimonoseki, to mine coal. Already there were 200 British and an equal number of Americans there. Seventy-five miles later, the train passed through Hiroshima, where 11 months later the United States would drop the first atomic bomb. It does not appear that any prisoners were left off in Hiroshima, but approximately 30 miles later, a contingent of 100 was taken off the train at Onomichi at 3:00 a.m. on the morning of 7 September. A short time later they were transferred to their camp on the Island of Mukashima, a short distance away. With these larger detachments of men, one or sometimes two medical officers were assigned to accompany them. The rest of the men continued on to Tokyo.

NORQUIST DIARY — 7 September 1944 — Got off the train at about 3:00 a.m. and were marched to some sheds where we were allowed to wash up and rest awhile. There was a rumor that some of us would work on a farm run by some Swedes there. Presently we had our breakfast. We each got a box of rice and another box containing a pickle, a salted plum, a bit of fish, a piece of cucumber and a little dried seaweed. To that hungry mob, this breakfast was a feast.

At 10:30 a.m. we got into some old wooden coaches that resembled U.S. coaches of Abraham Lincoln's day. They had straight-backed, leather-covered seats. Before long we were on our way, bouncing and lurching over the narrow-gauged railway to Tokyo. I was surprised at the scenic beauty of southern Japan, I must admit. There were lofty mountains, fertile valleys and mighty rivers to look at. Every piece of available land seemed to be farmed and even on the hillsides, crops flourished in step-like terraces from top to bottom. In the valleys, the farms resembled the lush truck gardens of Washington and Oregon. We could see corn, potatoes, onions, cabbage, squash, sweet potatoes, barley, tea, eggplant, and even such delicacies as apples and pears growing. We thought to ourselves that we were going to like Japan after all, perhaps if we could get some of these fine things to eat. The small but tasty boxed lunches we had on the train gave us the same idea.

After leaving Onomichi on the 7th, the prisoners continued on a 125-mile ride through the lush countryside of southern Japan before coming to their next large city, Kobe. When one considers that 50 got off at Omine Machi, 100 at Onomichi for Mukashima, 100 at Tokyo for Omori, and the final 500 at Hanawa, that leaves 285 unaccounted for. It's reasonable to assume that sometime on the 7th, 285 were deposited at Kobe or Osaka which was 30 miles farther north. Neither microfilm nor subsequent interviews have provided conclusive evidence. Colonel Fleming feels strongly that the men were assigned to one of these two camps or possibly both. If Drs. Jackson and John Lamy were assigned to Hanawa, Dr. Golenternek originally to Omori, and Dr. Altman to Mukashima, it is again reasonable to assume that the final two doctors, Max Bernstein and Adanto D'Amato, were assigned to the large 275-man detail that possibly went to Kobe or Osaka.

After the train departed these two industrial centers, the men had a 150-mile ride before they saw the Pacific Coast. From there it was a 125-mile trek to Shinagawa, just south of Tokyo.

NORQUIST DIARY — 8 September 1944 — Had an excellent boxed breakfast of rice, soy, sweet potatoes, fish patty, squash, greens, tea, and ginger all in minute quantities. At 10:00 a.m. we saw the long, gray horizon of the Pacific and rode along near a sea wall. Mile posts, or should I say kilometer posts, told us the distance left to Tokyo.

The railway seemed to be very well kept up indeed with an excellent uniform right-of-way, automatic signal equipment, massive bridges and good rolling stock. A few of the locomotives were covered with a semi-streamlined shell. All of them as well as the freight cars, followed the European pattern. The latter had only four wheels each and had buffers at either end. Switchers were the tank type, having no tenders. They looked pretty old. Passenger locomotives were of the light Pacific type. There were some pretty substantial electric engines too. The passenger cars were all "American" having eight wheels, vestibules, and no buffers. Unfortunately for us the seats were too small, very hard, and straight backed. And we were now crowded 150 to a car which necessitated doubling up. [Reverend Norquist's hobby is collecting miniature train engines and cars and no doubt stems from his job during the college summers prior to graduation from the University of Minnesota in 1940. His job? A cook on the Great Northern Railway.]

As we approached Tokyo, we saw many sluices and stone-banked rivers leading to the sea. I saw a bamboo scarecrow with a straw hat in a field. He didn't look realistic enough to scare a crow. The tracks multiplied; so did the houses, factories, and other buildings we could see. Presently the train jerked to a halt and we stepped out and lined up on a concrete platform in Shinagawa Station. I should explain that only 100 of us got off. I don't know where the others went.

Norquist was in that group of 100 that went to Omori along with the Chaplains, Fathers Braun and Baumann. Also in the group was Dr. Golenternek. "Where did the others go?" Norquist asks. After ten terrible days in the hold of the *Noto, Maru*, the remaining POWs thought the train ride was a fantastic stroke of luck. Not in their wildest dreams did they imagine what was to come next — a visit to a Japanese tea room for food and relaxation.

COLE — They took us to a big tea garden. We had bottles of hot water, and they gave us a big lunch in a little box. That lunch and hot water were like heaven. We cleaned ourselves up. I had a razor and a blade I kept sharp with a piece of broken glass. Everybody was bathing. The tea garden had a fence around it, and the guards all stood around and laughed at us. We cleaned ourselves up, got rested, and then, "*Hayaku! Hayaku!*" [hurry, hurry] and we left and boarded a train and started north.

FLEMING — We eventually arrived at a suburb of Tokyo called Shinagawa. We were taken out of the railroad station and up the hill to a little tea garden. The mamasan and papasan were on the hill waiting for us. The Japanese people there were very kind to us. When I went back to Japan in 1946 [War Crimes Trials], I made it a point in going out there a couple of times to see the papasan and mamasan who ran the place. They made tea for us while we were waiting for the next train.

After leaving the unexpected hospitality of the tea garden, the men were taken by subway to the railroad station in Tokyo, where they boarded another train for the 300-mile trip to Hanawa. By now most were impressed with the efficiency and condition of the Tokyo subway and railroad system.

COLE — When we got to Tokyo, we were impressed with the elaborate subway system. They had an electric system in Tokyo that exceeded some of our electric systems back home. They took us to street level and marched us down the street, and the Japanese people would throw things at us, women would scream at us, and the old men would just stare. As we were marching down the street, that was when we saw evidence that confirmed for us that rumor we had heard that Doolittle had bombed Tokyo in April 1942. When we got on the train, you know how when you got on they got a spot for baggage, well, I got on the top rack, and this big Jap came over. It was strange to see him with a big overcoat on. But that year it started snowing early, and it was chilly.

Uphill Ride to Hanawa

After leaving Tokyo, the 500 remaining prisoners settled in for the final 400 miles to Hanawa. From the relatively warm weather and large cities of the first leg of their journey, the prisoners now saw the quiet countryside as they climbed the mountains to Hanawa.

MANASSE — When we left Tokyo there were 500 of us left, and on this particular train trip from Tokyo to Hanawa, it was quite comfortable because we all had a seat, and it was not that crowded.

FLEMING — That evening sometime we transferred to another train, and the following morning we were in Sendai. We passed through Sendai and went on to the town of Morioka. We stopped there for the better part of an hour. I believe they changed engines there to a steam engine instead of electric. There we branched off to a line that snaked up the hills and through some tunnels and down into the valley where Hanawa was located.

PELTIER — As we went north the temperature got cooler but not unbearable. As we had so recently lived in a tropical climate, we were not in physical condition to stand this change.

Finally their three-day train odyssey came to a halt. The men got off the train in Hanawa, a small town in the northern portion of Honshu. Hanawa is over 4,000 feet above sea level, 40 miles east of the Sea of Japan, 40 miles west of the Pacific Ocean, and 40 miles south of the northern tip of Honshu. The route the men took from Tokyo is practically the same route that today's Bullet Train takes.

FLEMING — Somewhere around 5:00 in the afternoon we arrived in Hanawa, which is the railroad station. From there we walked to the little town of Osarizawa. That was actually the little town we were in, where our prison camp was, but we've always referred to it as Hanawa, and I'm certainly not going to try and change that.

MANASSE — When we got to Hanawa, it was not raining. It was the end of the rainy season and a beautiful Indian summer day. In September and October it was quite pleasant.

After getting off the train in late afternoon, the men marched 1½ miles to the newly constructed camp that Joe Zorzanello recalled "had the sweet smell of pine." Many remember the first meal to taste something like potato soup. Unlike the low flatlands of Las Piñas, Addie found Hanawa set in a beautiful valley surrounded by majestic mountains.

DR. JACKSON DIARY — 9 September 1944 — We got off train in Hanawa about 4:00 p.m. Rainy and damp. A small town. We marched to a wooden enclosure, put in a wooden building. Each given a single silk covered mattress and a cottonfilled silk comforter. Capt. E. Pearce Fleming is the C.O. First Lt. R. T. Pullen is the asst. C.O.

COLE — The hills and mountains around Hanawa were just beautiful. It was like a National Park with fir trees. There was a mountain over here and a mountain over there, and you'd look closely and see a cable car between them.

Chapter 11

Hanawa

Camp Organization/Barracks Life

The Hanawa Camp that Addie and the final 500 *Noto, Maru* POWs wearily marched into was newly constructed. The camp was one of the many small northern Honshu camps governed by military authorities in Sendai. Hanawa is officially referred to as Sendai Camp-6B. Many of the prisoners on earlier Hell Ships were sent to camps in southern Honshu. Addie's group was one of the first to be sent to the mountains of northern Honshu. Hell Ships like the *Haro, Maru* furnished men for other northern Honshu camps like nearby Kosaka and Odate. Many of the friends that remained at Las Piñas when Addie left in July 1944 dotted the rosters of these camps.

The sites in these mountains were designated as mining camps. Some mined nickel, some coal, some lead. The men at Hanawa became copper miners. The mine was located approximately two miles northwest of the camp. The daily walk to the mine was uphill. Although the men were paid for their work, the Japanese believed that this slave labor would be more effective and less costly than bringing in civilians. There were few civilians because the bulk of the country's young work force had by now been conscripted for the war effort. The mine itself was reputed to be a very, very old mine that recently had been run by a British firm. When the War started, the Mitsubishi Corporation was in charge. But for the first day or two the men didn't report to the mine. More pressing was the need for getting the camp organized.

The Japanese Commander of the Camp was Lieutenant Asaka. The Sergeant of the Guard was Takahashi, the most popular of the guards. Most if not all of the Japanese guards were men who saw action in China and not the Philippines. Some were recovering from previous wounds. The American contingent at Hanawa was composed of four officers: Major Calvin G. Jackson, M.D.; Captain E. Pearce Fleming; First Lieutenant Richard T. Pullen; First Lieutenant John Lamy, M.D.; and 496 enlisted men — 379 Army, 75 Navy, and 46 Marines. Of the 379 Army personnel, approximately 50 were

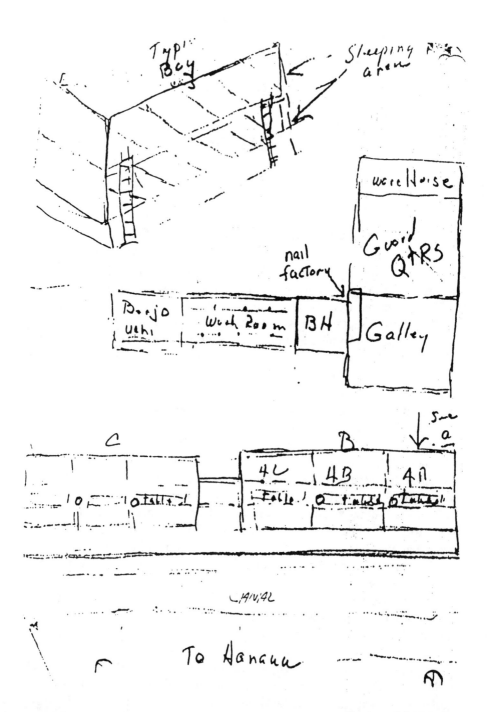

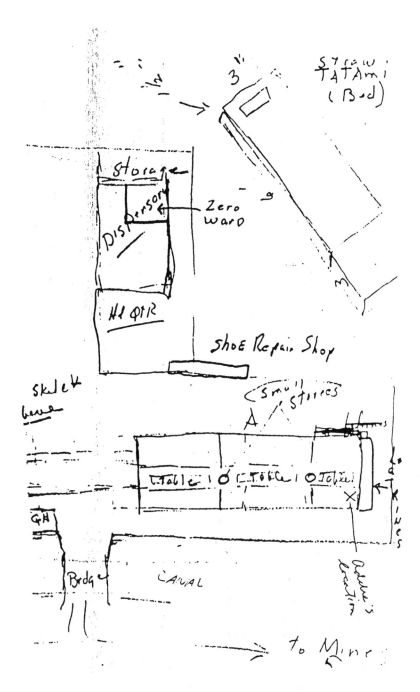

(Courtesy of Asbury Nix)

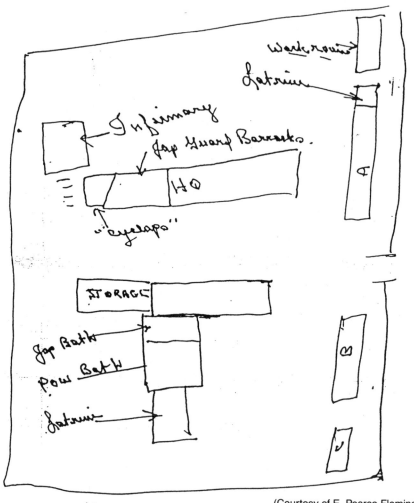

Work room
Latrine
Infirmary
Jap Guard Barracks.
HQ
"eyelaps"
STORAGE
Jap Bath
POW Bath
Latrine

(Courtesy of E. Pearce Fleming)

HANAWA

Pearce Fleming Diagram May, 1986

from Addie's original outfit: the 200th Coast Artillery Corps. Walter Schuette, who was inducted with Addie in March 1941 from Brown County, was also there.

One of the initial tasks confronting Captain Fleming, the Commanding Officer, was to arrange the men in the camp. First, POWs were given numbers from 1 to 500, according to rank and branch of service. These numbers were worn on the chest and on the front of the cap. Addie, being a First Sergeant, had a high ranking — #31.

After arranging them in order, the men were placed in work sections. Each section occupied one area of the barracks. They awoke together, ate together, and walked to and from work together. As time went on and the nasty winter set in, the men discovered that their circle of friends consisted of the few men in their section who ate, slept, and worked near them. Few got to know men in other sections or other barracks.

Some men believed the designation of what section they were in depended on their service record. Some believed the Japanese wanted those they hated the most, those who were "killers" during the war — Air Corps and Infantry — to be designated as miners, the most dangerous of mine jobs. Captain Fleming doesn't recall it quite that way. The sections were usually filled according to age and previous work experience.

> FLEMING — When we first arrived at Hanawa, there were several days before we went to work. One of the mine officials came down, and they were looking for certain skills. We were busily engaged in those first few days trying to find and isolate the talent that they wanted. We were trying our best to cooperate in the hopes of good treatment and food. I guess the last ones on the list were those with no skills. They were the ones who went underground.

Addie's section, 3A, consisted of approximately 32 prisoners. I say approximately because men were occasionally transferred from one section to another. Section 3A included many of the older men in camp and many of the Sergeants and First Sergeants. First Sergeant Emmanuel Hamburger, from Seattle, was a World War I veteran and 49 years old when he got to Hanawa. Many marveled at how he was able to survive the 3½ years of captivity. These men worked topside at the mine, a backbreaking but not necessarily dangerous job. The younger men, usually those with higher camp numbers, were sent to the more hazardous jobs in the mine.

The following information about the camp comes from a report about Hanawa written by John M. Gibbs in July 1946. He composed the report by reading accounts given by the released Hanawa men. The document is available through the American Ex-Prisoners of War Association. Although I have found a number of errors in the report, it does provide some interesting information:

Hanawa-Sendai 6

Size of the camp was 130'x325'. A 12' wood fence surrounds the installation and the entrance, or north end of the compound was flanked by a canal. . . .

The men were housed in 3 barracks measuring 20'x150' each, two of which were practically made into 1 building, and under a single roof, by being brought together end to end, with a communication

HANAWA 6

AREA DRAWN IS AS I REMEMBER.

BROKEN LINES INDICATE BUILDINGS OR
AREAS CONTINUE BUT I DO NOT RECALL HOW FAR
OR USES MADE OF AREA NOT INCLUDED.

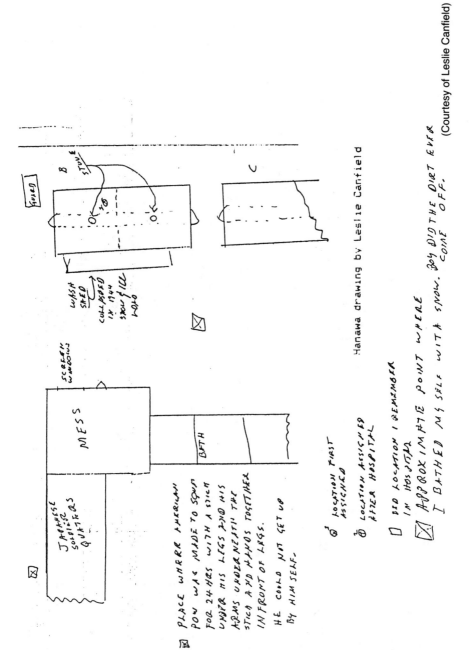

Hanawa drawing by Leslie Canfield

(Courtesy of Leslie Canfield)

The following four pictures are of Hanawa. They were sent to me by a former Hanawa prisoner, Crayton Burns of Portsmouth, Ohio. He believed the pictures were stolen from the Japanese by a fellow prisoner from New Mexico, who sent them to him after the war.

Front entrance to camp. Note the snow and mountains. Building in the foreground, right, is the shoe repair shop. The little building to the left is the latrine. To the left of the latrine is the barracks that Addie lived in — also the British and the American officers. To the left of Addie's barracks on the far left are other barracks, the second of the two just barely visible. Note that the small building jutting out toward the foreground is *Aeso* (jail).

covered passage way. The barracks were located at the north end of the compound. The 3 barracks were made communicable by a covered walkway on the outside. Sheltered outside paths connected the prisoner barracks with the Japanese administrative and sleeping quarters.

The barracks, adequately lighted, were constructed of wood with shingled wood roofs and packed dirt floors. They were very inadequately heated. The interior was of rough wood without sheathing on side walls or the 30' ceiling. Double-deck sleeping platforms lined either side of each of the 3 buildings into which straw sleeping mats had been placed.

Other buildings constituting prisoner facilities were 2 rectangular structures housing the hospital, first aid room, doctor's office and corpsman quarters. These buildings were connected at one end by two latrines. Another L-shaped structure contained the galley, a store

This is a propaganda photo. Men never had that much food. The bowls contain barley, which has little food value.

room, a bake shop, a prisoner bath, a wash room and a latrine. There were two latrines at the west end of one of the barracks.

Tables and benches were placed in the aisles of the barracks.

Three latrines, squat type, conveniently located, were adequate. The latrine buildings were floored with cement into which holes had been cut. Underneath were cement pits which were emptied about each 3 months.

For bathing two tubs of wood 12′ square and about 4′ deep constituted the bathing facilities. Each tub accommodated 6 to 8 prisoners simultaneously without a change of water. Hot water was available. The bathing facilities were augmented by 3 cold water taps.

The food was served in the barracks, therefore there was no mess hall. The mess was drawn from the galley in wood kegs by prisoner mess-men.

The hospital was located in a separate building which had been partitioned into 3 rooms, one of which was equipped with 20 wood bunks. The other 2 smaller rooms contained 5 wood bunks each. Heating facilties were poor and there was a persistent dearth of medicine. The heating unit was 1 stove. The only fuel available was what could be obtained by the prisoners, sometimes through unorthodox channels. The medical program was administered by a member of the Army Medical Corps under the jurisdiction of Japanese authorities. The doctors were assisted by 3 prisoner corpsmen. The Japanese medical officer would go through the form of examining the prisoners monthly, but no beneficial results followed these examinations. There were no bandages or sterilizing equipment; hence, the bandages were used over and over again in hope that they would not set up reinfection. Regardless of the physical condition of the prisoners, only a fixed number of them would be released from work.

Addie was assigned to the barracks to the right as one enters camp. Section 3A occupied the far end of the barracks. Addie slept in the second tier of the northwest section of the barracks. Each little sleeping bay held approximately

A prisoner, an unnamed sailor, dances on a table. In middle of the picture is a phonograph. Note the sign, "Take Off Hands."

These are the men of work group 3B. Addie's work group, 3A, would be in the background. Note the two-tiered *tutamis* for sleeping.

four men. His bunk mates were Solly Manasse from Las Cruces, New Mexico; Marvin Shearwood from Goodman, Missouri; and Willbourn "Lucky" Lacewell from Vienna, Illinois. Although he was only in the barracks for a few months before becoming a permanent resident of the "camp hospital," many recall his time in the barracks. Bob Stewart from Janesville remembers his walk, the short quick steps like he was always in a hurry. Bob also recalls that in the barracks was another Martin, M. K. Martin from Oregon, who was much bigger than Addie. The barracks called M.K. Martin, "Big Martin," and Addie, "Little Martin." Bob and Dick Taylor from Ohio as well as others recall Addie's hacking cough during the night, the onset of tuberculosis. Some originally thought it at first to be smoker's cough.

After the war, M. K. Martin initiated a lawsuit against the Japanese government for $46,880.00. Although the suit was never successful, its contents shed some light on barracks life in 3A at Hanawa.

MARTIN LAWSUIT — The living conditions in the barracks were deplorable. Our bedding consisted of one thin pad and five Japanese blankets, all of which were about five and one-half feet in length

[Martin is over six foot tall]. There was no running water; the toilets were a group of stalls built over a straddle trench in the end of each building with only a thin partition to separate them from the main barracks. The maggots, flies, and rats overran the place, and the stench from the toilets made living in this barracks acutely miserable. There were five heating stoves [in the barracks] and in this entire eight-month period of intense cold, our barracks was issued 12 kilos or about 24 lbs. of fuel. With this exception, all of the fuel used in these stoves had to be stolen in the mine, concealed on our persons, and carried into the camp. My group obtained sufficient fuel in this fashion to keep a fire in one stove for approximately one hour each morning and two hours each evening.

Life in barracks B and C was similar to life in barracks A. For a variety of reasons, few POWs were able to visit the other barracks to compare living conditions.

GRADY STANLEY — Our barracks were wooden buildings with small windows at the top. The walls were not insulated. A barn-like structure with a dirt floor. The sleeping bay was double-decked and made out of woven straw with a small ladder to get up to the top part.

GRANVILLE PREWETT — Beds? None! We had inlaid grass mats to sleep on. Fleas? Many!!

ART TRONESS — When they brought the rice and soup to our section at night, we'd set out our mess kit and canteen cup and someone would ladle it out. We'd stand around and watch with great interest to make sure it was even.

ZORZANELLO — Barracks life from September to May was dull because the barracks were cold, except for the brief period at meal time when the little sheet metal stoves were lighted. Conversation was the main form of recreation, and there was some visiting back and forth. In the main, we lay on our bunks and carried on our conversations from there. One outlet for our frustrations was our cursing the fleas. They were easier cursed than killed because they had such a hard shell. Sundays were usually spent in camp, and they were more relaxed, and we were more sociable.

The officers also lived in Barracks A, like Addie, but they were in the section right next to the main gate. With only four people in their section, there was initially plenty of room. This changed, however, in March 1945 when Lieutenant Colonel Arthur J. Walker (USA), First Lieutenant R. H. Thompson (Australia), and Captain I. C. Spotte (USA) arrived, and then again in May when 50 British were brought to the camp. Walker had been shot down during the war, and because he outranked Colonel Fleming, he became the number one ranking American in camp.

Work at the Copper Mine

Besides having larger living quarters than the enlisted men, the officers also weren't required to report to the mine for work. Captain Fleming recalls that this presented a problem.

> FLEMING — The Japanese initially told me that I would have to go to the mine. I said, "Nope. I'm not going to the mine." Then Lieutenant Pullen sort of undercut me a little bit. He was a graduate chemical engineer and spoke pretty good Japanese. So one day he went up to the Japanese and spoke to Lieutenant Asaka, I believe, or maybe it was Takahashi, and he signed up for a job in the chemical lab up there. This concerned me because under the Geneva Protocol of Warfare, I believe, the only work officers are required to do is work in the garden. I only went to the mine a half dozen times. The work was pretty rough. It was an all uphill walk to the mine. This mine was reputed to be some 2,000 years old and had miles and miles of tunnels. As a general rule, the armed guards, Japanese soldiers, went to the mine but in a reduced number because they had these civilian honchos, as we called them, who were in charge of each group.

Each day the men would have *tenko* in the area between the two barracks and then filed out the gate with their mess kit filled with lunch and march the approximately two miles up the mountain in a northwesterly direction to the mine. For many the walk to and from the mine provided numerous memories.

> FRANCIES — In the fall as we walked to the mine, we noticed 10 to 12 foot poles in the ground with a pole laying across them at the top. We asked what that was all about. The Japs told us that in the winter time, as we walked to the mine, we would hold on to that pole across the top of all the other poles. Snow at that point would be about 10 feet deep. At the mine we noticed all the buildings were connected by tunnels on top of the ground. We asked, "Why the tunnels?" We were told that in the winter time it snowed so much that they had to put tunnels over the train tracks, so the trains could get from building to building.

Despite the struggle with the snow that began to fall in late October, there were other sights on the daily walk to the mine.

> CANFIELD — If you allowed yourself to ignore the fact that you were a prisoner, the countryside and the walk to the mine weren't too bad. There was a school on the way up to the mine. I believe it was on the left-hand side of the roadway. It seems to me the road curved just past the school. I remember the little Japanese children staring at us as if we were part of a circus passing by. They all were carrying little wooden guns and in uniform.

The work schedule usually called for the men to rise around 5:00 a.m. and eat a breakfast of rice, barley, *lugao*, or millet. They would assemble in the area between the two barracks and march with their section up to the mine. They were usually accompanied by camp guards, who would turn them over to civilian honchos at the mine. At the day's end, usually around 5:00 p.m., the guards would come back to the mine and return the prisoners to the camp. This regimen was followed Monday through Saturday.

> M. K. MARTIN LAWSUIT — At Hanawa our day began at 5:00 a.m., at which time we had breakfast. Breakfast consisted of 400 grams of cooked grain and about one-half pint of soup. The grain ration was about a third rice and two thirds rolled barley or millet or soy beans. At 5:45 a.m. we left for the mine, arriving there at approximately 7:00 a.m., where we worked continuously until 5:00 p.m. with 30 minutes allowed for lunch. We were then returned to the barracks for supper.

Sunday was a day off. The Japanese, however, usually found a chore or two for the men to "enjoy" on Sundays. Sometimes the men worked in the vegetable garden located just south of camp. Another chore early in their stay at Hanawa was collecting grasshoppers.

> MANASSE — One Sunday we were taken out to pick up grasshoppers and shove them in boxes. We had one box for ten people, and when we filled them up, we were taken back into camp, where we were taken by the kitchen, and we dropped all the grasshoppers into boiling water. They dried them out, and we had them in our rice the following day.

> STAUDENRAUS — The grasshoppers were boiled quite crisp in sugar water and then mixed with the millet.

FLEMING — I recall that they toasted the grasshoppers in soy sauce, and it seems to me we had some sugar on them, but they were delicious. You just had to make the legs go down the right way.

Not everybody shared the culinary enthusiasm of Captain Fleming.

FRANCIES — We knew the grasshoppers were a delicacy for the Japs, so we caught all we could. Then when we got back into the compound, the Japs took part of the boxes we had put the grasshoppers in and said, "Here is your meat ration for the week."

The Japs had to show the cooks how to cook them in a huge, round, iron pot, three to four feet in diameter, on top of a huge stove. The pot was filled to the top with water and brought to a boil. Then the cooks stood over the top of the pot and dumped the boxes of grasshoppers into the boiling water. The grasshoppers turned red like a lobster. Then they were scooped out of the pot and mixed in with the rice. I ate three of them. Then I decided I didn't need any meat that week. Did you ever take a toothpick and chew it for a while? That's just what grasshoppers taste like.

Although some didn't relish these fall afternoon food hunts, all would take that duty over work at the mine. The work was long, strenuous, and back-breaking — the type of work Addie liked to avoid in his youth when he was healthy. Coupled with inadequate diet and three years of prison life, it was impossible for the prisoners to do the job the Japanese wanted. Whereas at Las Piñas the men toiled in a warm, tropical climate, at Hanawa they worked in the cold. This change in temperatures created havoc with Addie's already weak condition, and he didn't last long working at the mine.

The men in Addie's barracks, 3A and 3B, worked topside above ground. Others in Section 2 and Sections 4A and 4B worked in the blacksmith and electrical shop or in the smelter. Most of the others worked in the mine extracting copper, a necessary mineral for the war effort. According to the *American Ex-Prisoners' of War Report*, the men were paid ten to fifteen yen per day. Most never saw the money.

AMERICAN EX-PRISONERS OF WAR REPORT — The enlisted men worked in the copper mine and the smelting plant near the camp. Details were selected to work in the machine, blacksmith, and electrical shops. The prisoners working in the mines frequently were standing in water. The ore was broken up by use of sledge hammers and very large deposits required dynamiting to enable handling and loading in the mine cars. The work was dangerous, the lighting was poor and there were very few safety contrivances in the mine. The prisoners worked under the direction of civilian foremen who were claimed to be more brutal in their treatment of the men than military bosses.

RICHARD TAYLOR — I know Addie had been working with us up there at the mine before he went into the hospital. He didn't work topside very long. We were getting rid of waste sand on a conveyor. Addie was a real nice person, not too big, but a mild person. Solly Manasse was that way too. He never caused any trouble. Solly never shirked one bit on any of his work. He was fun to work with. If Addie hadn't had that TB problem, we'd have been close too.

LAWRENCE VAN LIERE — Dick Taylor and I would conceal pieces of wood to burn in our barracks pot belly stove. We stashed the wood in the overhead over our top bunk. Topside was the coldest, most miserable job at the mine. I had no feeling in my feet all winter. We huddled around a little stove on our breaks. They gave us some coal which would not burn. We sneaked gobs of grease, which turned the stove beet red as it burned. The Japs could never understand how we got such good heat from that damn coal.

CANFIELD — I worked as a millwright topside at the mine. The millwright's group worked with the roller crushers and the ball mills. They also had their hand in the care of the conveyor belts and the bubble tanks. The conveyor belts were made by Goodyear, complete with their logo. The mine ran out of the large size belts just before the end of the War. Everytime the conveyor belt split, it would shut down a large part of the copper reclaiming process.

FRANCIES — In the winter time it was extremely cold in our work location. They gave us a small wood stove that didn't throw much heat. So good old Yankee ingenuity made improvements on the wood stove. We found some coke. Then we took one of the air hoses that went into the floatation machine and put it in a hole at the bottom of the wood stove. The air turned that coke red hot, which in turn turned the stove red. We had plenty of heat then. The Japs were amazed. They had never thought of anything like that.

ZORZANELLO — I was one of the luckier ones. I worked in the electrical shop rewinding motors. It was a small group.

Deep in the Mine

DON BERGER — I worked underground at about 500 feet. I think it may have been deeper. Actually, it was warmer working below than topside unless you worked in the smelter, which I did for a few months until the end. The safety features on the mine tunnels and the dangers from the blasting were terrible — rickety cars, bad tracks, cave-ins or slides. The Jap foreman would even steal our ration, little as it was!

STAUDENRAUS — Cecil Ammons was our work detail leader — nice fellow. In the morning we had a mess kit of millet for breakfast, and those who worked in the mine would get a mess kit full to eat on noon time break. A civilian Jap would then guide our detail to and from the mine. He was quiet and courteous and never gave us any problem. We worked deep in the mine, and after arriving at our station, we would stash our mess kits and outer clothing. Two men would then be assigned to a tunnel. Each had a diamond-shaped hoe and shaped dust pan with handles, whereby we filled the ore cars. Then we pushed them to the dump tunnel. We had to get five loads in the morning and five in the afternoon. During the winter, we always looked forward to going to the mine just to get warm. Some tunnels we worked were cold, wet, and drippy with an inch of water. Others were dry and warm.

PELTIER — I worked as a miner. The work was extremely hard and backbreaking and as we worked on a quota system, the result was often long hours. The civilians, as a whole were decent; however, most of the foremen were on the cruel side.

POW Clothing

NIX — When we arrived in Japan, we were issued one overcoat, which was an English Army overcoat which had been taken in the capture of Singapore or Hong Kong. That was only permitted to be worn to and from the mine. Once you got to the mine, you had to put it in the storage area, and you worked in your uniform of a sort. It was made out of burlap and dyed a rather dark green. Anything that you added on to that was anything you happened to have. You wore all of your clothes so to speak. Shoes were Japanese issue shoes, similar to a tennis shoe that we wear today, except that it doesn't have laces. You slid it on from the back, and you fasten the snaps on the side of that, and that was your shoe. Your socks were whatever you had. I got the largest pair of shoes I could get, because I had two dental face towels, which I would use as socks. I would put them over my feet, and then I could stuff the extra part of the shoe, and that way my feet stayed fairly warm. It was warmer than one would think as long as you could keep the shoe dry. It was better than the leather boots that we had. I remember I made the mistake one day of wearing leather boots. I thought I'd be smart and save on my other shoes, but my feet froze the entire day. I never wore the leather boots again.

FLEMING — One of the things I remember about the winter of '45 was the shoes that they issued. These were straw shoes that came up well above the ankle. They were great for walking in the snow, but when you went into the mine to work, you wore them out in a hurry. I don't think we ever got it through to the Japs that we needed to carry leather shoes with us and then change shoes when we got to the mine.

Trying to Find a Decent Meal

As in the Phillippines, food was uppermost in the minds of the prisoners. Many had heard the rumor at Bilibid that they would find more food in front of them in Japan. Nothing could have been further from the truth at Hanawa.

AMERICAN EX-PRISONERS OF WAR REPORT ON HANAWA — The food was prepared by American prisoners in large iron cauldrons. Rice, of course, was the staple article of diet. The prisoners who worked in the mines were allowed 625 grams per man per day of grain-rice and barley. The sick prisoners were allowed 500 grams per man per day. On occasions all the prisoners were given soup made from vegetables and meat. At other times putrid fish were served. Whenever meat and/or fish were served the staple items were reduced to the calorific content of these diversions. On this diet the average lbs in weight lost per man was approximately 25 lbs in a little less than a year. The quality of all the items of food except the fish, was not complained of, although the lack of seasoning in cooking the food was mentioned by some of the prisoners.

The Mess Sergeant for most of the time at Hanawa was First Sergeant James Scruggs of West Monroe, Louisiana. He was assisted by David Van Hook from Nebraska, Al Protz from Wisconsin, Joe Merritt and Emerson Milliken from Michigan, and a few others. Theirs was the unenviable job of getting enough calories into the men to keep them alive and, at the same time, keeping the Japanese superiors happy by not using too much food.

JIM SCRUGGS — I was the Mess Sergeant when we first arrived at Hanawa. I was in charge when the men brought all those grasshoppers in. Rice was our staple product and everybody almost to a man was served the same diet. In the mess hall the cooks got to eat the scrapings, and because they didn't have to work in the mine, they maintained their weight better. The physical aspect of the mine work was greater than that on the mess hall people. We didn't have to walk to the mine and back like they did. This Japanese guard who was the direct overseer of the kitchen was the most sadistic person we had at Hanawa . I am very aware of his sadistic nature as he threw me over the semi-cemented floor on quite a few occasions.

ARTERBURN — We didn't eat much rice. I guess we got rice for the first week. Then we went on barley, and then we went on millet. You know what millet is? Chicken feed. Then they had us go and catch grasshoppers for our rice. The Japs, though, were just as hungry as we were.

JOHNSTON — At evening we had a small bowl of rice, three quarters of a canteen of soup. Sometimes it was a boiled radish soup and sometimes fish head soup. We had no meat, no sugar, very little salt but sometimes a few boiled greens.

FLEMING — In the fall and in the beginning of the spring, there was a garden that we worked in, maybe a half mile up the mountain on sort of a plateau. We had to lug honey buckets up there, and we planted radishes, cabbage, and beans. And I'll say this, those vegetables really grow with human excrement on it. I don't recall if we ever harvested any of it. During those weeks when the weather was permissible, the troops would work in the mine for six days, and on the seventh they worked in the garden.

FRANCIES — We ate our meals right where we slept. A number of times we would, as a group, go to one of the underground storage caves and bring back vegetables. I wasn't in a position to steal food. If I had been in that position, I would have stolen the food.

Many others were in positions to steal and were successful. Some were very open in their stealing while others were rather clandestine. Most shared their contraband with fellow prisoners, but all believed anything that belonged to the Japanese was fair game.

JAMES EMANUEL — I know some guys were going out through a hole in the fence and stealing radishes. The Jap civilians would have them hanging outside, kind of like in cold storage, and the Camp Commander got us together and said, "Now, look! These people are having a hard time getting food, too, so let's stop stealing theirs from them."

FLEMING — Some of our men, one named [Douglas] Brown from New Mexico and another named [Lee] Williamson from Oklahoma were designated as orderlies for the Japanese. They actually slept in a little nook by the mess, where they had a stove, and they were in high cotton. Every once in a while, they were able to steal something from the Japs. I recall getting an apple that way.

MERRILL RIDDLE — About March of 1945 my buddy, Noble Dudley, from Section 3B, and I stole quietly out of the barracks, past two guards asleep, at 2:00 a.m. In a snow storm we managed to break into the Jap store room and stole a 125-pound bag of rice. With difficulty we got it back into the barracks and placed it behind the pine boards where we slept. Our plan was to cook a portion each day, as we were allowed to boil water in small containers on the coal burning stove when we were lucky enough to scrounge a little coal. About the second or third day, a person in our barracks reported us to the Barracks' Officer, who as I recall was a Captain. I guess he feared the well-being of the rest of the men, so he took us down to the Japanese headquarters. The officer slapped us around for a while, verbally admonished us, and put us into the solitary confinement cell. I can't say I was bitter, but I felt scared and shocked that the Captain took us to the Jap Headquarters. I guess he was fearful that the Japs might punish the other men in camp as Japs were great to use mass punishment tactics.

Another time during work operations one day, word got around that a pure vegetable-type oil was in the shop. We located a five-gallon can sitting on the floor near one of the machine lathes. At great risk a number of us on different occasions sneaked over and put some in smaller containers. The oil was a salvation. Putting it over our rice ration made it very tasty and healthy to our diet.

PAYNE — One of my buddies come up with the idea that we should steal a sack of rice from the Jap warehouse, and we would have extra rice for a few days. We three talked it over, and myself and the other said it was too much of a risk, plus the penalty was death. I thought this was behind us; however, this buddy found himself another helper. They got the rice. It was snowing, wind blowing hard, and my buddy lost his cap [which had his prisoner number on it]. They could not stop to get it until they hid the rice — buried it in a snow bank near the rear of our barracks. Then he went to get his cap, and the guard caught him. The guard hit him over the head, which almost broke. The guard made him stand in front of the guard house for about 30 minutes. While the guard was refueling the fire, my buddy ran off. He came in, woke me up telling his story. Well, needless to say, I was not happy with the deed, but now I must try to save his life. We were almost the same size, so we traded caps and jackets. By that time, the guards had everybody up looking for the escaped man. They would call his number, and I would step forward. The guard would look at me and say, "You're not the one, no way." This went on for an hour. Lieutenant Asaka lost his temper, slapped the guard, and sent us off to work.

Like so many of the other remembrances of Japan, some of the men don't recall ever seeing an apple while in Hanawa, while others have very vivid recollections. Some recall getting an apple issue at Christmas, some recall pilfering them off a nearby tree, some trading for them at the mine, while others remember being in the right place at the right time.

TRONESS — One Sunday everyone jumped up saying, "I smell apples!" We ran outside and there was a cart of apples 50 yards away. We each got one.

As in the Philippines, Hanawa had a warehouse of Red Cross packages. And, as in the Philippines, the Japanese were reluctant to let the prisoners have the contents. When the men were given a package, they found the Japanese had already taken many of the items. Nevertheless, the Red Cross packages were extremely beneficial to the prisoners' health. The *American Ex-Prisoners of War Report on Hanawa* states that five Red Cross parcels were given to each man during his year at the camp.

FLEMING — There were a number of Red Cross boxes in the storage house and I tried to get Asaka to release them to us. He said, "No. We are saving that. We might have a bad winter. We are saving them for a rainy day."

I had the interpreter there at the time, and I said, "Tell him it's not only raining, but we got a storm going here." Our men were getting weaker, and I believe that if we had stayed there another winter, we probably would have lost another 50 men. Supposedly there were enough Red Cross packages shipped for each man to get one a week. I received 11 during the entire POW experience, and that was about average. Enough for one per week and I got eleven over a 3½ year period. The Japs took their "kumshaw" off at various levels, and we got what was left.

After three years of gradual starvation, it was no wonder that food was all the prisoners thought about 24 hours a day. Some even went as far as writing recipes or elaborate menus.

STEWART — This is Big Martin's birthday menu as I had copied it in Hanawa in August of 1945. This Martin was a chow hound — that is he was continually talking about food and drove us crazy with some of his menus. This is a good example. This was to be his first birthday menu after he got home. It seems he had a menu for every occasion.

BIRTHDAY MENU

Breakfast
Fruit, juice, oatmeal, bran muffins, Canadian bacon, fried eggs, fried potatoes, chocolate, toast, buckwheat cakes, creamed country sausage, maple syrup, jam, butter, coffee, cream, cream cheese, cigarettes.

Dinner
Fruit cocktail, cream of tomato soup, Swiss steak à la Martin-natural gravy, baked potato au gratin, creamed cauliflower, string beans — fried, sea food and vegetable salad, hot biscuits, whole wheat bread, pie, cheese, coffee, jelly, pickles, olives, celery, butter, honey.

Supper
Oyster stew, consommé, baked stuffed salmon, scalloped potatoes, creamed carrots and peas, buttered beets, mashed potatoes, salad, sliced tomatoes, cucumbers, onions, hot rolls, bread, angel food cake, frozen fruit custard, ice cream, salted nuts, "niblets," wine.

I have often wondered if he ever at any time after liberation had such a menu for the complete day. Many of us talked about the strangest things we were going to do when we reached the States.

M. K. MARTIN — As for those menus, as soon as I started eating good old U.S.-of-A. food again, I forgot all about such extravagant meals and concentrated on steak and eggs.

An Unbelievable Winter

One of the biggest challenges the prisoners faced was the severe weather conditions. In the Philippines the prisoners were used to year-round temperatures in the eighties and nineties. Some mentioned that during the *Noto, Maru* voyage they could feel the change to a cooler climate. During their three-day train trip from Shimonoseki to Hanawa they noticed the change in the Japanese clothing from the lighter to heavier garments.

Hanawa is located only 40 miles from the sea and yet is over 4,000 feet above sea level. As the winds move from the water over the land of northern Honshu, the rapid increase in elevation causes a tremendous amount of precipitation. In Hanawa that meant snow.

Although the first September days of 1944 in Hanawa were described as "beautiful, Indian summer days," by October winter had already set in. No one knows for sure how much snow fell that year, but all are in agreement that it was somewhere near 40 feet. The snow fell almost daily from November to mid-April and caused problems not only within the camp, but also for those who had to walk to the mine.

ZORZANELLO — The weather was cold from the minute of our entry into Hanawa. I thought it was because we had just come from the tropics, but our white breath convinced us otherwise. Hanawa was on the northern tip of Honshu, the main Japanese island, so the temperatures were naturally cool. It snowed from early October to May. The winter temperatures weren't much below freezing. Under normal conditions they wouldn't have had the effect on us that we experienced. Summer arrived around the first of June. It was warm, about mid-seventies, and greatly appreciated.

CANFIELD — In the middle of the winter season the snow was great enough that we had to form ice steps to get out of the barracks. The snow was heavy enough that the wash shed attached to Barracks B collapsed. We then had a choice, go dirty, wash in the snow, or try to get to the bath house if the water lines weren't frozen. Although the winter was cold and our clothing was not the best for cold weather, the snow would continuously drift down in very large flakes, catching in the branches of the tall pines and blanketing the area around. I very nearly had my head knocked in because I mentioned that the snowfall with the moon shining through was pretty.

DR. GOLENTERNEK — It snowed day and night for about three months. We had Japanese women come in and take the snow off the roof. I filled my canteen with hot water at night and put it under the covers. It was my drinking water the next day.

There was so much snow in the compound that one of the jobs for those too sick to work in the mine was to get rid of it by hand. With snow falling continuously for as long as it did, this became almost a daily work detail.

NIX — In March of 1945 I had double pneumonia. I went to see Dr. Golenternek, and all they could give me was some sulfa drugs. They could not put me in the camp hospital because the Japanese policy was that there could only be 25 sick in the hospital at one time. If you went into the hospital, someone sicker than you might be shoved out. When you were placed on quarters in your barracks, you were given less rations. The Japanese philosophy was that if you were sick, you got less rations than if you worked. It meant that your recovery would be prolonged rather than expedited. You could never convince the Japanese that this was wrong. So instead of going to the hospital, they put me on quarters, which meant I didn't have to go to the mine. As a Non-Commissioned Officer, a Staff Sergeant at the time, I didn't have to work, but I had to go and get other men to shovel all that snow out of the compound. The way we did that was we would rotate. I would take out five guys from this group and four guys from that group, etcetera, and we would rotate. My job was to go and get the guys who were shoveling snow at the end of their hour and bring out the next group, even though I had a 104-degree fever.

Addie by this time was one of those 25 who was in the hospital and didn't have to participate in the snow removal detail. Hunger and getting warmth were constantly on the prisoners' minds. Just as they stole food to satisfy one desire, they also stole fuel of any type to burn in their barracks stove to satisfy the other.

TAYLOR — We lit fires for the cold barracks with flint and dynamite. The Japs one time caught us. They thought we were going to blow the place up when we put dynamite in the stove.

PAYNE — We had a small fire going when I seen Royal Huston open the door to the 30-gallon drum converted into a stove. He looked at me, and with a little smile, reached into his overcoat pocket and pulled out a stick of dynamite putting it into the stove. Within a split second I came to the fast conclusion he had lost his marbles. There were others, too, that had the same feeling. It took place so fast you couldn't run.

He had three sticks, I think. The stove turned red, and we really had a fire for just a short time; however, all decided fast, don't bring any more dynamite. There is always the possibility that it would *blow*. This Huston was one of the best.

FRANCIES — At the mine, each of us would steal a piece of coal, wood, or coke to bring back to burn in the stoves. Sometimes we were searched, and the fuel was taken away. Sometimes a POW was beaten because of stealing the fuel. We got more fuel back to the barracks than we had taken away from us.

FLEMING — Sometimes the Jap guards would come in the barracks and warm their hands on the stolen wood burning in the stove. But if they caught you stealing the wood, they would raise hell.

Additional Work Details

Not everyone worked at the mine. There was a Special Duty work section. The 26 men of this detail included medics, cooks, dog robbers (orderlies), a shoe repairman, a carpenter, a dental technician, and administrative personnel. Some men were also assigned to work occasionally at the sawmill in town. Others were given jobs within the compound making rope and nails or working in shoe repair. And some were permitted to leave the camp to perform work for the Japanese.

FLEMING — I remember Bill Vice. He was 41 years old and still a private. He was the camp carpenter. He had been at Clark Field with me, too. Ted Leitz did administrative work. Leonard Larsen "Swede" ran the shoe repair shop. Lee Williamson was our "dog robber," or orderly, and Douglas Brown was the "dog robber" for the Japanese.

George Young of section 4D suffered a compound fracture of his left foot in a mine accident in November 1944. After recovery, he was not able to work at the mine, so he was assigned to various jobs in camp. For a period of time he worked in shoe repair and later in the camp hospital. He was there when Addie died. He aided the doctors and medics by helping drain lungs and feeding those too ill to feed themselves.

One of the other work details involved those in the hospital. They made rope. Robert Johnston was one of those who did. The rope was made from rice straw.

The nail detail was housed in a little wood building directly behind the bath house, galley, and warehouse.

JACK SHARP — I made nails from cable. There was a tram or cable, which ran from the town to the mine. It had buckets that transported stuff to and from the mine. The cable was about one inch in diameter, and one day it broke. That's what we made nails from. I'd heat one end, sharpen it, then heat the other end, and put it in an iron block filled with holes. Then I'd beat that end with a hammer to make the head.

Medical Care

The most important people in a prisoner-of-war camp are the doctors. Even without proper medicine, they were able to save lives with common sense, innovative treatments, and comforting words. Many of the smaller Japanese camps were without American doctors. At those camps Japanese doctors took care of the men. This led to many problems, as the Japanese medical practices were often inferior to the American. Such was not the case at Hanawa. Of the six doctors on the *Noto, Maru*, initially two, Dr. Calvin Jackson from Ohio and Dr. John Lamy from Missouri, went to Hanawa. Dr. Golenternek later replaced Dr. Jackson. Of the 20 medics on the Hell Ship, five — Frank Mayer, Hugh Hunt, Robert Warnock, James O'Keefe, and James Dugan — came to Hanawa. Dugan was actually a dental technician. This is not to say, however, that Japanese medical personnel were not stationed in Hanawa.

FLEMING — Now "Cyclops," I don't remember his real name, but he was the Medical Sergeant at Hanawa. He was sort of rough and especially bad about people who were sick. He tried to make them go to work. Dan Golenternek really succeeded in winning that man's confidence. I don't think Dan bent over and sent somebody to work when in his judgement they shouldn't go to work.

There was a Japanese doctor that would come into camp ostensibly to check on whether the men that Dan said were sick were really sick. He also checked on old "Cyclops," who was scared to death of him. Enlisted men in the Japanese Army lived in great fear of their officers and non-coms.

DR. GOLENTERNEK — Many of the prisoners disliked "Cyclops" and the Japanese doctor, — the "Black Knight," he was called. But I could see the predicament they were in. They treated the American soldier just like they treated the Jap soldier — with little compassion and tried to keep him functional. At times I think the Jap doctor and "Cyclops" played dumb and let me get away with keeping more men off work. But I also know that from their standpoint, they too were concerned with what might happen to them if they let the Americans

get away with too much. They were all part of a system based on fear
of their superiors.

The infirmary was a separate building located in the southwest corner of the
compound. When the men first arrived at Hanawa, not all were given a
physical. Time, space, lack of proper instruments, and the Japanese were the
reasons. Some of those, however, who had experienced problems already back
in Bilibid, were looked at by the doctors. Addie, who had "recovered" from
pellagra shortly before the *Noto, Maru* trip, was one of those to see the doctors
in September. Another was Asbury Nix, who had a severe vision problem and
almost missed the *Noto, Maru* trip because of it.

> NIX — Dr. Jackson gave me an eye exam shortly after we got to
> Hanawa to see if I was physically able to work. I was looking at the eye
> chart on the wall an' he says to me, "Can you read the bottom
> [smaller] letters?"
> "No."
> "How about the row above it?"
> "No."
> "How about the top letter?"
> "No."
> "Well, can you see the Goddamn wall?"

Fortunately, Asbury could see the wall and got to work at the mine. The
incident demonstrates Dr. Jackson's rather direct and frank manner of dealing
with people. He told you exactly what was on his mind. To the Japanese, who
have a strict discipline code, he appeared uncooperative. The Japanese found
little to like in his style. In November, after a blowup with the Japanese
medical staff at the camp, he was sent to Shinagawa near Tokyo.

> FLEMING — This Dr. Jackson was a funny guy. He antagonized the
> Japanese and made no progress, so one day he was asked to pack up
> and was taken down to Tokyo. When they shipped him out, that wasn't
> the first time he had crossed the Japs. The problem was whether
> "Cyclops," a Jap medic, should decide if men should stay on quarters
> or Jackson should.
> Jackson said, "I'm the doctor."
> "Cyclops" said, "I'm the doctor."
> Jackson said, "No you're just a Medical Corpsman!"
> We had some hard feelings there for some time before Jackson got
> shipped out.

What was it that raised the ire of the Japanese? His reaction to the 10

November 1944 death of Private Robert Ring of Litchfield, Ohio, who died of pneumonia? Fortunately Dr. Jackson recorded what happened in his diary.

> JACKSON DIARY — 10 November 1944 — I had a run in with the Nip doctor. A man [Ring] had died. He was all skin and bones! I was asking or trying to get more food and medicine. I went to uncover the body and I don't know how I did it, but that entire sheet just floated up to the ceiling as if it was a silk scarf in a dance. The Nip doctor fumed, grabbed his sword, though he left it in his scabbard, and hit me on the head and shoulders and said, "Get out!" So I left the hospital and was never in it again.
>
> 12 November 1944 — About noon I was told by the Nips to get all my belongings and that I was going away for a couple days. This is a rapid Shanghai for my telling off the Nip M.D. with the camp. They don't like the truth. Left Osarazawa at 1:30 p.m. taking two meals with us.

On the 20th, Dr. Golenternek arrived at Hanawa to join Dr. Lamy. His presence helped stabilize the medical situation in camp. Much of the change was due in no small part to his easygoing, diplomatic personality. Dr. Golenternek was in his early thirties when he arrived at Hanawa. Originally from Texas, he had been in practice in Beverly Hills before the war. He was in the Army Reserve and arrived in the Philippines and was stationed at Fort McKinley only weeks before Pearl Harbor.

> FLEMING — Dan Golenternek was one of the real morale boosters we had at Hanawa. He is one of the finest people to have with you in a tough situation that I ever knew. It must have been extremely frustrating for he and John Lamy to try and treat their patients with little or no medicinal supplies. The best thing we had going for us for getting over an injury or illness was "soak it in hot water" and "bed rest." Dan and I, and later Colonel Walker, we stood firm on that Dan should be the one to pronounce a man to quarters for being sick or injured rather than the Japanese. We won most of the time. After Dan arrived things began to get a lot more stable with respect to our sick, lame, and lazy.

The hospital was a separate wood building that had been partitioned into three rooms. The larger room had 20 wood bunks while the two smaller rooms had five bunks each. Usually the very, very ill were put into the smaller, private rooms to prevent the spread of disease and also to make their stay more comfortable.

In checking over the Hanawa medical records on microfilm from the National Archives, it seems that three men were put into the hospital immediately after arriving at the camp. Paul Miller, Robert Ring, and Earl Moravee do not appear in any of the section rosters. Miller from Virginia was the first to die at Hanawa, on 24 October 1944, of beriberi and malnutrition. Ring died in November of pneumonia, and later that month Moravee was transferred to Shinagawa. Microfilm also indicates that Moravee was in and out of Bilibid for many months prior to the *Noto, Maru* trip. These men were ill before they got to Hanawa, and the cold weather and lack of food and medicine just made their condition worse.

Addie worked at the mine in September and October, and sometime during November or December his cough became worse, and he was put into the infirmary, never to leave.

One of the other difficulties the doctors faced, besides lack of medicine and equipment, was being able to keep accurate and detailed medical records. All of these medical records were later turned over to American authorities when Hanawa was liberated in September 1945. On microfilm from the National Archives there exists a complete medical roster in numerical order on every man at Hanawa — his illness, tests, and treatments. It appears that some medical data was lost or not put on the roster. Some prisoners in their interviews indicated an illness or injury that did not appear on the medical chart. Also, there appear to be many more entries for 1945 than for 1944. When looking over the entries, one of the recurring problems was with worms.

Worms were a chronic problem in prison camps. Unsanitary conditions, weakened body conditions, lack of medicine, and poor personal hygiene caused the problem to worsen. Some also picked up the illness by eating the raw vegetables that had been fertilized with human waste. At Hanawa, Dr. Jackson, Dr. Lamy, and Dr. Golenternek often treated the men for *Ascaris Lumbricoides*. This species of pinworm lives in the human intestine, and its eggs are passed with the feces and transmitted by contaminated food, water, or hands. Also treated were *Necator americanus*, a type of hookworm; *Trichuris*, a type of whipworm; and tapeworms. Treatment to expel the worms usually included a dose of tetrachlorethylene, a colorless liquid.

The medical records indicate that 475 of the original 500 prisoners had their stool tested for worms sometime during their stay at Hanawa. Two hundred seventy-six, or 58 percent, had worms. Many more than once. Interestingly, of the 100 highest ranking men in camp, 56 tested negative and only 41 had worms, and 3 were not tested. Of the lowest ranking 100 men in camp, only 27 tested negative, while 65 had worms, and 7 were not tested. Why did the higher ranks not have as many cases of worms? I'm not sure. Few of the top 100 worked in the mine while most of the bottom 100 were miners. A large percentage of the top 100 lived in barracks A and were older. Many of the bottom 100 lived in barracks C and were younger. None of these differences on the surface, however, would seem to provide an answer.

Also interesting is the fact that in March, 50 British troops, 2 American officers, and an Australian officer were brought to Hanawa from the Tokyo area. When these men had their stool tested, 85% were negative and only 15% had worms. Generally these men were in far better health to begin with than the Battling Bastards of Bataan. The battle against the worms provided lingering memories.

ARTERBURN — I was in that infirmary a couple, three times. I had bronchial pneumonia once and worms. Course everybody there had worms. It wasn't tapeworms. I had 'em about four times. You'd see an ol' boy laying down outside, and after a while you could see some worms crawling out the mouth. Even the worms weren't getting enough to eat. A worm has to have something to survive on, too. They would crawl out your intestines into your stomach and throat. You could pass them both ways.

This one morning I could feel something hard in my rear end, so I took this piece of paper and grabbed it by the head and pulled it out, and the worm was over a foot long. I went to see Dr. Lamy and he said, "Arterburn, did that thing bite you on the way out?"

Medical Statistics

Keeping records and diaries while a prisoner of the Japanese during World War II was difficult, if not impossible. The Japanese feared the incriminating material that these would hold. They also worried that these written records might contain secret messages to the outside world. Besides, paper and pen were difficult to find. The conquerors had already confiscated most of the pens during shakedowns since the fall of Bataan. And where could one find paper?

At Hanawa the medical staff of Dr. Jackson, Dr. Lamy, and Dr. Golenternek were able to keep records on their patients. Sometimes men working in the mine would bring back four-inch square paper work tickets. The back of these tickets were usually blank. Also used were the backs of labels from the cans of food or powdered milk. In September 1945, these scraps of paper were turned over to American personnel onboard the Red Cross ship *Rescue*. These slips were then compiled on a numerical roster of the camp. When viewing copies of the Hanawa medical records 41 years later, Dr. Golenternek thought the writing might be his, that he compiled the record. On closer inspection he said in typical physician fashion, "The writing is too neat to be mine." Perhaps a non-prisoner onboard the *Rescue* performed this task. If this were the case, it might account for a few errors. For example, Desire Peltier #467, had crushed fingers and boils. Those medical problems, however, are recorded after the name of Harley Pierce, #466. Regardless, it does provide graphic evidence on the condition of the Hanawa men.

Forty-nine broken bones were treated by the doctors. Some of them, especially the broken ribs, could have come from beatings. The prisoners in the mine (Sections 4C, 4D, 4E, 4F, and 4G) accounted for most of the ankle, foot, and toe breaks. The darkness of the mine laterals, the rickety rail cars, and the occasional cave-ins were responsible.

The many lung problems — bronchitis, pneumonia, influenza, and tuberculosis — were the result of the change of climate from the heat of the Philippines to the cold of northern Honshu. Lack of proper clothing, poorly insulated buildings, improper diet, and lack of medicine contributed to the problem. One out of every seven men had bronchitis while at Hanawa. Many of those with pleurisy, according to Dr. Golenternek, probably had TB. Most of the time sulfa drugs were given to men with lung ailments. According to statistics, one out of every six was suffering from malnutrition. In actuality all were malnourished. If the War had lasted another year and the men had had to experience another Japanese winter, maybe 30 or 40 more men might have died.

The stomach disorders — diarrhea, dysentery, and enteritis — were not new to the men. Many suffered from these in the Philippines. But what made it difficult at Hanawa was the fact that often they were on a millet diet, and millet is almost undigestible. It goes right through you.

Two other diseases that followed the men to Japan were beriberi (65 cases) and malaria (39 cases). Rather than picking up the "bug" in Japan, the germs accompanied them on the *Noto, Maru*.

Although only five cases of scabies appear on the records, Dr. Golenternek, hoping to get men off work, one time tried to convince the Japanese doctor that it was small pox. When the "Black Knight" looked at the men, he chewed out the doctors, "You dummies! Don't you know a case of scabies when you see one?" One of the treatments for scabies was to cover it with a salve. Not having any available, Dr. Golenternek mixed axle grease and sulfa together to use as a salve. Lawrence Van Liere remembers it being a mixture of Barbersol and sulfa.

Most of the lacerations, sprains, and sores were the result of the work at the mine. Because these could not be cleaned properly, infection usually followed. Often bandages were used over again. Hot water and rest were usually prescribed.

One of the dangers at the mine was eye injury. Slivers of rock or metal would occasionally strike a man's eyes. Interestingly, three men from section 2 — Dix, Benedict, and John Nelson — all suffered from opthalmia from being exposed to the arc light while working near welding equipment topside at the

HANAWA MEDICAL REPORT

Broken Bones - 49
  rib - 7
  collar bone - 2
  hand-wrist-finger - 13
  arm - 3
  nose - 1
  ankle-foot-toe - 22

Lung Disorders
  tuberculosis - 3
  pleuris - 18
  pneumonia - 35
  bronchitis - 73
  influenza - 14

Stomach Disorders
  diarrhea - 45
  dysentery - 20
  enteritis
    (inflamation of intestines) - 49

Skin Disorders
  chickenpox - 3
  scabies - 5

Sores
  skin ulcers - 22
  furunculosis (boils) - 17
  infection - 28
  frostbite - 10
  hemorrhoids - 7

Lacerations and Sprains
  cuts and sprains - 110
  lower back pain - 9

Head Afflictions
  sinusitis - 8
  opthalmia (eye injury) - 9
  otitis media
    (inner ear damage) - 17

Tropical Diseases
  beriberi - 65
  malaria - 39

Other
  malnutrition - 82
  diptheria - 1
  epilepsy - 2
  meningitis - 1
  tachycardia
    (abnormal heart rate) - 1

mine.

Statistics indicate that the doctors had their hands full. Unfortunately, not all the little slips of paper records were recorded. Some were lost. Many men have mentioned medical problems that don't appear on the Hanawa medical roster. But the men do have vivid memories of their illnesses and afflictions. And they do remember what the doctors did for them.

PELTIER — The infirmary was rather small, but since a person had to be nearly dead or badly crippled for the Japanese to let anyone stay in the dispensary, it proved adequate. In any event, there was sympathy available as medication was practically nonexistent. One of the doctors operated on my left finger [crushed], and this was saved and amputated later on. I also had a series of 38 boils from mid-April to the latter part of May. The medication — lance and keep clean to avoid infection in the copper mine. I can only praise Captain Golenternek and Lieutenant Lamy for all they did and tried to do. They were just super human beings and, I feel, great doctors.

STAUDENRAUS — I acquired a sinus infection from working in the mine. It was infected so bad that my face was swollen. My eyes were mere slits. Dr. Golenternek would pack my nose with cotton soaked with a purple solution to help drain the sinuses. With this physical evidence [swelling], he finally persuaded the Japs to let me work topside on the timbers used for shoring, so I wouldn't have to work in the mine. He was a good man — kind and gentle. He seemed to have an empathy for the sick.

TRONESS — In November of '44 one morning, a pain began to develop in my left side, getting worse and worse. We started the walk to the mine, and half way up the mountain, the pain was so bad I began to vomit and fall down. I couldn't get up again despite the guard's kicks, so they rolled me into the ditch, left a guard with me, and they took off. I lay there all day. In the evening, they came back down the hill, and when they saw I still could hardly walk, they dropped off an American medic and a guard and told us to follow. I moved out slow, stumbling along. That damn medic didn't help me. The guard kept hollering "Speedo." The medic urged me to move faster, which I couldn't. The son-of-a-bitch was afraid the guard would get violent, and he might be hit.

We finally got to camp, and I went to my sleeping place to lay down. Gail Kelly brought me my rice. I told him to eat it, which was unheard of. Kelly went to the officers' quarters and told Dr. Lamy that I was in trouble. They had taken Dr. Lamy's medicine from him and had forbade him to treat us. Dr. Lamy sneaked down to me that night. He told Kelly it was a kidney stone or an infection. He gave me two codeine pills he had hidden from the Japs. Then I could sleep.

In the morning, it was mandatory to go on sick call to the Jap doctor whenever you missed work. Algen Hills helped me over to the sick call building. About 15 or 20 guys were ahead of me waiting for the son-of-a-bitch to decide to start. He sat on a chair on a platform. I felt comfort to see Dr. Lamy seated to his left and a couple feet back. Finally he started. The first guy in line would step about six feet in front of him, bow, and state his name and what was wrong with him. He didn't examine the patient, just looked at him, and decided whether "sick" or "not sick." I think for most he said, "Not sick. Go back to work!" Most of these, he'd come down in front of the guy and slap him hard. The sound would just crack through the room. Then he'd like to practice his judo, and he'd throw the guy over his shoulder and crash him to the floor a couple times. Meantime, it takes all my strength and will just to keep standing.

Finally it was my turn. He turned and asked Dr. Lamy something, and Dr. Lamy responded. I didn't see him consult Dr. Lamy regarding the others. Finally, he said, "You're sick. Rest!"

FLEMING — About a mile up the road toward the village of Osarizara there was a Japanese hospital. I don't know why we took the men there, maybe just to break the monotony. I went with them on a number of occasions, and the Japanese people were very nice to us. I was always given tea and one cigarette to smoke. These people at the hospital appeared to be very kind and considerate.

Hanawa medical records also indicate that 70 men had dental care during the months of May, June, July and August in 1945. John Dugan from Philadelphia was a dental technician who took care of the men. Not far from the camp was a dental clinic run by a Japanese dentist. Prisoners were taken to the clinic for checkups and treatment. The medical record seems to be records of that treatment at the clinic. Because of the absence of sugar from the diet for over three years, the prisoners didn't have many cavities. Gums and teeth were treated with zinc oxide and Eugenol, and approximately half of the men on the records had teeth extracted.

DR GOLENTERNEK — I went to the home of the dentist one time to get some kind of medication. They let me out of camp, and I walked up to his home. I remember I had never been in a Japanese home. I took off my shoes. I had a little tea and a nice visit, and then I came back to camp.

Some of the prisoners were quite ill upon their arrival at Hanawa. They were unable to perform any work and were, therefore, not of any use to the Japanese at the mine. Some also had ailments that could not be treated properly at Hanawa. In November, the Japanese decided to ship seven of the men to Shinagawa Prisoner-of-War Hospital, located a few miles south of Tokyo. The hospital was run by a sadistic Japanese doctor. The men were Earl Moravee, Dan Berger, Bob Stewart, James Knight, Gordon Hilton, Robert Sills, and Clifton Frazier. Addie was still working at the mine and not sick enough to be included. Berger had tuberculosis, Stewart had beriberi, and Sills was an epileptic. On 12 November, the men boarded a train. With them was Dr. Calvin Jackson, who was being shipped to Tokyo after his blowup with "Cyclops."

STEWART — Around November the top honcho for the Japanese prison camps came through and inspected our camp and they wanted everybody that could possibly walk to be at work so they could show good records. There were only about two over at the dispensary permanently, but there were another five of us that couldn't work at the mine. This inspector came by, and he pointed at me. I could understand "Tokyo," but I didn't know what "Shinagawa" meant. The next day we were on our way. The only guy I can remember being with me on the train was Frazier. I remember him because he had no teeth. They had all fallen out. I was so swollen when I left that they gave me the biggest pair of split-toed shoes they had in camp, and I still couldn't get them on. They sent this medic along with me. Every time we came to a stop, we got off of the train, even if it was a five-mile distance between stops. He tried to give me a shot but couldn't find my vein anymore than the man in the moon, because you couldn't locate it. I think he did that for propaganda to show the people that they were taking care of the prisoners.

My testicles were like basketballs, and the doctor who saw me when I got to Shinagawa said I was the funniest looking thing he ever saw, because when I lay on my right side, the right side of my head was flat, and the rest was like a balloon, and if I lay on my left, vice versa. I had to sleep sitting up because if I lay down, the water would choke me off, and I couldn't breathe.

At Shinagawa, this doctor had absolutely no medicine to treat me with, but he finally came up with the idea of Epsom salts. That was to get all the water out of my system. The funny part was I was worried about this Japanese doctor that was a sadist. What he did was perform autopsies upon patients that were still alive. I was always afraid that he might use me as a guinea pig. While I was there I contracted mumps, and for some reason or another, the Japanese were absolutely deathly afraid of mumps. They isolated me, and that was the nicest thing that ever happened to me as far as I was concerned. They put me in a room, and the Japanese didn't come and check on me at any time.

I must have spent two weeks or longer in that room all by myself. They brought my rations to me twice a day. I figure this is one of the things that kept me from falling into the hands of that sadistic doctor, the experimental operator.

BERGER — In November, I was sent to Tokyo under guard with other men to a so-called hospital camp at Shinagawa, a suburb of Tokyo. The Japs thought I had a lung problem, TB, and other things that they seemed to be very afraid of. Why, I'll never know. This camp was on reclaimed sea land, very cold and damp, lots of fog and no medical treatment for any of the problems. It was a mixed camp of British, Dutch, Aussies, Americans, and some Javanese POWs who didn't last long in that climate. I would have lost both of my feet if it hadn't been for an American medic who lanced and drained my toes as a result of chilblains infection.

The food was worse than Hanawa, and no heat in the same kind of barracks. During the air raids we would get nothing to eat as the Japs wouldn't permit fires except for their own people. Sometimes we got a chunk of very moldy bread, about four inches by four inches by two inches. Maybe I got a little form of penicillin and didn't know it. We had to be in the trenches during the air raids. I was there when the B-29s made their first raid on Tokyo and also the first carrier strike against the area in February of 1945. It got worse as the fire bombing grew. Sometimes we would see one of the bombers hit and go down, but we knew the terrible amount of damage being done to the Japs. It got so bad that the Japs sent prisoners back to their camps well or not, and I was back in Hanawa in March. Of course, I could tell the guys all what I had seen, and that we were winning.

Punishments, Guards, and Other Characters

Of considerable importance to the Japanese in maintaining discipline within their own ranks was the use of physical punishment. To hit one of a lesser rank was a common occurrence. That was the Japanese way of doing things. When it came time to discipline the American POWs, the Japanese naturally used these and other methods that bordered on torture. Initially in the prisoner experience, the Battling Bastards of Bataan had difficulty accepting what to them was an irrational form of discipline. By the time they got to Hanawa, however, most expected to be hit by the guards. They still didn't like it, but for the most part they accepted it. The beatings and tortures were not as frequent nor as violent as those incurred in the Philippines.

The Camp Commandant, Lieutenant Asaka, although fairly fluent in English, used an intrepreter, whose name was something like Yamaguchi.

Grayford Payne remembered that Yamaguchi was a good man — 52 years old, and had gone to Tokyo University. He was a writer in civilian life. He helped the prisoners more than they knew, according to Payne, by playing dumb and not seeing a lot of things. The second in command was Sergeant Takahashi. Many of the prisoners have fond memories of him. According to *American Ex-Prisoners of War Report on Hanawa*, there was "a two-star private who had considerable voice in the camp administration, and he was rated by the prisoners as cruel and despotic." That was Segae.

> FLEMING — Segae was the bull of the woods, I can guarantee you. Now he never struck me; to my knowledge he never struck one of the officers, but he came close to striking me on a number of occasions when I was interceding on behalf of some of my men. He was a veteran of the Chinese campaign — claimed he had not been in the South Pacific and had not fought against the Americans. He was infantry and he was a tough, tough guy. I visited him at Segamu Prison after the War, and later he went off his rocker, and he tried to commit suicide. It made the newspapers in this country. He would just as soon knock you down and stomp on you as look at you.

Lieutenant Asaka, however, was not as cruel as Segae nor prone to strike everyone who disobeyed. He had his job to do. If he didn't, he certainly would have incurred the typical Japanese wrath of his superiors in Sendai and Tokyo.

> RIDDLE — On one occasion, Lieutenant Asaka came to the mine and toured our blacksmith shop asking questions about what we were doing, etecetera. He spoke pretty good English. I believe he was educated at Columbia University in the U.S.A. Sometimes he would come in our building at 2 or 3 a.m. in the morning. We all had to stand at attention while he raved and ranted in a drunken stupor about nothing we could understand.

On the other hand, Takahashi was often looked at as a "friend." Although he had to distribute punishment as he saw fit, he often ignored severity and was actually kind to the men.

> FLEMING — Takahashi was tall, probably around five feet ten or eleven inches. He was about as tall as I am, and I am six foot. He had a pleasant personality. To the best of my knowledge, he never struck a man in anger. Now he might have feigned a blow and slapped them a little bit, but never very hard. He was not one to go out and get blood. Takahashi was good with us. We called him "Tak" and he liked that.

He liked the nickname. All in all, he was very helpful to us. He seemed to be an understanding young man, and I believe he felt sorry for us. He didn't take the attitude like a lot of Japs that you're not to surrender.

ZORZANELLO — Takahashi basically was a decent individual. His instincts were to be nice but CYA [cover your ass] came first. I felt sorry for him. He was a victim of circumstances.

"Cyclops" was the medic who saw the ill each day. All had little use for his sadistic, unmerciful style.

ZORZANELLO — "Cyclops" was aptly named. He was in charge and wanted to make sure you knew it. He really abused his authority! He didn't have one shred of compassion. His favorite form of cure was to whack us on the forehead with his bayonet practice pole.

Compared with the treatment the prisoners received from the guards in the Philippines, Hanawa was an improvement. Addie's bunkmate, Marvin Shearwood, called Hanawa a "rest home compared to Nichols Field." Perhaps the fact that the guards were not Philippine Campaign veterans had something to do with it. Perhaps it was the harsh winter, which kept most indoors. Perhaps it was the long hours in the mine that prevented the men from summoning any excess energy and converting it into trouble. Most likely it was a combination of all three plus more. But that is not to say there weren't punishments. Grady Stanley, who stole a turnip, was caught and made to stand in the snow. The big toe on his right foot is now dead from that experience.

FRANCIES — In most cases of punishment, we American POWs brought that treatment upon ourselves. We knew the rules, and we got caught. I remember men standing outside in freezing weather as a punishment.

CANFIELD — I recall one man beaten and made to sit with a stick behind his knees and with his arms under the stick. His hands were tied in front of him.

RIDDLE — [As punishment for stealing the rice] Dudley and I were put in the little aeso [jail]. It was March and no heat. Dudley was in one cell, and I was in the other. A small opening at the top of the wall allowed us to talk. My cell leaked, and only a small area of the floor was dry. In one corner, a large icicle hung down from the top of the ceiling to almost the floor. When I could no longer endure it, I talked it over with Dudley and we agreed that I would try the crazy act. I rolled around the floor screaming, moaning, and clutching my stomach. Shortly thereafter, footsteps came down the little hallway. A guard peered in the doorway. Soon a couple more came. Then I was carried on a sort of stretcher and was placed in the little hospital. I don't know what the Japs thought of my condition but it worked.

THRONEBERRY — Fortunately, I did not smoke, but those who did would reach for cigarette butts which the guards would throw on the snow. When the POWs reached for them, they [the guards] would spike the prisoners hands with their shoes.

One of the more memorable punishments occurred when the Japanese fire ladder was stolen, chopped up, and then used for fuel in Barracks B. The culprits were beaten and then put in the 4x4 foot *aeso* by the front entrance guard house.

COLE — One time Gordon Hilton and I stole a fire ladder from the guards' quarters and took it back to our bunk, broke it into smaller pieces, and put it into the pot belly stove in the barracks and had a hot fire going when the men got back from the mine that evening. We had to give ourselves up after the guards threatened to punish everybody in the barracks. The guards worked me over with their judo. I fell on one of the icicles and got it under my rib. We were then put in the guard house. I never carried any hatred toward Takahashi, although he permitted me to get a pretty severe beating for taking the fire ladder. I had it coming. Because of my injuries and frost bite, Dr. Golenternek came and got us out of the *aeso* two days later.

GORDON HILTON — The ladder was measured, then calculations made whether it could be safely moved inside through the sliding doorway opening. It could be done. It took a few minutes time getting the ladder into the correct angle to negotiate the doorway. The deed was done.

All was quiet inside. We were waiting for the mining detail to return to camp. Several hours had passed — no trouble was antici-pated from the ladder caper. Suddenly, Takahashi stormed in, asked me in English had I taken any part in cutting up the fire ladder? Yes, I said.

We were marched out into the area where work details were assembled. All the other men were moved to a location where honchos from the mine and Jap soldiers beat each man.

One of the punishments inflicted on a POW involved some of the men in Barracks C who caught one of the Americans stealing from them while they were at the mine. The thief already had been put in the *aeso* for other reasons.

FLEMING — Le Beau would come out of the *aeso* latrine, go into the barracks, and steal things, and then crawl back in the *aeso*. He was a constant source of trouble, so when the men in Barracks C caught him, they roughed him up pretty good and then took him to the Japs. I wasn't called in at this point. It was winter time and they put him back in the *aeso*. In that *aeso* you couldn't even lie down. It was four feet square. Just a little cell next to the guard house near the front gate. The weather was bitter and I think Le Beau spent 24 hours there. Dan Golenternek and I went to Asaka together. We were afraid the man was going to die there. We brought him out, and he was shivering so bad that he could hardly walk. That was probably the worst case of punishment we had at Hanawa.

Le Beau was #30 in camp. He was #209 on the *Noto, Maru*. He was always one number ahead of Addie. On the list of men being sent in August 1944 from Cabanatuan to Bilibid for the *Noto, Maru* trip, he again is listed one ahead of Addie's name.

But there were other interesting occurrences in camp. Gordon Hilton from Minnesota was the cause of some excitement.

DR. GOLENTERNEK — Hilton ran through the main gate right by the guards singing "God Bless America" and "California Here I Come." The Japs let him alone and let him wander the hillside stealing food. He was sent to Tokyo for a few weeks and then returned. The Japanese [thought it was] mental illness and were afraid [though they] had little compassion for physical illnesses.

HILTON — One night after supper, I got out of the sleeping bay and walked outside. Apparently I had blanked out. They said I walked out of the camp, past the Jap guarding the gate, and began climbing the hill behind the camp. The Jap guard didn't know what to do. He yelled and other Japs ran out after me. The Jap Medic caught up to me, slapped my face several times so they said. Finally I recovered consciousness. They marched me back to my sleeping bay and told me to stay there.

There were other camp notables besides Le Beau and Hilton. Master

Sergeant C. R. Jackson from San Diego, California, was in his forties when at Hanawa. He was one of the instructors at the "university" at Cabanatuan teaching Ancient and Medieval History. Brownell Cole recalls him as "one of the smartest men I've ever talked to." When looking for conversation, Dr. Golenternek used to seek Jackson and 48-year-old Sergeant Emanuel Hamburger from Seattle, Washington. Because both were in their forties, he tried to keep them off work as much as possible.

Trying to Stay Clean

During time of battle, personal hygiene is difficult but possible. In a POW setting, without self-discipline, it was hopeless unless drastic measures were taken.

> NIX — I have seen instances where some soldiers were introduced to the importance of taking a bath frequently by a procedure known as the GI Bath. This was usually supervised by an NCO and was usually a forced bath. Several soldiers would grab the offender; hustle him into the shower, clothes and all; strip him down to the skin; and proceed to scrub him with a GI scrub brush and laundry soap. This rather harsh method of instilling basic hygiene was effective, and usually the culprit did not have to be scrubbed a second time.

Keeping clean was an individual matter. Not only was the food contaminated, but often the prisoners themselves were covered with germs. Soap and water were luxury items in a prisoner-of-war setting. The Japanese weren't about to go out of their way to provide for POWs, whom they considered "inferior soldiers."

> NIX — From the Japanese viewpoint the concern for the minimum needs of the POWs stems from the Japanese position that to surrender was a sin, and the poor soldiers who were captured were considered lower than the lowest private in the Japanese Army. Death was honorable and never would a true soldier of the Emperor accept surrender. Consequently, the attitude of the Japanese was that the lower echelons of the Japanese Army did not and would not accept the POW as a human being.
>
> One of the contributing factors to the uncleanliness of the POW was the total lack of a single commodity that you hardly ever think of — *toilet paper*. Most of the time, men used what they could find. It might be grass, corncobs, paper if it could be gotten. Anything!
>
> When we got to Hanawa the latrines were unheated, and a visit there in cold weather was on an urgent basis. The washing facility for hands and face was cold water, so you can see that those not inclined to be very diligent in their cleanliness were to suffer the consequences.

But the men at Hanawa were allowed to take baths occasionally. The Japanese and American baths were located directly behind Barracks B and C and were part of the L-shaped building that also housed the mess and storage areas. The Japanese system of bathing was quite new to the American prisoners. The baths were not used as often as one might think. With 500 men waiting to use them, fatigue from work at the mine, and absolutely miserable weather, most found it easier just to bunk in every evening.

NIX — I've been going to a health club here in Stevens Point, Wisconsin. Just the other day I was sitting in this large Jacuzzi tub and thinking back to Christmas Day of 1944. The way the Japanese bath system worked was that once a week you were permitted to take a bath in the bath tub. The Japanese system calls for you to go to the tub and sit on the outside edge of the tub which is about six feet square and about five feet deep. You take a bucket and bail out some water and wash yourself completely and then get in the tub. The water was around 140-150 degrees, so it was a process of slowly getting used to it. By the time 500 men went through the bath in a day, it got kind of soupy, particularly if the men didn't take the time outside of bath and wash off before they got in the tub. But my group happened to be first on Christmas Day. I went about 9:00 that morning and stayed in that tub of warm water all day until 3:00 that afternoon. That was the first time I had been warm since I had been in Japan. How little things are so accepted in our society today.

FLEMING — The Japanese did do us the courtesy, if that is what it is, to permit the officers to take a bath in the Japanese bath house. I don't recall how often they let us do this; I'm inclined to think it was once or twice a month. The way you bathe is you take some wooden buckets and you dip your bucket into the hot water of the big tub which was probably 10 or 12 feet square and soap up and wash and get yourself clean. Then you jump into this tub and rinse. I'm telling you, about the time the 200th man went through, there was scum all over the top of that water and made us wonder if we were really getting ourselves sanitarily clean.

VAN LIERE — The first group into the water was rotated among our groups of 40 to 50 men. Of course, you were supposed to wash and rinse off Japanese style before soaking in the tub. Since we were so darn cold, most of us could not wait with the snow drifting on our shoulders from the vents above. So we jumped in pretty dirty. With about 450 men in camp and most of them working underground, that water got black fast. But it was warm, wet, and you always seemed to come out cleaner than you went in. It was supreme luxury to be the first group in the clean, hot water.

Christmas 1944

In December 1944, the Hanawa prisoners celebrated their third Christmas as captives of the Japanese. At Christmas 1942, most believed that in 1944 they would be observing the holiday as free men. Few would have guessed that they would still be prisoners in 1944, and none would have imagined they would be in Japan. And yet all the men at Hanawa thought back to happier Christmas days 7,000 miles away back in the States with their families. Some thought of the smell of the newly cut pine tree, some recalled unwrapping special presents from loved ones, and others remembered the bountiful Christmas dinner. At Hanawa, a few lucky ones actually got to observe December 25th. The celebration wasn't elaborate nor the food bountiful, but the few men who gathered in Barracks B remember the day as though it were yesterday.

FLEMING — We had a Catholic priest visit us in prison camp more than once. The Japanese gave us a Christmas holiday, though. We all gathered in Barracks B. We filled up both top and bottom bunks, hung over the sides, sang Christmas carols, and had some prayers. There were some tears shed. We just didn't know when we were going to get home. It was very emotional. It really was.

PELTIER — The central bay of one of the barracks was festively decorated and a makeshift altar put in. A Catholic priest came and said Mass and made it a truly great occasion. This was the only Mass that was said in the camp. Also this was the day we got a meat ration, and then we received Red Cross boxes — one box for every four men.

ZORZANELLO — I remember we had a show and some Red Cross rations. The German priest I remember. He seemed to be glad that he could be of service, but he had to watch his step — be neutral in other words.

SCRUGGS — At Christmas time we were given the Red Cross packages — one for every two men — and it was a grand and glorious occasion. We knew that the Japanese ransacked the packages before we received them.

We were also given an apple. I unthinkingly picked up my apple too soon and was severly beaten by a guard with his wooden cane that he

俘 虜 郵 便

FROM

NAME&NO Alfred R. Martin 36209798

NATIONALITY AMERICAN

RANK First Sergeant

CAMP Tokyo

TO

Mrs. William H. Martin

303 South Erie Street

De Pere, Wisconsin

PRISONERS OF WAR MAIL

DATE

Wonderful Christmas Confession And Communion Red Cross and other Gifts Best Wishes To All Have My Allotment To you Increased Few dollars if you WANT. God Bless you All Love

東
京
俘
虜
収
容
所

On opposite page and this page: Addie's last POW card from Hanawa. Sent in January 1945, the card arrived in DePere in late 1945 or early 1946. In the card Addie makes reference to Christmas celebration. On front of the card the number 31 after his name refers to his camp number.

carried with him at all times. It was real embarrassing in front of the whole group.

I also remember that Lieutenant Asaka took his sword and stuck Captain Fleming a number of severe blows during the Christmas time of 1944. This was very demeaning to the American Commander.

FLEMING — I don't remember why Asaka struck me with his sword, but we must have tangled over something. After all those months as a prisoner at Clark Field, I had learned to keep my cool in dealing with them. What could you do by retaliating? They would probably kill you, but it must have been over the issuance of Red Cross boxes in the store room. I believe that's what I was pleading for.

PAYNE — Don't let anyone tell you Fleming was afraid. Lieutenant Asaka did hate him, but also showed much respect for him as an American officer who would stand up to him. The Lieutenant also thought Fleming to be tough and mean. I worked the night shift in the mess hall and Asaka would ask me a few questions about Fleming. "Is everyone in North Carolina that mean?" I think he and Fleming must have had some words that day. I know there were men that didn't like Fleming but give that man his credit; there were senior officers in camp, but they didn't want the job. It was a very tough job. The POWs disliked you because you could not make the Japs feed you better or give you more medicine, and the Japs thought he should be magic, and held him liable for everything they didn't like about the POWs. Give the man his due.

Addie was present not only to receive a Red Cross package but also to help the German priest with Mass. According to Domenico Ferrari, a friend from the 200th CAC, Addie received Holy Communion on Christmas and Easter. The priest, who might well have been a Father Pohl, was sequestered in a nearby town along with members of the Italian Embassy who had been moved out of Tokyo during the winter bombing raids. By then Italy was no longer an Axis member with Germany and Japan. For Addie, the opportunity to receive Communion and help a priest was the highlight of his stay at Hanawa.

In Addie's only POW card that he sent from Hanawa to his mother, he mentions he had "A wonderful Christmas confession and communion. Red Cross and other gifts. Best wishes to all." This was the last his family heard from him. It was the family's first knowledge that he had been shipped to Japan. The return address was CAMP TOKYO while the previous five cards were all marked PHILIPPINES. The card was signed "Adrain R. Martin-31." Thirty-one was his age when he died at Hanawa. But the number did not refer to his age; that ironically was his camp number.

Not all Hanawa men recall sending a card home from Japan. In the Philippines, the prisoners wrote out the message, and it was typed for them. At Hanawa, the message was handwritten but not by the men themselves. Dick Francies recalls his mother receiving his card on 15 January 1945.

> FRANCIES — We were given cards to fill out. Then another group of several fellows had to recopy the cards. The Japs didn't trust us that we wouldn't try to use some codes in writing home, so everything had to be recopied.

Coming of the Brits

Because of the American bombing of the Tokyo area, the Japanese during 1945 moved prisoners to camps in northern Honshu. Lieutenant Colonel Walker, Captain Spotte, Flight Lieutenant Thompson (Australian) and the seven Hanawa POWs at Shinagawa were brought to Hanawa on 3 March 1945. Two months later, on 13 May, a larger contingent of British prisoners was brought in. Captain Robert Eagle, Lieutenant Wesley Willoughby, and 48 enlisted men arrived from the Yokohama Shipbuilding Camp. Practically all were in better health, and the new arrivals occupied the portion of Barracks A that previously had housed the four American officers. To make room, the American doctors moved into the infirmary.

The American enlisted men weren't too happy to see the Brits. Although the British had to work topside at the mine at the smelter, just like the Americans, the fact that the British looked like they had eaten better might have made the Americans a little envious. But the English attitude didn't help either.

> CANFIELD — To me they were very aloof and hard to get to know, but there were a few that I did get to know. It was because of these few that I later accepted an assignment to go to England. I really couldn't believe that the whole nation could be as bad as what I had perceived the others to be. Glad to say that I found the English in their home country to be very nice people.

> COLE — These English POWs had the most profane, obscene language, and they'd be sitting up in their bay making tea and talking about the "stalwart spirit of the English people in face of adversity" and how they had barrage balloons defending the island. Some smart American would holler up, "If they cut the barrage balloons, the damn island would sink."

> STAUDENRAUS — I got along with the British just so-so, but one of them, Eddie Begg, and I became very good friends and had many

interesting conversations. I still have a colored crayon drawing he made for me of his Scottish dress uniform, kilts and all. Yes, there was animosity between the groups.

PAYNE — They are completely different from us Americans. They will take orders to death. Americans will not. Because they did not fight at Shanghai, and they made that decision, and it was probably the right one. It was a no-win decision for them. We put that strike against them from the start and added anything else we could. By doing all these things, most POWs said, "I hate the British." They were different from the American soldier, but don't sell them short. They were also among the world's best fighting men.

JOHNSTON — I was never in the barracks the British were in. All 50 of them worked topside at the mine. I saw them once in a while. I noticed they had good woolen overcoats. We didn't. The rumors were that they got treated better than us Yanks.

FLEMING — The Brits were in darn good physical condition. They had been working on shipbuilding in the Yokohama area and were evacuated after the bombing started there. The Japs at least had the gumption to get the prisoners out of the targeted areas. I liked the Brits all right. Captain Eagle and Lieutenant Willoughby were a nice addition to our officer group. We got a little crowded. If I remember correctly, Dan Golenternek and John Lamy moved to the infirmary and lived there, which made room for a couple more officers, Colonel Walker and Captain Spotte, that had come up in March of 1945.

The enlisted personnel didn't get along too well with the British. The Brits hung off to themselves pretty much. They were friendly, but I guess part of it was due to the fact that they had been captured in Singapore, which fell before we did on Bataan. I don't recall anything specific, but they were different. They speak the same language with a different accent. They were sort of haughty and thought they were well above the bedraggled Americans at Hanawa, who had been the Battling Bastards of Bataan.

Death at Hanawa

Death was nothing new to the Battling Bastards of Bataan. Once the fighting started in 1941 in the Philippines, the word was on their lips and in their minds daily. After they surrendered in 1942 and the fighting stopped, death didn't go away. It followed them along the Death March to Camp O'Donnell, then to

Cabanatuan, later to Camps like Nichols Field and Las Piñas, and continued with them on the Hell Ships bound for Japan. Somewhat ironic about the Hanawa men is that after three years as prisoners and in a weakened condition, only eight died during the 12 months that Hanawa was in operation. Credit certainly has to go to Dr. Jackson, Dr. Lamy and Dr. Golenternek. Unfortunately, Adrian Raphael Martin was one of the eight to die. Knowing his background, many were amazed that he lived for three years as a prisoner under these intolerable circumstances.

As a young boy back in Wisconsin, Addie dreamt of his future and his death. He envisioned a long life and a quiet, peaceful death. His imagination as a young boy could not conceive of a lonely death 8,000 miles from home in the mountains of northern Honshu at the relatively young age of 31.

Addie's death at 10:30 p.m. on 8 June 1945 was the seventh of the eight deaths. The first to die was Private Paul Miller of Bridgewater, Virginia, on 24 October 1944, of beriberi and starvation. On 10 November, Private Robert Ring of Litchfield, Ohio, died of pneumonia. This was the death that caused Dr. Jackson's complaining to the Japanese, whose solution was to send him to Tokyo. Beriberi and starvation claimed Gilmore Smith of Lafollette, Tennessee, on 9 December 1944. Two months later on 5 February 1945, pneumonia snatched Ray Underwood of Fulton, Mississippi. A mine cave-in in March took the life of Joseph Werner of New Orleans, Louisiana.

For almost two months death took a holiday before claiming William Havilland of Cleveland, Ohio, on 31 May 1945. He died of tuberculosis, and eight days later, Addie died of the same illness. The final death in camp was Jasper Knowles of Three Forks, Montana, who died of beriberi and starvation on 8 July 1945.

Dr. Jackson, Dr. Lamy, and Dr. Golenternek were the reason that more men did not die. Keeping the ill alive without proper medicine was the ultimate challenge. Encouragement can only go so far. The man himself has to bring his own will to live to the crisis. Interesting stories about the will to live have been attributed to two of the men who died of starvation, Smith and Knowles. What is significant or tragic about the stories is what happens to a man after three years as a prisoner with no hope of liberation in sight.

Some of the men traded their cigarettes to Smith for his rice rations. Before Dr. Golenternek and Captain Fleming discovered what was going on, his condition had deteriorated. According to Dr. Golenternek, Smith had to be declared "bankrupt" so that no one could collect his debts (rice rations). That way, hopefully, he would start eating again.

Many recall Knowles dying in the barracks. His death in July, one month before the war ended, was a surprise to the doctors. After Addie's death in early June, the entry in the camp diary kept by Walker and Fleming indicated that the doctors expected no other deaths in camp.

The Death of Adrian R. Martin

For many prisoners of war captured in the Philippines, death came quickly. For some it was a bayonet or bullet, for others death was drowning in a sinking Hell Ship, and for a few it was a week or two of intense pain before dying in a "Zero Ward" of amoebic dysentery or tertian malaria. For Addie, death came after several months of suffering with tuberculosis.

DOMENICO FERRARI LETTER-1947 — Addie's health started failing him in November, 1944, when we were transferred to Japan. The change of climate had a lot to do with it, from tropical weather to winter weather in the northern part of Japan.

In January, 1945, his health broke completely and he was confined to a hospital. There it was discovered he had T.B. The American doctors who were stationed there did everything possible for him with little the medical aid that was supplied to them. They did everything possible to have the Japanese transfer him to Shinagawa Hospital south of Tokyo. The Japanese would not approve it.

By January and February when the request was made, the Americans were in the process of bombing the Tokyo area, and the Japanese were transferring men away from Tokyo rather than bringing them in. The Hanawa men who were sent to Shinagawa in November 1944 were returned in early March 1945 for that very reason. To the Japanese, sending Addie there was out of the question. Besides, according to Don Sollenberger, who was sent to Shinagawa with TB, treatment at Shinagawa was almost nonexistent.

Many of the men in Addie's section, 3A, recall his hacking cough, which started shortly after the September arrival. One of Addie's three bunk mates, Solly Manasse, wrote Addie's parents in November 1945, shortly after his arrival back in the States.

MANASSE LETTER-1945 — We were placed in the same work group and continued to see each other daily. Due to the change of climate Addie immediately took ill and after several weeks at this camp the American doctors placed him in our camp hospital. I may say at this time that the two American doctors we had were excellent men, and it was solely through their untiring efforts that those of us who survived can thank. We had almost no medicine, and what we did have was given to boys like Adrian who needed it most of all. This bronchial trouble developed into tuberculosis and although he rallied from time to time, the climate and all was against him. I frequently visited him in the hospital and he always maintained a clear perspective of everything. He never gave up hope and talked about what we were going to do after we got home. Around the middle of May [1945] his condition became worse, and on June 8 about 10:00 he passed out of this life.

Forty-one years later Solly, who had been confined to the infirmary during the spring of 1945, recalled Addie's death.

MANASSE — Adrian was not well and spent most of the time housed in the infirmary. Towards the end of April, I had a terrible sore throat, which they diagnosed as diphtheria and isolated me along with ten other men, including Adrian, in what they called the "Zero Ward." During the next three weeks I bunked next to Adrian and talked with him considerable. I tried to encourage him to hold on, if he possibly could, for a few more months. The poor fellow was apparently very ill and was not eating. I was discharged, and he died after I left the hospital. Fortunately, I was not as ill as they thought, or I was too mean to die.

According to the Hanawa medical records, Addie died at 10:30 p.m. of tuberculosis. The diganosis of his illness was done by the "positive examination of the sputum." Dr. Golenternek recalls that this exam was done at the local Japanese hospital and not in camp. There were no x-rays available to help in the diagnosis. Treatment included rest and improved diet, augmented occasionally by vitamins from the Red Cross parcels. Although known for his stateside appetite, Addie was having difficulty eating. Those who visited him during the last months recall his cheerful, encouraging personality, but also his emaciated look. He weighed around 65 pounds at death. Although he knew he was dying, Addie encouraged the healthy to hold on and not give up. Liberation was close at hand.

ZORZANELLO — The only guy I remember who passed away was an Army man. He was a close friend of Jim O'Sullivan, an Army Tech Sergeant from Massachusetts who was in my work group [3B]. Sully, as we nicknamed him, told us about this guy who had a bad case of tuberculosis. He suggested that a few of us go visit him in the hospital to cheer him up. The poor fellow was in a bad way. He was extremely thin and emaciated when I saw him, but his morale was good, despite frequent spells of a wracking cough. He was a devout Catholic, and we recited a rosary with him. Before we could visit him again, he passed away. My recollections are that he was a graduate of or attended Notre Dame and that he was highly respected and looked up to. I have never forgotten how I admired him. He had a wide circle of

friends who were solicitous and concerned about him to the end.
Normally, only a few very close friends spend time with a dying
person. I also remember having seen him in our barracks [A]. He was
in an adjacent bay [3A]. I feel privileged to have known him and
remember the favorable impression I have retained through all these
years.

One out of every ten men at Hanawa was from Addie's original outfit, the
200th Coast Artillery. The unit was heavily Catholic. Since there were no
Chaplains sent to Hanawa, many of the men from the 200th remembered
Addie as the Chaplain's Assistant and sought him out for prayer and comfort.
Knowing his passion for his religion, it pleased him that he could be of help to
others. Max Leyba from Albuquerque, New Mexico, a Sergeant in the 200th,
was one of those who visited with him in the hospital.

MAX LEYBA — I used to go to the "Zero Ward" on days off and visit
Adrian. He would tell me and the other guys to keep our chins up. He
gave me encouragement to hold on, that I could make it. He'd say,
"Don't give up!" For a dying man, he really made me feel at home.

As the ranking American officer at Hanawa, Captain Fleming did not have
to go to the mine to work. But there was plenty to do in camp. One of his jobs
was to visit the hospital each day to see how the sick were doing.

FLEMING — Now Adrian gave me the impression of being a very
ardent Christian. If I remember correctly, he conducted some religious services at Hanawa. I think Dan Golenternek diagnosed his
illness as tuberculosis through the local Japanese hospital. I suspect
we wanted to send him to Shinagawa, but at that time the Tokyo-
Yokohama area was being bombed by B-29s and then carrier-based
planes. Obviously we couldn't do anything for him. We knew that.
When he became seriously ill three or four weeks before he
actually died, I saw him a couple of times a day. He and I had worked
up a real close relationship, and I admired the man tremendously. It
was just a damn shame we couldn't get him to the Shinagawa hospital,
where they *might* have been able to save his life. He always had a smile
on his face. He was a happy man. He was happy in the Lord. He told
me that many times.

After his death at 10:30 p.m. the evening of 8 June 1945, his body was
prepared for a Japanese service — a Shinto funeral and cremation. One of the
men in the hospital at the time of Addie's death and Haviland's death eight

days earlier recalls what happened. Delbert Moore was admitted to the hospital near the end of May for treatment of pleurisy. He remembers that the clothes were removed from the body and immediately burned outside. The Japs had a fear of tuberculosis and figured burning the clothes would prevent the spread of the disease. The body was dragged outside and then taken by the Japanese.

> FLEMING — The Japs had a box [small coffin], which incidentally was difficult to get the larger Americans into especially if rigor mortis had set in. Usually, when we found out that an American had died, or knew it was about to happen, we tried to get the box within a few hours. The body was placed in this box and the lid nailed on it. We didn't see the box or the remains. There was a crematorium some- where in the vicinity. Sometime later the ashes were returned in a wooden box, a cubicle about 15 inches on a side.

The Japanese held a Shinto funeral. There were eight such services, but not everyone could attend. Usually the officers and selected enlisted men were present.

> DR. JACKSON DIARY — [on the first such ceremony for Paul Miller who died on 24 October 1944] — The body was put in a room alone, a bowl of apples set at his feet with a couple bouquets of flowers, and punk burned continuously. The funeral was right at supper time and us four officers had to attend.
>
> What sacrilege and show this Shinto funeral for OUR soldier. Our officers were ordered to attend and a few soldiers, a few Nip soldiers, a few civilians, the Camp C.O. [Asaka] and the Nip M.D. We all stood except the Nip officers. The body was in a pine box the size of a foot locker, upon a table. On top the box was a small box to hold the ashes. In front of the coffin box on another table was a bowl of apples, flanked by a bouquet of real flowers. These were flanked by a a tall bouquet of artificial golden water lilies about three feet high. In the front of the apples was a partitioned black box. On one side was burning incense; on the other a supply of incense. An armed guard kept piling on incense. The priest came in garbed in a kimona-toga affair, satin, and purplish black in color. Not very attractive. He sprinkled on incense, gabbled in a low, gutteral tone with a few nasal skirmishes. Then he rang a bell, then gabbled some more, and then an intermingling of clicking sounds; like bones together.

Notification of Death/Return of the Ashes

A similar Shinto ceremony was held for Addie. When his ashes were returned from the crematorium, they were put in a pine box, labeled, and kept with the other seven. At liberation in September 1945, the boxes were carried out of camp by the prisoners. When they arrived in Yokohama, the ashes were turned over to the authorities. As more camps were liberated and more boxes came in, the American authorities put hundreds of these boxes in a warehouse.

In late August, when Addie's parents in DePere had not heard from him, they submitted a message to the War Department asking that he contact his family when liberated. Unfortunately, the Hanawa men had not yet been returned to American control. By the end of September, when his parents had not heard from Addie, they wrote Wisconsin Senator Robert La Follette. A reply by telegram indicated that all lists of prisoners being liberated were being scrutinized, and as yet Addie's name had not appeared. Hanawa was one of the last to be liberated, a month after the War ended, so it's easy to see why his name did not appear.

As his family agonized over his fate through the early weeks of October, the news of his death came not from the War Department but from the *Chicago Tribune*.

My mother's family lived in Menasha, 30 miles south of DePere. My grandfather, a doctor, was also a prominent Democrat in the State Party having been a delegate to numerous National Conventions. To keep abreast of the national political situation, he was a daily subscriber to the *Tribune*.

The *Tribune* had authorized one of its reporters in Japan, Donald Stone, to seek information concerning the whereabouts of Edward Herbeck, a relative of a *Tribune* employee, who had not been heard from. Ironically, Herbeck had been at Las Piñas with Addie in 1943-1944. The following article appeared in the paper on 25 October 1945. My mother's family read the article on one of the back pages and immediately called DePere to let Addie's parents know the tragic news.

TRIBUNE FINDS ASHES OF CORP. HERBECK
by Donald Stone
(CHICAGO TRIBUNE Press Service)
Yokohama, Japan, Oct. 24

Two days ago a letter was delivered at the TRIBUNE office in Tokyo from a Chicagoan seeking trace of a relative captured by the Japanese on Corregidor.

In it Edward Herbeck, an employee of the CHICAGO TRIBUNE composing room, wrote that his nephew, Corp. Robert M. Herbeck, 34th Pursuit Squadron who had been taken prisoner on Corregidor in May, 1942 when last reported by the War Department in August this year was in a prison camp near Tokyo. Attempts to trace his nephew through the Red Cross and War Department failed, the elder Herbeck wrote, asking that any possible inquiries be pressed.

Upon invitation of an army officer in a chance meeting, we entered a one story stone building this morning to inspect a new established mortuary containing the ashes of 922 prisoners of war who died in Japanese camps. Search for the name of Chicagoans led to a little pine box which was placed along with others on neatly arranged shelves. The identification tag read: Robert M. Herbeck, POW 612 American Corporal: destination of report, Mr. James Herbeck, 6442 S. Washtenaw Ave., Chicago: date of death unknown.

Other identification tags found on similar boxes were: Sgt. A. R. Martin, died June 8, 1945, next of kin, Mrs. William H. Martin 303 S. Erie St., DePere, WI. . . .

The original article from the *Tribune*, that was sent by one set of my grandparents to the other, was one of the documents I found in that shoe box a decade ago. The War Department did not notify Addie's family of his death until 29 October by telegram. The official letter confirming their telegram was sent on 1 November almost a week after the *Tribune* article.

The "official" letter indicates that "He died on 9 June 1945 at Sendai Assembly Area, Camp Number 6 [Hanawa], Japan, as a result of tuberculosis." The Army's official file lists his death as 9 June 1945, but the camp diary, the camp medical record, and the tag on his box of ashes *all* indicate that he died on 8 June.

What happened was this. Sendai was the largest city in northern Honshu and was the headquarters for the approximately dozen camps in that area, including Hanawa. By the time Addie died in June, communications by phone were difficult. Because he died late at night, his death was not reported until the following day, and Sendai listed his death as occurring on the day they were notified. In going over microfilm from the National Archives, I discovered that the Sendai microfilm contained pages of deaths in Sendai-controlled camps. On one of the pages is found Addie's name, camp number, cause of death, next of kin, and date of death. The date given is "June 9, 1945." This list is the one that was turned over to the American authorities in Tokyo and the one that was given to the War Department.

All that remained was for the ashes to be returned for burial. According to Addie's cousin, Jim Martin, Addie's father when informed that the ashes were coming replied, "How do I know those ashes in the urn are Addie's and not some *bohunk's*?" How did any family know that the ashes being returned from

HUSTON, ROYAL W. 1ST. SGT., U.S. ARMY 6245902	3a	24
FLOWERS, HOWARD O. 1ST. SGT, U.S. ARMY 6948566	3a	25
LACEWELL, WILLBORN O. T/SGT, U.S. ARMY 6740194	3a	26
DOWMAN, DONALD A. T/SGT, U.S. ARMY 6980664	3a	27
CASTER, CHARLES F. T/SGT, U.S. ARMY 6862224	3a	28
HAMBURGER, EMANUEL 1ST SGT, U.S. ARMY R-2368127	3a	29
LeBEAU, ALFRED E. T/SGT, U.S. ARMY 6443335	4F	30
MARTIN, ADRIAN R. 1ST SGT., U.S. ARMY 36204798	3a	31
POPE, RALPH W. T/SGT, U.S. ARMY 6894597	3B	32
SCRUGGS, JAMES B. 1ST SGT, U.S. ARMY 6298060	3a	33
BEARDON, FRANK N. T/SGT, U.S. ARMY 6271471	5D	34
COBB, GEORGE E. SC.1/c, U.S. NAVY 372-84-75	2	35
DARNEAL, DILLARD A. M.M.1/c, U.S. NAVY 346-70-11	4G	36
DUDLEY, NOBLE O. MM1/c, U.S. NAVY 283-11-10	3B	37

Above and opposite: Hanawa Medical Report recovered from microfilm. Note Addie's death listed as 10:30 p.m. on 8 June. (National Archives)

12/28/44 TYNOSYNOVITIS LEFT WRIST.

Stool - Negative
Back Injury

Stool - Negative
1/19/45 BRONCHITIS

Stool - Negative
2/26/45 - Enteritis, recurrent

Stool - Neg.
11/25/44 MALNUTRITION (SEVERE)
2/27/45 EPIDIDYMITIS, BI-LATERAL

4/10/45 Stool - Ascaris Lumbricoides
11/29/44 BERI-BERI AND DIAHRREA.

Stool - Negative
2/12/45 OTITIS MEDIA 5/2 Infested rt foot
Recurrent malnutrition.

4/28/45 - Stool - Ascaris Lumbricoides.
DIED 10:30 P.M. 6/8/45 of TUBERCULOSIS
BODY EXAMINED. DIAGNOSIS PROVEN BY POSITIVE
EXAMINATION OF SPUTUM.

2/24 Influenza. 5/21 Contusion rt hand

Stool - Negative

3/19/45. Stool - Ascaris Lumbricoides
4/5/45. Tonsillitis, acute; acute extraction

4/22/45 - Stool - Ascaris Lumbricoides
Enteritis, persistent. Bleeding hemorrhoids

3/14/45 - Stool - Ascaris Lumbricoides
1/8/45 INJURED GREAT TOE 6/2 Lacerated rt ankle
Oct. '44: BERI-BERI. 7/24 Bunion

6/13/45 Stool - Ascaris Lumbricoides
Beriberi

MAT	UNN NO.	CARD NO.	RANK	NAME
A.	III 1	III 254	SGT.	CHAVEZ, RAMONSE A.
A.	III 2	III 247	SEA CAR MAN 1CLA	CARSON HENRY I.
A.	VI 1	VI 242	PVT.	HAVILAND WILLIAM JAMES
A.	VI 2	VI 31	1ST SGT.	MARTIN ADRIAN RAFAEL
A.	VI 3	VI 436	PVT.	KNOWLES JASPER R.
A.	VII 1	VII 2642	CIV.	EWING, JAMES
A.	VII 2	VII 2502	P.F.C. U.S.M.	JANSEN ROBERT O.
A.	V 1	V 1680	TEC. SGT.	SPARKS RAYMOND T.
A.	V 20	V 1763	CPL.	GASKIN EARL E.
A.	V 26	V 1743	P.F.C. U.S.M.	WALSH JUSTIN C.

Above and opposite: Sendai Camps' death list. Note Addie's death is recorded as 9/6/45 (9 June 1945). Recovered from microfilm. (National Archives)

REG. NO.	DIAG.	DEATH DATE	DEPT. of REPORT
20841750	PLEURISY PNEUMONIA	25/5/45	L. SANTILLANES 469 E. OLIVE ALBUQUERQUE N.M.
393- 39-46	BERI-BERI	26/5/45	M.I. CARSON 1147 HARVARD ROSEBURG, ORE.
35014809	PNEUMONIA T.B.	1/6/45	C. HAVILAND 9516 LEO AVE. CLEVELAND, OHI
36204795	T.B.	9/6/45	W.H. MARTIN 303 S. KNIB S MYERS, WIS.
19019930	ENTERITIS BERI BERI	8/7/45	I.E. TRATE THREE FORKS MON
	PNEUMONIA	10/7/45	A. EWING 3302 ELM ST. OAKLAND, CALS
	ENTERITIS BERI BERI	15/7/45	T.J. JANSEN 4211 W. LEIAN CHICAGO, ILL.
237627	CRUSHED	14/7/45	T.H. SPARKS EDEN, TEXAS
268825	BURN	9/8/45	B. GARCIA BOAZ ALA.
	BURN?	10/8/45	E.B. WAISM MOUNTAIN CIT TENN.

THE COMPANY WILL APPRECIATE SUGGESTIONS FROM ITS PATRONS CONCERNING ITS SERVICE

1201-S

WESTERN UNION

R. B. WHITE
PRESIDENT

NEWCOMB CARLTON
CHAIRMAN OF THE BOARD

J. C. WILLEVER
FIRST VICE-PRESIDENT

CLASS OF SERVICE

This is a full-rate Telegram or Cablegram unless its deferred character is indicated by a suitable symbol above or preceding the address.

SYMBOLS

DL = Day Letter
NM = Night Message
NL = Night Letter
LC = Deferred Cable
NLT = Cable Night Letter
Ship Radiogram

The filing time shown in the date line on telegrams and day letters is STANDARD TIME at point of origin. Time of receipt is STANDARD TIME at point of destination.

Received at
⌐AUA 336 105 GOV WUX

WASHINGTON D C 29 239PM

MRS ANNA MARTIN . 803 LEWIS ST DE PERE, W. S.

IT IS WITH DEEP DISTRESS THAT I MUST INFORM YOU THAT SINCE MY TELEGRAM

30 AUGUST INVITING YOU TO SUBMIT A MESSAGE FOR ATTEMPTED TRANSMITION TO

YOUR SON IN THE EVENT HE WAS RETURNED TO MILITARY CONTROL A REPORT HAS

JUST BEEN RECIEVED WHICH STATES THAT YOUR SON FIRST SERGEANT ADRIAN R.

MARTIN DIED IN JAPAN 9 JUNE 1945 WHILE A PRISONER OF WAR OF THE

JAPENESE GOVERNMENT AS RESULT OF TUBERCULOSIS. THE SECRETARY

OF WAR ASKS THAT I EXPRESS HIS DEEPEST SYMPATHY TO YOU IN YOUR TRAGIC

LOSS PERMIT ME TO ADD MY OWN PERSONEL EXPRESSION OF CONDOLENCE

CONFIRMING LETTER FOLLOWS

(OVER)

THE QUICKEST, SUREST AND SAFEST WAY TO SEND MONEY IS BY TELEGRAPH OR CABLE

Japan weren't someone else's, some hoax to somehow sooth the grieving families? I presented that dilemma to Captain Fleming.

FLEMING — We took those eight boxes with us and turned them over to the authorities at Yokohama. Can we be assured that the remains are those of First Sergeant Martin? No, we couldn't. We lost

---

MWG/cgf

WAR DEPARTMENT

THE ADJUTANT GENERAL'S OFFICE

IN REPLY REFER TO:
AG 201 Martin, Adrian R.   WASHINGTON 25, D. C.
PC-0 299106

1 November 1945

Mrs. Anna Martin
303 South Erie Street
DePere, Wisconsin

Dear Mrs. Martin:

It is with profound regret that I confirm the recent telegram informing you of the death of your son, First Sergeant Adrian R. Martin, 36,204,798, Coast Artillery Corps, who was previously reported a prisoner of war.

An official message has now been received which states that he died on 9 June 1945 at Serdai Assembly Area, Camp Number 6, Japan, as a result of tuberculosis.

I realize the great suspense you have endured during this unfortunately long period and now, the finality to those hopes which you have cherished for his safety. Although little may be said or done at this time to alleviate your grief, it is my fervent hope that later the knowledge that he gave his life for his country may be of sustaining comfort to you.

I extend my profound sympathy in your bereavement.

Sincerely yours,

Edward F. Witsell

EDWARD F. WITSELL
Major General
Acting The Adjutant General of the Army

1 Inclosure
WD Pamphlet No. 20-15

contact with the body when it left the prison camp. We knew nothing until they brought the ashes back.

But I believe the ashes are his, and I'll tell you why. There are several things there that make a difference. One: the Japanese had nothing to gain by not returning the ashes of the men that died. Another is that they had a great respect for the dead. It's a tradition in Japan, so I just can't believe that they would have violated that.

Later that month, Addie's ashes were returned to the town he had left in 1941 as a volunteer to see the country that was not yet at war. On 25 November a memorial service was held at St. Francis for his family and friends, and his ashes were later placed in the family plot in Mount Olive Cemetery. A simple flat marker states:

Adrian R. Martin
First Sergeant/200th Coast Artillery
Born: March 4, 1914 Died: June 9, 1945

When it came time to inscribe the marker, his family chose to believe the War Department and not the *Tribune*.

Camp Humor

A peacetime Adrian Martin had made humor an integral part of his life. Despite three years of starvation, the men at Hanawa found humor essential to their survival. Whether in the barracks, at the mine, or on the walk between the two, humor at Hanawa had a contagious effect.

M. K. MARTIN — There were two cowboys in 3A who were great storytellers and the best morale builders in the camp. Here is an example:

First Old Buddy: "What's worse than being cold?"
long pause
Second Old Buddy: "Being cold and wet."
long pause
First Old Buddy: "What's worse than being cold and wet?"
long pause
Second Old Buddy: "Being cold and wet and hungry."

This conversation took place every evening when we returned from the mine. We were all cold, wet, and hungry all the time. All of us looked forward to the little by-play as it was delivered in such a way that all of us were held in suspense during their pauses wondering if they would change the routine. They NEVER did!

STANLEY — Some guy would come through the barracks and yell, "Would you rather have a can of corn beef or Betty Grable?"
The guys would answer, "To hell with Betty Grable!"

One of the men, Warren Ghilardi of San Francisco, expressed his humor with cartoons. Leslie Canfield, a member of Ghilardi's section, saved the cartoons. Cartoon #1 (below) was drawn 14 July 1945 while listening to POWs tell what they were going to do upon return. Cartoon #2 (p. 266) was drawn on 3 August 1945 while listening to POWs' comments on the States' reaction to their return. It was drawn in five minutes — the time between muster and starting the march up the mountain to the mine.

The War Ends

History books record that the atomic bomb was dropped on 6 August 1945 on Hiroshima in southern Honshu and a few days later on Nagasaki, a port city on the island of Kyushu. These same books record that the Japanese surrendered on 15 August, and the formal surrender document was signed by MacArthur and representatives of the Japanese government on 2 September on the battleship *Missouri* and the War was over. But the men at Hanawa in northern Honshu, hundreds of miles away from the "action," did not experience this textbook ending. News of the bombing, surrender, and liberation came in bits and pieces. Phone communications were very poor.

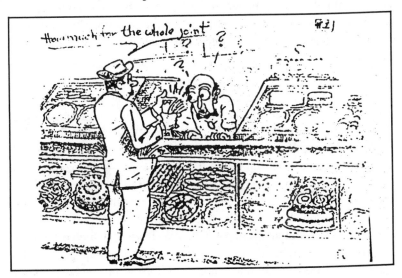

Besides, American Intelligence wasn't sure how many POW camps there were in northern Honshu. But even before the August A-bombs, the men at Hanawa had an inkling that the end was near. When Don Berger and the others returned in March 1945 from Shinagawa Hospital near Tokyo, they reported firsthand on the devastation caused by our bombers. Others heard "rumors" in a variety of ways.

FRANCIES — The civilians in charge of us at the flotations machines occasionally gave us hints as to what was going on at the war front. They would always tell us when the Japanese had won some kind of battle. But these battles that they were winning were always getting closer and closer to Japan. We knew the Americans were on their way.

FLEMING — One of the amusing memories that I have of Asaka was after our country had dropped the first atomic bomb on the 6th of August of '45. He called me in. He was reading a newspaper. He called the interpreter in, so I knew this was a serious meeting. Through the interpreter he told me that one *"B-ni ju kyu,"* which is Japanese for one B-29, flew over Hiroshima and dropped one bomb and destroyed the city and killed 100,000 people. It was so powerful that it even dried up water in streams as far as ten kilometers, which is about six miles away. So I listened to this through the interpreter, and I responded somewhat along the following lines.

I said, "Ah, Lieutenant, that is Japanese *senden*, (which is Japanese for propaganda). What they didn't tell you in that newspaper was that there were 1,000 B-29s that came over." Now of course we knew nothing of the atomic bomb. I discussed this with the other officers when I returned from the interview with Asaka. We just left it hanging. They got a big laugh out of my telling Asaka it was 1,000 B-29s.

At any event the second bomb was dropped on Nagasaki on August 9th 1945. So he called me over. He was reading the newspaper again, and the little moon-faced Japanese interpreter, who was afraid of his own shadow, turned to me and said, "They've done it again!" I almost had to laugh.

So we knew something was up. This time when I returned to the officer's quarters we huddled. Somebody, I think it was Dick Pullen, said, "You know they broke the atom somewhere before the war, and I wonder if they perfected an atomic bomb."

We had heard rumors that Okinawa had fallen. We knew that Iwo Jima had fallen. We knew that the Americans were bombing the hell out of Tokyo. We anticipated a landing. You always like to have the optimistic rumors, so we felt the Americans would land in Japan during the summer of 1945.

NIX — Hanawa was very isolated from the rest of Japan. It is not near the major metropolitan areas that were targets when the Americans started bombing Japan. From the time we arrived there in September of 1944 until August of 1945, we did not have a single air raid alert. We did not miss a day of work because of air raids nor did we see a single American plane. Somewhere around August 10th we had warmed up in the yard and had started to go out when the first air raid alert came on. They sent us back to the barracks and told us to stay inside and don't come out. The all-clear came on about an hour or two later, so they took us out again. On the way to the mine we had another air raid alert, so we went back in the barracks. That went on all day. That was the first day we had work interrupted by an outside source. We never did work a full day at the mine from August 10th to 15th. I heard the Japanese talking at the mine in their *kupae* shack [warming shack], and I could understand some of their conversation. This was after the bombing of Hiroshima and Nagasaki. They were shaking their head. They didn't realize that I was listening. They said, *"Echi Vakadon, Echi skoshi hati pot-I"* which means "One bomb, many soldiers killed." I didn't understand the impact of what this was, but I fathomed that something big was going on. We had no resources for news other than what we overheard. Some of the men had picked up the ability to read some of the newspapers, but what was appearing in the newspapers wasn't always what was going on.

The camp knew something was up when on 14 August the men were not sent to the mine, and they were not told why. This "No Work" order continued until the morning of 20 August at 9:30 when Lieutenant Asaka delivered his "peace" speech. The speech was given in Japanese but translated into English by the moon-faced interpreter. The speech in broken English was later posted and many copied it.

> Peace, peace comes to all the world again. It is great pleasure for me, to say nothing of you, to announce it for all of you now. The Japanese Empire acknowledges the terms of suspension of hostilities as given by the American Government even though these two nations do not still reach the best agreement of a truce. As a true friend from now on I am going to do my best in the future for the convenience of your life in this camp because of having been able to get friendly relations between them, and also the Japanese have decided their own Nation's Policy for your Nation. Therefore, I hope you will keep a comfortable daily life by the orders of your own officers from today while you are staying here. All of you will surely get much gladness in returning to your own lovely country. At the same time one of my wishes for you is this: your health and happiness will call upon you and your life henceforth will grow up happier and better than before by the honor of your own country. In order to guard your life I have been endeavoring in ability. Therefore you will please cooperate with me in anything more than usual, I hope. I enclose the statement in letting your honor again. The peace already has come.

The reactions to the speech were varied. Many of the men already knew that the war was obviously over. Many noted that the Asaka forgot to mention that the Americans were the victors and the Japanese the losers.

> COLE — Yeah, the Americans got Asaka's government's attention by dropping two atom bombs. Naturally, you would think that after the message that the war was over that there would be a tremendous explosion. There wasn't. You could hear a pin drop. We were supposed to be executed in the event that there were any landings on the Japanese mainland. They had a 50-caliber machine gun in the camp compound ready to go. They called us out, and we were worried about getting killed. After the announcement, we all turned around and went back to the barracks. When we got to the barracks, all hell broke loose. We cried, we prayed, we grabbed each other and hugged. The next thing we heard was, "Hey you owe me a ration of rice, I told you the gull darn war was over."

STAUDENRAUS — I still have a copy of the speech. I think we were quite subdued. Just the fact that there would be no more harassment and we could now take care of our physical needs was a tremendous relief. You must remember we were just plain exhausted.

THRONEBERRY — For three days we did not go to work in the mines. The guards were leaving camp with their guns. Everyone was whispering "The war must be over." We were told they were commemorating their war dead.

Later Asaka was asked if the war were over. He replied, "No, No!" Someone slapped him across the face which was of course a great insult. He yelled, "Kioski," and then standing at attention he said, "The war is now over. We have come to a friendly truce and agreement. We are now friends, and you will be treated as such." Everyone screamed and hollered saying that they wanted meat in camp. In no time, three fat steers were brought in, the warehouse opened up, and we had blankets and even some unopened Red Cross boxes.

ZORZANELLO — My reaction to Asaka's speech was, "Hallelujah, it's really over!!" We were still in hostile territory, however. Our barracks were like tinder. Any rash act by a diehard Jap could quickly end it for us, so I didn't stop praying.

Now that the men were "free," would anyone know where to look for them? Most of the American intelligence reports stated that the POWs were in camps in southern and central Honshu. Would anyone think to look in the mountains of northern Honshu? And if they did, how soon would it be before they were liberated?

Captain Fleming and others prepared the camp as best they could.

FLEMING — We had a bugler begin all the bugle calls all day that were appropriate like "first call" and "reveille." One of the things that we did that was helpful was we had a Navy signal man who knew the Morse code, and we took a piece of stove pipe and put a shaving mirror in the back of it, wired it with an electric bulb, and put a handle on it so you could hold it. We waited for the planes to find us.

And the planes came. . . .

PAYNE — The torpedo planes came about 3:00 p.m. [21 August] to drop K-rations for us. They circled the camp and signaled us to mark out a spot about 50 feet in diameter and place something white in the middle so they could drop. This we did, and we circled around the 50-foot circle with a Jap bed sheet in the middle. There were six planes; the first four dropped almost dead center with each making two drops. The fifth plane's bundle hung and went over our heads, hitting the side of a building knocking a 10 foot hole in it. That's when we realized how stupid we were. These bundles weighed about 40 pounds, and the speed of the diving planes made them somewhat dangerous. We spread out a bit after that. The first four were precise, lucky for us. They asked for 50 feet, and that's all we gave them, and they put it there. That's how good some of those bombers were.

DR. GOLENTERNEK — The planes asked us to print in white paint on the barracks roof what medications we needed. They dropped food by parachute and a case of canned food fell through the roof into the mess hall. The men had little fires and cooked and ate all day.

FRANCIES — It was great when the US Navy torpedo planes came over and dropped the message that when they developed the film of the reconnaissance plane and saw the "Hanawa-550 POWs" that we were in an unmarked prison camp, . . . they came back to investigate. They said they couldn't drop any supplies, but that they had already radioed Saipan and that the B-29s would be up the next day with our supplies.

These "Saipan Samaritans," as the B-29s were dubbed, carried enough food in 55-gallon drums to feed 200 prisoners. Usually 18 bundles were loaded in the bomb bay and dropped from less than 1,000 feet.

FLEMING — The first planes found us, I believe, on the 21st of August. They were Navy and off the carrier *Bennington*. Anyhow, these big torpedo bombers, a huge single-engine plane, came over and wagged their wings. We signaled up to them. I think we said we needed medicine. They dropped a message to us that "We're going back to the carrier and will be back in four hours." So shortly before dark they came back in and dropped all sorts of things to us including, as I remember, penicillin, which our doctors were unaware of. Penicillin had been discovered after we had been captured. As I remember it, the doctors had to learn how to use penicillin.

FRANCIES — The B-29s arrived the next day. We had never seen anything larger than a B-17. These B-29s were huge! They circled the camp for a short time and waved to all of us. Then they gained more altitude and dropped us supplies via parachute — clothes, food, and medicine. They dropped penicillin, and we had never heard of it or knew what it was. So back up on the roof of the barracks the men went and painted "PENICILLIN?" A short time after the planes flew over the next time, one came back and dropped a book on penicillin.

DR. GOLENTERNEK — We had a man, a tall blond, who had a kidney infection. He had a high fever, and we would treat him with sulfa and that would help him for three or four days. Then we would give him more sulfa. After the planes dropped the medicine, Dr. Lamy said. "Let's give him this penicillin."

I said, "No, we kept him alive this long. We don't know anything about this drug." What we knew I think we read in *Reader's Digest*.

I said, "Let's keep giving him the sulfa and get him home." We never did use the penicillin.

FLEMING — The B-29s came every other day for, I don't know, six or eight trips, and they dropped it all over the landscape. We had a 55-gallon drum of food or clothing that went through the Japanese headquarters building, but no one was injured.

On the second drop by the B-29s, a barrel full of peaches went through the roof of a nearby Jap house. The Jap was cooking over his hibachi, and the barrel hit him in the lap. I figured we better help this guy, or he'll make a claim against the American government for about $10,000.00. But the men I sent over to help him were eating the peaches on the way down to him. I heard he later died.

Not all the food came from the planes however.

DR. GOLENTERNEK — After the War ended, we told them we wanted a cow every day. They said they couldn't get one. I said, "I didn't ask you if you can get one. I said bring us a cow every day."

"There are no cows in this part of Japan."

"It doesn't matter. Just bring us a cow every day."

They brought us a cow.

FLEMING — One of the big things we did immediately after we knew the War was over was we fired up the bath house and kept the water hot all day and into the evening. Everyone got a decent bath. That was great!

They also dropped DDT powder. We had one helluva time with

fleas. So for the first time since winter, we managed to get rid of the
fleas.

LAWRENCE VAN LIERE — Those B-29s dropped Watkins flea
powder. We sprinkled, on the sleeping mats and watched as the fleas
started jumping — each time a little lower until finally all were dead.
We got our first good night's sleep without scratching all night.

Not only could the men eat, take a bath, and get a good night's sleep, but
they also could read.

FLEMING — One interesting thing, when the Navy came they must
have cleared out the officer's ward room of everything that was
readable. That night we stayed up all night with one man reading out
loud and everybody else listening. Strangely enough, to show you
what happened there, we had a newspaper, the *Honolulu Advertiser*,
that was only three-days-old. It was great sport to read *Time* and *Life*
and some of those magazines that they dropped to us.

Eating *real American* food for the first time in 3½ years was just what the
prisoners needed to restore their health and stem their weight loss. But the
sudden availability of food was not without problems.

FLEMING — We ate everything we could get a hold of, and with Dr.
Golenternek and Dr. Lamy's guidance, we restricted the amount of
food a person could eat at one time. We would serve several meals a
day. Even then some of us got sick. It was sort of hard to transition
from a bland diet to a full-fledged American diet.

CANFIELD — I remember well Dr. Golenternek's comments about
overeating of the rations. He said, "If you overeat you will probably
bloat, get diarrhea, and throw up." I did overeat and he was absolutely
right. I did all three! Such sweet torture at the time.

NIX — If the parachute didn't open, the 55-gallon drums couldn't
slow down. They hit pretty hard in the rice paddies and everything
would squirt out the end of the barrels like a cannon. We were sent out
to pick up the rations. I remember this can of peaches — the
concussion forced all the juice out one end, and all we had to do was
gorge ourselves on the peaches that remained. We had chocolate bars
— you name it. It was like taking things off the Christmas tree. Some
of the guys just overate, and they paid the consequences with a severe

case of diarrhea. But there was cigarettes, chewing gum, clothing, and medicine. You name it, and it was in those barrels. You could eat all you wanted, any time you wanted. The mess hall was always open 24 hours a day. We would get our mess kit filled up with rice first and a little bit of the rations. Gradually, after a few days, you couldn't give your rice away. Everyone wanted the food from the barrels.

Now the weather was warm, about 80 degrees because it was August. We would go to our sleeeping areas after stuffing ourselves, and we'd chew about five sticks of gum and get all the sweetness out, then throw it out the window. Then we'd light up a Camel cigarette. We thought this was great. When we were finished with the cigarette, then we started on another pack of gum. When that was done, then we'd smoke another cigarette.

But the men soon tired of doing nothing but eating, smoking, and chewing gum. Captain Fleming and Colonel Walker thought some exercise and sightseeing would alleviate the boredom.

FLEMING — We spent time until liberation with some training. We did some close order drill. We would split the men into groups of 50 or 100, and we'd go down to the river in the valley and go swimming. We went into town. We did not work in the mine. You can bet on that. We went on walking tours around the area we had been prevented from going to before.

NIX — Colonel Walker had us off drilling. I didn't give a damn because a little exercise wouldn't hurt me. But I got more fun watching the British drill because they did the "right," "left," and "stomp" much different than we did it. We used to crack up because we didn't care if we were in step or not.

Not all the men confined their exercising to the camp. Some ventured into Hanawa.

FLEMING — I got to town a number of times with Takahashi. I don't remember any untoward incidents that happened to me. It seems to me we stopped someplace one time and had a soft drink together. They had controlled houses of prostitution there, and I think some of the men managed to find one of them. I don't know what they used for money. Maybe it was free at that point.

CANFIELD — I went to town twice. Once a group of us just walked around. The shops were deserted. The streets were deserted. It looked as if the Japanese people were afraid of us weak, skinny Americans.

The second time was to pay a visit to the civilian in charge of the millwright section. He helped us when he could and in the end invited us to his house. I only wish I could remember more about the visit than removing my shoes and putting them back on!

Another group of men from Section 4D decided that having their picture taken in Hanawa would be a fine memento. After walking into a downtown studio to arrange for the picture, they were paid a surprise visit by Lieutenant Asaka. The picture was taken approximately three weeks after receiving the B-29 drop of food, clothing, and medicine. The men looked healthier, heavier, cleaner, and happier than they did in the months previous.

COLE — We were downtown and saw this little photography studio. Someone got the bright idea to go in and have our picture taken. We went in, took off our shoes, and walked in front of the camera. By this time, we were wearing semi-American clothes due to the fact that the B-29s had dropped clothes to us. While we were in yakking about having the picture taken, Lieutenant Asaka for one reason or another was walking the streets, and he saw us go in the studio. A hush fell over the room when he came in. He was a good looking guy, dark, and wore shiny boots. He smiled all over and told the lady to make one picture for every man, and he paid for it!

But there was just so much one could see in Hanawa, so by the time 1 September rolled around, the men were getting anxious about being recovered. They became extremely excited one day when a vehicle containing Recovery Personnel drove into the compound. The newly arrived Americans took some pictures, interviewed some of the men, and promptly left, leaving the disgruntled prisoners behind.

FLEMING — When planes began dropping the food, they also dropped a message: "Do Not Leave the Camp — We're Coming to Get You."

Well, they never did. The two or three men that came up the road one day in the jeep, I can't remember why they were there by themselves, but they did not "liberate" us.

COLE — They sent Non-Commissioned Officers into the camp, and they took pictures and interviewed us and checked out our rations. And boy, were they celebrities. There must have been three or four of them, and the guys took them into the barracks and ganged around them and made them unload their pockets. They made them take their money out of their pockets so they could see. "Look at the date on that bill. That came out after I was a POW." They talked to them about everything. We also heard them say that a detachment of WACs had been brought up from Australia. We thought it might be a new secret weapon or a group of those animals you find in Australia. It wasn't until we got aboard the rescue ship that we found out what a WAC really was — Women's Army Corps.

One of the reasons the men were requested to stay in camp was the American authorities were concerned with the possibility of revenge by the Japanese civilians.

FLEMING — On the day before the Emperor announced the unconditional surrender, we were still in hostile territory. There were occasions when men walking to work at the mine had a rock thrown at them or were spit on. We thought probably most of that was maybe somebody had a relative or son that was killed fighting the Americans. Most of the Japanese just disregarded us or looked at us with curiosity.

The interesting thing is that the day after the surrender, they were bowing and scraping. They changed from being all black to all white. No gray area — no transition. It was just like you turned a light switch on, the way they changed. Everybody was all smiles, and everybody was happy.

DR. GOLENTERNEK — After the Japs surrendered, the Jap officers wanted to have a little get-together with the American officers at the Mitsubishi Country Club, which was away from camp. The American officers wanted no part of that. We wanted to have it here in camp. We all sat around drinking saké, and Colonel Walker got up and sang a song that went something like, "I'll be seeing you when you're dead."

Leaving Hanawa

But it wasn't until mid-September that Hanawa was liberated. After the first week of September when no rescue team appeared in Hanawa, Colonel Walker and Captain Fleming feared that some of the men might leave on their own.

FLEMING — One of the things we were trying to avoid was the men taking off individually. In a number of other camps they did that. I

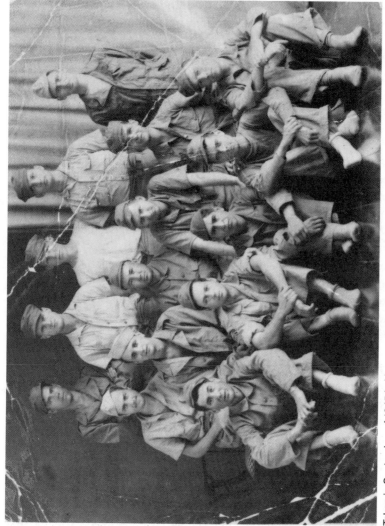

Taken in September of 1945 in Hanawa, Japan. Top row, left to right: Diaz Pablo, Jimmy Vaughn, Sedric Pearson, Prewett, Silverstein, Brownell Cole, S. F. Brooks, M. Vidaurri, L. Whichard, Al Lopez, M. Torres, R. Levis, Sisneros, J. Brundage, Clarence Shaw. (Courtesy of Brownell Cole)

did that. I think some of them got hurt or maybe even killed trying to get to Yokohama.

We might have been one of the last camps liberated. But really, no one came to liberate us. We eventually went out on our own. By the time it got to be the 8th or 9th of September, I was concerned that the men were going to start going on their own. I told the Japs to put a train on the track down at the station, which they did. We took a group of men down on one of our morning walks, and I pointed out the train to them. I said, "There's the train. As soon as the railroad tracks are fixed we'll go." That quieted the men down.

Getting liberation information was difficult. One afternoon Captain Fleming visited the nearby Italian Embassy to find out why the POWs hadn't moved.

FLEMING — I went over to the Italian Embassy one day by car and visited with them. They had been in the Mussolini Embassy in Tokyo. When Mussolini's government fell and Italy was taken over by America, they were no longer welcome in Japan. They moved them to an isolated area, six or eight miles from our camp.

But the Italians were of little help. Not until 14 September did word reach Hanawa that the prisoners were to leave.

FLEMING — Authorization for us to move came through channels unknown to me. I did not have control of that. If I did, I might have said, "Let's go now!" I think the authorities wanted the LSTs [landing craft] and the USS *RESCUE* in Shiogama Bay. That might have been the delay. There was no way they could handle us if we got there early. On the afternoon of the 14th of September, Asaka got word that we would leave at midnight.

Before the men could leave, there were a number of tasks to complete. One involved money.

FLEMING — The Japanese had been paying us a couple of yen a day for working at the mine, but there was no way we could spend the money. They didn't have a commissary, so we put it in the bank. We took the passbooks and about 15 men from our camp and went down to the bank and said, "We want our money!" They jabbered around for awhile. We pulled the rifles out that we had taken from the guards, and they bowed, "*Ahso, ahso!*" And started counting out the money.

And the other task involved food.

ROBERT JOHNSTON — The surplus things, we sent to the Chinese POW camp not far from ours. The rest of the things we didn't need, we gave to the Japanese civilians.

COLE — There was this old man who worked at the mine. We called him papasan. Old papasan was always good to us. He had this old skinny horse, and he'd come into camp with the horse and go and get the droppings in the honey buckets. There was a long trap door behind the *benjo* with this great big long ladle and he would put the droppings on his cart and go down into the valley and sell it as fertilizer.

This papasan was the one who told us that President Roosevelt had died. He always seemed pro-American. When we were getting ready to leave camp, we wondered what we were going to do with all the food. We decided to give it to papasan. We went out and found him, and he brought that horse and cart into camp. We loaded it with food. He just sat down and cried.

Once the prisoner's money and the excess food were taken care of, it was time to leave Hanawa.

COLE — I remember we marched out of camp around midnight on a damp, rainy night. I could hear the British singing a marching song.

> And they say there's a ship a leaving Bombay
> Bound for the old Blimy shore
> Heavily laden with time-expired men
> Bound for the shores they adore.
> Bless them all, bless them all, the long, the short, and the tall.
> Bless all of the sergeants and all of the guns.
> Bless all of the corporals and all of their sons,
> Cause we're saying good-bye to them all
> And back to their foxholes they crawl.
> Bless them all, bless them all.
> The long, the short, and the tall.
> You'll get no promotions this side of the ocean,
> So cheer up me lads, bless them all.

VAN LIERE — I'll never forget the British singing "God Bless Them All," etcetera. They did not *bless* us but substituted a common GI four-letter word.

FLEMING — We loaded on the train, and this is interesting. They even provided sleeping cars for the officers. I think Asaka and Takahashi were in these Pullman cars with us. I don't recall the other guards going with us. We arrived at Sendai the next morning close to noon. We found out that there was an American ship in the harbor at the port of Shiogama. They backed the train up and got off on a spur track. After an hour or so ride, sure enough there was the rescue team. Lying off the coast was the hospital ship *Rescue*. Pulled up on the beach was an LST landing craft. They loaded us into the belly of that thing. Suddenly somebody said, "Look, look guys. There's our flag." It brought tears to everyone's eyes. That's the first time I ever saw 500 grown men cry. You just can't imagine the emotion. I still get emotional when I think about it.

PELTIER — We arrived at Shiogama at 10:15 a.m. on the 14th. We boarded a landing barge, #252, which took us to the USN hospital ship *Rescue*. Later we took the troop transport and set sail for Yokohama. On September 15th, we arrived and landed at 7:00 a.m. on September 16th.

FLEMING — We were on the *Rescue* for a few hours. They only kept the most seriously ill men. Then we were put on a troop-carrying destroyer that night. The next morning we were in Yokohama. The money from Hanawa we had taken with us. On the dock at Yokohama we debated what to do with it. I eventually got a jeep and a driver and went from the port area and up to the Headquarters of the 8th Army. We gave it to the finance officer and labeled it to be used by the Red Cross. We didn't take any of it ourselves.

PELTIER — We finally set sail about 7:00 a.m. on September 19th and arrived outside the Manila breakwater about 11:00 a.m. September 25th. We disembarked at 9:30 a.m. September 26th. We boarded a Dutch ship, *Clip Fontaine*, on October 8th, and docked at Seattle, Washington about 9:00 p.m. October 27th and disembarked the next morning about 10:00 a.m.

Most of the Hanawa men who left the *Clip Fontaine* that October morning hoped for a return to a normal life. Many didn't realize that after being away for four years that their future would become anything but normal. What happened to them *after* the War is as important as what happened to them *during* the War. But for Addie, whose ashes remained behind in Yokohama, only his relatives and friends could guess what his future may have held.

Prisoner Remembrances of Adrian Raphael Martin

Another irony of war is that the participants often aren't the same people they were before they entered conflict. My generation fought the Vietnam conflict and numerous friends of mine all seemed changed after they returned in the early seventies.

If Adrian Raphael Martin had survived, what type of person would have returned to Wisconsin? For many of the Bataan-Corregidor survivors, the war and POW life changed them, and the effects, good or bad, have never left them. Would the postwar Addie have been different than the Addie that Harold Schumerth, Jim Martin, Virgil Kohlbeck, and John Toonen of DePere knew?

FERRARI LETTER — June 1947 — Addie was a man who had no enemies. Regardless who you may meet that knew him, they would say the same. He was loyal and faithful, always ready to help the other person regardless who he was, whether it was during battle or our internment in prison camp.

Mrs. Martin, you had a grand son. Always feel especially proud of him and try to feel happy when thinking of him for that's the way he'd want it to be. He will never be forgotten, that he knows, by you and his family and buddies.

MANASSE LETTER — November 1945 — Adrian was one of the swellest fellows I have ever been fortunate enough to know. He was a good soldier and believed in the inherent goodness of mankind, something that few of us can do.

FATHER DUFFY LETTER — November 1947 — You had a great son, Mr. and Mrs. Martin. He was a wonderful boy. He always fulfilled the highest traditions of his Church and nation. He was a credit to his parents, his teachers, and his country. Why God chose to call him home we do not know. But I'm sure that he is happy and still putting in a few punches for his Padre with the Big Boss up above. You should feel great consolation that you have a son to represent you before the Judgment Seat of God and who will be petitioning God to put some sense into this silly, senseless world that is so unappreciative of so many blessings.

WALTER GILLES LETTER — 30 October 1945 — Addie was one of the finest Catholic fellows I met during my three years and four months as a prisoner. There is no doubt he is in heaven because he surely spent his time in hell. May God rest his soul.

MARVIN SHEARWOOD (Hanawa bunkmate) — Adrian Martin was one of the finest, nicest men I ever knew in my life. He was always so kind and sympathetic to others. When he was so very sick and weak, his personality was still sunny and bright. If this world was full of Adrian Martins, there would be no need for armies, and this would be a much better place to live.

Epilogue

Ex-POWs Today

As I conducted this research, I often wondered why Addie didn't come back and others did. When I've asked the Vietnam veteran of my generation why he came home alive, his usual response was, "There wasn't a bullet with my name on it." I posed the question of survival to many Bataan veterans. Only one told me that your survival was predetermined even before the War started — when your time's up, it's up. Many, on the other hand, believed God and a positive attitude had something to do with their returning.

PELTIER — I prayed and put my trust in God. Perhaps I can say it this way — Thy Will Be Done.

THRONEBERRY — I survived due to my faith in God and the feeling that we *would* survive. I fixed a date in my mind when this would happen, and though I had to advance the date three times, I came very close to the date of actual liberation. Also, the fact that I did not smoke was in my favor. I saw too many men trade their rations for cigarettes. And they starved.

NIX — The only way a lot of guys survived was having faith in their country and faith in their God. When you go through these kinds of things, like torture, that's what you fall back on. If you allow yourself to think negatively, you are not going to have an easy course. In our time, the rumors were off of every latrine — "The War is going to be over" or "The Americans are coming." And it wasn't necessarily so. If you said that the Americans were going to be here on August 6th and you get to August 6th and nothing happened, you were disappointed. You were let down. My philosophy was that the War would be over in a six months' period. No certification of a date. I *never* set a date. I said, "Six months more and we'll be out of here." I remember one day we were chatting with the guys, and I started saying, "Six months more," and ultimately, I was right. Subsequent to this, anytime I found a "figmo sheet" in my section, a calendar that you laboriously marked off each day until you were out, I made the prisoner tear it up. It was not good for morale. If you said, "Six more months and we'll be out," that was fine. But no "figmo sheet." He was a better soldier without that "figmo sheet."

One who thought survival was merely luck lately has changed his mind.

TRONESS — I always thought it was luck. I missed Camp O'Donnell by luck. I missed the boat torpedoed at Sindangan Bay by a stroke of luck. Lately I've begun to think the luck was answers to my parents' prayers rather than luck.

And maybe in the decades to come more Vietnam veterans will consider that prayer had a role in their return. But POW survival was much different from that of the ordinary foot soldier. Many Bataan veterans believe that Depression upbringing before the War had much to do with surviving the POW experience.

DE BAUCHE — I was an orphan growing up in Milwaukee. I had to fight with the Blacks in my own neighborhood just to survive. Then during the thirties I worked in a Civilian Conservation Camp. I never had any money. I had a POW friend who always had his mother do things for him. He refused to eat the rice the Japs gave us. He died.

STEMLER — Sometimes you wonder how the hell you made it. From the beatings a guy took you wouldn't think there'd be an unbroken bone left in your body. The guy who wanted to live, he lived. That was about the size of it. You had to have the attitude, "The hell with you. You ain't goin' to get me!" Some of that stuff — givin' up easy, quitting, or fighting to hold on — that comes from home. A lot of these kids were brought up in a world with a fence around it. Half of them didn't make it because of too much dependence on everyone else. That was the big thing in prison camp. A guy who was getting the strap once in a while as a kid, he's the guy that came out of it. The guy who never had a fight in his life didn't have it in him. He died.

Those who did return soon found that the POW experience remained with them. For all, the 3½ years of incarceration affected their health. For many it also touched their minds.

> McVEY — Some of the guys came back and went right to work, settled down, and raised families. And then there were some guys who couldn't get the war out of their head. That's all they talked about was being in a Japanese prisoner of war camp. They traveled the country looking for the guys they served with to talk about the experience.

One group that didn't do a good job of listening was the Veterans Administration (VA). Returning Bataan soldiers found the VA often had a deaf ear to their problems. Examining doctors weren't familiar with POW life and illnesses. Many veterans found their stories of beatings and starvation doubted by the agency that was supposed to help them. Some found it safer just to go on with life and not talk about their problems. Some succeeded. Many didn't.

> McVEY — For a number of years after the War, I had to give myself vitamin B shots every day. I stuck the needle right here in my arm. It took two to three years before my body started to take American food again. After all, I ate nothing but rice for 3½ years. I went to the VA hospital and was checked out by the doctors. One young doctor told me to put down everything that I possibly thought could be wrong with me as a result of the war. He said, "Even if you're not sure, put it down." That was the best advice, because years later when I went to the VA for treatment, they would say it wasn't war related.
>
> I'd say, "Look at my record." Sure enough, they'd come back and treat me because of what I had written down years ago. One time I had a fungus growing on my neck. They weren't going to treat it, but when they saw my record, they treated it in a hurry.

> MANASSE — During all the time I spent in these camps, I tried to block out the unpleasant things. I only thought of the good things my life had been before I got into the Army and what it was going to be after I got out. I have since completely recovered from all of this, and I don't talk about this very much. Sometimes it becomes very painful for me to relate these stories. About the only time I do is when I've been drinking a lot. I say things and recall things that I really shouldn't. It doesn't do any good at all to look to the past. It's been 40 years since the War. I spend most of my leisure time playing golf, meeting people, and just thanking God that I am still alive and enjoying life. I think of the many friends I lost in the Philippines and Japan, and I have the deepest sympathy for their survivors.

Some not only had problems talking about captivity, but also just thinking about it was terrifying.

McVEY — I spent many a night where I would get a nightmare. I'd break out in a cold sweat. Sometimes this would be nightly. Nowadays I don't get them too often. In fact, I had made up my mind a long time ago that it was best to just forget about the experience and get it out of my mind. Sometimes that's hard to do. I don't like talking about it. I haven't even told my two daughters these stories. No one could possibly comprehend what happened to us over there.

STEMLER — People ask, "Why don't you take a trip back to the Philippines?" I don't want to go back. I've been there. Why stir up something that's been sleeping for so long. There was some good moments and some bad moments. The good moments was when you could put somethin' over on the Japanese. The bad moments was when they caught you.

But, on the other hand, there are many today who want to remember. They've retired from their jobs, their children are grown, and they have the time to contemplate what happened to them over 40 years ago.

LESTER RUZEK — Now that I've retired I'd like to go back and relive some of the POW experience. I figured the best thing to do when I got out of the war was to put all of that behind me and forget what happened. Now it's difficult to go back and get those memories, but I know they're there.

Ruzek is not alone. Many others who willingly want to remember those POW years now find that the 3½ years of malnutrition and physical abuse have shattered one's memory. In the interviews, I have tried to use artifacts — rosters, maps, pictures, etc. — to pry those prisoner-of-war experiences from the deep crevices of the mind. Sometimes these methods have been successful.

CANFIELD — Talking with you unlocked some memories that I had misplaced. As you heard in my voice while talking, I was happy about the situation as it unravelled. It seems a shame that stress and public reaction to the POWs' return can cause people to tuck information in some corner of the mind and not know what the key is to retrieve it. It's like programming a computer disk and then forgetting what the address was. No address — no retrieval.

And there are those who vividly recall the experience but haven't talked for another reason.

JAMES FAULKNER — It doesn't bother me to talk about POW life, but I seldom do because I've always felt most people don't want to hear about it. I might add that I never carried over animosity towards the Japanese. Other ex-POWs seem to hate them. I am a little different. I always thought, I didn't have to surrender. I made the choice, and took what they dished out.

Ernest Norquist, who later became a Presbyterian minister, feels the reason he's living today is because the Japanese kept him alive during those 3½ years. Dan Stoudt, who was at Cabanatuan, Davao, and Hanawa says, "I don't hate the Japanese. I have a Honda." But I also heard a story that was the opposite of Dan's. A 200th CAC ex-POW hadn't seen his son for a few weeks even though they lived in the same New Mexico city. Finally, the son drove up in his new Japanese-made car. The father met him at the driveway.
"How long have you had the car?"
"Three weeks."
"That's how long you have to get rid of it."
And the son got rid of the car.
But there are other, more subtle ways that ex-POWs "retaliated" against the 3½ years. Most methods had to do with diet. The men simply refused to eat rice upon return to the States. Those who eat it today took many, many years before attempting a mouthful. Augie DeBauche not only didn't eat rice, he even refused to say the word. At his wedding, he had the well-wishers throw barley. And the irony of all ironies occurred at the Bataan reunion banquet during the 1985 American Ex-Prisoners of War National Convention in Milwaukee. The first item on the elaborate smorgasboard was a huge mound of rice. I'm sure the hotel didn't realize its faux pas, but I sure did. I also noticed that most of the ex-prisoners put rice on their plate.
But regardless of whether the ex-POWs still hate the Japanese or not, or whether they eat rice or not, I found in my interviews that indomitable spirit of survival still evident over 40 years later. Most are still feeling the effects of those 3½ years, but yet they won't quit.

GALDE — During the time I was incarcerated I suffered from malaria many times, hepatitis twice, dysentery, beriberi, pellagra, tropical ulcers, hypo-protein anemia, hookworms, and lost the use of my legs and arms. Since I've retired from the Navy in 1959, I've had two coronary by-pass surgeries, four stomach surgeries, six leg surgeries, and four prostate surgeries. I also had cancer, and I suffer from headaches all the time, but I *still continue*. I sound like a hypochondriac, but all the surgeries had to be done. Oh, I had kidney stones too. I haven't been very vocal about my problems, but if this interview will help your research, then it's my last hurrah. My health isn't too good now. I suffer from asthma, arteriosclerosis, arthritis, headaches, and physical deterioration in general. But then I'll be 70 on my next birthday. Somebody up there must like me.

This spirit of cooperation with my research has fortunately been the rule rather than the exception. Many today have poured their hearts out. Decades ago that might not have been the case. Hanawa physician Dr. Calvin Jackson sums up this feeling of cooperation the best: "I am only too happy, or rather pleased, to be of any assistance. It's amazing the number of people who never heard of Bataan nor the Philippines, let alone a POW." If this work does anything I hope it will leave for posterity the fact that Las Piñas, the *Noto, Maru*, and Hanawa did exist.

Appendix

Las Piñas Men

The following men were contacted either orally or by the mail concerning Las Piñas. Approximately 67% responded with information.

Abie Abraham	Pete Gandy	Bishop McKendree
Jack Aldrich	Walter Gilles	Austin Moore
Milton Alexander	Offutt Goble	Delbert Moore
Willie Arterburn	Al Hale	Joseph Moore
Dan Borodin	Glen Haynes	Fausto Noche
John Brannon	Otto Hirsch	Julian Prada
Webster Burch	Pat Hitchcock	Glen Ream
Leslie Canfield	Carl Holloway	John Riley
John Cicha	Robert Johnston	Joe Romero
Leroy Cookingham	Lloyd Jones	Art Ross
Avril Davis	Morgan Jones	Johnnie Samarrippa
August DeBauche	Paul Kerchum	Bernard Sanders
Truman Deede	Dave Kimball	William Schaeffer
Clehan Dewey	Peter Kirghesner	Art Smith
August DePaulo	Manfred Kirk	John Stinson
George Dravo	Forrest Knox	Richard Taylor
Bill Evans	Y. C. Lindsay	Tallmadge Wallace
Thomas Flathers	James Martin	Roosevelt Watson
George Fox	Solly Manasse	
Burton Galde	Frank Mayhue	

LAS PIÑAS ROSTER
FROM BILIBID CARDS ON MICROFILM

Microfilm does not provide a complete list of the approximately 800 men who made up the Las Piñas detail. The following names came from cards stored at Bilibid. The cards provided name, rank, and branch of service. Each time a man passed through Bilibid a notation was added concerning his destination. Each of these men had Las Piñas typed on their cards. The problem, however, is that 99% of the cards were for Army personnel. A separate file must have existed for Navy and Marines. The names with an asterisk behind them are individuals who MIGHT HAVE BEEN at Las Piñas. Their names were derived from interviews or other readings.

Abraham, Abie	Aldrich, Jack	Allen, Henry
Adams, Jesse	Alexander, Milton	Allin, Sherdie

Almeraz, Manuel
Amos, Charles
Anderson, George
Anderson, Jut
Andrews, Herbbert
Antelope, George
Apodaca, George
Archuleta, Tellisvoro
Argeanes, James
Arterburn, Willie
Bacalski, Art
Ballow, Glen
Banegas, Lorenzo
Banta, Francis *
Bardin, Robert
Barnes, Lellon
Barnhart, Lucen
Barton, Irvin
Berlanga, Martin
Beus, William
Biedenstein, Arthur *
Black, Cecil
Bankenbreaker, Wayne *
Bolf, Tony
Bolinger, Frank
Borodin, Dan
Boswell, John
Bowers, Glen
Boyd, James
Brakebill, Roy
Branning, Adam
Brannon, Olliver
Braye, William
Breslin, Richard
Breeze, ??? Marine *
Bridges, Tallmadge
Brohm, Frank
Brooks, Seymour
Brown, Earl
Brunett, Henry
Bucholz, Chester
Bullock, Orlinza
Burch, Webster
Burchill, Raymond
Burlag, George
Burns, Robert
Byrne, Patrick
Cable, Dwight
Cale, Lester

Calkins, John
Callison, Billy
Cammarata, Joseph
Canfield, Leslie
Cape, Jack
Carlson, William
Carpenter, James
Carrier, David
Carrol, Thomas
Carter, Godfrey
Carter, Howard
Castel, Aubrey
C DeBaca, Benedicto
Cecil, Allen
Celusniak, Louis
Chandler, Arthur
Chappele, Curtis
Chenoweth, Mervin
Childs, Eldon
Chio, Wade
Christiansen, Harold
Cicha, Anton
Clark, James
Clemmor, George
Clifton, Ansel
Cloud, Milan
Cochrane, Harry
Cochrane, Henry
Coleman, Thomas
Combs, Aaron
Connor, James
Conover, Earl
Constant, John
Cookingham, Leroy
Cooksley, Richard
Corbi, Frank
Cotten, John
Coyle, James
Crane, Stanley
Crocker, Fred
Crosby, Harvey
Crossman, Donald
Cromwell, Royal
Crumley, Cleo
Davis, Alvin *
Davis, Avril
Davis, Harold
Davis, John *
Davis, Thomas III

Davis, Twitty
Dawson, Malcolm
De Augustine, Dan
De Bauche, August
De Boer, Arlen
Deede, Truman
Deemer, Carl
de Gottardi, Edward *
De Graff, Thomas
Dempsey, Evlyn
DeReemer, Harry
DeVinaspore, Ray
DeVivo, Frankie
DeVote, Robert
Dewey, Clelan
Dietrich, George
Di Paolo, August
Donai, Frank
Donelli, Robert
Doolos, Demetri
Drake, Roy
Dravo, George
Druey, Milton
Dunagan, Jewell
Du Puis, Charles
Durden, Jack
Durgin, August
Dzierlatka, Stanley
Edmonds, Homer
Eldrige, Robert
Ernst, Norman
Errington, Richard
Evans, Franklin
Evans, Herbert
Evans, Bill
Exceem, Leonard
Fackender, Ken
Fajnik, Nicholas
Fienberg, ??? Marine *
Fisher, Edward
Fisher, Leo
Fisher, William
Flathers, Thomas *
Fleming, Ernest *
Fletcher, Kirk
Flowers, Travis
Floyd, Lee
Fox, George
Fragale, Joseph

Fralick, D. *
Franceschi, Italio
Frederick, Joseph
Freeman, Ray
Gagnon, Joseph
Galde, Burton
Gandy, M. Z. *
Garnett, Franklin *
Garrison, John
Garside, George
Gebhard, Roy
Gelb, Dan
Gilles, Walter
Gilson, Owen
Glaab, William
Goble, Offutt
Godsil, Kevin
Gomez, Clyde
Gonzales, Rubel
Goodwin, Bill
Gordon, Jack
Grant, Lucian
Green, Chester
Greer, Edward
Gribble, Sam
Griffin, Bobbie
Grimes, Rollie
Groszek, Joseph
Guenther, Wm
Guiterrez, Eddie *
Gurganus, Leroy
Haerman, Frank *
Haines, Lucy
Hale, Alfred
Hall, Daniel
Hammond, Homer
Hampton, Jay
Hansen, Wilbur
Harris, Byron
Hart, Donald
Harvey, Charles
Harvill, Lyodd
Harvison, Ernie
Hatfield, John
Haynes, Glen
Heckman, Clyde
Hendon, Clifford
Henrich, Loyal
Herbeck, Robert

Herbert, Philton
Herreka, Albert *
High, Raymond
Hildebrand, James
Hill, Edward
Hitchcock, Pat
Hnidak, John
Hodges, Thomas
Hollan, Murray
Holloway, Carl
Houseman, John
Howard, R. L. *
Howland, Alfred
Huckstep, Robert
Hyatt, Boyce
Ison, Raymond
Iverson, Guy *
Jameson, Richard *
Jarycranzki, Edward
Jensen, Billie
Jerome, Albert
Jimenez, Antonio
Johns, Robert
Johnson, Albert
Johnson, Edward
Johnson, Howard
Johnson, Robert C.
Johnson, Sam
Joyce, Pierre
Jones, Clatus
Jones, Everett
Jones, John
Jones, Lloyd
Jones, Morgan
Karr, Austin
Katanskas, Fran *
Kean, Leo
Keltz, Charles
Kemp, Newton
Keena, Robert
Kerchum, Paul
Kimball, David
Kinler, William
Kipps, Harold
Kirk, Manfred
Kirley, Howard
Klein, Nicholas
Klinekole, Bruce
Knox, Forrest

Kolger, Louis
Kolinski, Stanley
Koury, George
Kutch, Joseph
La Bella, "Swede"
La Fountaine, George
Lara, Porfiro
Larson, Lloyd
Lary, Henderson
Lawhorn, Allen
Lawrence, Walter
Lawton, Robert
Lask, Warren
Leavitt, Milton
Lee Walter
Leighton, Reginald
Lewis, Homer
Lewis, Morris
Levba, Max
Lieb, Walter
Lieman, Charles
Limas, Ruben
Lindsay, Y. C.
Logan, Byron
Lohman, ??? Marine *
Long, Robert
Lopez, Ray
Lujahn, Leopoldo
Luper, Chester
Lutz, ??? Marine
Madero, Mel *
Maki, Arthur
Mann, Chester
Marshall, John
Marshall, ????
Martin, Adrian R.
Martin, James
Martin, Thomas
Martin, Wiley
Martinez, Belermo
Martinez, Eduardo
Mayhue, Luther Frank
Mc Clelland, Jim
Mc Cubbin, Eugene
Mc Daniel, Robert
Mc Dermott, Charles
Mc Donough, Donald
Mc Farland, Cecil
Mc Farland, James

Mc Gee, William
Mc Ham, Reese
Mc Kendree, Bishop
Mc Kenzie, James
Mc Knight, Arlon
Mc Louth, Estie
Mc Mahan, James
Mc Nulty, William
Medina, Miguel
Medina, Robert
Medwick, George
Mehegan, Edward
Meier, Emil
Meier, Hix
Mekulsia, Peter
Menini, Carlos
Menzies, Arthur
Meredith, Alonzo
Meyers, D. V. *
Mielo, John
Michesky, Frank
Milhep, Jesse
Miller, Louis
Minder, Joseph
Miner, James
Moen, Norman
Moldenauer, Lewis *
Montes, Aljandro
Montova, Onofre
Moore, Austin
Moore, Delbert
Moore, Joseph
Moore, Ralph
Morill, Eben
Morris, Claude
Morris, Lee
Morrison, Lester
Moscato, Michael
Mott, Eugene
Mullins, William
Murphy, Nathaniel
Murray, Grady *
Myers, ???? *
Nalezynski, Alexander
Nelson, ??? *
Newell, James
Nevarez, Manuel
Noche, Fausto
Novak, Henry

Oakes, Donald
O'Hara, Larry
Opis, Fred
Ordis, William
Ortiz, Fofila
Osborne, Ben
Osecky, Benny
O'Shea, Thomas
Owen, William
Padilla, John
Paiz, Juan
Parker, Don
Parker, William
Pasurka, Carl
Patterson, Bill
Peek, Jack
Perez, Anisto
Perkins, George
Perry, Edward
Perry, Frank
Peterson, Melvin *
Peterson, Robert
Petrosé, A.M.
Phillips, Earl
Pilson, William
Plodzien, Edward
Polk, Reginald *
Poulimenos, Ijanetos
Powell, George
Prada, Julian
Prehm, Ernest
Pribbernow, Robert
Purcell, Bill
Pietzke, Merrill
Quast, Nelson
Quintana, Aurelio
Ragicto, Paul
Rael, Marcus
Rahe, John
Ramos, Juan
Rea, Everett
Read, Louis
Ream, Glen
Reed, Morton
Reeves, Larry
Rertan, Robert
Rexrode, Roy
Reyes, Eusebio
Rhke, Heinz

Riley, Edwin
Riley, John
Rinas, Bruno
Rio, Lewis
Ritchie, Bert
Ritchie, Ken
Rivet, Louis
Roach, James
Roberts, Eustace
Roberts, Melvin
Robertson, Joseph *
Robinson, Albert *
Rodriguez, Juan
Rogers, Climita
Rollie, Edward
Ramanelli, Joe Marine *
Romero, Joe
Rose, Frank
Ross, Arthur
Rowan, James
Rowell, Ralph
Rowland, Albert
Ruchalski, Tony
Ruelas, Albert
Ruiz, Sirenio
Russell, Francis
Russell, James
Rutledge, Tillman
Ruzek, Lester
Saccone, Ben *
Samarippa, Johnnie
Samek, Thomas
Sanchez, Charles
Sanchez, Frank
Sanchez, Joe M.
Sanchez, Stephen
Sanders, Harry
Santillanes, Valentine
Saunders, Bernard
Savedra, Teodore
Scarboro, Pearly (2nd Lt)
Scott, Daley
Scott, Robert
Schasel, Robert
Schenk, Harold
Schmidt, Emil *
Schmidt, Otto
Schmidt, Leroy
Schnieder, Hilbert

Schraml, Henry
Schultz, Albert
Schultz, Delbert
Schwausch, Herman
Seiderman, Louis
Senkyrik, Ignac
Senna, Al
Shanks, Harold *
Sharp, Geral
Shaw, Charles
Shearles, James
Shirley, Ralph
Shoof, John
Shropshire, George
Sigala, Charles
Silva, Duane *
Sivola, Walter
Skowronski, Taduaz
Slabinski, Tony
Smack, Edward
Smith, Arthur
Smith, Earl
Smith, Elmer
Smith, Elza
Smith, Emmett
Smith, John *
Smith, Oscar
Smith, Tim
Spanovich, Julius
Spiranza, Eugene
Spurlock, Charles
Sora, Pragedis
Sotak, George
Southard, Walter
Stevens, Curtis
Stevens, Jesse
Stevenson, Rolly
Stever, Archie
Stewart, Robert
Stileo, Paris
Stine, Lee
Stinson, James "John"

Stotler, Ernest
Strickland, Lacy
Strompolis, John
Stroope, Winfred
Stumbo, Marion
Swartz, Forrest
Swearingen, Dallas
Swope, Fred
Taylor, Fred
Taylor, Jack
Taylor, Richard
Taylor, William
Tellez, Henry
Tennig, Elmer
Terrazas, Nick
Thenell, Norman
Thomas, George
Thompson, Arthur
Thompson, Francis
Thompson, John *
Thompson, Richard *
Thurston, Eugene
Tighe, Robert
Toland, Philip
Tome, Louis
Torres, Joseph
Traino, Michael
Triplett, Preston
Trujillo, Juan
Trucker, Carl
Trucker, Raymond
Trupiano, Pete *
Underwood, J. R.
Urban, Anton
Valdez, Armando
Vanish, George
Vandenbroucke, Ray
Virgil, Albino
Villa, Freeman
Von Schumaker, Maurice
Vest, Richard
Walker, Gaylon

Wall, John
Wallace, Tallmage
Ward, James
Warth, Henry
Wasson, Paul
Waters, Bennett
Watson, Roosevelt
Waterud, Glenn
Webb, James
Webb, Louis
Wec, Fred
Weingartner, Jerome
Welch, Robert
Werner, Melvin
Wexler, Robert
Wideman, Charles
Wight, Donald
Wilkerson, Vincent
Wilkes, Joseph
Wilson, Arthur
Wilson, Joe
Winter, Chris
Whitman, James
Wittke, Donald
Woda, Ed
Wolf, Ed *
Woulf, Clarence
Wolfenbarger, Leonard *
Wood, John
Working, Nelson
Worley, George
Wyatt, Ed
Wylie, George
Wypon, Menzies
Yates, Otis *
Yohn, Leonard
Youman, Billy
Youngblood, Vernon
Zimmerman, Willard
Zumwalt, Gilbert

NOTO, MARU ROSTER
sailed from Manila on 15 August 1944
arrived in Moji, Japan on 6 September 1944

Company One

1. Charles Samson, Capt.
2. David Kirk, 1st Lt.
3. Harold Kipps WO (jg)
4. Stanley Crane, M/Sgt.
5. Howard Flowers 1st Sgt
6. Lloyd Meador, Pvt.
7. Loyal Huston, 1st Sgt.
8. Willbourn, Lacewell, T/Sgt.
9. John Abramowicz St/Sgt.
10. Cecil Ammons, St/Sgt.
11. Jack Boyd, St./Sgt.
12. Sam Derryberry St/Sgt.
13. Anthony Duino, St/Sgt.
14. Archie Golson, St/Sgt.
15. Walter Howard, St/Sgt.
16. Gordon Jensen, St/Sgt.
17. Fred Opis, St/Sgt.
18. Harry Sanders, St/Sgt.
19. Marvin Shearwood, St/Sgt.
20. James Tribby, St/Sgt.
21. James Benedict, Sgt.
22. Paul Cahill, Sgt.
23. Harold Christianson, Sgt.
24. Thomas Litch, Sgt.
25. Thomas Mathews, Sgt.
26. Percy Mooney, Sgt.
27. Delbert Moore, Sgt.
28. Earl Moravee, Sgt.
29. James T. Murphy, Sgt.
30. Chester Nicholson, Sgt.
31. Lee Pelayo, Sgt.
32. Gustave Rosenfeldt, Sgt.
33. Bob Rutledge, Sgt.
34. John Slownick, Sgt.
35. George Sotak, Sgt.
36. Lawrence Stubblefield, Sgt.
37. Mitchell Telendo, Sgt.
38. Anton Urban, Sgt.
39. George Vanish, Sgt.
40. Clyde Winters, Sgt.
41. Ken Bodine, Cpl.
42. Leslie Canfield, Cpl.
43. Jack Cape, Cpl.
44. William Carlson, Cpl.
45. Robert Chambers, Cpl.
46. Arlen DoBoer, Cpl.
47. Jack Erickson, Cpl.
48. George Felty, Cpl.
49. Ralph Jacques, Cpl.
50. Vern Knapp, Cpl.
51. Herbert Markland, Cpl.
52. Arthur Mohr, Cpl.
53. Carol Moore, Cpl.
54. Carrell Morton, Cpl.
55. Felix Seems, Cpl.
56. Tony Slabinski, Cpl.
57. John Snellen, Cpl.
58. Don Sollenberger, Cpl.
59. Robert J. Stewart, Cpl.
60. John Aldred, Pfc.
61. Francis Bain, Pfc.
62. Richard Baldwin, Pfc.
63. John Ballow, Pfc.
64. Roy Bean, Pfc.
65. Elmer Bowers, Pfc.
66. Seymour Brooks, Pfc.
67. George Clemmer, Pfc.
68. Brownell Cole, Pfc.
69. Goff Coleman, Pfc.
70. Louis Cusans, Pfc.
71. Raymond Demers, Pfc.
72. Lee Floyd, Pfc.
73. Malcolm Foster, Pfc.
74. Clifton Frazier, Pfc.
75. Adrian Gentry, Pfc.
76. Werner Ghilardi, Pfc.
77. Leslie Greenlee, Pfc.
78. Eddie Guiterrez, Pfc.
79. Ferrill Harrison, Pfc.
80. John Henry, Pfc.
81. Patrick Higdon, Pfc.
82. Vance Horn, Pfc.
83. Archie Hughes, Pfc.
84. Lyle Hulbert, Pfc.
85. Henry Inman, Pfc.
86. Andre Fox, Pfc.
87. Jay Lawler, Pfc.
88. Whitney Leritt, Pfc.

89. Robert Levis, Pfc.
90. Henry Liskowski, Pfc.
91. Tony Mariangello, Pfc.
92. Maurice Mazer, Pfc.
93. Murrell McClure, Pfc.
94. Albert E. McFarley, Pfc.
95. Thomas McDill, Pfc.
96. James Mctigue, Pfc.
97. Paul Miller, Pfc.
98. Harry Neece, Pfc.
99. Wilson Parks, Pfc.
100. Wayne Pennington, Pfc.
101. Aurelio Quintana, Pfc.
102. Gay Ring, Pfc.
103. Albert Roth, Pfc.
104. Clarence Sequin, Pfc.
105. Carl Shaw, Pfc.
106. Glen Simonds, Pfc.
107. Anselmo Sisneros, Pfc.
108. Harold Taves, Pfc.
109. Eugene Thurston, Pfc.
110. George Webb, Pfc.
111. Bill Wheeler, Pfc.
112. James Whitman, Pfc.
113. Carl Wuhrmann, Pfc.
114. Leonard Yohn, Pfc.
115. Gordon Alton, Pvt.
116. Don Adair, Pvt.
117. John Arnold, Pvt.
118. Willie Arterburn, Pvt.
119. Harrison Avery, Pvt.
120. Mathew Barker, Pvt.
121. Millege Bartley, Pvt.
122. J. M. Baxhart, Pvt.
123. Amos Beach, Pvt.
124. Jack Brundage, Pvt.
125. Nestor Bustmante, Pvt.
126. John Butler, Pvt.
127. Chester Burks, Pvt.
128. Ken Calvits, Pvt.
129. J. D. Carner, Pvt.
130. William Clifton, Pvt.
131. Emil Moritz, F/C USN
132. Eugene Cox, Pvt.
133. John Crown, Pvt.
134. Earl Cunningham, Pvt.
135. Bill Curtis, Pvt.
136. Bert Dehr, Pvt.
137. Adolph Dickson, Pvt.
138. Joseph Dilella, Pvt.
139. Ronald Donaldson, Pvt.
140. William Edmonds, Pvt.
141. Warren Elder, Pvt.
142. John Emerick, Pvt.
143. Bernard Fennell, Pvt.
144. Earnest Fleming, Pvt.
145. Ben Garcia, Pvt.
146. Norman Ford, Pvt.
147. Robert Gilbert, Pvt.
148. Lonnie Gray, Pvt.
149. Howard Gundrum, Pvt.
150. Clay Harris, Pvt.
151. W.L. Harris, Pvt.
152. John Haywood, Pvt.
153. Leon Heinz, Pvt.
154. Wayne Hietanen, Pvt.
155. Edward Hill, Pvt.
156. John Hoback, Pvt.
157. Fredrick Howard, Pvt.
158. Vincent Imme, Pvt.
159. Jack Jones, Pvt.
160. John H. Jones, Pvt.
161. Leo Kean, Pvt.
162. Robert Keesley, Pvt.
163. David Kimball, Pvt.
164. Alfonso Lopez, Pvt.
165. John Kiser, Pvt.
166. Jasper Knowles, Pvt.
167. Harold Lane, Pvt.
168. Jesse Lane, Pvt.
169. Walter Lee, Pvt.
170. Paul Lindermuth, Pvt.
171. Herman Link, Pvt.
172. Albino Lopez, Pvt.
173. Benjamin Manzanares, Pvt.
174. Wiley Martin, Pvt.
175. A. C. McGrew, Pvt.
176. Joe Merritt, Pvt.
177. Arthur Miller, Pvt.
178. William Moore, Pvt.
179. Burl Morris, Pvt.
180. George Muller, Pvt.
181. James Murray, Pvt.
182. John Nelson, Pvt.
183. Noel Olson, Pvt.
184. Harley Pierce, Pvt.
185. Desiree Peltier, Pvt.
186. Dwight Pendleberry, Pvt.

187. Joe Perez, Pvt.
188. Fowler, Brain, CBM, USN
189. Earl Phillips, Pvt.
190. Edward Pine, Pvt.
191. Joseph Politz, Pvt.
192. Homer Preston, Pvt.
193. Roy Rankins, Pvt.
194. George Risher, Pvt.

195. Forrest Richeson, Pvt.
196. Robert Ring, Pvt.
197. Samuel Robertson, Pvt.
198. Marion Rodgers, Pvt.
199. Robert Roehm, Pvt.
200. Jay Rye, Pvt.
201. Campbell Sadler, Pvt.
202. Paul Sanford, Pvt.

Company Two

203. Peter Perkins, 1st Lt.
204. John Kunick, M/Sgt.
205. William Atkins, T/Sgt.
206. Donald Bowman, T/Sgt.
207. Charles Caster, T/Sgt.
208. Emmanuel Hamburger, 1st Sgt.
209. Alfred E. LeBeau, T/Sgt.
210. Adrian R. Martin, 1st Sgt.
211. James Mathieson, 1st Sgt.
212. Ralph Pope, 1st Sgt.
213. James Scruggs, 1st Sgt.
214. Cecil Berry, St/Sgt.
215. Harold Bryant, St/Sgt.
216. Curtis Gartman, AMM 2c, USN
217. Ken Davis, St/Sgt.
218. Dick Francies, St/Sgt.
219. Asbury Nix, St/Sgt.
220. James O'Sullivan, St/Sgt.
221. Robert Peterson, St/Sgt.
222. Lewis Brittan, Sgt.
223. Crayton Burns, Sgt.
224. John Carle, Sgt.
225. Lawrence Coker, Sgt.
226. Malcolm Crowe, Sgt.
227. Shelby Emery, Sgt.
228. Colby Fields, Sgt.
229. John Howard, Sgt.
230. Pat Howell, Sgt.
231. Max Leyba, Sgt.
232. Vincent Likeday, Sgt.
233. Francis Macey, Sgt.
234. Sidney Marcom, Sgt.
235. Stanton Price, Sgt.
236. David Summons, Sgt.
237. Jesse Adams, Cpl.
238. William Ballou, Cpl.
239. Phillip Brain, Cpl.
240. Stanley Casanove, Cpl.

241. Ben Creagle, Cpl.
242. Volney Deal, Cpl.
243. Austin Karr, Cpl.
244. James Mills, Cpl.
245. John Murphy, Cpl.
246. Joseph Powell, Cpl.
247. Vernon Reen, Cpl.
248. Louis Silverstein, Cpl.
249. E. R. Barkhart, Pfc.
250. Charles Bolt, Pfc.
251. Angelo Borruano, Pfc.
252. Claude Box, Pfc.
253. Leslie Carr, Pfc.
254. Clifton Coffin, Pfc.
255. Pablo Diaz, Pfc.
256. James Drake, Pfc.
257. James Farmer, Pfc.
258. James Flowers, Pfc.
259. Ernest Haddox, Pfc.
260. Gordon Hilton, Pfc.
261. Joseph Jacque, Pfc.
262. Elven Jones, Pfc.
263. Stephen Lambathas, Pfc.
264. Richard O'Connor, Pfc.
265. Frank Piburn, Pfc.
266. Granville Prewitt, Pfc.
267. Edward Schott, Pfc.
268. Rudolph Schuster, Pfc.
269. Edward Wilkerson, Pfc.
270. Charles Bain, Pvt.
271. Gordon Barnes, Pvt.
272. Carl Begley, Pvt.
273. Howard Bowers, Pvt.
274. Leonard Browder, Pvt.
275. James Brown, Pvt.
276. Howard Carter, Pvt.
277. Edward Free, Pvt.
278. Carl Harris, Pvt.

279. Dan Holder, Pvt.
280. Ray Kimball, Pvt.
281. John Lemanski, Pvt.
282. Roger Lowhead, Pvt.
283. James Mines, Pvt.
284. Lee Morris, Pvt.
285. John Nelms, Pvt.
286. Donald Oakes, Pvt.
287. Cruz Ortiz, Pvt.
288. Ted Paris, Pvt.
289. Joe Quinn, Pvt.
290. Ernest Prehm, Pvt.
291. Bill Purcell, Pvt.
292. Walter Samson, Pvt.
293. Walter Schuette, Pvt.
294. Phil Tripp, Pvt.
295. William Self, Pvt.
296. Jason "Jack" Sharp
297. George Sheldon, Pvt.
298. Robert Sills, Pvt.
299. Taduaz Skowronski, Pvt.
300. George Smith, Pvt.
301. Gilmore Smith, Pvt.
302. John Spencer, Pvt.
303. Walter Stefanski, Pvt.
304. Albert Stengler, Pvt.
305. Ken Stone, Pvt.
306. Lacy Strickland, Pvt.
307. Raphael Thorneberry, Pvt.
308. Ernest Taylor, Pvt.
309. Richard Taylor, Pvt.
310. Joseph Torres, Pvt.
311. Michael Trains, Pvt.
312. Francis Tucker, Pvt.
313. Pat Turner, Pvt.
314. Ray Underwood, Pvt.
315. Charles Urban, Pvt.
316. William Van Almen, Pvt.
317. Lawrence Van Lier, Pvt.
318. Jimmy Vaughn, Pvt.
319. Robert Strahl, CY, USN
320. Leon Waldrip, Pvt.
321. Lewis Wallace, Pvt.
322. Fred Watkins, Pvt.
323. Clarence Webber, Pvt.
324. Lafayette Whichard, Pvt.
325. Alexander Wills, Pvt.
326. George Young, Pvt.
327. Lee Dix, CCSTD, USN
328. Oscar Gullickson, CEM, USN
329. J. T. Jarrett, CMSMTH, USN
330. William S. Stacks, CWT, USN
331. Basilo G. Zorzanello, CEM, USN
332. George Cobb, SC 1/c, USN
333. Dillard Darneal, MM 1/c, USN
334. Noble Dudley, MM 1/c, USN
335. Arthur Feher, MM 1/c, USN
336. James Gray, MM 1/c, USN
337. Leonard Hallman, RM 2/c, USN
338. Earl Johnson, RM 1/c, USN
339. Phillip L. ?????, MM 1/c, USN
340. Frank Margiotto, Y 1/c, USN
341. James McCarthy, BMER 1/c, USN
342. George McCullough, GM 1/c, USN
343. Robert Montgomery, RM 1/c, USN
344. Gustav Mubhigh, RM 1/c, USN
345. Al Parrish, MM 1/c, USN
346. Earl Rector, BM 1/c, USN
347. Virgil Sauers, BM 1/c, USN
348. Robert Sheats, EM 1/c, USN
349. Herman Tinen, EM 1/c, USN
350. Ted Galeavy, CM 2/c, USN
351. Thomas Gale, EM 2/c, USN
352. John Kenney, TM 2/c, USN
353. Paul Town, QM 2/c, USN
354. Patrick Wheat, WT 2/c, USN
355. Walter Carter, SM 3/c, USN
356. Arthur Chandler, GM 3/c, USN
357. Howard Fisher, COX, USN
358. Ken Gmeiner, EM 3/c, USN
359. Warren Hawkes, EM 3/c, USN
360. Pritchard Hoggard, CW, USN
361. William McDuffie, CM 3/c, USN
362. Clarence Nelson, EM 3/c, USN
363. William Shawhan, FC 3/c, USN
364. Harold White, EM 3/c, USN
365. Dale Hahn, SEA 1/c, USN
366. Robert Johnston, SEA 1/c, USN
367. Jenro Lambasio, SEA 1/c, USN
368. Albert O'Meara, Pvt.
369. Robert Vondette, SEA 1/c, USN
370. Peter Kirchgesner, F 2/c, USN
371. Thomas McClean, OSEA, British Navy
372. Ivan Buster, M/Sgt. USMC
373. Charles Jackson, Sgt/Maj., USMC
374. M. Keith Martin, Sup/Sgt., USMC
375. Ed White, T/Sgt., USMC
376. Al Protz, S/Sgt., USMC

377. Wilfred Schlatter, Sgt., USMC
378. Stanley Allen, Cpl., USMC
379. Jesse Davenport, Cpl., USMC
380. Alvie McDaniel, Fld. Cok., USMC
381. Wilfred Mensching, Fld. Cok., USMC
382. Melvin Mikkelson, FM. Cpl., USMC
383. Junior Newman, Cpl., USMC
384. Merrill Riddle, Cpl., USMC
385. Clayton Rundle, Cpl., USMC
386. John Sinders, Cpl., USMC
387. Franklin Abrahams, Pfc., USMC
388. Billy Arney, Pfc., USMC
389. John A. Best, Pfc., USMC
390. James Faulkner, Pfc., USMC

391. Jack Fish, Pfc., USMC
392. William Helfing, Pfc., USMC
393. Arthur Hunt, Pfc., USMC
394. Francis Jensen, Pfc., USMC
395. Robert Schroeder, Pfc., USMC
396. Arthur Jones, Pfc., USMC
397. Julius Kindel, Pfc., USMC
398. Delmer Meyers, Pfc., USMC
399. Frederick Saeffke, Pfc., USMC
400. William Vardeman, Pfc., USMC
401. Frank Wagner, Pfc., USMC
402. Richard Watson, Pfc. USMC
403. Joseph Werner, Pfc., USMC

Company Three

404. George Sense, 1st Lt.
405. Charles Audet, WO (jg), USN
406. Hampton Drake, M/Sgt.
407. Lloyd Milkey, M/Sgt.
408. Alvin Arundell, 1st/Sgt.
409. Phillip Neverson, Pvt.
410. George Norris, T/Sgt.
411. James Randolph, T/Sgt.
412. George Shirk, 1st/Sgt.
413. William Smith, T/Sgt.
414. Edward Wright, T/Sgt.
415. Elbert Coleman, S/Sgt.
416. Gifford Dixon, S/Sgt.
417. Robert Dunsworth, S/Sgt.
418. Dale Dyches, S/Sgt.
419. William Hicks, S/Sgt.
420. William York, Pfc.
421. John Krowl, S/Sgt.
422. Lloyd Leckey, S/Sgt.
423. Ward McFadden, S/Sgt.
424. Mike Ready, Pfc.
425. John Stein, Pfc.
426. Malcolm Wallace, S/Sgt.
427. Milton Weaver, S/Sgt.
428. Paul Womack, S/Sgt.
429. Edgar Adams, Sgt.
430. Robert Boyer, Sgt.
431. Richard Dahm, Sgt.
432. George Dixon, Sgt.
433. Edward H. Domrochs, Sgt.
434. Hulan Goodnight, Sgt.
435. George Green, Sgt.

436. Walter Hess, Sgt.
437. John Hobbs, Sgt.
438. Harold Holmes, Sgt.
439. Bernard LeBeau, Sgt.
440. Dewey Lloyd, Sgt.
441. Johnny Lujack, Sgt.
442. Marvin Miller, Sgt.
443. George Nord, Sgt.
444. James Parents, Sgt.
445. Phil Parish, Sgt.
446. Clarence Roeske, Sgt.
447. Robert Showalter, Sgt.
448. Lee Stephens, Sgt.
449. Robert Thames, Sgt.
450. Paul Trujillo, Sgt.
451. Rufus Whiteman, Sgt.
452. George WhiKavage, Sgt.
453. Harold Bergbower, Cpl.
454. Norman Brenner, Cpl.
455. Thomas Calderone, Cpl.
456. Richard Carter, Cpl.
457. John Cobb, Cpl.
458. Ken Day, Cpl.
459. Alonzo Dotson, Cpl.
460. Joseph Dye, Cpl.
461. James Faulkner, Cpl.
462. John Fuentes, Cpl.
463. Nelson Hale, Cpl.
464. John Hansen, Cpl.
465. Wilbur Houser, Cpl.
466. William Kellene, Cpl.
467. Clifton Lee, Cpl.

468. Earl McCombs, Cpl.
469. Eugene McDonough, Cpl.
470. Fred Melnick, Cpl.
471. Frank Shimko, Cpl.
472. Vincent Silva, Cpl.
473. Dewey Smith, Cpl.
474. Clude Stone, Cpl.
475. Harold Sturt, Cpl.
476. Alton Swann, Cpl.
477. Thomas Thompson, Cpl.
478. Ken Wents, Cpl.
479. Charles West, Cpl.
480. Donald Anderson, Pfc.
481. Charlie Ante, Pfc.
482. Charles Ashcraft, Pfc.
483. Charles Barnett, Pfc.
484. Robert Beard, Pfc.
485. John Blackwood, Pfc.
486. Fred Bolinger, Pfc.
487. Rex Bray, Pfc.
488. Charles Brown, Pfc.
489. John Chambers, Pfc.
490. Jack Cole, Pfc.
491. James Collins, Pfc.
492. Gibson Davidson, Pfc.
493. John M. Dempsey, Pfc.
494. Bill Edwards, Pfc.
495. Peter Eresh, Pfc.
496. Frederick Fullerton, Pfc.
497. Miguel Gallegos, Pfc.
498. Paul Vetter, Pfc.
499. Charles Gooddiffe, Pfc.
500. Francis Graham, Pfc.
501. Joseph Grossman, Pfc.
502. Everett Harless, Pfc.
503. Hoyt Haynie, Pfc.
504. Louis Herring, Pfc.
505. James Holston, Pfc.
506. Jack Holt, Pfc.
507. George Howard, Pfc.
508. Otha Johnson, Pfc.
509. Bill Kilby, Pfc.
510. Dave Kincaid, Pfc.
511. Bert Klein, Pfc.
512. Reino Tuomala, Pfc., USMC
513. Lester Lacy, Pfc.
514. William LaFitte, Pfc.
515. Frank Lane, Pfc.
516. John Lawson, Pfc.

517. Victor Lear, Pfc.
518. Curtis Marlton,m Pfc.
519. Herbert McCants, Pfc.
520. Malcolm McClaugherty, Pfc.
521. Delbert McDaniel, Pfc.
522. Armand McClain, Pfc.
523. Donald Moore, Pfc.
524. Luther Oaks, Pfc.
525. Richard Peschel, Pfc.
526. Francis Paparo, Pfc.
527. Clarence Ray, Pfc.
528. General Lee Shelton, Pfc.
529. Ellis Shorthill, Pfc.
530. Hubert Smith, Pfc.
531. Francis Sokolik, Pfc.
532. Alfred Sorensen, Pfc.
533. Don Spaulding, Pfc.
534. Joe Stemler, Pfc.
535. Robert Stevens, Pfc.
536. Dale Strong, Pfc.
537. John Thompson, Pfc.
538. Albert Tomcavage, Pfc.
539. Frank Trieda, Pfc.
540. Bernie Valecic, Pfc.
541. Lee Vercher, Pfc.
542. Pete Armijo, Pvt.
543. Jan Berman, Pvt.
544. Ralph Boyle, Pvt.
545. John Cabeza, Pvt.
546. Glen Caudill, Pvt.
547. Elroy Patrico Cardenas, Pvt.
548. Clovis Chavez, Pvt.
549. John Chesebrough, Pvt.
550. John Connor, Pvt.
551. Vernon Craig, Pvt.
552. James Crookshank, Pvt.
553. Sherman Crookshank, Pvt.
554. Ralph Cullinan, Pvt.
555. Juan De Luna, Pvt.
556. Raymond DuPont, Pvt.
557. Joe Duran, Pvt.
558. Roy Emkin, Pvt.
559. Robert Endres, Pvt.
560. Dwight Felts, Pvt.
561. David Ferratti, Pvt.
562. Don Forsythe, Pvt.
563. Louis Fredieu, Pvt.
564. Vern Knappenberger, Pvt.
565. Phillip Goodman, Pvt.

566. Thomas Griffin, Pvt.
567. Lloyd Hill, Pvt.
568. Algen Hills, Pvt.
569. Toney James, Pvt
570. Gail Kelley, Pvt.
571. James Knight, Pvt.
572. Joseph Krinock, Pvt.
573. Walter St. John, Pvt., USMC
574. Jerry Lambo, Pvt.
575. Cecil Little, Pvt.
576. Vincent Marcella, Pvt.
577. Ralph Martinez, Pvt.
578. Gordon Morris, Pvt.
579. David Osborn, Pvt.
580. George Overly, Pvt.
581. Julius Ororozy, Pvt.
582. John Padget, Pvt.
583. Sedric Pearson, Pvt.
584. Patrico Quintana, Pvt.
585. Edward Ross, Pvt.

586. Carlos Schmidt, Pvt.
587. Edward Sergeant, Pvt.
588. Al Schuman, Pvt.
589. James Speckens, Pvt.
590. Alden Spencer, Pvt.
591. Henry G. Stanley, Pvt.
592. Gerald Staudenraus, Pvt.
593. Charles Stewart, Pvt.
594. Dan Stoudt, Pvt.
595. John Suskie, Pvt.
596. Howard Taylor, Pvt.
597. Miguel Torres, Pvt.
598. Arthur Troness, Pvt.
599. Manuel Vidaurri, Pvt.
600. Antonio, Virgil, Pvt.
601. Roy Walton, Pvt.
602. Wilton White, Pvt.
603. Grover Willis, Pvt.
604. Barney Zack, Pvt.

Company Four

605. E. Pearce Fleming, Capt.
606. William Andrews, T/Sgt.
607. Frank Bearden, T/Sgt.
608. Wilson McGuire, 1st Sgt.
609. Frank Minnis, 1st Sgt.
610. Joe B. Gutiurrez, T/Sgt.
611. Harold Spooner, 1st Sgt.
612. Melvin Waltmon, T/Sgt.
613. Charles Burgan, St. Sgt.
614. Ed Canfield, St. Sgt.
615. Horace Clark, St. Sgt.
616. Lawrence Elkins, St. Sgt.
617. Henry Gourdeau, St. Sgt.
618. Wayne Hinkle, St. Sgt.
619. Edward Johnson, St. Sgt.
620. William Langfelt, St. Sgt.
621. Alf Larson, St. Sgt.
622. Bill Mergan, St. Sgt.
623. Byron E. Pope, St. Sgt.
624. Herbert G. Smith, St. Sgt.
625. Walter Unic, St. Sgt.
626. David Van Hook, St. Sgt.
627. Thomas Watts, St. Sgt.
628. Rudie Apel, Sgt.
629. Willie Baxter, Sgt.
630. Leon Beasley, Sgt.

631. Lloyd Byers, Sgt.
632. John Campbell, Sgt.
633. Ted Cook, Sgt.
634. Thomas G. Davis, Sgt.
635. Raymond Densmore, Sgt.
636. Roy Fines, Sgt.
637. Roy House, Sgt.
638. Woodrow Hutchison, Sgt.
639. James Jones, Sgt.
640. Leonard Larsen, Sgt.
641. George Lawhorn, Sgt.
642. Albert Leach, Sgt.
643. Norman Lorenzen, Sgt.
644. Albert Maxwell, Sgt.
645. Peter MosKalick, Sgt.
646. W. A. Noffsker, Sgt.
647. Louis Sachwald, Sgt.
648. John Shadoan, Sgt.
649. Joseph Smith, Sgt.
650. Jack Swearingen, Sgt.
651. Dan Webb, Sgt.
652. Charles Williams, Sgt.
653. Harold Ahlstedt, Cpl.
654. Arthur Anderson, Cpl.
655. Melvin Chato, Cpl.
656. Phillip Coleman, Cpl.

657. Francis Fontana, Cpl.
658. Nathan Garner, Cpl.
659. Art Gilcrease, Cpl.
660. Richard Joder, Cpl.
661. Johnny Love, Cpl.
662. Ralph Moore, Cpl.
663. Grayford Payne, Cpl.
664. Joe Rossotto, Cpl.
665. Gregorio Sanchez, Cpl.
666. Ken Schoonover, Cpl.
667. Fred Smith, Cpl.
668. John Stoddard, Cpl.
669. Robert Williams, Cpl.
670. Richard Angus, Pfc.
671. Ivan Ball, Pfc.
672. Douglas Brown, Pfc.
673. Joseph Brown, Pfc.
674. Mavis Brown, Pfc.
675. Dennis Coucet, Pfc.
676. Domenico Ferrari, Pfc.
677. Frank Goldstein, Pfc.
678. Lawrence Hugaboom, Pfc.
679. Rolland Hutchins, Pfc.
680. Burk Larchmiller, Pfc.
681. Willis Lee, Pfc.
682. Charles McClanahan, Pfc.
683. Harold Moody, Pfc.
684. James Morehead, Pfc.
685. Earl Platt, Pfc.
686. Rueben Rathjen, Pfc.
687. Same Romero, Pfc.
688. Soine Torma, Pfc.
689. Hobart Trout, Pfc.
690. David Vandal, Pfc.
691. Harry Whittinghill, Pfc.
692. Elmer Wilcoxson, Pfc.
693. Johnnie Wisneski, Pfc.
694. Everett Wood, Pfc.
695. John Wood, Pfc.
696. Roland Zwelser, Pfc.
697. Russell Alt, Pvt.
698. Clarence Daniels, Pvt.
699. George Boyd, Pvt.
700. Charles Brown, Pvt.
701. Thomas Charlie, Pvt.
702. James Lehner, Pfc., USMC
703. Dana Cogair, Pvt.
704. James Collier, Pvt.
705. Walter Deans, Pvt.

706. Charles Dickson, Pvt.
707. Stanley Mroz, TM 2/c, USN
708. Franklin East, Pvt.
709. Henry Foster, Pvt.
710. Arthur Franzwa, Pvt.
711. Al Galloway, Pvt.
712. Joseph Gollasch, Pvt.
713. Jose Grego, Pvt.
714. William Havilland, Pvt.
715. Wynton Hestor, Pvt.
716. Ernest Hornback, Pvt.
717. Chester Irvin, Pvt.
718. Willie Kemp, Pvt.
719. David Kirk, Pvt.
720. Robert Knight, Pvt.
721. Russel Larkin, Pvt.
722. Oskar Mackey, Pvt.
723. Tone Maurion, Pvt.
724. James McCormick, Pvt.
725. Thomas Mikita, Pvt.
726. Merle Miller, Pvt.
727. Sam Nex, Pvt.
728. Bernard O'Brien, Pvt.
729. Edwin Preston, Pvt.
730. Harry Pruss, Pvt.
731. Aubrey Renfro, Pvt.
732. Keyton Roberts, Pvt.
733. John Rodriguez, Pvt.
734. James Rose, Pvt.
735. Tony Salcedo, Pvt.
736. Albert Schooley, Pvt.
737. James Secrist, Pvt.
738. Virgil Sherwood, Pvt.
739. James Siple, Pvt.
740. Thomas G. Stewart, Pvt.
741. Joe Svrcek, Pvt.
742. Bill Vice, Pvt.
743. Floyd Wade, Pvt.
744. Jack Warnick, Pvt.
745. Herbert White, Pvt.
746. Clyde Wolf, Pvt.
747. Franklin Workman, Pvt.
748. Marvin Wright, Pvt.
749. Archie Branbury, CBM, USN
750. Robert Merechal, CBM, USN
751. Norman Markwell, CBM, USN
752. George Morrison, CBM, USN
753. Wesley Thomas, CBM, USN
754. Robert Wilson, CS 1/c, USN

755. James Bordwell, SK 1/c, USN
756. Francis Dennis, TM 1/c, USN
757. Martin Gorman, CM 1/c, USN
758. John Lafferty, MM 1/c, USN
759. Emerson Milliken, TM 1/c, USN
760. Herbert Neumann, MM 1/c, USN
761. Sylvester North, TM 1/c, USN
762. Charles Peda, SC 1/c, USN
763. William Ritter, BM 1/c, USN
764. John Ryan, SF 1/c, USN
765. Andrew Wiley, AMM 1/c, USN
766. Alton Byran, BM 2/c, USN
767. Russell Hansen, SM 2/c, USN
768. John Howton, BM 2/c, USN
769. Donald McConn, AEROG 2/c, USN
770. Alfred Wilson, BM 2/c, USN
771. Lynn Rinker, CTM, USN
772. Wilson DeVoss, SC 3/c, USN
773. Russell Frazee, MM 3/c, USN
774. Frederick Garza, TM 3/c, USN
775. Harold Gearhart, MM 3/c, USN
776. Alfred Goudge, GM, 3/c, USN
777. Raymond Hoffman, RM 3/c, USN
778. James Hooten, SK 3/c, USN
779. William Hooten, SK 3/c, USN

780. Glen Michels, EM 3/c, USN
781. Homer Roach, COX, USN
782. Leo Casey, F 1/c, USN
783. Clarence Bjork, M/Sgt, USMC
784. Floyd Schilling, 1st/Sgt., USMC
785. Claude Harrill, Sgt., USMC
786. William Vaiden, Pl-Sgt., USMC
787. Tony Gasper, Sgt., USMC
788. Paul Graham, Sgt., USMC
789. Ollie Hill, Sgt., USMC
790. Elmer Long, Sgt., USMC
791. Frank Murphy, Sgt., USMC
792. Ray Provencher, Sgt., USMC
793. Lyoyd Anderson, Fld. Cr., USMC
794. George Bass, Cpl. USMC
795. Frank Dillman, Cpl., USMC
796. Francis Hooker, Cpl., USMC
797. Charles Horvath, Cpl., USMC
798. Ray Howard, Cpl, USMC
799. Shirk Jansen, Cpl., USMC
800. Carl Johansen, Fld. Cl., USMC
801. Gerald Parker, Cpl., USMC
802. Charles Patterson, Cpl. USMC
803. Albert Pickett, Cpl., USMC
804. Earl Anderson, American Civilian

Company Five

806. Richard Pullen, 1st Lt.
807. Bryan Doughty, M/Sgt.
808. Elmer Thomas, Pfc.
809. Harry Kulas, 1st/Sgt.
810. Lewis Rosenberg, 1st/Sgt.
811. Joe Annss, St/Sgt.
812. Wilson Dolde, St/Sgt.
813. James Emmanuel, St/Sgt.
814. Solly P. Manasse, St/Sgt.
815. Charles Stein, St/Sgt.
816. Ed Alcorn, Sgt.
817. Bill Baits, Sgt.
818. Edsel Bartle, Sgt.
819. John Baskin, Sgt.
820. Thomas Bogie, Sgt.
821. James Copeland, Sgt.
822. Ferren Cummins, Sgt.
823. Daino Daum, Sgt.
824. Jack Gregory, Sgt.
825. Thomas Harrell, Sgt.
826. Robert Horn, Sgt.

827. John Hryn, Sgt.
828. Houston Lowe, Sgt.
829. Issac Piercy, Sgt.
830. Brada Rayburn, Sgt.
831. Armando Reveglia, Sgt.
832. Homer Shannon, Sgt.
833. Orval Simpson, Sgt.
834. Alphonse Tondrealt, Sgt.
835. Milton Uphoff, Sgt.
836. Vernon Wheatley, Sgt.
837. Ed Zielinski, Sgt.
838. Charles Barnum, Cpl.
839. Rhodun Bussell, Cpl.
840. Arturo Comacho, Cpl.
841. Cipriano Chavez, Cpl.
842. Adam Ciborek, Cpl.
843. James Davis, Cpl.
844. Arel Escalente, Cpl.
845. Lawrence Howell, Cpl.
846. Herbert Johnson, Cpl.
847. Terrel Johnson, Cpl.

848. Leonard Korpal, Cpl.
849. George Milhalipoulous, Pvt.
850. Clifford Omtvelt, Cpl.
851. John Perrette, Cpl.
852. William Twigg, Cpl.
853. Lee Vistuba, Cpl.
854. Alfred Angert, Pfc.
855. Howard Baker, Pfc.
856. William Black, Pfc.
857. Lawrence Bowman, Pfc.
858. Alfred Cook, Pfc.
859. Jax Couper Pfc.
860. Dale Earing, Pfc.
861. James Edwards, Pfc.
862. Stanley Fort, Pfc.
863. Laurel Gillespie, Pfc.
864. William Gunnup, Pfc.
865. Hoyt Haynie, Pfc.
866. Howard Hicks, Pfc.
867. Homer Hobbs, Pfc.
868. Edward Hoffman, Pfc.
869. Floyd Horton, Pfc.
870. Raymond Howard, Pfc.
871. Paul Jakubowski, Pfc.
872. Otto Kafer, Pfc.
873. Ray Knight, Pfc.
874. John Kusiak, Pfc.
875. Francis Malikowski, Pfc.
876. George Martinez, Pfc.
877. Thomas McGee, Pfc.
878. Wayne McHenry, Pfc.
879. Eliza Millsap, Pfc.
880. Albert Moore, Pfc.
881. Cecil Plymale, Pfc.
882. Edgar Pope, Pfc.
883. John Ptris, Pfc.
884. George Scott, Pfc.
885. Joseph Semanchick, Pfc.
886. James Shuford, Pfc.
887. Melvin Stambaugh, Pfc.
888. Andrew Stanley, Pfc.
889. Edward Tyrell, Pfc.
890. Leo Wagner, Pfc.
891. Golden White, Pfc.
892. Norace Whitecotton, Pfc.
893. George Williams, Pfc.
894. Lee Williamson, Pfc.
895. August DeBauche, Pvt.
896. Floyd Adamson, Pvt.

897. James Aragon, Pvt.
898. Walter Arwood, Pvt.
899. Raymond Baker, Pvt.
900. Robert Barton, Pvt.
901. Joseph Blackman, Pvt.
902. Chaucey Calvin, Pvt.
903. Donald Carabine, Pvt.
904. Aubrey Chism, Pvt.
905. Edward Chovan, Pvt.
906. Claude Coats, Pvt.
907. Eugene Coxey, Pvt.
908. Francis Davis, Pvt.
909. Floyd J. Meyer, Pvt.
910. Leonard Pickett, CRM, USMC
911. Donald Gerola, Pvt.
912. Ramon Carona, Pvt.
913. Glen Himes, Pvt.
914. George Holman, Pvt.
915. Wallace Hopkins, Pvt.
916. John Hutson, Pvt.
917. Ray Joplin, Pvt.
918. Wayne Lawrence, Pvt.
919.
920.
921. Dean Macey, Pvt.
922. Lawrence Martin, Pvt.
923. Landys McClamma, Pvt.
924. Roy McGuinness, Pvt.
925. Stanley Nadolney, Pvt.
926. George Paiden, Pvt.
927. Charles Phillips, Pvt.
928. Ralph Pote, Pvt.
929. Mike Ryan, Pvt.
930. Stanley Santoyo, Pvt.
931. Ralph Shaffer, Pvt.
932. Ralph Torvillo, Pvt.
933. Cyrus Young, Pvt.
934. Harold Hirschberg, Pvt.
935. Thomas Hurtt, SSM, USN
936. Arnold Johnson, CSK, USN
937. Ted Lietz, CY, USN
938. Lyle Orcutt, CMM, USN
939. Floyd Conn, BM 1/c, USN
940. Wilbert Gustafson, PRTR 1/c, USN
941. John Pasino, CM 1/c, USN
942. Stephan Yurchak, SK 1/c, USN
943. Roy Washburn WT 1/c, USN
944. Alvin Andrews, MM 2/c, USN
945. Rollie Blair, CM 2/c, USN

946. Robert Burton, MM 2/c, USN
947. Clifton King, SC 2/c, USN
948. Jack Kirby, QM 2/c, USN
949. Wendell Stone, Y 2/c, USN
950. Robert Welch, BM 2/c, USN
951. John Benson, BM 3/c, USN
952. Charles Lowdy, COX, USN
953. Lance Loring, CM 3/c, USN
954. Charles Pruitt, CM 3/c, USN
955. Herbert Linton, F 1/c, USN
956. Louis Duncan, Sgt., USMC
957. Dan Ditzel, Sgt., USMC
958. Gerald Turner, Sgt. USMC
959. Edmund Barler, Cpl., USMC
960. Malvern Meyers, Cpl., USMC
961. Vito Pepitone, Cpl., USMC
962. John Ray, Cpl., USMC
963. Adolph Richter, Cpl., USMC
964. William Russell, Cpl., USMC
965. Raymond Smith, Cpl., USMC
966. Kenneth Strickland, Cpl., USMC
967. William McClung, Sgt., USMC
968. Benjamin Vinson, Pfc., USMC
969. Raymond Amirant, Pfc., USMC
970. Roger Baker, Pfc., USMC
971. John Corley, Pfc., USMC
972. Dale Coulson, Pfc., USMC
973. Thomas Craigg, Pfc., USMC
974. Frank Etterm, Pfc., USMC
975. Culver Fisher, Pfc., USMC
976. George Fisher, Pfc., USMC

977. Homer Gilbertson, Pfc., USMC
978. Thorton Hanby Pfc., USMC
979. Walter Hawthorne, Pfc., USMC
980. James Hosler, Pfc., USMC
981. Warren Jorgenson, Pfc., USMC
982. George LaFluer, Pfc., USMC
983. William Lang, Pfc., USMC
984. John Latham, Pfc., USMC
985. Charles Lee, Pfc., USMC
986. Wilfred Matheny, Pfc., USMC
987. Owen Ratliff, Pfc., USMC
988. Lester Ruzek, Pfc., USMC
989. Albert Sautter, Pfc., USMC
990. Charles Scott, Pfc., USMC
991. Irvin Scott, Pfc., USMC
992. George Smith, Pfc., USMC
993. Donald Vidal, Pfc., USMC
994. Verdie Wells, Pfc., USMC
995. James Haynes, Pfc., USMC
996. Garland Anderson, American Civilian
997. Fred Anhorn, American Civilian
998. Alfred Chung, American Civilian
999. George Cook, American Civilian
1000. Elvard Davis, American Civilian
1001. Courtney Forth, American Civilian
1002. Alvin Ing, American Civilian
1003. Harold Lake, American Civilian
1004. Frank Smith, American Civilian
1005. Rein Merisaar, Estonian Civilian
1006. Olaf Storhaug, Norwegian Civilian

Medical Detachment, etc.

1007. Ralph Artman, Major, MD.
1008. Calvin Jackson, Major, MD
1009. Max Bernstein, Captain, MD
1010. Adanto D'Amato, Captain, MD
1011. Dan Golenternek, Captain, MD
1012. John Lamy, 1st. Lt., MD
1013. Hugh Hunt, Sgt., Medic
1014. Leslie Long, Sgt. Medic
1015. Frank Mayer, Cpl., Medic
1016. Robert Warnock, Cpl., Medic
1017. Robert Adams, Pfc., Medic
1018. John Hervat, Pfc., Medic
1019. James O'Keefe, Pfc., Medic
1020. Clyde Porche, Pfc., Medic
1021. Donovan Ricks, Pfc., Medic

1022. Morris Rifkin, Pfc., Medic
1023. Norman Roberts, Pfc., Medic
1024. Joseph Wilkens, Pfc., Medic
1025. Horace Young, Pfc., Medic
1026. James Dugan, Pvt., Medic
1027. Wilbur Lense, Pvt., Medic
1028. Ira Morgan, Pvt., Medic
1029. Ernest Norquist, Pvt., Medic
1030. Charlie Smith, Pvt. Medic
1031. Charles Sorochtey, Pvt. Medic
1032. Lawrence Wolf, Pvt. Medic
1033. Fr. Albert Braun, Major, Chaplain
1034. Fr. Herman Baumann, Chaplain
1035. James Boyce, Sgt., Interpreter

NOTO, MARU

Men on the *Noto, Maru* came from the following camps.
August 17, 1944 Bilibid — 150
August 17, 1944 Cabanatuan — 517
August 19, 1944 Clark Field — 150
August , 1944 Murphy — 150
August 20, 1944 Clark Field — 195
TOTAL: 1162

REPLACED MEN ON THE *NOTO, MARU*

first change

1. Capt. Charles Samson replaced Capt. Charles Mueller as Unit Commander
2. 1st Lt. Davis Kirk replaced Phillip Farley as Company 1 Commander
100. Wayne Pennington replaced Aurellio Quintana
116. Don Adair replaced Willard Anderson
146. Norman Ford replaced Martin Grachino
164. Alphonso Lopez replaced Don King
203. Peter Perkins replaced Charles Bennett - 2nd Lt.
289. Joe Quinn replaced Charles Pettis
294. Phillip Tripp replaced Charles Scawright
319. Robert Strahl replaced Ben Vidal
404. George Sense replaced William Beard
424. John Reidy replaced Albert Schla???
513. Lester Lacy replaced Marvin Lackey
565. Ralph Knappenberger replaced William Garleb
574. Walter St. John replaced Joseph Knabe???
611. Joe Gutierrez replaced Joe Smith
699. Clarence Daniels replaced James Black
780. William Hooten replaced John Kanaaaa???
786. Claude Harrell replaced Emmett Nolan
806. Richard Pullen replaced Charles Samson - Capt.
849. George Mihaldroulus replaced Ray McGee
965. William McClung replaced Fred Taylor

LAST MINUTE CHANGES

6. Lloyd Meador replaced T/Sgt Phil Harmon
131. Emil Moritz replaced Pvt. Henry Cochrane
188. Brian Fowler replaced Pvt. Joseph Petrosius
216. Curtis Gartman replaced S/Sgt. Floyd Cooney
368. Albert O'Meara replaced David Latharn
409. Phillip Niverson replaced Eugene Lossett T/Sgt
420. William York replaced S/Sgt Otha Holladay
498. Paul Vetter replaced Pfc. Eugene Gibson
512. Reino Tuomala replaced Pfc. Harold Knighton
702. James Lehrer replaced Pvt. Reginald Evraets
707. Stanley Mroz replaced Anthony DeQuette-Pvt.
767. Alton Bryan replaced SC 2/c, USN Mike Cihulia

772. Lynn Rinker replaced COX USN George Deisinger
895. August DeBauche replaced Pfc. James Woodson
909. Floyd J. Meyer replaced Pvt. Roy Flippen
910. Leonard Pickett replaced Al Gasteluh

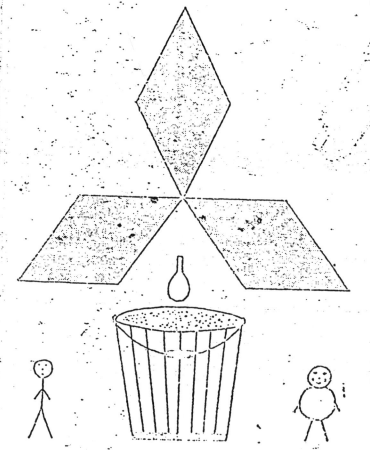

CONTACT YOUR P.O.W. PALS

Souvenir Booklet

including

NAMES AND ADDRESSES OF ALL PERSONNEL

who were P.O.W. in

HANAWA CAMP, JAPAN

Compiled by Acey RUDKIN

KINO - KINO
MISHI SCOSHI

EMA - ASTER - ASTER
MISHI TAXAN

(Courtesy of Max Leyba, Albuquerque, NM)

~ Calvin Jackson ~

No.
-1 Capt. E. P. FLEMING, Jr., 234, Shelburne Road, Arkville, N.C., U.S.A.
-2 Capt. D. GOLENTERNEK, c/o Los Angeles Medical Assn., Los Angeles,
    California, U.S.A.
3 1st-Lieut. R. T. PULLEN, 4360, Lime Avenue, Long Beach, California, U.S.A.
-4 1st-Lieut. J. E. LAMY, 500 So. Grand Street Sedalia, Missouri, U.S.A.
4 M-Sgt. S. H. CRANE, Crane's Tavern, Seattle, Washington, U.S.A.
6 M Sgt. J. KUNICK, R.D.1, Box 43, Ebensburg, Pennsylvania, U.S.A.
7 MdSgt. I. L. BUSTER, 171 S. Cottage Street, Salem, Oregon, U.S.A.
8 C.B.M. F. M. BRIAN, R.2, Camden, Arkansas, U.S.A.
9 C.Y. R. E. STRAHL, 2545, S.W. Vista Avenue, Portland, Oregon, U.S.A.
10 C.C.S. L. E. DIX, 331, Kalama, Washington, U.S.A.
11 C.E.M. O. T. GULLICKSON, Rt.1, Box 1449, Elk Grove, California, U.S.A.
12 J. T. JARRETT, 1650, Santista Street, Singalong, (Sub. Div.), Manila, P.I.
13 C.W.T. W. S. STOCKS, Ayden, N.C., U.S.A.
14 C.E.M. B. G. ZORZANELLO, West Stockbridge, Mass., U.S.A.
15 C.B.M. A. N. SANBURY, Forest Grove, Oregon, U.S.A.
16 C.B.N. R. MARECHAL, 83, Jetter Street, Redwood City, California, U.S.A.
17 C.T.M. L. K. RINKER, 237, Summit Avenue, Cedar Heights, Conshokschen,
    Pa., U.S.A.
18 C.S.M. T. S. HURTT, 1110, South 14 Street, Tacoma, Washington, U.S.A.
19 C.S.K. A. L. JOHNSON, 2906, Logan Ave. No., Minneapolis, Minnesota,
    U.S.A.
20 C.Y. T. L. LIETZ, 236, Shelbourne Road, Burlington, Vermont, U.S.A.
21 C.M.M. L. ORCUTT, U.S. Navy
22 Sgt.-Mas. C. R. JACKSON, 1865, Goldfield Street, San Diego, California,
    U.S.A.
23 M-Sgt. C. L. BJORK, 1735, Granada Avenue, San Diego, California, U.S.A.
24 1st Sgt. R. W. HUSTON, Brandon, Colorado, U.S.A.
25 1st Sgt. H. B. FLOWERS, 343, Rogan Street, Rogersville, Tennessee, U.S.A.
26 T.Sgt. W. O. LACEWELL, Vienna, Illinois, Gen. Del., U.S.A.
27 T.Sgt. D. A. BOWMAN, c/o B. H. Bowman, Lockwood, N.Y., U.S.A.
28 T.Sgt. C. F. CASTER, Underwood, Iowa, U.S.A.
29 1st. Sgt. E. HAMBURGER, 3216, West McCraw St., Seattle, Washington,
    U.S.A.
30 T.Sgt. A. E. LE BEAU, 1477, South 7th East, Salt Lake City, Utah, U.S.A.
31 1st Sgt. A. R. MARTIN (Deceased), De Peere, Wisconsin, U.S.A.
32 T.Sgt. R. W. POPE, Berryville, Virginia, U.S.A.
33 1st. Sgt. J. B. SCRUGGS, 911, Cypress Street, West Monroe, Louisiana,
    U.S.A.
34 T.Sgt. F. N. BEARDON, Gen. Del., Brownwood, Texas, U.S.A.
35 S.C. 1-c G. E. COBB, 425, Magellan Avenue, San Jose, California, U.S.A.
36 M.M. 1 c D. A. DARNEAL.
37 M.M. 1-c N. C. DUDLEY, 3057, Daleford Avenue, Canton, Ohio, U.S.A.
38 A. J. FEHER, 601E. 101st Street, Cleveland, Ohio, U.S.A.
39 R.M. 1-c J. F. GRAY, 312, Benicia Road, Vallego, California, U.S.A.
40 R.M. 1-c L. E. HALLMAN, Holcland Store, El Centro, California, U.S.A.
41 R.M. 1-c E. C. JOHNSON, 23351, Hollander Street, Dearborn, Michigan,
    U.S.A.
42 B.M. 1-c P. L. MANN, Marshall, Minnesota, U.S.A.
43 Y. 1-c F. MARGIOTTO, Jr., 122, Fulton Spring Road, Medford, Mass., U.S.A.
44 B.M. 1-c J. H. McCARTHY, 7, Crescent Street, Lynn, Mass., U.S.A.
45 G.M. 1-c G. W. McCULLOUGH, Cassville, Missouri, U.S.A.
46 R.M. 1-c R. A. MONTGOMERY, 137, S. Kenwood Street, Casper, Wyoming,
    U.S.A.
47 R.M. 1-c G. J. MUENICH, 1613, Otte Avenue, Cincinnati, Ohio, U.S.A.
48 B.M. 1-c A. H. PARRISH, Rt. E2, Box 121, Mill Valley, California, U.S.A.
49 B.M. 1-c E. W. RECTOR, Chautauqua, Kansas, U.S.A.
50 B.M. 1-c V. L. SAUERS, Box 96, College Place, Washington, U.S.A.
51 B.M. 1-c R. C. SHEATS, R.2, Delta, Colorado, U.S.A.
52 E.M. 1-c H. J. TIKEN, 316, Unicar Avenue, Jefferson City, Mo., U.S.A.

3

No.
53 S.M. I/c J. D. BORDWELL, 5005, South East Boycic Street, Oregon, U.S.A.
54 C.M. I/c M. J. GORHAM, 56, Federal Street, Portland, Maine, U.S.A.
55 T.M. I/c E. J. MILLIKEN, 18489, Parkside Avenue, Detroit, Michigan, U.S.A.
56 T.M. I/c S. F. NORTH, Junction City, Kansas, U.S.A.
57 B.M. I/c W. L. RITTER, 426, West 8th Street, Davenport, Iowa, U.S.A.
58 B.M. I/c F. O. CONN, Indianolo, Iowa, R.F.D., U.S.A.
59 Ptr. IIc W. T. GUSTAFSON, 311, East 25th Street, Erie, Penna., U.S.A.
60 W.T. I/c R. M. WASHBURN, 247, McKinley Street, Chabot Terrace, Vallejo, California, U.S.A.
61 T/Sgt. E. W. WHITE, 52, Fort Greene Place, Brooklyn, New York, U.S.A.
62 S/Sgt. J. V. ABRAMOWICZ, U.S. Army, 6767415, Adj.-Gen.
63 S/Sgt. C. AMMONS, 1528, N. Kingsley Dr., Hollywood, California, U.S.A.
64 S.Sgt. J. BOYD, c/o A.G.O., Washington, D.C., U.S.A.
65 S.Sgt. S. T. DERRYBERRY, Ranier, Penn., U.S.A.
66 S.Sgt. A. G. DUINO, 69, E., 2nd Street, Dunkirk, N.Y., U.S.A.
67 S.Sgt. A. M. GOLSAN, Jr., 1010, S.W. 22nd Avenue, Miami, Florida, U.S.A.
68 S.Sgt. W. HOWARD, Sayersville, Ky., U.S.A.
69 S.Sgt. G. T. JENSEN, Rt. 5, Box 345, Modesto, California, U.S.A.
70 S.Sgt. H. E. SANDERS, P.O. Box 593, Caldwell, Idaho, U.S.A.
71 S/Sgt. M. SHERWOOD, Goodman, Mo., U.S.A.
72 S.Sgt. J. S. TRIBBY, Ladoga, Indiana, U.S.A.
73 Sgt. J. H. BENEDICK, 3603, Walker Avenue, Kansas City, Kan., U.S.A.
74 Sgt. P. F. CAHILL, 4927, Seminary Avenue, Richmond, Va., U.S.A.
75 Sgt. H. C. CHRISTENSEN, A.G.O., Washington, D.C., U.S.A.
76 Sgt. T. M. LITCH, P.O. Box 205, Seaside, California, U.S.A.
77 Sgt. T. V. MATTHEWS, Box 321, Queensborough Station, Shreveport, La., U.S.A.
78 Sgt. P. C. MOONEY, Ruston, Louisiana, Gen. Del., U.S.A.
79 Sgt. D. MOORE, Logan, West Virginia, U.S.A.
80 Sgt. E. R. MORAVEE, Adj. A.G.O., Washington, D.C., U.S.A.
81 Sgt. J. T. MURPHY, 204, Liberty, Texas, U.S.A.
82 Sgt. C. L. NICHOLSON, Artesia, New Mexico, U.S.A.
83 Sgt. L. R. PELAYO, Beming, New Mexico, U.S.A.
84 Sgt. G. ROSENFELT, 3322 N., 15th Street, Philadelphia, Penna., U.S.A.
85 Sgt. R. H. RUTLEDGE, 520, Rencher Street, Clovis, New Mexico, U.S.A.
86 Sgt. J. W. SLOWNICK, 2007, Sidney Street, St. Louis, Missouri, U.S.A.
87 Sgt. G. SOTAK, Preble Avenue, North Side, Pittsburg, Penna., U.S.A.
88 Sgt. L. E. STUBBLEFIELD, Box 112, Fairhope, Alabama, U.S.A.
89 Sgt. M. J. TELENDO, 9, Isabella Street, Northampton, Mass., U.S.A.
90 Sgt. A. URBAN, 1007, 7th Street, International Falls, Minnesota, U.S.A.
91 Sgt. G. VANISH, 443, Hudson Street, Jermyn, Pa., U.S.A.
92 Sgt. C. E. WINTERS, 118, St. Clair Avenue, East Liverpool, Ohio, U.S.A.
93 S.Sgt. C. A. BERRY, Box 255, Oil City, Louisiana, U.S.A.
94 S.Sgt. H. E. BRYANT, 621, 17th Street, Corbin, Kentucky, U.S.A.
95 S.Sgt. K. E. DAVIS, 612, 5th Street, Bemidji, Minnesota, U.S.A.
96 S.Sgt. R. E. FRANCIES, 1033 E., 79th Street, Cleveland, Ohio, U.S.A.
97 S.Sgt. A. L. NIX, 905, Turner Street, Waco, Texas, U.S.A.
98 S.Sgt. R. E. PETERSON, 906, South 9th Avenue, Maywood, Ill., U.S.A.
99 S.Sgt. J. N. O'SULLIVAN, 153, Cottage Street, Norwood, Massachusetts, U.S.A.
100 Sgt. C. BURNS, Wheelersburg, Ohio, U.S.A.
101 Sgt. J. L. CARLE, 18, Locke Vo., Ansonia, Conn., U.S.A.
102 Sgt. M. P. CROWE, Oak Grove, Louisianna, U.S.A.
103 Sgt. S. G. EMERY, 2118, Howard Street, Apt. 2, Yourdville, K.Y., U.S.A.
104 Sgt. C. T. FIELDS, 321, Eighth Street, Burk Bennett, Texas, U.S.A.
105 Sgt. J. C. HOWARD, 1111, Arlington Avenue, Atlanta, Ga., U.S.A.
106 Sgt. P. R. HOWELL, Bingham, Nebraska, U.S.A.
107 Sgt. M. LEYBA, 1604, South Williams, Albuquerque, New Mexico, U.S.A.
108 Sgt. S. L. MARCOM, Combs, Arkansas, U.S.A.
109 Sgt. S. PRICE, R.F.D.2, 273, Rochester, Washington, U.S.A.

4

No.
- 110 Sgt. D. H. SUMMONS, 157, W. Broadway, Salem, New Jersey, U.S.A.
  111 S Sgt. A. L. PROTZ, Three Lakes, Wisconsin, R.R.I
  112 Sgt. W. A. SCHLATTER, Jennings Lodge, Oregon, U.S.A.
  113 S Sgt. E. C. CANFIELD, R.F.D., Stewartsville, New Jersey, U.S.A.
  114 S Sgt. H. J. GOURDEAU, 397, Lowell Street, Methuen, Mass., U.S.A.
  115 S Sgt. W. P. HINKIE, Mansfield, Louisiana, U.S.A.
  116 S Sgt. E. M. JOHNSON, 116, 17th Street, Cloquet, Minnesota, U.S.A.
- 117 S Sgt. D. C. VAN HOOK, 503 N., 23rd Street, Lincoln, Nebraska, U.S.A.
  118 Sgt. W. O. BAXTER, Casby, Tenn., U.S.A.
  119 Sgt. L. D. BEASLEY, Cramford Hotel, Carlsbad, New Mexico, U.S.A.
- 120 Sgt. L. R. BYERS, Bayard, New Mexico, U.S.A.
  121 Sgt. T G. DAVIS, Jones Bourgho, R.I, Ind., U.S.A.
- 122 Sgt. W. M. HUTCHISON, Highlands, U. Las Vegas, New Mexico, U.S.A.
  123 M./Sgt. L. O. LARSEN, 103, N. Spring Street, Luverne, Minn., U.S.A.
  124 Sgt. P. MOSKALICK, 725, South 3rd East, Salt Lake City, U.S.A.
- 125 Sgt. W. A. NOFFSKER, 1099, Rencher Street, Clovis, New Mexico, U.S.A.
  126 Sgt. L. SACHWALD, 611, Pearl Street, Lancaster, Pa., U.S.A.
- 127 Sgt. C. N. WILLIAMS, Box 653, Lordsburg, New Mexico, U.S.A.
  128 S Sgt. J. ANNESS, R.F.D.4, Harrodsburg, K.Y., U.S.A.
- 129 S Sgt. W. F. DOLDE, 1327, Van Burnt Blvd, Kansas City, Mo., U.S.A.
- 130 S Sgt. J. W. EMANUEL, Route I, Ft. Collins, Colorado, U.S.A.
- 131 S Sgt. S. P. MANASSEE, 117E, Griggs Street, Las Cruces, New Mexico, U.S.A.
  132 S Sgt. C. S. STEIN, I, Long Street, La., U.S.A.
  133 Sgt. E. E. ALCORN, 1020, Indiana Avenue, South Passadena, California, U.S.A.
  134 Sgt. E. BARTLE, Parker, S. Dakota, U.S.A.
  135 Sgt. H. D. HUNT, Box 241, Carthage, Texas, U.S.A.
  136 A.M.M. 2/c C. S. GARTMAN, 2640, Int. s2, Herran Street, Manila, P.I., U.S.A.
  137 C.M. 2/c T. J. GALBARY, 2610, W. 26th Street, Chicago, Illinois, U.S.A.
  138 E.M. 2/c T. D. GALE, c/o Teata-Apt., 11-11., 41, West 92nd Street, New York City, U.S.A.
  139 T.M. 2/c J. KENNEY, 309, Hersom Street, New Bedford, Mass., U.S.A.
  140 W.T. 2/c P. H. WHEAT, Lonoke, Arkansas, U.S.A.
- 141 S.M. 3/c W. W. CARTER, 3000/1, Spaulding Avenue, Long Beach, California, U.S.A.
  142 G.M. 3/c A. W. CHANDLER, Princeton, Ill., R.F.D.3, U.S.A.
  143 H. R. FISHER, U.S.N. Dep., Personal D., Washington D.C., U.S.A.
  144 E.M. 3/c K. F. GMEINER, Elm Street, Harrington Park, New Jersey, U.S.A.
  145 E.M. 3/c W. K. HAWKES, 653, Downington Avenue, Salt Lake City, Utah, U.S.A.
  146 P. R. HOGGARD, Colerain, N.C., Rt.I, U.S.A.
  147 C.M. 3/c W. G. McDUFFIE, 312, 2nd Avenue, Big Rapids, Michigan, U.S.A.
  148 E.M. 3/c C. H. NELSON, Jr., 311, W. Center Street, Woodbury, N.J., U.S.A.
  149 W. I. SHAWKAN, R.F.D.2, 65, Clarkesburg, W.V., U.S.A.
  150 E.M. 3/c H. B. WHITE, 510, Sweetwater Avenue, Florance, Ala., U.S.A.
  151 T.M. 2 c S. MROZ, Frankton, Ind., R.R.I, U.S.A.
- 152 G.M. 2/c A. B. BRYAN, R.T.2, Luther, Oklahoma, U.S.A.
  153 B. M. 2/c J. I. HOWTON, Edinburg, Texas, U.S.A.
  154 A 2/c D. W. McCONN, 1216, 6th Avenue N.E., Minn., N. Dakota, U.S.A.
  155 W. DEVOSS, R.R.6, Lafayette, Indiana, U.S.A.
  156 T.M. 3/c F. GARZA, 2915, Wilborne Street, Dallas, Texas, U.S.A.
- 157 G.M. 3/c A. L. GOUDGE, 4410, Monroe Avenue, San Diego, California, U.S.A.
  158 H. E. ROACH, Westport, Clifornia, U.S.A.
  159 M.M. 2/c A. A. ANDREWS, McPherson, Kan., U.S.A.
  160 M.M. 2/c R. V. BURTON, P.O. Box 35, Petersburg, Alaska, U.S.A.
  161 Q.M. 2/c J. P. KIRBY, 1112, Kichwaukee Street, Rockford, Ill., U.S.A.
  162 B.M. 2/c R. H. WELCH, 905, East 5th Place, Tulsa, Oklahoma, U.S.A.

5

No.
163 C.M. 3'c L. E. LORING, Caldwell, Idaho, U.S.A.
164 Pltn,Sgt. W. S. VAIDEN, 2421, Rosewood Avenue, Apt. 4, Richmond, Va., U.S.A.
165 Sgt. C. H. HARRELL, P.O. Box 24, Winters, Texas, U.S.A.
— 166 Sgt. E. E. LONG, Jr., 123, North Market Street, Frederick, Maryland. U.S.A.
— 167 Sp Sgt. M. K. HARTIN, Holmes Lane, Oregon City, Oregon, U.S.A.
168 Cpl. K. J. BONINE, 2702, N. Euclid Street, St. Louis, Missouri, U.S.A.
⌐ 169 Cpl. L. L. CANFIELD, 412, Burdick Street, Stillwater, Okla., U.S.A.
— 170 Cpl. J. CAPE, 701, East Charles Avenue, Pauls Valley, Oklahoma, U.S.A.
171 Cpl. W. CARLSON, U.S. Army
172 Cpl. R. L. CHAMBERS, 6041, Hoeveler Street, East Liberty, Pittsburgh, Pa., U.S.A.
173 Cpl. A. M. DE BOER, Route 1, Arpin, Wisconsin, U.S.A.
174 Cpl. J. ERICSON, Los Angeles, California, Gen. Del.1, U.S.A.
175 Cpl. G. E. FELTY, 1 Rt, Bristol, Virginia, U.S.A.
176 Cpl. R. J. JACQUES, 1703½, South Union Avenue, Los Angeles, California, U.S.A.
177 Cpl. V. R. KNAPP, 4301, Garfield Avenue, Kansas City, Mo., U.S.A.
178 Cpl. H. F. HARKLAND, 3, Circle Drive, Fort Smith, Arkansas, U.S.A.
179 Cpl. A. A. MOHR, South Cairo, New York, U.S.A.
180 Cpl. D. E. MORTON, Grandy, Mo., U.S.A.
181 Cpl. F. J. SEEMS, 316, Water Street, Perryville, Mo., U.S.A.
182 Cpl. A. K. SLABINSKI, 11, Jones, Street, Hudson, Penna., U.S.A.
183 Cpl. J. P. SMELLEN, Hugo, Okla., c/o J. T. Holton, U.S.A.
— 184 Cpl. D. E. SOLENBERGER, 11400, Laurelcrest Drive, North Hollywood, California, U.S.A.
— 185 Cpl. R. J. STEWART, Ablemon, Wisconsin, U.S.A.
186 Cpl. J. H. ADAMS, 314, Woodsboro, Texas, U.S.A.
— 187 Cpl. W. G. BALLOU, Artesia, New Mexico, U.S.A.
188 Cpl. P. S. BRAIN, 4620 33rd Avenue, So. Minneapolis, Minnesota, U.S.A.
— 189 Cpl. S. CASANOVE, 2000, 60th Street, Brooklyn, New York, U.S.A.
190 Cpl. B. L. CREAGLE, 8115, Myrtle Street, Houston, Texas. U.S.A.
— 191 Cpl. A. C. KARR, 1523, East Archer, Tulsa, Oklahoma, U.S.A.
192 Cpl. J. A. MILLS, Converge, Louisiana, U.S.A.
193 Cpl. J. MURPHY, Bedford, Penna., U.S.A.
194 Cpl. J. A. POWELL, R.2, Box 4, Falkner, Mississippi, U.S.A.
195 Cpl. V. C. REED, 400, Bonita Avenue, San Jose, California, U.S.A.
196 Cpl. L. A. SILVERSTEIN, 2801, West, Atkinson Avenue, Milwaukee, Wisconsin, U.S.A.
197 Cpl. S. G. ALLEN, R.3, Box 97, Santa Cruz, California, or 1720, Riverside Drive, Los Angeles, California, U.S.A.
198 Cpl. J. H. DAVENPORT, 721, Pine Street, Perrysburg, Ohio, U.S.A.
199 Fld.Ck A. McDANIEL, Riceland, Mo., Star Route, U.S.A.
200 Cpl. H. W. NIKKELSON, 205, Upper Terrace, San Francisco, California, U.S.A.
201 Cpl. J. H. NEWMAN, c/o A. W. Finley, Sapulpa, Oklahoma, Box 53, U.S.A.
◄ 202 Cpl. M. B. RIDDLE, 4445½, E. Fifth Street, Los Angeles, California, U.S.A.
203 Cpl. C. T. RUNDLE, 320, Portland Avenue, Oglesby, Ill., U.S.A.
204 Cpl. J. W. SINDERS, c,o Postmaster, Clifton, Texas, U.S.A.
205 Cpl. F. A. FONTANA, Pence, Wisconsin, U.S.A.
⟍ 206 Cpl. A. H. GILCREASE, R.1, Box 651, Albuquerque, New Mexico, U.S.A.
⤴ 207 Cpl. J. E. LOVE, 221, N. Carlisle Avenue, Albuquerque, New Mexico, U.S.A.
⟶ 208 Cpl. G. C. PAYNE, Bovington, New Mexico, U.S.A.
209 Cpl. J. F. ROSSOTTO, 133, Lincoln, Avenue, Dunkirk, N.Y., U.S.A.
210 Cpl. K. H. SCHOONOVER, Salkum, Washington, U.S.A.
211 Cpl. J. STODDARD, Liberal, Kansas, U.S.A.
212 Fld Ck L. G. ANDERSON, Nora Springs, Iowa, U.S.A.
— 213 Cpl. G. L. BASS, Box 551, Reedsport, Oregon, U.S.A.
214 Cpl. F. H. DILLMAN, Box 145, Lander, Wyoming, U.S.A.
215 Cpl. F. C. HOOKER, 44, Pemberton Road, Cochituate, Mass., U.S.A.

No.
- 216 Cpl. C. S. HOVARTH, 321, Carlton Avenue, Bethlehem, Penna., U.S.A.
  217 Cpl. C. E. PATTERSON, Valley Mills, Texas, U.S.A.
- 218 Cpl. V. PEPPITONE, 17, Mt. Vernon Street, Bridgeton, New Jersey, U.S.A.
- 219 Fld, Ck J. F. RAY, c/o Mrs. Herbert Burgess, 273, Summer Street, Somerville,
         Mass., U.S.A.
- 220 Cpl. F. H. MAYER, Harrold, Texas, Box 63, U.S.A.
  221 Cpl. R. G. WARNOCK, 5935, Monte Vesta Street, Los Angeles, California,
         U.S.A.
  222 Pvt. H. S. BROWN, R.I., Box 240E, West Carlsbad, New Mexico, U.S.A.
  223 P.F.C. D. F. BROWN, 134 S., Pickering Avenue, Whittier, California, U.S.A.
- 224 P.F.C. D. FERRARI, 14120, Mapleridge Avenue, Detroit, Michigan, U.S.A.
  225 PFC. F. GOLDSTEIN, 2030, Montrose Avenue, Chicago, Illinois, U.S.A.
  226 P.F.C. W. LEE, Keene, Texas, U.S.A.
  227 P.F.C. H. MOONEY, 36, South Penn Street, Shippensburg, Penna, Pa., U.S.A.
  228 P.F.C. J. M. MOREHEAD, Bynum Mont., U.S.A.
  229 P.F.C. S. ROMERO, Tass, Pueblo, Tass, New Mexico, U.S.A.
  230 P.F.C. H. A. TROUT, 929, Pershing Road, Zanesville, Ohio, U.S.A.
  231 P.F.C. D. L. VANDAL, 403, State Street, Centralia, Washington, U.S.A.
  232 H. WHITTINGHILL, Jr., Jamestown, Ind., U.S.A.
  233 P.F.C. E. E. WILCOXSON, Box 167, Tormersvill, Texas, U.S.A.
  234 P.F.C. J. WISNESKI, 415, Gray Ave., Houston, Texas, U.S.A.
  235 P.F.C. E. L. WOOD, 629, North Hammond Bethany, Oklahoma, U.S.A.
  236 P.F.C. J. R. WOOD, 1022 E., Hamilton Street, Tampa, Florida, U.S.A.
  237 Pvt. G. H. BOYD, c/o Mrs. A. L. Boyd, Cornish, Maine, U.S.A.
  233 Pvt. T. CHARLIE, Norfolk Street, 2303, Albuquerque, New Mexico, U.S.A.
  239 P.F.C. J. J. LEHNER, 1317, North Western Avenue, Chicago, Illinois, U.S.A.
  240 Pvt. C. S. DICKSON, 90, Brenham Avenue, Natchez, Miss., U.S.A.
- 241 Pvt. A. P. GALLOWAY, G.D. Des. Moines, Jono., U.S.A.
  242 Pvt. W. J. HAVILLAND, (Deceased), c/o Mrs. Celia Havilland, Cleveland,
         Ohio, U.S.A.
  243 P.F.C. W. H. HESTER, 1237, Forest Avenue, Wichita, Kansas, U.S.A.
  244 Pvt. C. H. IRVIN, c/o Mrs. J. B. Hoover, Northfield, Texas, U.S.A.
  245 Pvt. R. H. LARKIN, 1021, East State Street, Algona, Iowa, U.S.A.
  246 Pvt. T. MAURINO, 410, North 1st, Albuquerque, N. Mexico, U.S.A.
  247 Pvt. T. MIKITA, Jr., Maple Grove Street, Hubbard, Ohio, U.S.A.
  248 Pvt. J. I. ROSE, Jr., 12, Bigelow Street, Westerly, Rhode Island, U.S.A.
  249 Pvt. A. T. SCHOOLEY, Crossroads Street, Houston, Texas, U.S.A.
  250 Pvt. V. E. SHERWOOD, c/o Troy Sherwood, Clovis, New Mexico, U.S.A.
  251 Pvt. T. G. STEWART, Clifton, Colorado, U.S.A.
- 252 Pvt. W. L. VICE, Oxford, Indiana, U.S.A.
  253 Pvt. J. M. WARNICK, 284, 26th Avenue, San Francisco, U.S.A.
  254 Pvt. C. C. WOOD, Jr., 3235, Roxboro Road, Atlanta, Ga., U.S.A.
  255 Pvt. M. L. WRIGHT, 5801, Maywood Avenue, Huntington Park, California,
         U.S.A.
  256 P.F.C. E. A. THOMAS, 273, Clinton Street, Greenville, Penna., U.S.A.
  257 Pvt. D. A. MACY, Eagle, Idaho, R.R.I., U.S.A.
  258 P.F.C. L. B. WILLIAMSON, Homing, 117, West Main, Oklahoma, U.S.A.
  259 P.F.C. B. B. HAYNIE, Jr., Prescott Ark., Gen. Del., U.S.A.
  260 P.F.C. A. W. COOK, c/o James D. Cook (father), Julia, Texas, U.S.A.
  261 P.F.C. J. J. O'KEEFE, 2923, Broad Avenue, Altoona, Penna., U.S.A.
  262 P.F.C. H. R. HAYNIE, 304, Laurel Street, Prescott, Arkansas, U.S.A.
  263 P.F.C. D. F. FELTS, Duguoy'm, Illinois, U.S.A.
  264 P.F.C. D. L. FERRATTI, Jr., Long Hill Road, Chatham, New Jersey, U.S.A.
  265 P.F.C. D. B. FORSYTHE, 612, Canby Laramie, Wyoming, U.S.A.
  266 P.F.C. L. FREDIEU, 1192, Gilbert Street, Beaumont, Texas, U.S.A.
  267 Pvt. P. P. GOODMAN, 1/04, North 7th Street, Philadelphia, Penna., U.S.A.
  268 Pvt. T. J. GRIFFIN, 155, West 102nd Street, New York, N.Y., U.S.A.
  269 Pvt. L. J. HILL, Box 74, Fillmore, California, U.S.A.
  270 Pvt. A. E. HILLS, Corasegold, California, U.S.A.
  271 Pvt. T. JAMES, Fort Wingate, New Mexico, U.S.A.

No.
272   Pvt. G. J. KELLEY, 533, Harrison Street, Gary, Ind., U.S.A.
273   Pvt. J. E. KNIGHT, c/o Mrs. Ira C. Arnedt, Ralston, Oklahoma, U.S.A.
274   Pvt. J. A. KRINOCK, 247, Main Street, Ipern Glen, Penna., U.S.A.
275   Pvt. J. P. LAMBO, Strawberry Hill, New Canaan, Conn., U.S.A.
276   Pvt. C. H. LITTLE, Columbia, Miss., U.S.A.
277   Pvt. V. S. MARCEIA, 1119, School Street, Pueblo, Colorado, U.S.A.
278   Pvt. R. J. MARTINEZ, Box 675, Durango, Colorado, U.S.A.
279   Pvt. G. L. MORRIS, Mt. Enterprise, Texas, U.S.A.
280   Pvt. G. R. OVERLY, 1836, N. 15th Street, Lafayette, Indiana, U.S.A.
281   Pvt. J. J. OZOROZY, c/o Mrs. H. E. Knofler, Mill Creek Road, St. Augustine,
        Florida, U.S.A.
—282 Pvt. J. PADGET, Yahoku, Florida, U.S.A.
283   Pvt. S. V. PEARSON, Hot Springs, 310, Albert Pike, Arkansas, U.S.A.
✓ 284 Pvt. P. J. QUINTANA, Mora, New Mexico, Box 294, U.S.A.
285   Pvt. E. W. ROSS, Chewelah, Washington, Route No. 1, U.S.A.
286   Pvt. C. A. SCHMIDT, 1691, B Street, Fresno, California, U.S.A.
287   Pvt. E. A. SEARGEANT, 1450, Kearney Street, El Cerrito, California, U.S.A.
←288 Pvt. A. M. SHUMAN, 939, Washington Street, Reading, Penna, U.S.A.
289   Pvt. J. V. SPECKENS, 412, Soledad Street, Salinas, California, U.S.A.
290   Pvt. A. L. SPENCER, 3930, Mitilda Street, Miami, Florida, U.S.A.
—291 Pvt. H. G. STANLEY, McRae, Ga., R.F.D. 2
—292 Pvt. G. D. STAUDENRAUS, Rosholt, South Dakota, U.S.A.
293   Pvt. C. L. STEWART, 6660, Gaviota Avenue, Long Beach, California, U.S.A.
—294 Pvt. D. N. STOUDT, Shartlesvill, Penn., U.S.A.
295   Pvt. J. L. SUSKIE, Y.M.C.A., Johnstown, Penna., U.S.A.
296   Pvt. M. R. TORRES, Pharr, Texas, Gen. Del., U.S.A.
✗ 297 Pvt. A. TRONESS, 133, S. Oak Street, Sauk Centre, Minnisota, U.S.A.
298   Pvt. M. VIDAURRI, Jr., Ignario, Texas, U.S.A.
✓ 299 Pvt. A. J. VIGIL, Rt. 1, Box 34, Rociada, New Mexico, U.S.A.
300   Pvt. R. T. WALTON, R.F.D. 6, 60 ½, Texarkana, Texas, U.S.A.
301   Pvt. W. E. WHITE, c/o Mrs. Minnie Clark, 109½, Mimosa Place, Wilmington,
        North Carl., U.S.A.
302   Pvt. G. E. WILLS, Lilabee, Texas, U.S.A.
303   Pvt. B. S. ZACK, 950, East Church Street, Jacksonvill, Florida, U.S.A.
—304 P.F.C. C. R. BOLT, Paducah, Texas, U.S.A.
305   P.F.C. A. BORRUANO, Plaguemine, La., U.S.A.
306   P.F.C. C. W. BOX, P.O. Box 351, Sand Spring, Oklahoma, U.S.A.
—307 P.F.C. L. J. CARR, Avoca, Nebraska, U.S.A.
✓ 308 P.F.C. P. A. DIAZ, Lordsburg, New Mexico, U.S.A.
—309 PFC. J. F. DRAKE, Batesville, Mississippi, U.S.A.
310   P.F.C. J. H. FARMER, 1502, 15th Street, Lubbock, Texas, U.S.A.
311   P.F.C. J. A. FLOWERS, Laurel, Mississippi, R.F.D. 1, U.S.A.
✓ 312 P.F.C. E. S. HADDOX, P.O. Box 626, Deming, New Mexico, U.S.A.
313   P.F.C. G. K. HILTON, 707, Prevle Street, St. Paul, Minnisota, U.S.A.
314   P.F.C. R. D. O'CONNOR, 105, S. Sargent Avenue, Glendive, Nebraska,
        U.S.A.
315   P.F.C. F. H. PIBURN, 2718, N. 8th Street, Kansas City, Kan., U.S.A.
✗ 316 P.F.C. G. V. PREWITT, 314, Hudson Lane, Monroe, Louisiana, U.S.A.
317   P.F.C. E. E. SCHOTT, 1207, Lincoln Avenue, Yakima, Washington, U.S.A.
318   P.F.C. R. W. SCHUSTER, Evansville, Wisconsin, U.S.A.
✓ 319 P.F.C. E. L. WILKESON, 519, St. Thoyse, Hobbs, New Mexico, U.S.A.
320   Pvt. C. V. BAIN, Santa Fe, New Mexico, U.S.A.
321   Pvt. G. W. BARNES, Box 524, Blum, Texas, U.S.A.
322   Pvt. C. BEGLEY, Saumerset, Kentucky, U.S.A.
323   Pvt. H. F. BOWER, R.F.D. 2, 489, South Bend, Ind., U.S.A.
324   Pvt. L. M. BROWDER, Humphery, Arkansaw, U.S.A.
325   Pvt. J. R. BROWN, 2258, East 15th Street, Oakland, California, U.S.A.
✗ 326 Pvt. H. W. CARTER, ASN. 6294751, c/o War Dept., U.S. Army
327   Pvt. D. H. HOLDER, Titusville, Fla., U.S.A.
—328 Pvt. R. W. KIMBALL, Sealim, West Virginia, U.S.A.

3

No.
329 Pvt. J. S. LEHANSKI, 166, 7th Street, Jersey City, New Jersey, U.S.A.
330 Pvt. R. R. LOWHEAD, Route 4, Box 322, Vancouver, Washington, U.S.A.
331 Pvt. J. E. MINES, Russellville, Alabama, P.O. Box 225, U.S.A.
332 Pvt. L. M. MORRIS, P.O. 444, Laguna Beach, California, U.S.A.
333 Pvt. D. D. OAKES, Minneapolis, N.C., U.S.A.
334 Pvt. C. ORTIZ, c/o 323, So. Flower Street, Los Angeles, California, U.S.A.
335 Pvt. T. T. PARAS, 702, W. Market Street, Salinas, California, U.S.A.
336 Pvt. E. D. PREHM, Carrizozo, New Mexico, Gen. Del., U.S.A.
337 Pvt. W. W. PURCELL, Stroud, Oklahoma, Box 303, U.S.A.
338 Pvt. W. R. SAMSON, 690, 3rd Avenue, San Francisco, California, U.S.A.
339 Pvt. W. F. SCHUETTE, 1462, Kurtz Avenue, Green Bay, Wis., U.S.A.
340 P.F.C. P. B. TRIPP, 3857, Garfield Avenue, Mpls., Minn., U.S.A.
341 Pvt. W. G. SELF, Smichdale, Mississippi, U.S.A.
342 Pvt. J. L. SHARP, 600, W. 94th Street, Los Angeles, California, U.S.A.
343 Pvt. R. B. SILLS, 2154, Mission Street, San Francisco, California, U.S.A.
344 Pvt. G. J. SMITH, 1536, N. 8th Street, Milwaukee, Wisconsin, U.S.A.
345 Pvt. G. W. SMITH (Deceased), Lafallette, Tenn., U.S.A.
346 Pvt. J. C. SPENCER, 385, Western Avenue, Jamesville, Wisconsin, U.S.A.
347 Pvt. W. STEFANSKI, Box F.141, R.F.D., Roland Street, Valley Falls, Rhode Island, U.S.A.
348 Pvt. A. D. STENGLAR, 201, West Hill Street, Louisville, Ky., U.S.A.
349 Pvt. K. STONE, 7, W. 101st, Street, New York City, New York, U.S.A.
350 Pvt. L. STRICKLAND, c/o A.G.O., Washington D.C., U.S.A.
351 Pvt. R. THRONEBERRY, Pixley, California, Route 2, U.S.A.
352 Pvt. E. G. TAYLOR, 527, South Avenue, Rockford, Illinois, U/S.A.
353 Pvt. R. TAYLOR, 181, Lechner Avenue, Columbus, Ohio, U.S.A.
354 Pvt. J. TORRES, Galleys, 301 Third, New Mex., U.S.A.
355 Pvt. M. X. TRAINO, 31, Canary Street, Rochester, New York, U.S.A.
356 Pvt. F. O. TUCKER, Box 514, Sitka, Alaska, U.S.A.
357 Pvt. P. TURNER, Silver Creek, Miss., R. 1, Box 30, U.S.A.
358 Pvt. R. C. UNDERWOOD (Deceased), Fulton, Miss., U.S.A.
359 Pvt. C. L. URBAN, 2143, Carter Avenue, Ashland, Ky., U.S.A.
360 Pvt. W. J. VAN ALMEN, Atwood, Kansas, U.S.A.
361 Pvt. L. W. VAN LIEKE, 535, Lexington Avenue, Clifton, New Jersey, U.S.A.
362 Pvt. J. VAUGHN, 1811, E. Broadway Street, Ft. Worth, Texas, U.S.A.
363 Pvt. L. H. WALDRIP, Allisan, Texas, U.S.A.
364 Pvt. L. N. WALLACE, Box 718, Holtville, California, U.S.A.
365 Pvt. F. W. WATKINS, 2220, S. Santa Fe Street, Oklahoma City, Oklahoma, U.S.A.
366 Pvt. C. R. WEBBER, 1220, N. Grant Street, Indianapolis, Indiana, U.S.A.
367 Pvt. L. C. WHICHARD, 127, S. Market Street, Petersburg, Virginia, U.S.A.
368 Pvt. A. WILLS, 129, Railroad Avenue, Fresno, California, U.S.A.
369 Pvt. G. E. YOUNG, Lakeview, Oregon, Gen. Del., U.S.A.
370 Pvt. O'MEARE, 121, Lincoln Avenue, Gardiner, Maine, U.S.A.
371 Pvt. L. J. MEADOR, 420, Ralph 3, San Gabrale, California, U.S.A.
372 P.F.C. J. B. ALDRED, 2312, West Kentucky Street, Louisville, Kentucky, U.S.A.
373 P.F.C. F. BAIN, 7023, Gammage, Huston, Texas, U.S.A.
374 P.F.C. R. C. BALDWIN, 121, West Patriot Street, Somerset, Pa., U.S.A.
375 P.F.C. J. A. BALLOW, 130, North Avenue, Dunellen, N.J., U.S.A.
376 P.F.C. R. C. BEAN, Bridger, Montana, U.S.A.
377 P.F.C. E. E. BOWERS, 539, University Avenue, San Antonio, Texas, U.S.A.
378 P.F.C. S. F. BROOKS, 1205½, S. La Cienega Blvd., Los., California, U.S.A.
379 P.F.C. G. W. CLEMMER, Fairfield Va., R. 1, U.S.A.
380 P.F.C. B. H. COLE, Lisbon, North Dakota, U.S.A.
381 P.F.C. G. L. COLEMAN, Fort Snitu, Arkansas, R. 3, Box 268, U.S.A.
382 P.F.C. L. G. CUSANO, 271, Davenport Avenue, New Haven, Connecticut, U.S.A.
383 P.F.C. R. A. DEMERS, 1029, S.W. 5th Street, Miami, Florida, U.S.A.
384 P.F.C. M. S. FOSTER, 110, North Street, Calais, Maine, U.S.A.

No.
385 P.F.C. C. L. FRAZIER, 718, Pierce Street, Denton, Texas, U.S.A.
386 P.F.C. A. O. GENTRY, Leonard, Texas, Route 2, U.S.A.
387 P.F.C. W. A. GHILARDI, 82, Gates Street, San Francisco, California, U.S.A.
388 P.F.C. E. GUITTEREZ, 422, P.O.B., Colusa, California, U.S.A.
389 P.F.C. F. E. HARRISON, Newburg, Missouri, U.S.A.
390 P.F.C. J. H. HENRY, Box Elder, Montana, U.S.A.
391 P.F.C. P. J. HIGDON, 6440, Ellsworth Street, Detroit, Michigan, U.S.A.
392 P.F.C. A. HUGHES, 410, Lincoln Street, Snohomish, Washington, U.S.A.
393 P.F.C. L. G. HOLBERT, c/o Mrs. Roy C. Hulbert, 903, East Street, Lead., South Dakota, U.S.A.
394 P.F.C. A. Z. JEFFRE, 754, E. 82nd Street, Los Angeles, California, U.S.A.
395 P.F.C. J. B. LAWLER, Route 1, Thrall, Texas, U.S.A.
396 P.F.C. W. J. LERITTE, 1016, St. Phillip Street, New Orleans, La., U.S.A.
397 P.F.C. R. E. LEVIS, 311, Kelly Avenue, Willsinsburg, Penna., U.S.A.-
398 P.F.C. A. D. MARANGIELLA, 15, First Street, Glen Cove, New York, U.S.A.
399 P.F.C. M. A. MAZER, 5820, Jackson Street, Pittsburgh, Penna., U.S.A.
400 P.F.C. A. E. McFARLEY, 342, S. Lincoln Street, Denver, Colorado, U.S.A.
401 P.F.C. T. P. McDILL, Chadron, Nebraska, U.S.A.
402 P.F.C. J. J. McTIGUE, South Cairo, New York, U.S.A.
403 P.F.C. P. H. MILLER (Deceased), Bridgewater, Virginia, U.S.A.
404 P.F.C. H. E. NEECE, 13050, Sonarfe Street, Resecho, California, U.S.A.
405 P.F.C. W. G. PARKS, 2235, Queens Huey, Shreveport, La., U.S.A.
406 P.F.C. W. H. PENNINGTON, Box 223, Drumright, Oklahoma, U.S.A.
407 P.F.C. G. R. RING, 420, Daisy Avenue, Sodi, California, U.S.A.
408 P.F.C. A. L. ROTH, Plainview, Minnesota, c/o Herbert Marshman, U.S.A.
409 P.F.C. C. L. SEQUIN, Gervais, Oregon, U.S.A.
410 P.F.C. C. SHAW, 204, S. Sixth Street, Gallup, New Mexico, U.S.A.
411 P.F.C. A. SISNERDS, Ojo Caliente, New Mexico, Gen. Del., U.S.A.
412 P.F.C. H. R. TAVES, 1111, State Street, Alamosa, Colo., U.S.A.
413 P.F.C. E. M. THURSTON, Locust Valley, N.Y., U.S.A.
414 P.F.C. G. D. WEBB, 301, Jackson Street, Decatur, Alabama, U.S.A.
415 P.F.C. W. S. WHEELER, 19, Vernon Street, W. Medford, Miss., U.S
416 P.F.C. J. J. WITHAM, 2703, Moore Street, Phila., Pa., U.S.A.
417 P.F.C. C. G. WUHRMANN, 1351, State Street, Raane, Wisconsin, Blythe, California, U.S.A.
418 P.F.C. L. E. YOHN, 40, South Prince Street Lancaster, Pa., U.S.A.
419 Pvt. G. H. ALTON, Deer River, Minnesota, U.S.A.
420 Pvt. D. C. ADAIR, Bloomfield, New Mexico, U.S.A.
421 Pvt. W. H. ARTEBURN, 2010, Taylor Street, Amarillo, Texas, U.S.A.
422 Pfc. H. L. AVERY, Sandy Lake, Pa., U.S.A.
423 Pvt. M. F. BARKER, 801, 19th Street, Columbus, Georgia, U.S.A.
424 Pvt. M. L. BARTLEY, Walnut Hill, Florida, U.S.A.
425 Pvt. J. M. BAYHART, 627, South Front Street, Steelton, Pa., U.S.A.
426 Pvt. A. BEACH, Gen. Del, Bloomington, Indiana, U.S.A.
427 Pvt. J. K. BRUNDAGE, 501, E. Garfield Street, Phoenix, Arizona, U.S.A.
428 Pvt. N. M. BUSTAMANTE, San Jose, New Mexico, U.S.A.
429 Pvt. J. F. BUTLER, 3938, Hidalgo Pl., Riverside, California, U.S.A.
430 Pvt. C. D. BURKS, Girard, Rt. 1, Texas, U.S.A.
431 Pvt. K. L. CALVIT, Jackson Street, Ext., Alexandria, La., U.S.A.
432 Pvt. W. H. CLIFTON, 1447, East 8th Street, Jacksonville, Fla., U.S.A.
433 Pvt. J. CROWN, 1633, Canterbury Street, Jacksonville, Florida, U.S.A.
434 Pvt. B. M. CUNNINGHAM, Rufe, Oklahoma, Y.S.A.
435 Pvt. W. A. CURTIS, Route 1, Box 523, Muskogu, Oklahoma, U.S.A.
436 Pvt. B. W. DEHR, Climax, Colorado, U.S.A.
437 Pvt. A. D. DICKSON, 421, South 4 Avenue, Paragoda, Ark., U.S.A.
438 Pvt. J. M. EMERICK, Mt. Pleasant, Penna. R.F.D. 1, U.S.A.
439 Pvt. B. J. FENNELL, 612, Lafayette Street, Santa Clara, California, U.S.A.
440 Pvt. B. T. GARCIA, 2023, W. Trive's Street, San Antonio, Texas, U.S.A.
441 Pvt. N. C. FORD, Chattaroy, Washington, U.S.A.
442 Pvt. R. C. GILBERT, Oquawka, Illinois, U.S.A.

No.
443 Pvt. C. T. HARRIS, Route 1, Box 26, Casecy, Kansas, U.S.A.
444 Pvt. W. L. HARRIS, Valliant, Oklahoma, c o Dr. W. L. Harris, Rt., U.S.A.
445 Pvt. J. T. HAYWOOD, 505, N. Madison Street, Magnolia, Ark., U.S.A.
446 Pvt. L. E. HEINZ, 192, E. Stanton Street, Streator, Illinois, U.S.A.
447 P.F.C. W. V. HIETANEN, 1806, S. Barber Street, Bessemer, Michigan, U.S.A.
448 Pvt. J. HOBACK, c o Mrs. R. O. Lewis, Ten Sleep, Wyoming, U.S.A. ✱ *bathing force?*
449 Pvt. V. P. IHDE, 551, 3rd Street, Tracy, Minnesota, U.S.A.
450 Pvt. J. JONES, Boswell, Oklahoma, Gen. Del., U.S.A.
451 Pvt. J. A. JONES, Jr., Dougherty, Oklahoma, Gen. Del., U.S.A.
452 Pvt. R. A. KEESEY, c o De La Galle College, Manila, Philippines
453 Pvt. D. B. KIMBALL, 1109, 33rd Street, Parkersburg, West Virginia, U.S.A.
454 Pvt. A. A. LOPEZ, 211, W. 28th Street, Los Angeles, California, U.S.A.
455 Pvt. J. 3. KISER, Supply, Oklahoma, U.S.A.
456 Pvt. J. R. KNOWLES (Deceased), Three Forks, Montana, U.S.A.
457 Pvt. J. P. LANE, R.F.D. 1, Deerlodge, Mont., U.S.A.
458 Pvt. W. M. LEE, 3113, West 25th Street, Fortworth, Texas, U.S.A.
459 Pvt. A. LOPEZ, Sandoval, New Mexico, U.S.A.
460 Pvt. B. MANZANARES, Optimo, New Mexico, U.S.A.
461 Pvt. W. MARTIN, Route 2, Box 33, Chilcowe, Virginia, U.S.A.
462 Pvt. J. D. MERRITT, 6959, Lilley Road, Plymouth, Michigan, U.S.A.
463 Pvt. A. R. MILLER, 1239, Sparkbuk Avenue, East Akron, Ohio, U.S.A.
464 Pvt. J. T. NELSON, Titusville, Fla., U.S.A.
465 Pvt. N. M. OLSON, Story City, Iowa, U.S.A.
466 Pvt. H. H. PIERCE, 5112, North 39th Street, Tacoma, Washington, U.S.A.
467 Pvt. D. S. PELTIER, 70, Alexander Street, Springfield, Massachusetts, U.S.A.
468 Pvt. H. G. PHILLIPS, Box 11, Selkirk, New York State, U.S.A.
469 Pvt. E. C. PINE, 13, Holleck Street, New Ark., Y.J., U.S.A.
470 Pvt. H. I. PRESTON, 3655, South 9th Street, Tucson, Arizona, U.S.A.
471 Pvt. G. S. REISHER, Jr., R.R. 4, Chambersburg, Pennsylvania, U.S.A.
472 Pvt. F. E. RICHESON, 327, West Main Street, Barnesville, Ohio, U.S.A.
473 Pvt. R. V. RING (Deceased), Litchfield, Ohio, U.S.A.
474 Pvt. S. R. ROBERTSON, 320, Faraday Avenue, Peoria, Illinois, U.S.A.
475 Pvt. C. K. SADDLER, 411, Tucas Avenue, Owensbero, Kentucky, U.S.A.
476 Pvt. P. H. SANFORD, Marks, Mississippi, Box J, U.S.A.
477 Pvt. J. J. DUGAN, 2676, Braddock Street, Philadelphia, Penn., U.S.A.
478 P.F.C. O. R. RATLIFFE, New Albany, Mississippi, U.S.A.
479 P.F.C. W. G. JORGENSON, 116, 3rd Avenue N., Mount Vernon, Iowa, U.S.A.
480 P.F.C. W. St. JOHN, Perryville, Arkansas, U.S.A.
481 P.F.C. F. E. ABRAHAMS, Wayne, Kansas, U.S.A.
482 P.F.C. B. J. ARNEY, 2421, Wilshire Blvd, Houston, Texas, U.S.A.
483 P.F.C. J. A. BEST 630, E. Locust Street, Du Moines, Iowa, U.S.A.
484 P.F.C. J. O. FAULKNER, 20, N.W. 7th Street, Oklahoma City, Oklahoma, U.S.A.
485 P.F.C. J. E. FISH, 3355, Pine Street, Eureka, California, U.S.A.
486 P.F.C. F. E. JENSEN, Central City, Colorado, U.S.A.
487 P.F.C. A. W. JONES, Rush Springs, Oklahoma, U.S.A.
488 P.F.C. J. H. KINDLE, Forest Grove, Oregon, Route 2, U.S.A.
489 P.F.C. D. V. MEYERS, Post Office, Los Angeles, U.S.A.
490 P.F.C. F. E. J. R. SAEFKE, 306, S. Elmwood, Fargo, N. Dakota, U.S.A.
491 P.F.C. W. H. VARDEMAN, Hubbard, Texas, Route 1, U.S.A.
492 P.F.C. R. WATSON, 513, N. Madgland Street, San Angelo, Texas, U.S.A.
493 P.F.C. J. F. WERNER (Deceased), c/o J. F. Werner (sen.), 2414 Jackson
      Avenue, New Orleans, La., U.S.A.
494 F.M. 1/c L. F. CASEY, Jr., Belmont, Mass., U.S.A.
495 F 2/c P. J. KIRHGESNER, 1303, Wilbur Avenue, Akron, Ohio, U.S.A.
496 P.F.C. E. M. MORITZ, 1313, Layard Avenue, Racuil, Wisconsin, U.S.A.
497 S. 1/c S. F. VONDETTE, 33, Grant Avenue, Rutland, Vermont, U.S.A.
498 S. 1/c D. F. HAHN, 710, N. 3rd Street, Rochelle, Illinois, U.S.A.
499 S. 1/c R. W. JOHNSTON, Route 1, Anacortis, Washington, U.S.A.
500 S.M. 1/c G. LAMBASIO, 407, W. Adams Street, Abingdon, Illinois, U.S.A.

No.
501 Lieut.-Col. A. J. WALKER, c/o Adj. Gen., Washington, D.C., U.S.A.
502 Flt.-Lieut. R. H. THOMPSON, c/o R.A.A.F. H.Q., Victoria Barracks, Melbourne, Australia
503 Capt. I. C. SPOTTE, c/o Mary C. Simpson, 516, S. Rampart Blvd, Los Angeles, U.S.A.
     A. CRAPPER, 34, Rangeley Road, Sheffield 6, Yorkshire
     J. ARMSTRONG, 12, West Row, Freehold, Fence Houses, Co. Durham
     F. McLACHLAND, 56, Eldon Street, North Shields, Northumberland
     G. WOOLFORD, 13, Rosebank, Row, Burley Road, Leeds 3
     F. BARKER, 19, Cooper Street, Sidcup, Lancs.
     J. APPLEYARD, 98, Highbury Road, Lytham-St.-Annes, Lancs.
     C. HARVIE, 47, Strawberry Lane, Carshalton, Surrey
     F. FREEMAN, " Lyndhurst," Titchfield Avenue, Mansfield Woodhouse, Notts.
     C. JONES, 17, Grafton Street, St. Silas, Bristol 2
     J. BATEY, 64, Dalton Avenue, Daneside, Seaham, Co. Durham
     R. WORBOYS, 171, Bournemouth Road, Parkstone, Dorset
     D. CRABBS, 19, Piccroft Road, North End, Portsmouth, Hants.
     E. BROWN, 44, Hendon Valley Road, Sunderland, England
     B. LEGGE, 7, Summit Avenue, Wakeman's Hill, Kingsbury, N.W.9
     J. HENDERSON, c/o Hamilton, 75, Bridge Street, Kirkcaldy, Fife, Scotland
     F. RUDKIN, " Vogelenzang," 24, Compton Road, Colchester, Essex
     W. REID, 79, Fairview Avenue, Woodstock, Capetown, South Africa
     G. GRANTHAM, 61, Spencer Road, Wealdstone, Harrow, Middlesex
     R. BELL, 12, Sturdee Avenue, Gillingham, Kent
     E. HUBBOLD, c/o 77, Cavendish Street, Barrow-in-Furness, Lancashire
     T. McVEY, 3, Campbell Street, Newmilns, Ayrshire, Scotland
     B. STONER, 51, Central Avenue, Ibstock, Leicestershire
     E. BEGG, 72, Tophill Road, Hamilton, Lanarkshire, Scotland
     E. ILIFFE, 56, New Street, Earl Shilton, Near Leicester
     E. HILLS, 5, Commonside Street, Airdrie, Lanarkshire, Scotland
     J. WILSON, 392, Inverleith Street, Camtyne, Glasgow, E.2, Scotland
     H. SHENTON, 9, Saxen Street, Stapenhill, Burton-on-Trent, England
     W. GIBSON, 44, Ashburnham Road, Belvedere, Kent
     V. THOMAS, 17, West Bank, Nr. Openshaw, Manchester, Lancashire
     J. EVITTS, 2, Lord Street, Gin. Pit, Artley, Lancs.
     C. RUSSELL, 201, Low Quarry, Hamilton, Lanarkshire, Scotland
     T. O'ROURKE, c/o Mrs. Bradly, Leagrave, Luton, Bedfordshire, Eng.
     J. CAMPBELL, 64, Nelson Road, Gourock, Renfrewshire, Scotland
     J. FARREN, 27, Seldon Street, Kensington, Liverpool 6
     W. REID, 154, Candren Road, Paisley, Scotland
     F. CLEARY, 5, Dalfield Terrace, Dundee, Scotland
     C. DEAKINS, 113, Armstead Walk, Dagenham, Essex
     D. SALMON, 11, Tower Avenue, Chelmsford, Essex
     H. RICHARDS, 17, Dent's Road, Bedford, Beds.
     J. COOK, 74, Courthill Crescent, Kilsyth, Stirlingshire, Scotland
     A. FERGUS, 44, Charles Street, Kilsyth, Stirlingshire, Scotland
     J. GIBSON, 9, Kendigern Terrace, Bishopbriggs, Glasgow, Scotland
     A. CAMPBELL, 11, Seaforth Gardens, Dingwall, Ross-shire, Scotland
     G. BICKETT, 2, High Street, Halesowen, Near Birmingham, England
     T. LAWSON, 57, Quorrellhall Crescent, Carronshore by Falkirk, Stirlingshire, Scotland
     C. SCHOALES, " Station House," Liscooly, Castlefin, Co. Donegal, Eire
     H. ROBERTS, 32, Rupert Grove, Liverpool 5
     C. WILLOUGHBY, 17, Friars Close, Bear Lane, Southwark, London, S.E.1
     A. WEDGE, 161, Northumberland Park, Tottenham, London, N.17
     C. TUTON, 19, Cotton Road, Strood, Rochester, Kent

     HERBERT SMITH   545. DALLAS .b E

THE ESSEX TELEGRAPH LTD., PRINTERS, 38, HEAD STREET, COLCHESTER, ENGLAND.

HANAWA MEN

The following men were contacted either orally or by the mail concerning Hanawa. Approximately 67% responded with information.

Willie Arterburn
Matt Barker
Don (Sollen) Berger
Charles Bolt
Alton Bryan
Crayton Burns
Leslie Canfield
Jack Cape
Leslie Carr
Howard Carter
Stanley Casanove
Brownell Cole
Ken Davis
W. F. Dolde
James Drake
John Emerick
James Emmanuel
James (Jack) Faulkner
E. Pearce Fleming
Dick Francies
Al Galloway
Art Gilcrease
Dr. Dan Golenternek
Warren Hawkes
Gordon K. Hilton
Chuck Horvath

Woodrow Hutchinson
Dr. Calvin Jackson
Ed Johnson
R. W. Johnston
Austin Karr
Peter Kirhgesner
Dave Kimball
Dr. John Lamy
Max Leyba
Elmer Long
Tony Marangiello
M. Keith Martin
Solly Mannase
Thomas Mathews
Maurice Mazer
George McCullough
Emerson Milliken
Delbert Moore
Stanley Mroz
Asbury Nix
John Padgett
Grayford Payne
Lee Pelavo
Desire Peltier
Dwight Pennington
Vito Pepetone

Ralph Pope
Granville Prewitt
John Ray
Earl Rector
Merrill Riddle
Bill Ritter
Lester Ruzell
James Scruggs
Jack Sharp
Marvin Shearwood
Al Shuman
Grady Stanley
Gerald Staudenraus
Bob Stewart
Dan Stoudt
David Summons
Richard Taylor
Ray Throneberry
Phillip Tripp
Art Troness
Tony Urban
David Van Hook
Lawrence Van Liere
Bill Vice
George Young
Basilio Zorzanello

RECORD OF CHANGES. HANAWA PRISON.

DATE		STR.
SEPT. 1	MAJ. CALVIN G. JACKSON, M.C.; CAPT. ELMER P. FLEMING, JR. P.R. 1ST. LIEUT. RICHARD T. PULLEN, JR. + QR.C., 1ST. LIEUT. JOHN E. LAMY, M.C. AND 496 AMERICAN REMT. NAVY, MARINE ENLISTED MEN ARRD. FR. P.I.	500.
OCT. 24	PVT. PAUL H. MILLER. DIED	499
NOV. 12	FOLLOWING MEN TRFD. TO HOSPITAL AT TOKYO. #1,80,184, 185, 273, 313, 343, 366.	
NOV. 10	PFC. ROBERT V. RING, U.S.A. DIED	491
NOV. 20	CAPT. DON GOLENTERNEK, M.C. USA ARRD. FR [illegible], TO FRANCE	490
DEC. 1 1945	MAJ. JACKSON AS SENIOR M.O. AT THIS CAMP	490
	PVT. GRAMORE W. SMITH, U.S.A. DIED.	490
FEB. 16	PVT. ROY C. UNDERWOOD, U.S.A. DIED	489
MAR. 3	LT. COL. ARTHUR J. WALKER, U.S.A.A.F., CAPT. IRVIN C. SPOTTS, C.E., U.S.A. FL. LT. ROBERT H. THOMPSON, R.A.A.F. TRFD.,FR. TOKYO HR. CAMP THIS DATE: FOLLOWING NAMED MEN RETURNED FROM TOKYO HOSPITAL. #184,185, 273,313, 313, 343, 385.	
MAR. 10	PFC. JOSEPH F. WEBNER, U.S.M.C. KILLED IN MINE ACCIDENT.	488
MAY 13	CAPT. ROBERT C. EAGLE, LIEUT. WESLEY F. WILLOUGBY R.E. AND 48 BRITISH ENLISTED MEN TRFD. TO BUILDING CAMP.	441
MAY 31	PVT. WILLIAM J. HATFIELLAND DIED	541
JUNE 8	1ST. SGT. ADRIAN R. MARTIN DIED	546
JULY 8	PVT. JASPER R. KNOWLES. DIED.	545
		544

Hanawa Strength Roster recovered from microfilm.

HANAWA PRISON CAMP

Section 2

Buster, Ivan
Cobb, George
Murphy, James
Francies, Richard
Price, Stanton
Nelson, Clarence
Shawman, William
Adams, Jesse
Horvath, Charles
Trout, Hobart
Bower, Howard
Ghilardi, Werner
Hoback, John
Walton, Royt

Stocks, William
Feher, Arthur
Nicholson, Chester
Nix, Asbury
Stein, Charles
White, Harold
Canfield, Leslie
Creaglem, Benjamin
Dickson, Charles
Piburn, Frank
Holder, Daniel
Webb, George
Lane, Jesse
Montgomery, Robert

Dix, Lee
Benedict, James
Rosenfelt, Gustav
Fields, Collby
Carter, Walter
Andrews, Alvin
Morton, Darrell
Davenport, Jesse
Lee, Willis
Schuster, Rudolph
Oakes, Donald
Cunningham, Burl
Nelson, John

Section 3A

Banbury, Archie
Bjork, Clarence
Caster, Charles
Hallman, Leonard
Duino, Anthony
Berry, Cecil
Gale, Thomas
Loring, Lance
Cape, Jack
Payne, Grayford
Roth, Albert

Marchal, Robert
Lacewell, Willborn
Hamburger, Emmanuel
Johnson, Earl
Shearwood, Marvin
Manasse, Solly
McDuffie, William
Martin, M. Keith
Stewart, Bob
Parks, Wilson
Huston, Royal

Bowman, Donald
Martin, Adrian R.
Ritter, William
Cahill, Paul
Galbary, Theodore
Roach, Homer
Bonine, Kenneth
Gilcrease, Arthur
James, Toney
Gilbert, Robert

Section 3B

Gullickson, Oscar
Brian, Fowler fr. 3A
Rinker, Lynn
Jackson, Charles fr. 3A
Pope, Ralph
Dudley, Noble
McCarthy, James
Tihen, Herman
Tribby, James
Gourdeau, Henry
Kenney, John
Gmeiner, Kenneth
Long, Elmer
Riddle, Merrill
Wright, Marvin
Marcelja, Vincent
Speckens, James

Begley, Carl fr. 3A
Traino, Michael
Van Liere, Lawrence fr. 3A
Lawler, Jay
Butler, John
Harris, William
Preston, Homer fr. 3A
Burns, Crayton
Fredien, Louis
Jarret, Jessie
Zorzanello, Baselio
Orcut, Lyle
Flowers, Howard fr 3A
Scruggs, James
Gray, James
Rector, Earl
Gustafson, Wilbert

O'Sullivan, James
Dolde, Wilson
Wheat, Patrick
Hawkes, Warren
Carlson, Wm from 3A
James, Tony
Thomas, Elmer
Morris, Gordon
Haddox, Ernest
Taylor, Richard fr. 3A
Urban, Charles
Cusano, Louis
Leritte, Whitney
Harris, Clay
Pierce, Harley
Moritz, Emil
Haviland, Wm

Section 3C

Ammons, Cecil fr. 4E   Staudenraus, Gerald fr. 4E
Guitterrez, Eddie fr. 4E   Burks, Chester fr. 4F

Section 4A

Crane, Stanley   Kunich, John   Sauers, Virgil
McCullough, George   Parrish, Albert   Derryberry, Sam
Bordwell, James   North, Sylvester   Jensen, Gordon
Sheats, Robert   Golsin, Archie   Slownick, John
Moore, Delbert   Rutledge, Robert   Urban, Tony
Sotak, George   Stubblefield, Lawrence   Bryant, Harold
Vanish, George   Winters, Clyde   Howell, Pat
Crowe, Malcolm   Embry, Shelby   Beasley, Leon
Schlatter, Widfred   Canfield, Edward   Moskalick, Peter
Byers, Lloyd   Hutchison, Woodrow   Bryan, Alton
Gartman, Curtis   Hoggard, Pritchard   Goudge, Alfred
DeVoss, Wilson   Garza, Frederick   Slabinski, Anthony
Harrel, Claude   Felty, George   Murphy, John
Allen, Stanley   McDaniel, Alvie   Rosotto, James
Newman, Junior   Love, Johnny   Romero, Sam
Stoddard, John   Dillman, Frank   Little, Cecil
Haynie, Bill   Haynie, Hoyt   Curtis, William
Mazer, Maurice   Neece, Harry   Pine, Edward
Hietanen, Waino   Miller, Arthur   Arney, Billy
Richeson, Forest   Robertson, Sam   Christensen, Harold
Meyers, Delmer   Bayhart, Joseph
Jones, Arthur   Strahl, Robert

Section 4B

Johnson, Arnold   Ozorozy, Julius   Mills, James
Hinkie, Wayne   Barruano, Angelo   Bass, George
Baxter, Willis   Self, W, fr. 4E   Sinders, John
Sachwald, Louis   Harrison, Ferrille fr. 4E Goldstein, Frank
Alcorn, Ed   Wuhrman, Carl   Wisneski, Johnnie
Burton, Robert   Imme, Vincent fr. 4E   Wood, John
Chambers, Robert   Jorgenson, Warren fr. 4E Haviland, Wm.
Erickson, Jack   Vardeman, William   Rose, James
Markland, Herbert   Mikkelson, Melvin   Moorehead, James
Ballou, William   Kiser, John   Felts, Dwight
Casanove, Stanley   Peterson, Robert fr. 4E   Shuman, Albert
Powell, Joseph   Johnson, Edward   Carter, Howard fr. 4E
Hooker, Francis   Noffsker, W.A.   Turner, Pat, fr. 4E
Peppitone, Vito   Annes, Joe   Alton, Gordon
Ferrari, Domenico   Bartle, Edsel   Beach, Amos fr. 4E
Wood, Everett   Welch, Robert   Manzanares, Benjamin
Boyd, George   DeBoer, Arlen   Abrahams, Franklin
Mikita, Thomas   Knapp, Vernon   Hahn, Dale
Mooney, Harold   Seems, Felix   Malcolm Sidney
Macy, Dean   Brain, Phillips   Werner, Joseph

Section 4C

Gorham, Martin
Williams, Charles
Schoonover, Kenneth
Ray, John
Hester, Wynton fr. 4B
Larkin, Russell
Schodley, Albert
Vandal, David
Warnick, Jack
Ferratti, David
Goodman, Phillip
Hills, Algen
Knight, James
Ross, Edward
Stanley, Henry
Suskie, John
Vigile, Antonio
Farmer, James
Wilkerson, Edward
Schuette, Walter
Sills, Robert

Taylor, Ernest
Tucker, Francis
Willis, Alexander
Aldred, John fr. 4E
Clemmer, George fr. 4E
Foster, Malcom fr. 4E
McDill, Thomas fr. 4E
Clifton, Wm fr. 4E
Saddler, Campbell fr. 4E
Frazier, Clifton
Howard, Walter
Silverstein, Louis
Anderson, Lloyd
Galloway, Alfred
Irvin, Chesley
Maurino, Tony
Sherwood, Virgil
Wilcoxson, Elmer
Wood, Clyde
Forsythe, Don
Griffin, Thomas

Kelley, Gail
Krinock, Joseph
Schmidt, Carlos
Stewart, Charles
Troness, Arthur
Carr, Leslie
Flowers, James
Bain, Charles
Morris, Lee
Stefanski, Walter
Torres, Joseph fr. 4E
Wallace, Lewis fr. 4E
O'Meara, Albert fr. 4E
Baldwin, Richard fr. 4E
Demers, Raymond, fr. 4E
Hughes, Archie fr. 4E
Sequin, Clarence fr. 4E
St. John, Walter
Brown, James

Section 4D

Boyd, Jack
Mooney, Percy
Davis, Kenneth fr. 4B
Carle, John fr. 4E
Jacques, Ralph
Mohr, Arthur
Snellen, John
Patterson, Charles
Charlie, Thomas
Martinez, Ralph
Overly, George
Padget, John
Pearson, Sedric
Seargeant, Edward
Torres, Miguel
Vidaurri, Manuel
Bolt, Charles
Box, Claude
Hilton, Gordon
O'Connor, Raymond

Prewitt, Granville
Shott, Edward
Lowhead, Roger
Mines, James
Paras, Theodore
Prehm, Ernest
Jones, John fr. 4E
Martin, Wiley
Samson, Walter
Sharp, Jason fr. 4E
Strickland, Lacy
Smith, George
Spencer, John
Throneberry, Raphael
Van Almen, William
Vaughn, Jimmy
Watkins, Fred
Webber, Clarence fr. 4E
Whichard, Lafayette
Young, George

Bowers, Elmer
Cole, Brownell
Gentry, Adrian fr. 4E
Higdon, Patrick
Hulbert, Lyle
Jeffre, Andre fr. 4E
Levis, Robert fr. 4E
Shaw, Carl fr. 4E
Sisneros, Angelmo fr. 4E
Wheeler, Wm fr. 4E
Whitham, James
Brundage, Jack
Fennel, Bernard
Ford, Norman
Jones, Jack fr. 4E
Lopez, Al
Johnston, Robert
Drake, James

Section 4E

Leyba, Max fr. 4B
Karr, Austin fr. 4B
Brown, Mavis fr 4C

Cook, Alfred fr. 4C
Stoudt, Dan fr. 4D
Zack, Barney fr. 4D

Barnes, Gordon fr. 4B
Kimball, Raymond fr. 4D
Stengler, Albert

Waldrip, Leon fr 4D
Bain, Francis
Brooks, Seymour fr 4D
Henry, John
Ring, Gay fr 4D
Lee, Walter fr 4D
Watson, Richard fr 4D
Davis, Ken

Davis, Thomas
Fontana, Francis fr 4B
Lerner, James fr. 4E
Spencer, Aldon fr. 4C
White, Wilton fr. 4C
Diaz, Pablo fr. 4B
Browder, Leonard fr. 4B
Purcell, William fr 4D

Meador, Loyd fr. 4D
Bean, Roy
Coleman, Geoff fr. 4C
McTigue, James fr. 4D
Taves, Harold
Fish, Jack
Ballow, John

Section 4F

LeBeau, Alfred
Sanders, Harry
Emmanuel, James
Vaiden, William
Avery, Harrison fr 4E
Gustamante, Nestor
Dehr, Bert
Garcia, Ben
Kessey, Robert
Olson, Noel
Best, John
Saefke, Frederick

Pelayo, Lee
Fisher, Howard
Thurston, Gene
Adair, Don
Calvit, Kenneth
Dickson, Adolph
Haywood, John
Kimball, David
Phillips, Henry
Faulkner, James
Casey, Leo
Muenich, Gustaf

Howard, John
Kirby, Jack
Yohn, Leonard
Barker, Mathew
Crown, John
Emerick, John
Heinz, Leon
Knowles, Jasper
Sanford, Paul
Jensen Francis
Lambo, Jerry

Section 4G

Margiotto, Frank
Telendo, Mitchell
Summons, David
Reed, Vernon
Tripp, Phillip
Arterburn, Willie
Merritt, Joe
Kindel, Julius
Lambasio, Jenro

Abramowicz, John
Litch, Thomas
Mroz, Stanley
Quintana, Patrick
Marangiello, Tony
Bartley, Milledge
Peltier, Desire
Vondette, Robert
Darnell, Dillard

White, Edward
Mathews, Thomas
Sollenberger, Donald
Lemanski, John
Pennington, Wayne
Lopez, Al
Reisher, George
Kirhgesner, Peter
Ortiz, Ckuz

Special Detail (SD)

Hurtt, Thomas
Mann, Phillip
Washburn, Roy
Larsen, Leonard (shoe repair)
Howton, John
Mayer, Frank (medic)
Whittinghill, Harry
Williamson, Lee (dog robber)
Willis, Grover

Lietz, Theodore
Miliken, Emerson
Protz, Albert (cook)
Hunt, Hugh (medic)
McConn, Donald
Warnock, Robert (medic)
Stewart, Thomas
O'Keefe, James (medic)
Dugan, James (medic)

Bearden, Frank
Coon, Floyd
Van Hook, David
Chandler, Anthony (cook)
Rundle, Clayton
Brown, Douglas (dog robber)
Vice, William (carpenter)
Hill, Lloyd

DEBTS REPAID

When Solly Manasse returned to the States after the War, he sent Addie's prayerbook to his mother and father. Included with the book was a sheet of paper. On one side, written in Japanese, was a Japanese civilian's work ticket from the copper mine. Prisoners would occasionally steal these tickets to use as toilet paper. On the back side, Addie made a list of all the people he owed money to. Joseph Martin and Mark Lee were uncles. Most of the other names were high school or college friends. The Union Hotel was also mentioned. One of the names was Master Sgt. Jesse Finley from whom Addie borrowed money while a soldier. The Burr Jones Fund and Fr. Alvin Kutchera were also mentioned. Evidently Addie wanted these debts repaid. I checked with the University concerning the Burr Jones Loan and found out that they had forgiven the loan as he was "missing in action." Knowing Addie's wishes, I repaid these last two debts.

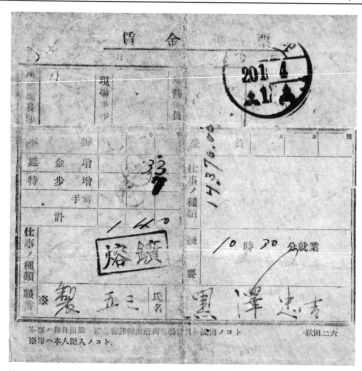

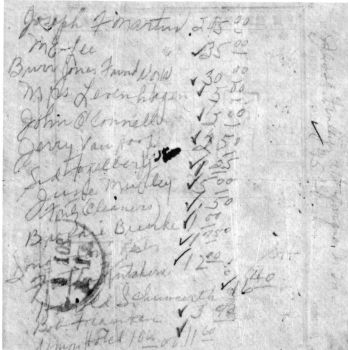

Japanese mine ticket from Hanawa with names on back of people to whom Addie owed money. Found in shoe box when my mother died.

Extended to 9/28/39

Martin Adrian
Name

No. 5782

$30.00

Jones
Fund

Madison, Wis., APR 28 1938

On or before _____ months after date, for value received, I promise to pay to THE UNIVERSITY OF WISCONSIN, or order, the sum of Thirty & no/100 _____ Dollars, with interest after date, at the rate of ___3___% per annum until maturity and ___7___% per annum after maturity until paid.

This is a debt of honor and the obligation should be sacredly kept in the interest of others who like myself may be worthy to profit by the fund.

I also promise to report to the Secretary of the Board of Regents of The University of Wisconsin, any change in my postoffice address until this note is paid.

Signed Adrian Martin

_____ Guarantor _____

Date	Payments	
	Princ.	Int.

APR 21 '86
BURSAR
UNIV OF W S
MADISON

3 PAID

Index

Compiled by Lori L. Daniel